When I'm Bad, I'm Better

When I'm Bad, I'm Better

MAE WEST, SEX, AND AMERICAN ENTERTAINMENT

MARYBETH HAMILTON

University of California Press
Berkeley   Los Angeles   London

University of California Press
Berkeley and Los Angeles, California

University of California Press, Ltd.
London, England

First Paperback Printing 1997
Previously published by HarperCollins Publishers 1996

Quoted material from the plays, *Sex, The Drag, Diamond Lil*, and *Pleasure Man* is reprinted with permission of the Receivership Estate of Mae West. All Rights Reserved. Represented by the Roger Richman Agency, Inc., Beverly Hills, California.

The author has made every effort to locate and credit owners of copyrighted photographs.

Library of Congress Cataloging-in-Publication Data

Hamilton, Marybeth.
    When I'm bad, I'm better : Mae West, sex, and American
  entertainment / Marybeth Hamilton.
       p.   cm.
    Originally published: New York : HarperCollins Publishers, 1996.
    Includes bibliographical references and index.
    ISBN 0-520-21094-8 (alk. paper)
    1. West, Mae.   2. Sex in the performing arts—United States.
  I. Title.
  PN2287.W4566H36   1997
  791.43'028'092—dc21   97-8277
                                                                CIP

1   2   3   4   5   6   7   8   9

The paper used in this publication meets the minimum requirements of American National Standard for Information Sciences—Permanence of Paper for Printed Library Materials, ANSI Z39.48-1984. ♾

For my parents and Ken

Contents

Acknowledgments   ix

Prologue		1
1	Tough Girl	3
2	"That Touch of Class"	19
3	*Sex*, *The Drag*, and the Comedy-Drama of Life	46
4	Sex on Trial: The Politics of "Legit"	70
5	A Little Bit Spicy: *Diamond Lil*	104
6	"I'm the Queen of the Bitches"	136
7	The Honor of White Womanhood	153
8	Mae West Mania	173
9	It Ain't No Sin	194
10	Mae West in Exile	218
11	The Queen of Camp	235
Epilogue		251

Notes   *255*
Bibliography   *281*
Index   *291*

Photographs follow page 148.

Acknowledgments

Many people have helped me to write this book, and it is a pleasure to have the chance to acknowledge them here.

My early interest in American history was encouraged by Paula Fass at the University of California at Berkeley, and for her support I remain very grateful. As a doctoral student at Princeton University I was lucky to find several splendid teachers. Sean Wilentz led me to Mae West's arrest records at the New York City Municipal Archives, the documents that first gave me the idea for this study. As both feminist and historian, Christine Stansell sharpened my thinking, and I owe a great deal to her insightful criticism. My adviser, Daniel Rodgers, deserves special thanks for his imaginative readings of even the roughest first drafts and for encouraging me, from the beginning, to trust my own instincts.

In Princeton, New York, Washington, and London I have benefited greatly from friends and colleagues who have helped me to pull my ideas into shape. For their insightful comments, advice, and encouragement, I am grateful to Barbara Balliet, Peter Buckley, Frank Couvares, Daniel Czitrom, Lizzie Francke, Jane Hill, Richard Maltby, Charles McGovern, Kathy Peiss, Rob Snyder, Andrea Stuart, and Julie Wheelwright. For the financial assistance that allowed me to write, I owe thanks to the National Museum of American History for a Smithsonian Institution Predoctoral Fellowship, the Woodrow Wilson National Fellowship Foundation for a Research Grant in Women's Studies, and the History Department of Princeton University for a Postdoctoral Fellowship. I owe a special debt of gratitude to my colleagues at Birkbeck College, who provided me with time in which to complete my research and whose good cheer and moral support brightened the final year of writing. My editors at HarperCollins, Joy Johannessen, Wendy Wolf, Larry Ashmead, and Jason Kaufman, have worked hard to make this a better book. I am grateful for their help and encouragement, as well as for the unflagging enthusiasm of my agent, Geri Thoma.

John Carson is one of a kind, an extraordinary reader and a wonderful friend, and I thank him for his help and devotion. Laura Mason, with her boundless generosity and passion for history, has been a constant source of inspiration. Laura Finster, Michele Gillespie, Katherine Stern, Beth and Ray Arnold, and Diane Michalek have lifted my spirits with their lively curiosity and infectious good humor. To my brother, Keith Hamilton, I owe special thanks for firing my interest in movies and my love of the process of writing. My debts to my parents, Bill and Cora Hamilton, are incalculable. Here I can only thank them for their understanding, generosity, and moral support.

My debts to Ken Arnold extend well beyond these pages, but even here he has provided enormous help. His skeptical but always constructive comments have consistently pushed me to expand my analysis and sharpened my awareness of the issues at stake. Throughout the last eight years, he has challenged me, provoked me, and made me think. For that, and for much more, I thank him.

When I'm
Bad, I'm
Better

Prologue

BYSTANDER: *You're a fine gal, Lady Lou, a fine woman.*
MAE WEST: *One of the finest women that ever walked the streets.*

In her 1933 film *She Done Him Wrong*, Mae West swaggered onto American screens making comedy out of the life of a street-smart New York City prostitute. Though the film made her Hollywood's biggest star, ten years later she was out of work, the victim of one of the most dramatic falls in the history of mass entertainment.

There are few more familiar figures than West, few pop culture icons we seem to know more completely. She was a temptress, a promiscuous woman, a Gay Nineties throwback, a satirical sex bomb, a taboo-breaker who outraged the censors, a female drag queen who personified camp.

Mae West was threatening—and she was ludicrous. She was a sex symbol—and she was a joke. The tools of biography do little to explain her: West left no diaries, no letters, no personal documents that might have shed light on her private self. The focus of her life was her work. She so threw herself into the business of being Mae West that in time the "private" West faded completely into the haze of the screen character's legends and myths. In fact, we actually don't know West at all.

This book sets out to unmask Mae West by tracing the history of her public persona, the process of theatrical experimentation by which she constructed and promoted herself. West won her place in American folklore in the guise of an amiably implausible, swivel-hipped

siren given to outsized mannerisms that at once projected and parodied sex. So central is that role to our image of West that it is hard to
imagine her as anything else. But that Westian pose was the end product of a tumultuous evolution that long predated her arrival in Hollywood—a thirty-year career in disreputable theater, climaxed in the
1920s on Broadway by spectacular notoriety as a low-rent playwright
and actress who showcased the sexual underworld.

Unraveling the threads that wove West's persona means setting
her in the context of social history. West's career spanned the twentieth century and unfolded against a backdrop of dramatic change:
a revolt against Victorian values, the code of sexual restraint and
reticence prized by the nineteenth-century middle class. Spearhead-
ing that rebellion were middle-class women, who decked themselves
out in lipstick and silk stockings and became ardent patrons of
movies, nightclubs, and dance halls. In West's hometown, New
York, they forged a new craze for "slumming," for exploring cultures and styles beyond the respectable pale: the "primitivism" of
African-Americans in Harlem, the flamboyance of the city's gay
men, and the aggressive eroticism exhibited by prostitutes, who put
sexuality on public display.

For Mae West all this was a godsend. The Brooklyn-born daughter of immigrant parents, sexually active since the age of twelve, she
grew up as (in turn-of-the-century parlance) a "tough girl," a sexually uninhibited working-class woman who flaunted a raunchy
streetwise style. To the Victorians, such women were outcasts,
deemed immoral, deviant, little different from prostitutes; but to
adventurous slummers they were objects of curiosity, fantasy, and
desire. West turned that fascination to her advantage. Her rough-
edged identity as a tough girl provided her with sensational raw
material that she would refine, refract, and in time veil in irony in
the process of creating an enduring stage self.

West reshaped her persona to suit new audiences, and often this
was her own choice. At other times that change was forced upon her.
In vaudeville, on Broadway, and in motion pictures, she brought a
style that transgressed boundaries, with its echoes of underworld theatrical traditions like burlesque, the drag show, and the black honky-
tonk. As a result she set off controversies among performers, producers, critics, and the public over the limits of legitimate performance.
West is remembered now as a quaint comic artifact, a saucy and
rather trivial icon, but that sentimentalizes her real outrageousness.
Hollywood saw it all along.

Chapter 1

TOUGH GIRL

On August 4, 1913, it was the hottest ticket in New York City. Hammerstein's Victoria Theater, a vaudeville palace in the heart of Times Square, had stolen a march on every other theater in town. So proud was its manager, Willie Hammerstein, of his triumph that he instructed his sign painters to blazon the attraction in four-foot-high letters. "Modern Ballroom Dancing," screamed the marquee, "Performed by EVELYN NESBIT THAW."[1]

Even the most cloistered New Yorker knew who Evelyn Nesbit was. A former chorus girl and artist's model, she had coquetted her way into one of the biggest sex scandals in the city's history when on a summer's evening in 1906 her husband, Pittsburgh millionaire Harry Thaw, strode into the Roof Garden Theater atop Madison Square Garden, aimed his pistol, and killed her former lover, eminent architect Stanford White. The resulting trials gave the public a lurid view of New York high society: of White, the city's leading arbiter of taste, revealed as a sensualist and a seducer of young girls; of the demented Harry Thaw, who enjoyed beating Nesbit as well as protecting her, and whose rage at her premarital affair with "that beast" had become an obsession; and of the renowned beauty herself, "betrayed," as she put it, at age fifteen, when Stanford White posed her in a red velvet swing and served her a glass of drugged champagne.[2]

After seven years in seclusion Evelyn Nesbit had surfaced, and to anyone who knew anything about New York City theater, it came as no surprise that Willie Hammerstein nabbed her. In his ten years as the Victoria's manager he had made it synonymous with unabashed sensationalism. Under his guidance the Victoria became New York's top-grossing vaudeville playhouse, renowned (or notorious) for its garish attractions—in Hammerstein's phrase, for its "freak acts."

These freak acts took many forms. Some were transparent humbugs, sleazy curiosities that Hammerstein promoted with the panache of a sideshow barker. There was Shekla, Court Magician to the Shah of Persia (in reality an Indian he discovered in a London music hall)[3]; Abdul Kadar, Court Artist to the Turkish Sultan, and His Three Wives (Adolph Schneider, music hall player from the Swiss "small time," and his wife, daughter, and sister-in-law)[4]; Willard, "The Man Who Grows—Seven-And-A-Half Inches Before Your Eyes!"[5]; and Mademoiselle Fatima, Escaped Harem Dancer: "Two years ago, during the Turko-Italian War, she fled from the palace of PRINCE ABDUL HAMID in Constantinople and has since been appearing in all PRINCIPAL CITIES OF EUROPE. She has a distinctive Turkish personality and dances with original movements all her own, accompanied by her two Eunuch servants."[6] But more compelling than these physical and geographical oddities were the freaks of publicity, the city's most notorious inhabitants, men and more frequently women who had made names for themselves through their links to New York's criminal and sexual underworld, in headline-grabbing vice raids, "love nest" scandals, and murders.

"Anything's a good act that will make 'em talk," Willie Hammerstein said, and his Victoria Theater had been provoking comment for years.[7] It was virtually a three-dimensional tabloid, giving New Yorkers a face-to-face glimpse of the infamous stars of the urban panorama. The emphasis was on sexual scandals, especially those featuring young, attractive women. Evelyn Nesbit was only the most show-stopping example. The theater had already presented Nan Patterson, a showgirl who shot her boyfriend in a Manhattan taxi, and Florence Carman, the wife of a Long Island doctor, who shot her husband's mistress and who entertained the audience with a demure rendition of "Baby Shoes."[8] In 1911 it headlined Lillian

Graham and Ethel Conrad, chorus girls then out on bail after shooting Graham's wealthy lover in the Veruna Hotel. Hammerstein brought them to vaudeville with true sensationalist flair, billing them as "Those Two Girls" and "The Shooting Stars," and promoting their appearance with posters so lurid they were used in court to damage the women's reputations.[9] So great did the vogue for female killers and near-killers become that "every pawnshop gun sold to a woman practically carried the guarantee of a week's booking," wrote one vaudeville old-timer.[10]

With Evelyn Nesbit the theater had snared what one commentator called "the freak act of all time."[11] No one could match her sensational appeal. New York's newspapers had written of little else for days, and by curtain time on opening night, the largest crowd in the Victoria's history had pushed its way into the theater's roof garden. Occupying every inch of available floor space were underworld gunmen and blasé Hammerstein regulars, shoulder to shoulder with society ladies and gum-chewing readers of the popular press. When the orchestra sounded and the curtain went up, the crowd strained forward as one. But first they had to endure several opening acts, definitely some of Hammerstein's lesser lights—The Three Ambler Brothers ("Sensational Equilibrists"), The Three Gertzes ("Acrobatic Marvels"), Dainty Marie ("Venus in the Air")—all facing the unenviable task of diverting an increasingly restless audience, tensely awaiting its first glimpse of the most notorious woman of the twentieth century.[12]

Far down on the Victoria's bill that evening, struggling to make an impression on the sweltering multitudes, was another little-known performer from Hammerstein's stable, "Popular Comedienne" Mae West. At nineteen West had just begun as a vaudeville "single," but she had served a long apprenticeship in cheap theaters, variety troupes, and stock-company melodramas. Playing Hammerstein's was potentially a big career breakthrough. Plenty of acts had begun at Hammerstein's and gone on to national stardom—vaudevillian Eva Tanguay, for example, currently the top attraction on the "big time," as the highest ranks of the vaudeville world were known to performers and fans.

But Mae West got nowhere on that hot August night. She tried every trick she could think of—a low-cut dress, a few provocative songs, an assortment of raunchy bumps and grinds—but her viewers were not to be swayed.[13] They had come for Nesbit and Nesbit alone. Most of the newspaper critics ignored her too, though one, Joshua Lowe in *Variety*, did notice how hard she tried. "Mae West," he commented, "sang loud enough to be distinctly heard in the rear."[14]

There is something deliciously apt in Mae West's futile labors in front of the Victoria's footlights in 1913: the woman later mythologized as a "sex bomb," the woman whose racy quips scandalized a nation, totally upstaged by a seductress still remembered, thanks to E. L. Doctorow's *Ragtime*, as the emblem of Gilded Age sexual indulgence. This episode illustrates more vividly than any other I know West's most significant contemporary context. Like Evelyn Nesbit and the Shooting Stars, she was trying to make her way in a time-honored style of performance, a tradition of commercial amusement with deep roots in New York's lower-class culture. One might call this tradition urban sensationalism: popular theater that catered to prurience by lifting the veil on metropolitan vice.

As a young performer West was instantly drawn to that sensationalist tradition. In time she would develop her own brand of "freak act," giving vaudeville audiences an unfettered portrayal of a hard-boiled, sharp-tongued, sexually adventurous woman—a "tough girl," in the parlance of the times. That she adopted this performance style had everything to do with her youthful experience as an immigrant's daughter growing up in working-class Brooklyn at the turn of the century.

It's not easy to root the young Mae West in her contemporary context. She herself always discouraged the attempt. West was reluctant to discuss her childhood. She refused to give interviewers precise dates and addresses; she muttered vaguely when faced with reporters who pressed her for details about her background. In her autobiography she was no more forthcoming, describing her parents in the most hackneyed of Gay Nineties clichés. Her mother might have doubled for Lillian Russell; her father was a rough-hewn, mustachioed brawler.

West's vagueness made perfect sense. She had no interest in being too specific, in allowing outsiders to see the social forces that shaped her. At the heart of her public mythology was the assertion that she created herself. She was *sui generis*, unique and unprecedented, by nature an erotic free spirit. No other performers, no theatrical traditions helped her to assemble her style. She simply appeared at the age of seven on a Brooklyn Elks Club amateur night, already flamboyant and imperious. Right from the start she was "Mae West":

> I stepped out on the stage, looked up angrily at the spotlight man in the balcony, stamping my foot. "*Where* is *my* spotlight!" I stamped it again and the spotlight moved across stage onto me and caught me in the act of demanding my light. The audience saw me and laughed and applauded. The angry expression on my little face as I impudently stared up at the spotlight man, and my exasperated stamping of dancing shoes, explained my delayed entrance. . . .
>
> With the spotlight on my shoulders like white mink, I went to center stage and sang my song, "Movin' Day." I did my skirt dance without missing a word or a step. Instead of having stagefright I was innocently brazen. My angry mood overcame any nervous doubts I might normally have felt. I've never had stagefright in my life.
>
> I was a hit with the audience. They were fine in their applause. I received a gold medal from the Elks organization. Papa was proud.[15]

Since she portrayed herself as a larger-than-life sex goddess, naturally she gave herself mythic beginnings, springing to the stage with a completely formed persona, a modern-day Venus strutting full-grown from the sea. The real story of her origins is more complicated, though many details remain elusive, with primary documents woefully sketchy and West so adept at rewriting her past.

One fact, however, is incontrovertible: Mae West was a child of plebeian culture. Born in Brooklyn on August 17, 1893, she grew up immersed in the sights, sounds, and smells of the rough-edged immigrant community of Greenpoint, with its mix of Irish, Italians, Germans, and Poles.[16] A down-at-the-heels industrial district, Greenpoint was famous as the most insular of Brooklyn's working-class neighborhoods and notorious for some explosive nightlife.[17]

Mae's father, John Patrick West, fit comfortably into this milieu. Born in 1866, of Irish extraction, he earned a living as a boxer and then as a bridlemaker until automotive technology made his trade obsolete. He seems to have drifted between jobs thereafter. Over the years, doubtless with considerable invention, West described him variously as a chiropractor, a realtor, a physician, a livery stable owner, and, in what must have been an unguarded moment, a bouncer in a Coney Island dance hall. Among his later occupations, he ran what his daughter termed a "private police force"—which seems to have meant that he worked as a bodyguard for local racketeers.[18]

West's father can be glimpsed through the cracks as a onetime craftsman on the margins of Brooklyn's underworld. Her mother remains so thickly veiled in West's mythologies that she's even more difficult to make out. Matilda Doelger was born in 1871 in Wurttemberg, Germany, emigrated to America in the 1880s, and never lost her German accent.[19] She married John West around the end of that decade and bore a daughter, Katie, who died in infancy. Three other children arrived at intervals: Mary Jane, soon nicknamed Mae, in 1893; Mildred, who renamed herself Beverly, in 1896; and John Edwin in 1899.

As her daughter described her, Tillie West was a paragon of female decorum: elegant, charming, with a delicate beauty. She was firm yet soft-spoken, aloof yet tender; above all, she was genteel. "There was a power and a vitality about Mother that made a man melt before her glance," West recalled. "She was sexy, but refined, see?" West repeatedly retouched the one surviving photograph of Tillie, adding thick layers of lipstick and eyeshadow to produce an immaculate, lifeless maternal ideal.[20]

The Wests' Brooklyn neighbors painted an earthier portrait. The Tillie West they remembered was shrewd, hardheaded, and immensely ambitious, a tough-minded stage mother. Unhappy and isolated in her own marriage, she discouraged her daughter from romantic attachments and cheered her every attempt to perform. She urged Mae early onto the stage and often neglected her housekeeping duties in her zeal to further her daughter's career. In return for her unswerving support, West showed her mother a wholehearted devotion that she would demonstrate for no other person, certainly no other woman, for the rest of her life.[21]

The ambition Tillie West passed on to her daughter was broadly shared among turn-of-the-century working-class children. But those children differed dramatically in how they expressed it, and within plebeian communities, as the Wests' neighbors might have put it, one distinguished the "rough" from the "respectable" on precisely this point. Respectable plebeians sought advancement through education. As the labor unions and workingmen's societies counseled, the dogged pursuit of intellectual achievement was the surest road to mainstream success.

Though West insisted on her family's upstanding morals, it's clear that she had little use for the tradition of sober self-improvement that marked the respectable working class. At the age of seven she left school for good. Taking to the stage before her eighth birthday, West took up New York's working-class youth culture, a world whose racy theater, gaudy fashions, and suggestive dance styles had become the bane of local social reformers. West's experience of that world would shape her future, eventually leading her to the stage of the Victoria, where she vied for an audience with sideshow oddities and murderesses, gun molls, sex-scandal luminaries, and freaks.

From 1900 to 1911 Mae West apprenticed in the urban popular theater. After her professional debut at seven she joined a shabby East New York stock company run by Brooklyn actor Hal Clarendon, who specialized in "blood-and-thunder" melodrama. West worked with Clarendon's company for nearly four years, playing in such standards as *Ten Nights in a Barroom*, *Little Lord Fauntleroy*, and *Uncle Tom's Cabin*, in which she played Little Eva. In her teens, too old for child parts, she took work where she could get it, tap dancing, singing, and performing acrobatics in New York theaters geared to burlesque and small-time vaudeville.[22]

The venues of West's early years were situated far down the theatrical hierarchy, well below Manhattan's "legitimate" showplaces and first-class big-time vaudeville palaces. With dime museums and nickelodeons, they formed a low-rent amusement network centered in working-class immigrant neighborhoods in Brooklyn, Queens, and the Lower East Side. New York's social workers, who loathed these places, called them the "cheap theaters"—a description that from their perspective suited not just the price range but the moral tone too.

Cheap theater flaunted a distinctive style that stood in sharp contrast to the tradition of genteel uplift, the hallmark of middle-class drama. From the garish productions of melodrama to the blatant sensationalism of burlesque and vaudeville, cheap theater bypassed heart and mind to grab hold of the body, to assault the central nervous system. Its lure was openly, unashamedly visceral: flamboyant costumes that dazzled the eye, vivid special effects that excited the pulse, raucous dancing that stimulated desire.

West's first training ground, Hal Clarendon's stock company, exemplified this style. As part of what was called the "ten-twent'-thirt' " circuit (ten, twenty, and thirty cents was the range of admission prices), it produced rowdy melodramas, all straining for the utmost in garish appeal.[23] This was not called blood-and-thunder theater for nothing. Specializing in hair-raising visual effects—fires, earthquakes, runaway horses—and lurid displays of violence and seduction, it gave West her first lesson in how to draw audiences. She recalled:

> There were sassy things with music in which any excuse to get the girl into tights and drawers was all right, if they showed their lacy derrieres. Murder, rape, forest fires, wrecks of famous river boats, crooked jockeys and forged wills also served us.[24]

Fast-paced, expressive, above all sensational, ten-twent'-thirt' was also localized and timely. Its playwrights, who often doubled as journalists, crafted quick cheap dramas out of press scandals, usually within days of the event hitting print. (One frequent play topic, unsurprisingly enough, was the tale of Evelyn Nesbit and Harry Thaw.) One writer of melodrama, Owen Davis, remembered:

> If a particularly horrible murder excited the public, we had it dramatized and on the stage usually before anyone knew who was guilty of the crime. Frequently I have had a job of hasty rewriting when it became evident that my culprit from real life was an innocent and perfectly respectable citizen.[25]

Cheap theater openly catered to prurience, flaunting sex, crime, and scandal, all that was salacious in urban life. Jane Addams, respected social worker and reformer, viewed it as yet another blight on the city landscape, another means of exploiting the poor. In her 1909 treatise *The Spirit of Youth and the City Streets*, she attacked its "trashy love stories," straight from the pages of the Sunday supplements, and its songs and numbers set to "flippant street music," celebrating such spectacles as "the vulgar experiences of a city man wandering from amusement park to bathing beach in search of flirtations."[26] Reveling in the city's random excitements, cheap theater mired the audience in the sensual drives that made urban streetlife so very degrading.

Other reformers, like Cleveland's Robert Bartholomew, agreed. Cheap theater provoked and aroused its audiences through sexual display, as Bartholomew's account of a local stage performance emphasized:

> Many verses of different songs have been gathered which would not bear printing in this report. Dancers were often seen who endeavored to arouse interest and applause by going through vulgar movements of the body. . . . A young woman after dancing in such a manner as to set off all the young men and boys in the audience in a state of pandemonium brought onto the stage a large python snake about ten feet long. The snake was first wrapped about the body, then caressed and finally kissed in its mouth.[27]

To Addams and her fellows, this was not theater at all. It violated their fundamental convictions about the purpose, the social importance, of drama. Middle-class children of Victorian parents, urban social reformers followed their elders in valuing theater as a means of "self-tillage," an opportunity for personal cultivation. Its job was to educate and uplift the viewer, to engage the heart and develop the mind by illuminating moral and spiritual truths. Only by attuning the mind to the realm of the spirit could one hope to conquer the pull of the body, to elevate oneself above the sensual stimuli that social reformers deemed both vulgar and dangerous.[28]

Cheap theater most definitely did not elevate anyone. For that reason, social workers considered it unsuitable for all, but particularly for the lower-class young people who formed its largest and most loyal audience. Uneducated, impressionable, and already the victims of a "hyperstimulating" urban environment, city youth lacked the inner resources, or so the reformers argued, to cope with its garish, frenetic stage spectacles. By agitating their senses while leaving their spirits untouched, cheap theater corrupted their youthful exuberance and aroused sex urges beyond their control.

The result, Jane Addams argued, was ominous: a population awash in unthinking pleasure, for whom sensuality was "merely a dumb and powerful instinct without in the least awakening the imagination and the heart." One need only examine urban America to see the corruption that inevitably followed. "Every city contains hundreds of degenerates who have been over-mastered and borne down by [the sex impulse]," wrote Addams. "They fill the casual lodging houses and the infirmaries." From that perspective, cheap theater was as pressing a threat as the saloon or the brothel, unleashing a force of sufficient power to work "as a cancer in the very tissues of society and as a disrupter of the securest social bonds."[29]

To the seven-year-old Mae West, taking her first steps on the stages of the blood-and-thunder showplaces, such arguments would doubtless have seemed remote. But it was precisely the style Jane Addams abhorred, the style reviled as lewd and low-class, that West herself was fast absorbing. Her years in the cheap theaters gave her a love of sensationalism that would color her work for the rest of her life—a gut sense, which she never fully discarded, that the way to grab an audience was to shock and arouse them, to titillate them with the lurid life of the streets.

If West took her lessons in performance from the cheap theaters, she learned about sex on the working-class streets. By all accounts, her own and her acquaintances', Mae West was a sexual adventurer early. She had her first intercourse before her first period, with a dancing instructor in the basement of her family's home. "I wasn't frightened," she recounted years later. "What was there to be frightened of, for god's sake?"[30] Thereafter she eagerly sought out encounters with dancers, musicians, and backstage admirers. None remained her single focus for long, as one early lover, ragtime musician Joseph Schenck, could attest: no sooner had she started sleeping with him than she began working her way through the rest of the band. Pregnancy she avoided with primitive but evidently effective contraception: a water-soaked sponge tied on a silk string.[31]

One might well marvel at this teenager's boldness and nerve. Her behavior flew in the face of turn-of-the-century middle-class culture, which exalted female purity. Venerated as men's moral superiors, women gained respect in that culture by displaying distaste for the body: by speaking with decorum, dressing with modesty, and refraining from sex before marriage. With her multiple lovers and saucy looks, West displayed sheer indifference to middle-class standards. But then she was not a middle-class product. She learned about sex from the world she grew up in, and in Greenpoint her brand of behavior, while by no means acceptable, was widespread enough to be familiar to all.

West's neighbors had a name for young women like her. She was a tough girl, a rowdy and flamboyant young woman who flaunted an aggressive erotic style. In the era of West's adolescence tough girls were a controversial modern phenomenon. They sprang out of, and thrived on, the industrial city. Jobs as shopgirls and factory workers gave them a bit of extra money to spend, and the patriarchal mores of immigrant families sparked a fierce desire to escape their fathers' control. They sought that escape in the city's new commercial amusements. Dance halls and cheap theaters drew them in droves. There they found freedom from prying parents, a space for pleasure on their own terms—terms that left many contemporary observers troubled. As social workers like Jane Addams saw with dismay, for many immigrants' daughters the contest between Old World traditions and the lure of the city was no contest at all.[32]

Tough girls were wild and made no secret of it. They decked themselves out for their nights on the town in uninhibited attire: low-cut dresses in gaudy colors, flamboyant feathered hats and cheap costume jewelry, elaborate pompadours filled out with artificial hairpieces, and an abundance of powder and paint. They moved their bodies on the dance floor in a fashion called "spieling," a "tough" style that stressed vigorous pelvic movement and blatantly alluded to sexual intercourse. Off the dance floor they bantered freely with men, trading provocative quips. No man could match them for coarse, graphic humor. A social investigator in a Brooklyn saloon heard a tough girl deliver the following toast: "Here's to the girl that smiles so sweet, she makes things stand that never had any feet."[33]

To social worker Lillian Wald, tough girls constituted a recognizable subculture—and a distinctly worrying trend. Their "pronounced lack of modesty in dress, . . . their dancing, their talk, their freedom of manner," she wrote, "all combine to render them conspicuous."[34] As a middle-class lady Wald veiled her language. What made tough girls "conspicuous" was their handling of sex—or more precisely, the attitude toward sex that their appearance and behavior seemed to connote. Their bold manner, loud clothes, and garish cosmetics had always been the marks of the prostitute. Whatever their private sexual behavior may have been (and social workers who knew them reported that it varied), they took pride in a scandalous public persona. They relished their bodies, their men, and their good times, and they appeared to be sexually proficient.

The tough-girl phenomenon appalled social reformers. And the fact that these girls were everywhere—in the audiences of the popular melodramas, strutting through the grounds of amusement parks, spieling and shouting and gyrating in dance halls—was damning evidence of the corruption cheap amusements brought in their wake.

Tough girls *had* been corrupted—of that the reformers were certain. The girls were naive dupes of dance hall and theater managers who preyed on their innocent hunger for pleasure and perverted their untutored tastes. "Let us see the amusement exploiter just as he is, for he lies in wait for the spirit of youth at every corner," argued social investigator Richard Henry Edwards. "He is not a playful person. . . . He buys youth's freshness of feeling in return for sundry ticklings of sensation, and blights its glad spontaneities with his itching palm."[35]

Social workers could only see tough girls as victims. As middle-class men and women shaped by their parents' Victorian values, they viewed sexual purity—and the appearance of purity—as the basis of female power and dignity. No sane woman would choose to abandon it. Tough girls, by these lights, were victims, and entertainment entrepreneurs no better than white slave traders, luring gullible young women into their clutches and degrading them into a vicious life.

Yet in attempting to minister to their charges, social workers bumped up against one immovable obstacle: too many tough girls, Mae West included, simply did not see themselves as victims. Relishing sex as a source of pleasure and power, they embraced New York's gaudy nightlife and scorned the new, wholesome civic recreations—the folk dancing clubs and dramatic societies—established to rescue them from their plight. Over time such defiance would provoke harsher and harsher critiques. To mental health experts in the 1910s, tough girls appeared "psychopathic," "moronic"; to social investigators, increasingly, they were not victims but "deviants," indistinguishable from prostitutes in their sexual aggression and physical flamboyance.[36]

This hostility was undergirded by fear. Tough girls were an ominous sign of things to come, a frightening indication of how women of all classes might elect to behave, might choose to handle their sexuality. This was no groundless speculation. By the 1910s there was already considerable evidence that the tough-girl style was spreading to urban daughters of white middle-class parents, "respectable" women, who were beginning to patronize the dance halls too.

At the turn of the century the debate was only beginning, but over the next thirty years female patronage of commercial amusements would become a hotly contested cultural issue. How to protect the female audience, how to prevent its corruption by "amusement exploiters," would occupy the minds of key moral guardians. And it would help provoke a furor around Mae West when this authentic tough girl became not just a consumer but a producer of popular entertainment.

As a child performer and a sexual adventurer West was shaped by sensationalist working-class theater and by the controversial subculture of tough girls. Since she was clearly a wild young woman, it is intriguing to learn that she took one brief step in the direction of respectability. On April 11, 1911, in a civil ceremony at Milwaukee City Hall, Mae West, not quite eighteen, married a twenty-one-year-old jazz dancer, Frank Wallace.

They had met in 1909, when West was touring New York's small-time vaudeville houses as a girlish comic in a "Huck Finn" act. Wallace quickly caught her eye. Born Frank Szatkus, the son of a poor Lithuanian tailor, he was thin and wiry, with an intense, cunning face, and his eccentric dancing won over audiences. At West's suggestion they teamed up in a song-and-dance act. They made a good pair—her sultry voice complemented his high-spirited footwork—and were soon getting regular bookings in small-time theaters around New York. In 1911 a bigger break came their way: they were hired as a juvenile couple for *The Sporting Widow*, a small-time playlet, which set off on a tour through the Northeast and Midwest. Heretofore their relationship had been strictly professional, but by the time they reached Wisconsin they were lovers—although West, true to form, was working her way through the rest of the cast too.[37]

Like most touring companies, this one was filled with veteran performers, a clannish assortment of older men and women who took a dim view of wild behavior. West's conduct soon created a stir among them. In Milwaukee Etta Woods, a German character actress, took West aside and informed her that the company was shocked by her antics. More pointedly, she warned of the danger of pregnancy. At least if West was married, Woods concluded, she could preserve some veneer of respectability. West was shaken enough to agree to go through with it—but only after swearing Wallace to secrecy.

To be sure, this was West's account of the incident. Wallace, who gave his story to a reporter in 1935, portrayed her as a dewy-eyed, infatuated young girl. But here, for once, West seems more reliable, since only her version makes sense of the whole tangled story. And even Wallace did not dispute West's account of the wedding's immediate aftermath: within a matter of days, she violently recoiled from what she had done.

As the company made its way through the northern Midwest the young newlywed was dallying with more men than ever. The end of each evening's performance saw West locking her husband in their hotel room, slipping out to a local nightclub, and returning, disheveled, at 3 A.M. Her carousing was not lost on the rest of the troupe. In Buffalo lead actor Hugh Herbert angrily told her that the whole company resented her treatment of her husband. West, bristling, retorted that she was just having fun.[38]

Once the tour ended, West's mind was made up: the wedding had simply never happened. She returned alone to New York and moved back in with her parents, flatly denying all rumors of marriage, even when confronted point-blank by her mother. As for Wallace—who certainly seems to have loved her, if complete submission to her wishes should be taken for love—he dutifully returned home to Maspeth, Long Island. Loyal despite West's cavalier treatment, he kept quiet about the marriage for the next twenty-five years.

On April 21, 1935, a Milwaukee Works Progress Administration worker who was indexing the city's marriage records unearthed the 1911 certificate issued to Mae West and Frank Wallace. By then an international star, West had always insisted that she was single. The news flashed to wire services around the country, and the press beat a path to Wallace's New York City door.

Even then, at least initially, Wallace equivocated. He claimed not to be certain whether they were married or not. He came out with the truth several days later, but only after West had hurt his feelings, truculently insisting the story was false and adding, "Wallace? I never hearda the guy." His decision may also have been influenced by more pressing financial matters. In 1935 West was a millionaire; Wallace was languishing in what was left of vaudeville. Though he had never asked her for money before, he quickly made up for lost time, commencing a nightclub tour as "Mr. Mae West" and suing his estranged wife for maintenance payments. West, who did not admit the marriage for another two years, finally granted him a bit of money and divorced him in 1943.

Most accounts of West's marriage treat it with humor, and it did have its comic moments. But what strikes me about its place in West's life is how painful the episode seems to have been. West fled from her marriage as though for her life. She avoided divorce simply because she preferred to pretend that the marriage had never happened. In later years she pushed Frank Wallace firmly out of her mind. By the 1960s she routinely told interviewers that she had been single all her life. As is not the case with all of West's misstatements of fact, one senses that she'd come to believe this herself.

It's not hard to see why the memory was painful. In marrying Wallace West had betrayed herself: she had given in to external pressure, to the force of community scorn. In the cloistered world of the touring company her sexual adventures provoked a scandal, and her co-workers demanded that she conform to convention. Not yet eighteen, far from familiar surroundings, West was sufficiently unnerved to succumb.

Mae West's dilemma was by no means unique. To be a tough girl at the turn of the century was to be subject to unceasing contempt. Deemed unruly and wild by parents and neighbors, immoral and deviant by social workers and clergy, tough girls were constantly admonished to shed their rough manners and flamboyant ways. For West giving in to that pressure proved a disaster. Yet all the same it was a productive disaster, one of those momentous events that shake up one's whole life and starkly illuminate the way forward. On the verge of adulthood West was about to yield to the demands of social respectability, like countless tough girls before her. She was preparing to abandon her independence, her pleasure in hedonism, and behave as the community dictated. But no sooner had she begun than she knew she could not go through with it. Her decision to dump Frank Wallace without a backward glance marked a critical turning point: West would remain defiantly tough and would never be so easily cowed again.

As a sexually active working-class woman Mae West was treated with scorn and exclusion. In the years that followed she learned not to care. Building a wall around herself, she shut out her fellow performers' contempt. Over time she came to relish her backstage notoriety. "She kept to herself," one fellow vaudevillian told her biographer George Eells, "but she gloried in the stir she caused wherever she went."[39]

Stirs never failed to surround her: West encouraged them. Rather than hide her carousing, she paraded it before her like a shield. She came to delight in preemptive strikes, buttonholing likely antagonists, often well-bred young women, with bawdy descriptions of her sexual prowess, disarming potential critics before they could launch an attack of their own. In 1918, in a small role in the Broadway musical *Sometime*, West pounced on Helen Ford, a patrician young dancer, sparing no details of her sexual exploits, clearly enjoying her genteel listener's embarrassment. "That kind of talk continued until I learned not to blush," Ford told George Eells. "Then Mae lost all interest in me and never said more than hello or good night."[40]

West learned, in short, to use sex as a weapon. She wore her disreputability like a suit of armor, a source of protection and personal power. Just as important, she grew supremely confident in using sex as a tool onstage. Beginning on her eighteenth birthday, shortly after leaving Frank Wallace, she set out for stardom as a featured performer in vaudeville, determined to make her mark with a raunchy expressive style. Over the next few years she took on the role she would play to the hilt—the hard-edged, slangy, rough-talking tough girl, glorying in her sexual allure.

Chapter 2

"THAT TOUCH OF CLASS"

*I*n July 1912 a visitor to downtown Philadelphia might have been intrigued by notices flooding the city streets, advertising a vaudeville engagement by a woman of unique and enticing talents. Her act would feature her specialty, "a muscle dance in a sitting position." "It is all in the way she does it," the flyers promised, "and her way is all her own!"[1]

As her earliest notices indicate, Mae West was always a provocative performer, and in vaudeville that would prove both an asset and a drawback. Her style certainly drew attention in her first vaudeville bookings, in the Northeast in March 1912, as the star of Mae West and the Gerard Boys. Backed by the "Gerards" (dancers Bobby O'Neill and Harry Laughlin), West took center stage in a low-cut dress and gave a raucous performance highlighted by her "muscle dance," a blatantly suggestive number in which she wriggled to a pulsating ragtime beat while seated in a chair. In the carefully engineered "accident" that ended the performance, as West writhed with enthusiasm, a strap on her already revealing gown broke, leaving her to readjust the gown over her nearly exposed breast with studied indifference.[2]

The ribaldry of West's act earned her some attention, but it also brought critical warnings: she would never make it in the big time, where managers demanded clean and reputable entertainers. The criticism continued over the next several months, after West dropped the Gerards to debut as a vaudeville single. The harshest complaints came from the critic most respected by vaudevillians— Sime Silverman, founder of the vaudeville journal *Variety*. Silverman assailed West's explicit sexuality, arguing that it deprived her of "that touch of class that is becoming requisite nowadays in the first-class houses." Moreover, big-time audiences expected a performer to have a vivid and instantly recognizable persona with direct appeal. West hadn't yet learned to "get" her audience in that fashion; she "should be coached," he urged, "to derive the full value from her personality."[3]

Over the next four years West attempted to take Silverman's advice. By 1913 her career seemed to be headed in a promising new direction. In the fall she premiered an act co-created by writer Thomas Gray, who had penned material for some of vaudeville's biggest names. Though it gave ample scope to West's predilection for suggestive musical numbers and undulating dance, it added a newly personable touch: a stream of tough wisecracks and jovial banter that helped West establish a rapport with the crowd. At least one vaudeville critic, *Variety*'s "Jolo" (the same Joshua Lowe who had remarked dryly on her singing at the Victoria a few months earlier), saw it as an effective addition: "The surprise of the bill to those familiar with her recent work around here was Mae West. She is doing less 'singing' and has a lot of new 'kidding' talk that is very good. She put it over in a manner to unmistakably indicate that this is her forte."[4]

West's new act served her well for its first several months. Though low on the bills, she obtained occasional bookings at the large East Coast houses controlled by the Keith Circuit, vaudeville's most prestigious theatrical chain. Catering primarily to a middle-class family crowd, the Keith Circuit defined big-time vaudeville: plush theaters offering high-salaried stars in two fast-paced, brightly polished performances a day.

West played on the Keith Circuit intermittently until early 1914. But by May of that year she had dropped from sight, to resurface in July under contract to tour the urban Northeast and Midwest on the small-time vaudeville circuit controlled by New York's Marcus Loew. However attractive steady employment may have been after months of irregular appearances in Keith houses, West indisputably took a step downward in moving to the Loew Circuit. Small-time theaters, with their lower-grade performers, cheaper prices, and working-class crowds, were widely regarded as the end of vaudeville most quickly to be escaped.[5]

For the remaining three years of her vaudeville career, try as she might (and she tried a great deal), West never managed to escape the small-time ranks. She herself had a ready explanation. In her 1959 autobiography she admitted she occasionally had difficulty in vaudeville, particularly when playing outside New York, but she attributed those problems to her pioneering sexual forthrightness and her "sophisticated ideas and style," which offended her provincial audiences' "country cousin standards."[6]

West did have a point. She was always most at home as a New York City performer, playing within a tradition that big-time managers deemed unsuitable for the hinterlands. But in fact the story of Mae West's failure in vaudeville is a more complex and more interesting one. Provincial vaudeville audiences were not universally prudish, and "country cousin" performers were as likely as not to meet an indifferent reception. If West failed to win their approval, it was not because she gave a sexual performance but because she gave a particular style of sexual performance—one that continued to lack "that touch of class."

The examination of West's career in vaudeville is constrained by the evidence. In the 1910s, when she was just starting out, she naturally received few press notices, and those she did get were usually brief mentions. As a result we can see her only in flashes: through song titles and descriptions of costumes, through comparisons to other performers, and through suggestions, often hostile, that her vaudeville style was better suited to very different theatrical venues. But even this fragmentary evidence points to the key issues raised by West's failure to break into the big time, issues of sexuality and class, of local taste versus mass appeal. West's problems in vaudeville bring into focus the themes that would define her career.

On paper Mae West's act looked no different from that of many of her female competitors in vaudeville: a mix of ragtime music, nonsense lyrics, and what publicists labeled "eccentric" dance. In person, however, she created a stir. Her style of delivery made theater managers nervous. As West herself put it at the close of each performance, "It isn't what you do, it's how you do it."[7]

Just how West did what she did—her looks, her mannerisms, and the resonances they carried—convinced more than one critic that she was simply unsuited to vaudeville. That was clearly the opinion of a *Variety* reporter who saw her perform in Philadelphia in 1912:

> May [*sic*] West and the Gerard Boys were another big letter act, and this trio put one over which made the uptown theater-goers, most of whom had probably never seen a burlesque show, sit up and take some notice. This May West is pretty near a duplicate of Babe La Tour, with a burlesquey style, some funny clothes which she handles freely and carelessly, and a couple of nifty looking boys who can step neatly. The act is a bit rougher than the usual order of things at the Liberty, but it went over and there was plenty of applause, also some talk caused by the frowsy headed May. The burlesque stage is her place and she can make a name there.[8]

Over the course of West's years in vaudeville critics regularly echoed *Variety*'s judgment that, as a vaudevillian, she was misplaced—her real home lay in burlesque. Rarely, however, was that assessment made as above, as a piece of helpful criticism. More often it was voiced in a tone of disgust and hostility. "Unless Miss West can tone down her stage presence in every way," wrote *Variety*'s Sime Silverman in 1916, "she just as well might hop right out of vaudeville into burlesque."[9] As Silverman's animosity made clear, linking West to burlesque was no compliment, but tantamount to consigning her to the theatrical wrong side of the tracks.

By 1910 burlesque was everything that vaudeville disdained: baldly sexual, ostentatiously sleazy, still awash in all the venal qualities vaudeville claimed to have shed in its elevation as "family amusement." Though it emerged in the United States as a European import, first appearing in the 1860s in the hands of British traveling troupes who performed travesties on classical plays, burlesque quickly discarded its parodic framework and pointed political satire in favor of scatological comedy and erotic feminine movement. Composed by the 1880s of a mishmash of suggestive songs, dances, and comedy sketches, burlesque became a fixture of working-class, male-oriented districts like New York's Bowery, vying for space with minstrel shows, concert saloons, and variety theaters, whose content it often duplicated and whose audience it shared.[10]

But variety theater, as we shall see, rose in social status at the turn of the century, moving from lower-class neighborhoods to central shopping and theatrical districts and forging bonds with a citywide, cross-class, sexually integrated public increasingly oriented toward leisure and consumption. Burlesque, in contrast, sank, left behind as a decaying remnant of the nineteenth-century netherworld of men-only entertainments. Districts like the Bowery, where New York's burlesque theaters congregated, deteriorated, their once-flashy streets fronted by crumbling and ill-ventilated buildings housing burlesque, cheap sideshows, and a few decrepit saloons. Such commercial establishments, once the province of a broad spectrum of workingmen, now drew only the most determinedly seedy—the failed laborers and the small-time crooks. So, at least, they seemed in the eyes of observers from the popular press, like one Boston journalist who visited a burlesque house in 1909:

> Before you a sadly questionable array of artisans, cheap drummers, petty clerks, temporarily opulent malefactors, and, plainly discernable, certain daring souls from the rural glades. . . . A little farther back, a glummer and less decent company, though more at ease. Beyond them, a noticeably viler herd. In the balcony a blend of pickpocket, day-laborer, and unwashed ne'er-do-well. Thronging the topmost gallery . . . a rabble of tramps, thugs, jailbirds and noxious urchins. The higher, the lower![11]

In truth, burlesque capitalized on its disreputability, flaunting its wickedness and purporting to offer what was unshowable in mass-market amusements. A night in a burlesque house was no less than riotous. The standard practice of playing with the house lights ablaze, begun to enable managers to spot police, allowed the division between entertainers and entertained to blur. Lewd comics directed their satire at noticeably youthful, balding, or uneasy patrons; patrons talked back to comics, often giving their humor an even raunchier bent ("What the comedians do not say on the stage," noted a disgusted *Variety* writer in 1915, "the inmates of the gallery say for them"); intermission "butchers" bartered with audience members in selling pornographic books and pictures; and skimpily dressed dancers tickled men with feather dusters and lured them to the stage for kisses.[12] Small wonder that to middle-class social workers who visited burlesque houses, accustomed, as in the legitimate theater, to a strict division between audience and entertainer, such raucousnesss connoted a sexual familiarity that extended beyond the performance. The reaction of investigator George Kneeland, who surveyed New York nightspots for a 1913 study of commercialized vice, was typical: "It may be said that practically all of the women in burlesque shows are professional prostitutes."[13]

Burlesque made a point of blurring the line between sexy performance and sexual commerce. The sheer stupidity of the shows contributed to reformist outrage, laying a thin veneer of coarse sight gags and wordplay over the parade of gutter indulgence. Plot, of any kind, was nonexistent. Instead, shows revolved around comic "bits"—brief skits marked by rapid-fire double entendre and ending in a salty one-liner. Not all such jokes were handled by male comics. Many burlesque troupes featured "talking women," female players adept at both insinuating humor and suggestive undulations.[14] Whoever the speaker, the intention to titillate was so transparent that some observers tagged the comedy "single entendre"—or, in the words of one outraged San Francisco journalist, "double meaning, so lopsided and tilted by indelicacy [that] the assumption of its being taken any other than the way intended was an insult to the intelligence."[15]

Those comic overtures did serve one purpose—they worked up anticipation for the evening's genuine focus. As *Billboard* magazine attested, "90 per cent of the burlesque audiences go to see the girls."[16] From the chorus dancers to the headlining soubrette, burlesque women made a flamboyant sexual appeal. Social reformers were not alone in assuming that they were "professional prostitutes." That assumption undergirded every burlesque display, and probably every man in the audience shared it.

Drawn from the ranks of working-class tough girls, burlesque women communicated a tough girl's aggression in a manner designed to look straight from the streets. Their heavyset bodies (burlesque managers boasted of their "elephantine" or "Beef Trust" choruses) evoked the animalistic, fully-fleshed sensuality attributed to prostitutes in contemporary artistic, medical, and social science discourse.[17] Their clothing was tight-fitting and skimpy. (They were never completely nude—the striptease did not become standard burlesque fare until the 1920s.) Above all, they put their portly, scantily clad bodies in motion, enticing their observers not just by the display of flesh, but by its rhythmic, undulating movement.

Most provocative of all was "cootch" dancing, a purposeful wriggling of the hips and torso that formed the burlesque show's explosive finale. Adopted from highly publicized Egyptian dancers who created a sensation at the 1893 Chicago World's Fair, the cootch highlighted the "suggestively lascivious contorting of the abdominal muscles" in a manner that struck some original observers as "extremely ungraceful and almost shockingly disgusting."[18] Transported to burlesque, performed with a dearth of grace and a wealth of abandon, the cootch exuded an air of exotic indulgence. Its powerful effect on audiences was captured in 1915 by a reporter for the *Philadelphia North American* who was at once fascinated and repelled by burlesque's reigning "cootcher," "The Girl in Blue," Millie De Leon:

Slowly, and in a manner hardly noticeable even through the transparent net which constituted the middle portion of her gown, the muscles of her body took on a wave-like motion. The undulations increased in rapidity. A purely muscular side to side movement, generally deemed the peculiar gift of horses, complicated the pattern and introduced a chaotic activity that probably lasted five minutes.

Finally, Millie De Leon became unspeakably frank. Every muscle became eloquent of primitive emotion. Amid groans, cat calls and howls of approval from the audience, she stopped. Standing suddenly erect, with a deft movement she revealed her nude right leg from knee almost to waist.

A strut to the right, a long stride back, and the abdominal "dance" was resumed. The large pink rose in her belt nodded confusedly, and her hands clasped and unclasped spasmodically under the strain of the stimulated emotion. Streaked and sweaty, her face took on the aspect of epilepsy. She bit her lips, rolled her eyes, pulled fiercely at great handfuls of her black, curly hair.

Indescribable noises and loud suggestions mingled in the hot breath of the audience. Men in the orchestra rose with shouts. A woman—one of six present—hissed. Laughter became uproarious. And then, sensing her climax, Millie De Leon gave a little cry that was more a yelp, and ceased.[19]

Mae West did not train in burlesque, but she exuded "primitive emotion" too. Taking the stage with a tough girl's swagger, she threw a cootch into everything she did. Hers was a raunchy, untrammeled cootch whose sexual resonance hit viewers full in the face. Her "muscle dance in a sitting position" showcased the movements of her hips and pelvis with an extravagance worthy of Millie De Leon.

Like burlesque performers, West wriggled her body in dances redolent of "primitive" cultures: not just the cootch, but the Grizzly Bear and the Turkey Trot, raucous steps that were rooted in African tradition and were all the rage in the urban working-class dance hall. Boisterous animal imitations that placed a premium on pelvic gyration, they struck social reformers as nothing short of obscene. As one dance hall investigator put it in 1912, the steps derived from "disreputable origins" and constituted "not dancing at all, but a series of indecent antics."[20]

Mae West performed the Grizzly Bear and the Turkey Trot in a fashion that brought that lower-class "indecency" to the foreground. To critics, that rendered her a "rough soubret" and her Turkey Trot "too coarse" for vaudeville's "two dollar audience."[21] At a time when social reformers and dance instructors were urging urban youth to temper their dances, West, if anything, inflamed hers even further. She took inspiration from places the respectable strictly avoided, like a "low colored cafe" in Southside Chicago where in 1914 she learned a new dance step, the shimmy:

> We went to the Elite Number One and the colored couples on the dance floor were doing the "shimmy-shawobble." Big black men with razor-slashed faces, fancy high yellows and beginners browns—in the smoke of gin scented tobacco to the music of "Can House Blues." They got up from the tables, got out to the dance floor, and stood in one spot, with hardly any movement of the feet, and just shook their shoulders, torsos and pelvises. We thought it was funny and were terribly amused by it. But there was a naked, aching sensual agony about it, too.
>
> The next day on stage at the matinee, the other actors were standing in the wings watching my act. I always did a dance for an encore. Then, inspired by the night before, during the dance music I suddenly stood still and started to shake in a kidding way, for the benefit of the actors in the wings backstage, recalling to them what we had seen the night before at the Elite Number One. The theater began to hum.[22]

With her shimmying and shaking and bumping and grinding, West palpably embodied the disreputable world of the burlesque show, the dance hall, and the black honky-tonk. Critics lambasted her vulgarity and roughness and urged her to reform, and fast. Unmodified, her low-grade undulations would scare off big-time audiences. The "muscle dance," predicted *Variety*, "will never go at Keith's Philadelphia."[23]

West, however, disagreed. Far from muting her undulations, she made them the core of her stage persona as a "rough hand-on-the-hip" tough girl who, one early fan remembered, strutted and cootched and sang songs full of boasts about her sexual prowess.[24] Unlike her critics, West believed that there *was* an audience for seamy vaudeville, and for vaudevillians who deliberately evoked the low-grade theatrics of the underworld streets.

Her calculations about audience taste differed dramatically from those of the Keith Circuit, with its chain of theaters stretching across the country. Keith Circuit big-time made its assumptions about audience desires by envisioning an unpredictable national public, regionally and temperamentally various crowds. Mae West made her assumptions about audience desires by envisioning the public she knew best—the theatergoing public of New York City. Trained in New York's popular theater and imbued with its traditions, she had good reasons for believing that there was a vital, broad-based market for raunchy and titillating vaudeville—and the chief embodiment of those reasons was none other than Hammerstein's Victoria Theater, the city's top vaudeville house, which drew crowds not with the rhetoric of wholesomeness that distinguished the Keith Circuit but rather by flaunting its ties to gritty underworld amusements. Via Hammerstein's, urban sensationalism had been broadening its audience since the turn of the century, attracting middle-class New Yorkers and tourists eager for a taste of the wicked metropolis. By the 1910s New York City supported a wide and enthusiastic public that prided itself on its "sophisticated" appreciation of urban vice.

It is worth taking a closer look at Hammerstein's Victoria, for its style and its fate illuminate the context of Mae West's vaudeville career. Built in 1889 by Metropolitan Opera House founder Oscar Hammerstein I (the grandfather of the lyricist-librettist Oscar Hammerstein II), the Victoria was located at Broadway and Forty-second Street in the emerging theatrical mecca of Times Square. It

was originally established as a legitimate theater but fared indiffer-
ently until 1904, when Hammerstein's son Willie took over its
management and turned it into a vaudeville house.

Willie Hammerstein came into vaudeville thoroughly familiar
with the seedier ends of show business. Beginning his career as a
press agent, he soon turned to burlesque, creating his own entertainment palace, Little Coney Island, on 110th Street.[25] As manager
of the Victoria he gave free rein to his taste for the sensational.
Granted a monopoly over big-time vaudeville in Times Square by
the Keith Circuit's booking office, and possessing sufficient power
to disregard the circuit's strictures, he devised a strategy that made
Hammerstein's theater New York's "undisputed queen of variety
theaters," drawing crowds even in periods of theatrical slump.[26] In
its eleven years as a vaudeville showcase the theater would gross
$20 million, enabling Oscar Hammerstein, in the words of his son
Arthur, "to build more opera houses."[27]

Willie Hammerstein gave his "unique place of entertainment" its
distinctive aura by evoking the seamy world of Bowery entertainments—both the burlesque house and the dime museum, a gallery
of human and animal deformities and dubiously "exotic" curiosities. He actively trumpeted his theater's links to the netherworld of
men-only amusements, even inventing them, if necessary. In presenting his 1909 headliner, "Princess Rajah in her Cleopatra Dance" (a
thinly disguised cootch), he embellished her already sleazy background by surreptitiously placing her in Huber's Fourteenth Street
dime museum, where she writhed for the all-male clientele; after a
few weeks he brought her to the Victoria, loudly heralding his "discovery" and making much of her migration "direct from Huber's to
Hammerstein's."[28] He tried the same maneuver in 1913 with "The
Half Woman," advertised as "The Only Legless Lady Ever Born,
Discovered Last Summer By Mr. Hammerstein at a Remote Five-
Cent Side Show." This time, however, the attraction proved too
tawdry even for the usually supportive *Variety*:

> One of the acts at Hammerstein's this week is of the freak variety,
> called the "Half Woman." She isn't an edifying object to look at.
> Loney Haskell, who lectures on her, says she is happily married.
> Let's hope so, and if she is, why doesn't she stay at home, or exhibit
> herself in a museum, where she belongs, not on a stage before peo-
> ple who go to be entertained, and then have nightmare[s] at night

because of imagining all sorts of things in connection with severed limbs, after the exhibition. . . . Because Huber's has gotten out of the dime museum business is no reason that Hammerstein's should try to take its place. . . . That this is not a deceit is proven by the half portion being carried through the audience.[29]

But Hammerstein did not transport the dime museum unaltered to the sophisticated terrain of Times Square. In adopting dime museum conventions, he reshaped them with a blend of urban topicality and tongue-in-cheek humor. As in the dime museum, Hammerstein employed a lecturer to instruct the audience on the curiosities; at the Victoria, however, that lecturer was comic Loney Haskell, like Willie Hammerstein a veteran of burlesque, who convulsed his listeners with droll, off-color disquisitions on the likes of "Venus on Wheels" and "The Diving Seal with the Human Brain." Even more important, as we have seen, Hammerstein broadened the definition of the freak show itself, giving it a new and specifically metropolitan twist by engaging notorious figures like Evelyn Nesbit and the Shooting Stars. Setting his prices low enough to accommodate most classes of patron (and quenching their thirst by selling alcohol at intermission), he devised snappy, outlandish promotions for appearances by the stars of the city's biggest scandals. Rarely did these freaks of the headlines possess any real performing ability. A few were capable of contriving an innocuous song and dance, but others simply stood onstage while Loney Haskell lectured on their history and merits. Of course, ability hardly mattered here. As vaudeville observer Caroline Caffin noted in 1914, the thrill of such performances lay in the peculiarly "real and tangible" air that surrounded these figures once they left their usual metier to face an audience on the vaudeville stage.[30]

Metropolitan sensations of all sorts found a home at Hammerstein's, from boxing champion Jack Johnson to women's rights activist Inez Milholland, who took the stage in 1912 on a "Suffragette's Day."[31] The emphasis, however, was on sex scandals and murders, and their provocative female embodiments. Evelyn Nesbit in August 1913 brought Willie Hammerstein his greatest triumph. The theater's all-time money-maker for a four-week "Exclusive Engagement," Nesbit's stint received an unexpected boost during the third week—a boost so perfect that some accused Willie Hammerstein of engineering it. Harry Thaw, committed for insanity, made a cloak-and-dagger escape from a mental institution in Matawan, New Jersey. Nesbit, naturally, "feared for her life," and the theater provided her with an armed escort, generating a wealth of free publicity.[32]

Mae West's appearance as one of the openers for Nesbit was not her first booking at the Victoria. In 1912 and 1913 she played eleven week-long engagements at the theater, close to half of her total during her first two years in vaudeville. For a relatively unknown performer to play frequently at Hammerstein's was not unusual: Willie Hammerstein always aimed to present huge vaudeville bills at minimal cost, and so peopled his shows with a few high-priced feature attractions and a stable of low-salaried novelties, a category in which Mae West undoubtedly fit. She meshed perfectly with the theater's style. Like the rest of the Victoria's slew of metropolitan oddities, she held audiences through her evocation of the notorious. As Sime Silverman noted of an early West appearance at the Victoria: "She's one of the many freak persons of the vaudeville stage, where freakishness often carries more weight than talent."[33]

At Hammerstein's West aimed her performances at an audience of loyal Victoria regulars. The theater's prices ranged from twenty-five cents to a dollar, so that all but the poorest could attend, from immigrant young people who crowded the gallery to the middle-class wives Sophie Tucker spotted at a 1906 matinee, women who were "all so smart looking. They came in couples or four or five together, all laughing and chatting."[34] But contemporaries described Hammerstein's habitual crowd less by its class affiliation, its relation to social categories of respectability or ill repute, than by its affectation of a distinctive style.

With its lobby a hangout for Willie Hammerstein's underworld and show business cronies (press agents, theater bookers, gamblers, actors, liquor salesmen), the Victoria drew a crowd that emulated their conspicuously jaded demeanor and their "wise" and racy banter. No other vaudeville audience, *Variety* attested, was wiser than the "Hammersteiners" to "the refinements of stage slang," a cynical, pseudo-underworld lingo marked by black humor. (An unresponsive audience was "handcuffed"; a theater doing poor business was a "morgue.")[35] At the Victoria an act could afford to let loose, to exaggerate its sexual expressiveness, to sharpen its innuendo, to parade its debts to the ribaldries of the Bowery. At other houses this might be inadvisable, but, noted *Variety*, "the Hammersteiners like that sort of thing." Hammerstein's patrons cultivated a cool impassivity of manner and a warm appreciation of the seamy; they prided themselves on being among "the knowing ones who passed the Victoria doorman with a vacant stare."[36]

The emergence of the Hammersteiners was part of a wider social development in early twentieth-century New York City: the expansion of a public enchanted with the underside of urban life. The same years that saw the ascendance of Hammerstein's saw the spread of cabarets in theatrical and restaurant districts with a citywide patronage. Transplanted versions of the underworld "joints" and "dives" that dotted the Bowery, these establishments continued to draw some of their old clientele. For new patrons, rubbing shoulders with the seamy was the cabarets' chief delight, and the spectacle that resulted often astonished observers: "a hodge-podge of people in which respectable young married and unmarried women and even debutantes dance, not only under the same roof, but in the same room with women of the town."[37]

For the respectable to exhibit a fascination with urban vice was not in itself new. Middle-class New Yorkers in the late nineteenth century had been avid readers of guidebooks like *Lights and Shadows of New York Life, or Sights and Sensations of the Great City*, which interspersed chapters on civic institutions with surveys of "Blackmailing," "Female Sharpers," and "The Heathen Chinee." But such guides, often written by clergymen, peppered their explorations of New York's notorious haunts with strong statements of moral condemnation. However lightly these strictures may have been taken by readers, they were still deemed necessary to legitimate any discussion of vice— "the eye of the needle," in William Taylor's phrase, "through which any consideration of sexual conduct was forced to pass."[38]

What was new in New York in the 1910s was the absence of all such moral distancing. Hammerstein's flaunted its connections to the urban underworld, and its patrons gleefully adopted that underworld's trappings. Hammerstein's and the cabarets paved the way for the expanded popularity of "slumming," long a practice of the urban elite but by the 1920s a leisure-time staple of middle-class New Yorkers who patronized speakeasies, Harlem nightclubs, and drag balls held by an emerging gay subculture.[39]

It was one thing for Mae West to become a Hammerstein's regular. It was quite another for her to become a big-time vaudevillian. For any performer as ambitious as West, real success meant reaching vaudeville's top rank, the national chain of theaters managed by B. F. Keith.

Even had West wanted to base herself at Hammerstein's, it would not remain an option for long. In March 1913, in what *Variety* called "the most brazen and unscrupulous piece of double-crossing ever recorded in theatricals," Willie Hammerstein's exclusive control of Times Square vaudeville came to an end with the opening of the Keith Circuit's Palace Theater at Forty-seventh Street and Seventh Avenue.[40] Paying Oscar Hammerstein an estimated $225,000 to suspend their contract and encroach on his territory, Keith and his partner, Edward Albee, launched a theater that cultivated an atmosphere radically different from Hammerstein's. To the Victoria's seedy sensationalism, the Palace opposed what it heralded as refined glamor; to the Victoria's stable of cheap urban curiosities, it counterpoised vaudeville's biggest stars, most of whom the Keith Circuit had under contract.[41] Most decidedly, Keith and Albee did not seek the Hammerstein's public on its own terms: as Albee would say in 1915, they considered "criminal proceedings freaks" like the Shooting Stars an "insult" to any reputable theatrical manager.[42]

The establishment of the Palace fettered Hammerstein's, making it increasingly difficult for the theater to book acts; performers were understandably wary of linking themselves to Keith Circuit competitors. Yet its demise did not begin in earnest until June 1914, when Willie Hammerstein died and the theater's management passed into the hands of his brother Arthur, who sought to place Hammerstein's on a more conventional big-time path. Under his guidance the Victoria followed the Keith Circuit's lead, ending its presentation of freak acts and even canceling slated appearances by Mrs. Lefty Louie and Mrs. Gyp the Blood. Deprived of its distinctive appeal, the Victoria lost its audience, and its receipts declined rapidly until it closed in May 1915.[43]

The collapse of the Victoria cemented a process that had been under way for more than a decade—the consolidation of vaudeville into a centralized amusement industry with one corporation dominating the field, routing standardized entertainment to a national audience. The Victoria had been a quintessential New York City theater, drawing primarily on local scandals and thriving on the public appetites fed by the local sensationalist press. Willie Hammerstein had no vaudeville interests outside New York, and thus no need to develop acts that would go over in other locales. Secure in his position as Times Square's sole vaudeville purveyor, he had a free hand to create his product and shaped a theater that emblematized a vital local style.

Hammerstein's harked back to vaudeville's early days, when theaters were owned singly and their bookings determined by the owners themselves in accordance with local tastes. By the 1910s, however, that world was fast disappearing. The Keith Circuit, which in the 1890s had owned five theaters in the Northeast, by the mid-1910s controlled dozens more, with eight in New York City alone. More important, the circuit had powerful affiliations with subsidiary vaudeville chains across the country, links that gave it a complete monopoly over big-time vaudeville, the elaborate, expensive shows mounted in plush theaters across the nation, offering performances by vaudeville's biggest names.[44]

In short, by the mid-1910s vaudeville was no longer a variegated enterprise. The Victoria had managed to be both idiosyncratic and prestigious, big-time without falling in the Keith Circuit mold. But with growing Keith Circuit domination, there was less and less room for such deviations. If Mae West was serious about vaudeville stardom, she would have to conform to Keith Circuit demands. For that reason, we must examine how the circuit defined big-time style—a matter that is not as simple as it might initially appear.

From the earliest days of their enterprise Keith and Albee had definite ideas about precisely what vaudeville ought to be. As northeastern theater proprietors in the 1880s, they had built their reputation on "clean, wholesome amusement," entertainment suitable for women, children, and the respectable middle class. The "clean and wholesome" was crucial, for when Keith and Albee began, vaudeville was linked to disreputable brands of theater from which the Victorian middle class strictly kept its distance.

Vaudeville traced its roots to several amusement traditions that flourished among the nineteenth-century working class: the circus, the melodrama, the dime museum, and most notably the concert saloon, a notorious hangout for laborers and slumming gentlemen seeking drink and bawdy diversion. To entertain their raucous clientele, saloonkeepers offered "variety theater" in their back rooms and cellars—random collections of dancers, singers, acrobats, and comics who performed and mixed with patrons in an atmosphere thick with smoke and alcohol. Featuring coarse scatological humor and promiscuous mingling of audience and entertainers (female singers, or "waiter girls," were often paid to solicit drinks and occasionally made assignations with customers), concert saloons were strictly male preserves that few women of any class could patronize with comfort.[45]

Keith sought to broaden variety's audience by making it palatable to the middle class. In establishing his chain of theaters—first in Boston in 1883 and later in Providence, Philadelphia, and New York—Keith banned alcohol from the premises and enforced strict censorship of performance content. His circuit's widely advertised emphasis on "polite" entertainment was no mere rhetoric; as performers discovered from signs posted backstage, theater regulations were minutely detailed, and disregarding them brought immediate dismissal from the stage:

> NOTICE TO PERFORMERS: You are hereby warned that your act must be free from all vulgarity and suggestiveness in words, action and costume, while playing in any of Mr. [Keith]'s houses, and all vulgar, double-meaning and profane words and songs must be cut out of your act before the first performance. If you are in doubt as to what is right or wrong, submit it to the resident manager at rehearsal.
>
> Such words as Liar, Slob, Son-of-a-Gun, Devil, Sucker, Damn, and all other words unfit for the ears of women and children, also any references to questionable streets, resorts, localities, and barrooms, are prohibited under fine of instant discharge.[46]

Keith's version of variety theater was tailor-made for genteel audiences; not only risqué performers but indecorous patrons came in for managerial censure. In its concert saloon setting, variety theater had been defined as much by the antics of customers as by the efforts of entertainers—by yelling, joking, whistling, and booing, the kind of unrestrained behavior that had come to typify "debased" working-class amusements in the eyes of critics.[47] In Keith theaters, by contrast, where prices were geared to the middle class but low enough for some workingmen, small cards were discreetly distributed to remind unruly patrons that they had entered a place of leisure for ladies and gentlemen:

Gentlemen will kindly avoid the stamping of feet and pounding of canes on the floor, and greatly oblige the Management. All applause is best shown by the clapping of hands.

Please don't talk during acts, as it annoys those about you, and prevents a perfect hearing of the entertainment.[48]

The Keith Circuit's policy produced, in the words of one booker, "the prettiest, coziest, daintiest theater in New York"—hardly a description that could ever have been applied to a Bowery concert saloon.[49] Throughout the Northeast in the last decade of the nineteenth century, the circuit proved phenomenally successful in drawing its intended audience: the urban middle-class family trade, men, women, and children eager for diverting amusement but still imbued with older notions of public decorum.

By the time Mae West entered vaudeville the Keith Circuit was still trumpeting its clean family amusement. Keith himself, when interviewed in 1911, stressed that the wholesomeness of his line of vaudeville had in no way diminished with its expansion into a national enterprise:

> I made it a rule at the beginning, when I first opened my Washington Street museum, that I must know exactly what every performer on my stage would say or do. If there was one coarse, vulgar or suggestive line or piece of stage business in the act, I cut it out. And this rule is followed in every Keith theater in the United States today and just as rigidly adhered to now as it was then.[50]

Measured simply by the degree of scrutiny accorded individual acts, Keith Circuit censorship indeed continued in the old, rigid tradition. Circuit officials maintained a close supervision of performers, originally at the level of the individual theaters, and by the mid-1910s at the level of the central booking office as well. Contracts issued by the Keith Circuit's United Booking Office ensured that theater managers could censor acts at will: material judged inappropriate at the Monday matinee would be ordered cut by Monday evening, and a report on the act's offense against decency would be sent to the United Booking Office in New York. Too many damning "blue envelopes" in a performer's file could create difficulty in securing UBO bookings; if a performer refused to comply with a manager's order, he or she would be banned from the Keith Circuit, and thus big-time vaudeville, altogether.[51]

In theory the vaudevillians who succeeded in big-time were those who toed a universally inoffensive line, whose acts were as free from suggestiveness as in the circuit's early days. Yet despite B. F. Keith's assurances to the contrary, the situation was more complex. By the 1910s the Keith Circuit's biggest stars were injecting more than a hint of innuendo and more than a trace of provocative movement in their performances. These were never overtly, unambiguously sexual, but sexuality was there for the viewer who wanted to find it.

Keith Circuit vaudeville had to change; its audience demanded it. Though it continued to cater to middle-class families, those families' tastes were growing less predictable by the year. The decades around the turn of the century had seen the disintegration of the middle-class worldview that valorized purity, duty, and self-restraint. By the 1910s vaudeville journalists were calling attention to the startling diversity of big-time crowds, not just from city to city, but within a single city, even a single audience. The middle-income fans who frequented big-time vaudeville had come to represent a range of moral viewpoints, from the most censorious to the most freewheeling, and not even a preperformance peek through the curtain could help a manager predict whose standards would prevail. External appearances had become a poor gauge of audience taste, as journalist Hartley Davis noted of his experience with Keith Circuit crowds: "When one has sat through an act that calls for expletives and resignation on one's own part, it is rather disconcerting to hear one's neighbor praise it as being 'real refined and genteel,' especially when one is certain that the nice spectacled old lady is far less tolerant of moral shortcomings than one's self."[52]

The Keith Circuit's official response to the disruption within its audience was to ally itself with the moral traditionalists. Its commitment to thoroughly wholesome entertainment was more than just a public relations tactic, at least as far as top management was concerned. Both Keith and Albee, who assumed complete control of the circuit after Keith's death in 1914, were notorious among performers for their unbending conservatism in matters personal and professional. In tightening and centralizing UBO censorship after abuses had been reported at some theaters in the mid-1910s, Albee made it clear that whatever the desires of some among its patrons, the Keith Circuit would not swerve from its original path. As he announced through *Variety*:

> The stringent instruction [stemmed from] . . . a desire by Circuit management to replace vaudeville on the cleanly path the late B. F. Keith first set it, and also to protect the matinee attendance, largely composed of the country's youth. The trend of the times, with its night amusements after theater hours and [styles of] dressing, not forgetting the afternoon dances, has been toward a liberality and a "wiseness" that greeted "fly stuff" on the stage with a welcome designed to deceive a manager, who could accept from its reception his audiences wanted that sort of matter. The U.B.O. intends to correct the abuses and return vaudeville to where it stood and belongs—the entertainment for the masses, children and adults, to be given without bringing a blush and a shiver.[53]

But Keith Circuit management was fighting a losing battle, trying to impose a traditional vision of family entertainment on families who were themselves divided in their ideas of appropriate conduct. Even in their stricter and more centralized form, the circuit's censorship practices proved ineffective, dependent as they were on the willingness of theater managers to restrain and report delinquent performers. However sympathetic managers may have been to the Keith Circuit's aims, their primary consideration had to be getting and keeping a paying crowd. An openly salacious act would doubtless offend many customers, but a wholly clean bill of fare, it was clear by the early twentieth century, would drive away even more. To draw an audience consistently, managers had to try, as journalist Caroline Caffin noted, to "fill in the breach" created by the new diversity: "There must be something for everyone and, though the fastidious may be a little shocked (the fastidious rather like to be shocked sometimes), they must not be offended, while the seeker for thrills must on no account be bored by too much mildness."[54]

Performers learned a similar lesson. By the 1910s the most successful Keith Circuit acts were those that could please a broad range of moral temperaments. Offering raciness for the thrill-seekers but crafting it for acceptance by the traditional, performers manipulated the increasingly uncertain boundaries of "respectable amusement" to make room for their acts.

No one did this more effectively than Eva Tanguay, a self-styled "eccentric comedienne" with connections to burlesque and to Hammerstein's Victoria Theater. Born in Canada in 1878, in 1904 she left Broadway musical comedy for vaudeville, where she became an immediate sensation. Over the next twenty-five years Tanguay remained the biggest draw on the vaudeville stage, its most highly paid and wildly trumpeted star.[55]

Tanguay rocketed to stardom because, as both friendly and hostile critics noted, she aggressively shattered accepted notions of what a female performer ought to be. She was not beautiful. As her critics flatly stated, she was often decidedly fat. She could neither sing nor dance in any conventional sense, with her screech of a voice and her graceless, undisciplined movements. Nor did she attempt, as did other women in vaudeville, to enact character sketches. Eva Tanguay made no pretense of appearing onstage as anyone but herself. Indeed, it was that self—her crazy, vivacious, unpredictable, "cyclonic" personality—that formed the subject of her act, which would remain unchanged, discounting minor variations, for all the years of her reign.

A Tanguay performance took place well into the evening's program, after six or seven acts had come and gone and the audience sat rigid with expectation. At the appointed moment a spotlight hit the corner of the stage and trombones blared. One hostile critic, writing in 1908, gave a concise description of what ensued:

> Eva Tanguay ran into view, with her shapely form encased in a short frock, her legs toddling freakishly, and her arms flung out on a level that was never for an instant lowered below her shoulders. She gyrated wildly while yelling a song about the kind of fascinating girl she was. Throwing off some of her attire, she gave vociferously a doggerel of which the refrain was "I don't care," her defiance being directed to those who disputed her talent. Finally, stripped of skirts, she finished her exploit in skin tights from neck to toes, jiggling about the stage and screaming that, no matter what anyone might say of her immodesty, she was a success, success, success.[56]

Composed of equal parts physical display, frenetic energy, and vehement self-promotion, Tanguay's act mesmerized audiences and critics alike. Reviewers unleashed a torrent of adjectives in their attempts to describe her "unique" and "explosive" style, all the while proclaiming her indescribable. Just what was it, they asked in bewilderment, that made her so compelling? Certainly, all were agreed, it was not talent.

As every observer noted, Tanguay riveted her viewers by her forceful physical appeal. Her costumes were scanty, "the most daring undress ever seen on a stage outside of the resorts under police surveillance," and she loved to spotlight her impropriety—boasting to reporters, for example, that she could carry her "Salome" costume in one closed fist.[57] Her songs were often provocative ("I'm Crazy About That Kind of Love," "I Want Someone to Go Wild With Me"), and her extravagant physical displays were reminiscent of burlesque. Indeed, Tanguay imitations became a standard feature of burlesque in the 1910s, with performers like Babe La Tour ("The Eva Tanguay of Burlesque") presenting "I Don't Care" in a manner that emphasized Tanguay's most suggestive contortions.[58]

But for all that she delighted in public indelicacy, Tanguay disassociated herself from her raunchier mimics. As she argued in a press release, such imitators as "Mademoiselle Fougere" entirely distorted her act:

> She has picked me out because she thinks she can wiggle. Anyone seeing her, who had not seen me, might get the wrong impression. I doubt if after seeing her imitation people who didn't know would be willing to be seen looking at my act, which I consider one a lady might do or see without shame.[59]

Tanguay exaggerated her act's innocence, but she had a point: while elements of her performance were certainly sexual, by no means all of it was. Tanguay's success in big-time vaudeville rested on her ability to defuse her sexual appeal, to provide alternative interpretations for behavior that might otherwise have seemed lewd and unrefined.[60] Her costumes may have been immodest, but they were also ridiculous: skimpy dresses covered in pennies, evening gowns stitched together out of pencils and memo pads. For every song she sang about passion, she sang three about herself ("The Tanguay Song," "I'm Happy, That's All," "Egotistical Eva," "Personality, Vitality, Pep and Originality Make My Spesh-ee-ality"). Finally, the physical exuberance with which she delivered all her numbers—the gyrating figure, waving arms, and restlessly pattering feet—might suggest the wantonness of a burlesque dancer; with sufficient outside suggestion, however, it could as readily evoke the unchecked raving of an asylum escapee. It was the latter impression that Tanguay, aided by voluminous press releases, sought to give her audience—an impression not of lewdness but of lunacy.

For an early twentieth-century middle-class audience, lunacy was a far more marketable commodity than an outright avowal of sensual passion. Even Tanguay's most adventurous fans might have been uncomfortable with the latter, their taste for rowdiness tempered by powerful older notions of the need for self-control. Tanguay played on that tension within her crowds, promising complete self-abandon and hinting at the madness that turn-of-the-century psychologists warned would inevitably follow the discarding of all restraint.[61] "She is a tornado," read one Tanguay press release, "a whirlwind, a bouncing bundle of perpetual motion. She screams, she shouts, she twists and turns, she is a mad woman, a whirling dervish of grotesquerie."[62]

Tanguay held her audience by conveying that abandon across the footlights, charging the theater with an electric energy that was by all accounts infectious. "There's no passive way of watching the Cyclonic One," observed the *New York Dramatic Mirror*: jittery and restless before she took the stage, her fans stamped, shouted, and screamed throughout her twenty-minute performance.[63] For that brief interval they could afford to be swept away by an exhilarating frenzy. As one formerly skeptical convert explained after witnessing her act, "What was the use of trying to be sane in the face of such inspired insanity?"[64] In an era when commercial amusements like Coney Island had found a lucrative middle-class market by creating safe, contained spaces for "inspired insanity," for momentary release from decorum, Tanguay exerted a similar appeal: Eva Tanguay, one critic noted, was "the only singer who makes you feel like 'holding tight' as the car is 'going around a curve.'"[65]

Tanguay drew in a public eager to flirt with her brand of outrageous abandon. They could toy with it without committing themselves to it, without being forced to live with its consequences. At the same time Tanguay's supposed lunacy prevented her from alienating more traditional audience members. While her scant costumes and frenetic gyrations satisfied those with a taste for the risqué, her pretensions to craziness disarmed those who might have found her immodesty threatening or immoral.

Indeed, a Tanguay performance was all about disarming criticism. She herself raised and repeated it, turning the furor around her into the focus of her act. Her songs, half-chanted, half-shrieked, were extended harangues cataloguing her eccentricities and mocking her attackers. Critics' charges that she could not sing, reviewers' swipes at her portly physique, fans' speculations about her personal mores, reporters' attacks on her outrageous salary (at $3,500 a week, the highest in vaudeville)—all were blithely reiterated and answered in the Tanguay repertoire:

> They say I'm crazy and got no sense, but—I don't care! My voice may sound funny but it's getting me the money so—I don't care![66]

> I don't believe I'm fat the way our Mr. Alan Dale did say, so—I don't care![67]

> They say I flirt and steal away from ladies fair their husbands gay, but it doesn't bother me![68]

> There's a method in my madness, there's a meaning for my style; the more they raise my salary, the crazier I'll be![69]

Tanguay made sure that the press attacks kept coming. Through her agents, she bombarded newspapers with accounts of her explosive temper, her abnormal vivacity, her atrocious voice, and her clumsy dancing. Even advertisements for her performances highlighted the Tanguay controversy, quoting critics who lambasted her as often as those who praised her. This barrage of verbiage ignited a furious debate: why was this woman, possibly a lunatic and definitely talentless, the most popular attraction in vaudeville? Fought out in nationally circulated press accounts and posed afresh each night onstage, it was a debate in which Tanguay encouraged her audience to participate.

And participate they did, with enthusiasm. Observed Tanguay of her fans' behavior, precisely the behavior she herself had helped to foster, "They go to see me as they go to the Zoo. They don't give me credit for ability; they repeat the most terrible tales about me, and believe them; and they go away from the theater saying, 'Well, you just can't do anything with that Tanguay woman.' "[70] Contemporary accounts support this contention: her fans vociferously debated the secret of her fame. Like most successful vaudevillians, she cultivated a friendly, informal stage presence, opening her act with a boisterous "Hello, everybody!" to which all were encouraged to respond and bantering agreeably with audience members whose comments she overheard. That direct appeal bred a sense of intimacy between Tanguay and her fans. Armed with information gleaned from press accounts, they yelled their opinions mid-performance. "Eva," shouted one man at a 1908 New York show, "you're a beauty!" Added another, in answer to her critics, "Your salary should be—," and then stopped, unable to think of a figure high enough.[71] By challenging her audiences to account for her fame, Tanguay kept them talking, arguing, trying to figure her out. Wrote critic Ashton Stevens in 1911 in the *Chicago Examiner*:

> She came like a meteor, but there is a lasting quality. What is that quality? Radium? Electricity? Sheer nerve? Or, as Eva Tanguay herself comically suggests, madness? I give it up. Every time I try to explain her it's another reason. She won't be still under the microscope. She yells, "I don't care!" and wriggles away. Her ego baffles. The more she flares it in your face the further you are from herself. . . . Eva Tanguay is hard, impenetrably hard.
>
> I listened to the crowd at the Majestic yesterday—such a crowd as only Eva Tanguay attracts—and the sum of its remarks was that she is a "genius" and a "freak." Most folks that do the extraordinary are. What isn't really accounted for is commonly called "freak" or "genius" or both.[72]

Tanguay had begun in vaudeville as a New York City attraction, first gaining notice in a series of hugely successful appearances at Hammerstein's Victoria. There, unsurprisingly, she fit easily into the panorama of freak acts, and even urged Willie Hammerstein to bill her as a "Theatrical Freak."[73] Yet Tanguay could make the leap to the Keith Circuit big-time where Mae West and the Shooting Stars could not; in contrast to them, she created a broad and multifaceted persona capable of appealing to a varied national audience. The notoriety of the Shooting Stars was linked to a specific New York City scandal; their appeal was thus purely local and of limited duration. Tanguay's scandal was more durable, was in fact self-renewing as she circulated it across the country in print and in performance. And while West's appeal was openly one of sexual impropriety, Tanguay's was not. She submerged her sexual impropriety in her broader assault on decorum, in a more global dismissal of convention. A Tanguay performance defied not only conventions of sexual modesty but of public dignity, seemly attire, graceful dancing, melodious singing—all flouted with an air of charming disregard that earned her, as her audience well knew, that unfathomable salary. Given the cheerfulness of her self-admittedly crazy assault on norms of all kinds, few could seriously label her antics immoral. As a Boston journalist wrote:

> Miss Tanguay freely admits that she hasn't a voice; she even confesses that she isn't much to look at, and certain people, moreover, have hinted quite plainly that she's a "fright." But she doesn't care (so she sings), nor, in sober truth, does her audience. . . . It only wants to hear her shriek slang and to see her smile. It likes her swing and swagger. And how spontaneous is that swagger and how deliciously wholesome is that smile! Indeed, it is easy to suggest that many another performer dressed in some of Miss Tanguay's costumes and singing some of Miss Tanguay's songs might easily become coarse and perhaps a trifle vulgar. But with Miss Tanguay the zest for fun is too keen, the delight in innocent roguishness is too sincere to cheapen or dull the edge of it.[74]

Eva Tanguay exerted a twenty-five-year hold over vaudeville audiences by mastering the secret of mass-market success: bridging the gaps created by regional variations, differences of class and gender, and divergent shades of moral opinion. She drew fans nationwide, from the cheaper seats in the gallery to the pricier spots in the orchestra, and among women as well as men. (One reporter particularly noted her female fans, who swarmed "the stage door wherever she appears . . . in order to catch a fleeting glimpse of her as she enters her carriage."[75]) She drew those fans not, as the Keith Circuit officially maintained, by excising questionable material from her act, but by reshaping it, giving it a range of possible meanings, putting it in the service of a colorful, amiable, and endlessly debatable personality.

It was Mae West's inability to do the same that kept her off the Keith Circuit's stages. At Hammerstein's she could afford to indulge in a low-class brand of performance: it suited the theater's style and the preferences of its audience. But in big-time vaudeville, West's conspicuous roughness limited her appeal. To please a national public, she needed a more nuanced performance style, one like Tanguay's, sufficiently enigmatic to accommodate the varied temperaments of her spectators.

West did try to recast her style, largely by shamelessly imitating Tanguay, as the notices for the act she put together with Thomas Gray indicate. "She dresses her hair a la Tanguay and affects costumes just as startling as the effervescent Eva," wrote a Philadelphia reviewer.[76] "She talks to the audience, makes them her confidants and otherwise follows the giddy footsteps of the Tanguay," observed the *Columbus Journal*.[77]

But West could only follow those giddy footsteps so far. For one thing, she could not hope to make a distinctive mark in vaudeville by replicating another performer's act. In addition, and crucially, in attempting to clothe her rough sexuality in an "eccentric" persona West was less than completely convincing. Her lower-class raunchiness always showed through in her pointedly provocative movements and banter. She had a wealth of ideas, billing herself variously as a "firefly girl" and a "Brinkley girl," experimenting with a rolled-out red carpet, harem pants, even male drag, but despite all her best efforts, she remained a "rough hand-on-the-hip character portrayer" rather than a Tanguayesque "cyclonic comedienne."[78] "Mae West is, plainly, vulgar," fumed one Detroit reviewer when West appeared in a local Loew theater. "This woman is all that is coarse in Eva Tanguay without that player's ability."[79] *Variety*'s Sime Silverman agreed. As he saw it, the problem was not West's ability but her style: her vulgarity came to her so naturally that it was virtually unmaskable. In a review of a New York appearance by West and her sister Beverly in their short-lived double act, Mae West and Sister—the same review in which he urged her to "hop right out of vaudeville into burlesque"—he wrote:

> Mae West in big-time vaudeville may only be admired for her persistency in believing she is a big-time act and trying to make vaudeville accept her as such. After trying out several brands of turns, Miss West is with us again, this time with a "Sister" tacked onto the billing and the stage. "Sister"'s hair looks very much like Mae's and there the family resemblance ceases in looks as well as

work, for "Sister" isn't quite as rough as Mae West can't help but being. . . . This working out new acts, buying new wardrobe and worrying will get to Miss West's nerve in time (but it will probably be a long time).[80]

West's descent into burlesque would come later, at a particularly low point in her career in the early 1920s, but by 1917 she had stopped working as a touring vaudevillian and abandoned her ambition to break into the big time. Whether from lack of ability or lack of will, she simply could not manage to smooth out her rough edges. As a working-class woman schooled in sensational theater, West would confront this problem throughout her career: how to reshape her native style of performance to accommodate a diverse middle-class public. But in the 1920s she would confront it within a very different context—not in the mass-market industry of vaudeville but in the legitimate theater of Broadway.

Chapter 3

SEX, *THE DRAG,* AND THE COMEDY-DRAMA OF LIFE

*M*ae West's years of obscurity in the theater came to an end in 1926–27 when she burst upon the notice of the New York City public through her association with two sensational—and, according to many, pornographic—productions.

In April 1926, with financial backing from two businessmen she treated to a private reading, West rented a Broadway theater, hired a director, and on what little money remained, staged a play she had written especially for herself, a tale of a Montreal prostitute to which she gave the provocative title *Sex*. The play was unanimously panned by New York's theater critics, all of whom predicted its immediate failure and some of whom called for police intervention. Yet despite this condemnation—or no doubt in part because of it—*Sex* confounded all expectations to become one of the major hits of the 1926 season, playing to largely full houses for almost a year.

West's production of *Sex* was sufficiently sensational in itself to guarantee its creator citywide notoriety. But West augmented her reputation in early 1927, writing and staging a play in which she did not appear, but which she proudly advertised as her own work. Billed as a "homosexual comedy-drama," *The Drag* played a series of widely publicized preview performances in Connecticut and New

Jersey in January 1927. By early February, against the united opposition of theatrical producers, social reformers, and public officials,
it stood poised on New York's city limits, making loud preparations
for a Broadway run.

Mae West's invasion of Broadway was prompted by a new level
of determination in charting her professional course. By early 1926
West's career had reached its nadir. At age thirty-two she had spent
twenty-five years in the popular theater, and not only did few New
Yorkers know her name, but to make matters worse, she had
recently been reduced to particularly humiliating work.

When she left the vaudeville circuits in 1917, after four frustrat-
ing years of nationwide touring, West had initially enjoyed a bit
more success. In 1918 she created a minor sensation in *Sometime*, a
Broadway musical comedy, and in 1922 she received warm notices
in a song-and-dance act with pianist Harry Richman. West and
Richman earned quality bookings in vaudeville theaters throughout
Manhattan, including New York's premier vaudeville showplace,
the Palace. But in September 1922 Richman left to join a nightclub
revue starring vaudeville headliner Nora Bayes. With his departure,
West's brief moment in the spotlight was over.

What happened next remains unclear. West's autobiography,
never very strong on dates, leaves the full four years after Richman's
departure entirely unaccounted for and conveniently obscures the
fact. Given her silence, it is hard not to believe film historian Jon
Tuska when he suggests that despite a lifetime of denials Mae West
had moved into burlesque.

Citations Tuska unearthed in *Billboard* suggest that West became
a featured player on the Mutual Burlesque Wheel (or Circuit)
between 1922 and 1925, appearing in Mutual's New York and
Brooklyn theaters in such revues as *Playmates, Girls From the Follies, Round the Town, Snap It Up,* and *French Models*—a sign of
just how far her career had plummeted.[1] Burlesque in general was
avoided by all ambitious performers, and the Mutual Wheel carried
the greatest stigma of all. Founded in July 1922, it was infamous for
its cheap, sensational revues flaunting no-holds-barred lewdness—in
the words of one chronicler, "such feverish shimmying and shaking," "cootching and undressing," as had never been presented in
burlesque theaters before.[2] By taking work on the Mutual Wheel,
West entered the roughest end of the burlesque business, the end
that approached outright pornography.

Though Mae West could not have relished being reduced to burlesque, it was certainly consistent with her earlier work. Throughout all West's efforts at stage success, one element of her strategy remained constant: she would get ahead by her talent for sexual expression, her vaudeville-honed ability to titillate audiences with a flamboyant persona. What little attention she won in the early 1920s had come when she stretched the sensuality of her roles to the limit. In *Sometime* she took the spotlight with the "shimmy," a "cootch above the waist" that West had learned in Southside Chicago and that was then creating a sensation in clubs around Times Square, dancing with sufficient abandon that her performance gained a reputation as Broadway's rawest.[3] Still, too many dancers were doing shimmies for hers to stand out all that much, and besides, in musical revues she was simply one of the crowd. What she needed was a vehicle in which she would be the unquestioned star, in a medium where there were no prohibitions to tone her down.

Broadway was the obvious answer: the "legitimate stage," as it had been labeled in the nineteenth century to distinguish it from vaudeville, burlesque, and the musical revue. In the 1920s the Times Square legitimate district was enjoying an unprecedented boom, even in the face of motion picture competition. The number of Broadway's legitimate houses had risen rapidly over the past two decades, from sixteen in 1900 to sixty-five in 1925; the number of plays premiering each season had nearly tripled; and as increased patronage helped drive ticket prices upward, the revenues associated with successful shows skyrocketed.[4] Broadway was the logical goal for the driven and ambitious Mae West: the rewards of stardom, in prestige and profits, far outstripped what she could hope to gain on the vaudeville circuits, where competition from the movies had already begun to take its toll.

Even more important was Broadway's freedom of expression. If the Keith Circuit's insistence on "family appeal" had kept Mae West from performing as she pleased, there was no such difficulty on the legitimate stage. Despite occasional threats of municipal interference and a few halfhearted efforts at theatrical self-regulation, sexual expression in Broadway plays had always been limited only by the boundaries of public tolerance—boundaries that seemed remarkably elastic in the 1920s and that Mae West tested to the limit with *Sex* and *The Drag*.

*   *   *

Sex starred Mae West as Margy Lamont, a bitter, imperious prostitute who presides over the roughest brothel in all of Montreal. Over
the course of three acts, the play follows Margy from Montreal to
Trinidad to the affluent suburbs of New York, where she travels in
pursuit of money, adventure, and sex. The plot is convoluted—an
absurd and at times incoherent blend of comedy and melodrama—
but, for the play's original viewers, its crucial moments came in acts
one and two, when we see Margy in her element, the reigning figure
in the Montreal brothel and the presiding entertainer in a sleazy
Trinidad nightclub that caters to visiting sailors. In these largely
comic scenes, Margy herself is always the focus, joking suggestively
with her sponging pimp, exciting the lust of her male customers,
and dispatching unwanted admirers with derisive comments on
their sexual prowess.

It is almost impossible to exaggerate the condemnation critics
heaped upon *Sex*, and on these scenes above all. These were not
simply negative reviews, dismissing the play in the vocabulary of
dramatic criticism; rather, they were reviews by people who were
genuinely appalled by what they had seen onstage. One typical
example, from the *New York Daily Mirror*, was headlined "SEX AN
OFFENSIVE PLAY. MONSTROSITY PLUCKED FROM GARBAGE CAN, DESTINED
TO SEWER." The reviewer continued, "This production is not for the
police. It comes rather in the province of our Health Department. It
is a sore spot in the midst of our fair city that needs disinfecting."[5]

The *Daily Mirror* was a tabloid, and thus habitually given to
hyperbole. Yet in making the case against *Sex*, even the more
restrained papers employed the vocabulary of infection, disease, and
filth. The script, said the *New Yorker*, was composed of "street
sweepings";[6] the play, declared another critic, left the audience
afflicted with "that 'dark brown' taste which results from proximity
to anything indescribably filthy."[7] The reviewer for the *New York
Herald Tribune* was somewhat more subdued, but he too came to
essentially the same conclusion. *Sex*, he wrote, was

> an ostensible reflection of the underworld as it is supposed to exist
> in Montreal and Trinidad. A world of ruthless, evil-minded, foul-
> mouthed crooks, harlots, procurers and other degenerate members
> of that particular zone of society. Never in a long experience of the-
> ater-going have we met with a set of characters so depraved. . . . All

the barriers of conventional word and act that the last few seasons of the theater have shown us were swept away and we were shown not sex but lust—stark, naked lust.[8]

Sex, in short, created a furor, and one that Mae West in subsequent years was never at a loss to explain. Her play had appeared at a time when Broadway shied away from all mention of physical passion. According to West, the legitimate theater in 1926 did not present sexual subject matter—it did not, for that matter, even employ the word. Before she used it as a play title, West claimed, the word "sex" had never appeared in the mass media, at least not to indicate physical acts; it was only used in medical journals or as a synonym for gender—"the fair sex," "the gentler sex." No city newspaper, she asserted, would advertise her play under its real title; instead, the press ran notices for "Mae West in That Certain Play."[9]

The truth is considerably more complex. Mae West did not introduce sex to Broadway. By 1926 Broadway abounded in plays dealing with sexual relations, including prostitution. The 1925–26 theater season featured such hits as *The Shanghai Gesture*, the story of China's most successful madam, and *Lulu Belle*, the tale of a mean, merciless, unrepentant mulatto hooker seducing black and white lovers from Harlem to Paris. Advertisements for *Sex*, with the title appearing in large boldface capitals, appeared in every New York City newspaper, alongside ads that far outshone them in garish suggestiveness.

It is true, however, that this was a relatively new state of affairs, and one that was provoking no end of criticism from New York's religious leaders and civic reformers. Ever since the mid-nineteenth century, when the legitimate theater first marked itself off as a discrete performance genre, it had geared itself specifically toward a middle-class public. Not only had its ticket prices catered to such patrons (and discouraged poorer ones), but its entertainment had as well. Until the early years of the twentieth century, the legitimate theater had specialized in decorous, sentimental productions tailored for a Victorian middle class that found any staged representation of sexuality dangerous and degrading.[10]

But by World War I a new generation of middle-class patrons began to fill Broadway theaters, a generation that was much less suspicious of sexual matters than their parents or grandparents. By the 1920s the old genteel productions had by no means disappeared, but far more producers were catering to the younger crowd with distinctly racier fare. Indeed, though productions like *The Shanghai Gesture* and *Lulu Belle* aroused comment and vigorous protest from social reformers, they were common enough to be perceived as part of an established Broadway genre, the "sex play."

With those facts in mind, we must interpret the critical response to *Sex* in a different light than suggested by Mae West. Broadway critics in the 1920s, no less than audiences, were a product of generational change, and were accustomed to sexually expressive plays. In many cases they praised them, and they prided themselves on their sophistication, their bemused tolerance for even inept producers' infatuation with sex. Their response to bad sex plays was typically ridicule, not condemnation; moreover, they were always capable of analyzing these productions in the terms of dramatic criticism, with attention to structure, technique, and execution.

But *Sex*, clearly, was different. With *Sex* the critics' carefully wrought tone of urbanity disintegrated, replaced by sputtering talk of disease and filth. Something more complex than prudery was at work here. Reviewers did not simply hate West's play—they were incapable of responding to it in terms of their trade, incapable of responding to it as theater.

Indeed, that it was not theater was precisely their point. Remember the distinction drawn by the *Herald Tribune* reviewer: that West's play presented "not sex but lust—stark, naked lust." The critics' vocabulary continually implied that *Sex* was no theatrical representation of a brothel, that it was not merely *about* sex but was somehow a literal presentation of it, a "sore" to be removed by the Health Department or the vice squad. It did not belong on Broadway, said *Variety*, but in another neighborhood entirely: it was "a nasty red-light district show."[11]

Critics labeled *Sex* offensively "realistic," a word whose meaning is always hard to pin down. We can more readily penetrate the controversy if we investigate not the "realism" of the play but its style of representation, the meanings and resonances that style carried. *Sex* shocked the critics because it presented sexuality in a style that legitimate theater scorned. It created its brothel by drawing on illegitimate sources that made it unusual and distinctly unnerving in the context of Broadway.

In part, *Sex* took its unsettlingly "authentic" tone from its humor.

The first act gained what coherence it had not from any development of character or situation but from a series of comic sketches, rapid-fire exchanges between Margy Lamont and her pimp, her fellow prostitutes, and her male customers. In one of *Sex*'s most notorious scenes, Lieutenant Gregg, a customer, loomed provocatively over Margy while explaining what he had been waiting three months to give her:

> GREGG: Oh, I've got something for you, wait until you see this, wait until you see this.
>
> MARGY: Well, come on and let's see it.
>
> GREGG: You'll get it, you'll get it. I don't mind telling you I had an awful time saving it for you. Why, all the women were fighting for it.
>
> MARGY: It better be good.
>
> GREGG: It's good alright. It's the best you could get, but you've got to be very careful not to bend it.[12]

In speaking the final line, Gregg made what one critic described as "a Rabelaisian gesture to indicate a certain anatomical virtuosity,"[13] then reached into his pocket and pulled out Margy's gift—an ostrich feather.[14]

This style of humor, marked by breakneck comic banter, transparently sexual double entendre, and graphic physical movement, characterized one type of theater above all: the burlesque show. Nearly all the critics who condemned *Sex* mentioned just that resemblance.

By the 1910s burlesque had firmly established itself as the outcast of the popular theater—insofar as it was regarded as theater at all. By the 1920s burlesque's reputation for seaminess had, if anything, intensified. Not only had it added a new convention, the striptease, it was also in the hands of new entrepreneurs, men who had even less concern for reputability than their predecessors. The Mutual Wheel, the Minsky theater chain, and dozens of independent "stock burlesque" operators set up business outside the Broadway mainstream on the Lower East Side and in Harlem, areas associated with an underworld of drugs and prostitution. Because they prided themselves on their ostentatious wickedness, on showing what was unshowable in respectable entertainments, such theaters were periodically investigated by the Committee of Fourteen, a group of New

York social reformers intent on combating the spread of commercialized vice. To many observers in the 1920s, burlesque theaters seemed little removed from brothels, and burlesque actresses themselves were widely assumed to be prostitutes.[15]

With *Sex*, Mae West brought burlesque humor to Broadway. In itself that might not have merited calling out the vice squad. More outrageous still was West's own performance, her physical style and the body language she used to bring her prostitute heroine to life. Critics were riveted by West's Margy Lamont—riveted not with pleasure, but with a kind of horrified fascination. Over and over in the words they used to describe her—"raw," "crude," "unvarnished"—one senses their discomfort at finding themselves faced not with a conventional theatrical portrait of a prostitute, but with something very like their idea of the real thing.

West's performance drew part of its disturbing power from her plainspoken definition of prostitution as an economic and specifically working-class activity. Margy Lamont was clearly, unmistakably a working prostitute, explicitly linked, as all real-life prostitutes were, to the cash nexus fueling the urban vice economy. She took money for sex, and West made no attempt to gloss over that fact, on which much of the play's "repellent" humor turned. Take the following moment, when Margy responds to a rival prostitute's accusation that she has stolen one of her customers:

> MARGY (flipping through her customer book): Sailor Dan from Kansas, Sailor Dan from Kansas—oh Sailor Dan from Kansas. Yeh Sailor Dan from Kansas, flat feet, asthma, check came back, o, baby, I'll make you a present of that bird, he's yours.[16]

Jokes like this made glaringly clear the fundamental reality of prostitution: a meeting of bodies and an exchange of cash, and often (as the bounced check reminds us) very little cash at that. It was a jarring truth, at least in a theatrical context. Prostitutes had long been depicted on the legitimate stage, but in a relatively romanticized form that obscured what they actually did, its place at the bottom of the economic order, and its nature as paid labor.

Margy, in contrast, was explicitly a sexual commodity, an ill-paid sex worker who traded her body on the streets. As West embodied her, Margy was palpably from the lower orders: she spoke in working-class slang, and she voiced a violent hatred of "decent folk," the supposedly respectable who sin on the side and exhort the poor to uplift themselves while denying them all means to do so. Margy is bitterly conscious of herself as a member of an oppressed class, and the harshness of her manner is reflected in the world she inhabits. Her Montreal red-light district is a mean and distinctly unglamorous place, rife with class antagonisms. As one critic noted, "It may be said of [Mae West] and *Sex* that they do not make sin attractive. The hell they picture is uninviting, a horrible place whose principal lady-viper has a tough hiss, an awkward strut and an overplump figure."[17]

As this comment suggests, West's portrait of Margy Lamont would not have been nearly so unsettling had it not been reinforced by her seemingly authentic lower-class sexuality. In *Sex* West exhibited what had become her distinctive physical style, developed during her years in the cheap theaters and refined according to burlesque conventions. Entering a scene, she did not so much walk as ooze, moving with a controlled, deliberate slouch, her full hips swaying in a languid rhythm. She delivered her lines in nasal yet resonant tones that spilled from the corner of her mouth, lending every word an insinuating sexual toughness.

To anyone who has ever seen Mae West onscreen, all that might sound familiar, but in *Sex* there was a crucial difference: there was not the least hint of irony. *Sex* contained none of the amiable self-mockery that we have come to think of as distinctively "Mae West"—no suggestion, either in the script or in West's performance, that she was parodying a sexy woman as well as playing one—and this point is crucial to understanding the startling impact of her physical presence. As contemporary reaction makes clear, when Mae West's sexual style was unmediated by self-mockery, it evoked a lower-class world with nearly tangible force.

In the 1920s Broadway did not shy from female sexual expressiveness, but its representation of female sexuality reflected the fashions and tastes of a middle-class public that was not nearly as sexually sophisticated as it often liked to pretend. High fashion in the 1920s had brought sexual expressiveness into respectable women's wardrobes more directly than ever before, but in restrained or teasing ways—through bound breasts, a straight silhouette, and a slender, boyish look that suggested cosmopolitanism or sporty independence rather than overt eroticism. Broadway's mainstream entertainment reflected this unease. The Ziegfeld Girls took the stage in the *Follies* with their breasts bared, but they did so with a near-motionless elegance that gave them a detached, aristocratic allure.[18] *Lulu Belle* put its prostitute heroine emphatically in motion, but as portrayed by actress Leonore Ulrich she was a stylishly slim, buoyant woman whose sexiness emerged flapper-style, through jazzy physical exuberance.

What Mae West displayed in *Sex* was indeed, as critics charged, raw by comparison: eroticism conveyed through an insolent sibilance of her voice and her graphic undulations. (One police observer reported that West moved "her buttocks and other parts of her body in such a way as to suggest an act of sexual intercourse."[19]) In the 1920s, when a boyish figure defined respectable sexuality, a thickset body like West's brought seamy associations to mind: prostitutes, who were marked, doctors claimed, by a "peculiar plumpness," and burlesque actresses, whose famously overblown figures signaled their supposedly aggressive embrace of sensual passion.[20]

Like a burlesque chorus girl, Mae West as Margy Lamont manipulated her full figure to convey a voracious sexual appetite, freely indulged and unabashedly savored. So convincing was she that most critics could not see it as a performance. While none accused West of being a prostitute herself, a few implied that she took actual sexual pleasure in her performance—in their minds the most offensive "realism" of all. In the words of one disgusted reviewer, "West cavorts her own sex about the stage in one of the most reviling exhibits allowed public display. She undresses before the public, and appears to enjoy doing so."[21]

Within months of the premiere of *Sex* Mae West embarked on a new project, one that would prove even more explosive than her first.

Long after the furor subsided Mae West explained in the pages of her 1959 autobiography how she had come to write her "homosexual comedy-drama" *The Drag*. Her interest was sparked, she related, by her acquaintance with an intensely magnetic, attractive man, a Mr. Dupont, who despite his "he-man charm" turned out to be bisexual. "I wasn't too familiar with this phase of sex," West admitted. Though in her long apprenticeship in the theater she had met many gay men, they had communicated their sexuality through a markedly effeminate manner. "The homosexuals I had met were usually boys from the chorus of some of the shows I'd been in," she recalled. "I looked upon them as amusing and having a great sense of humor. They were all crazy about me and my costumes. They were the first ones to imitate me in my presence."[22]

But Dupont was something different—a rugged, virile man who nonetheless was sexually drawn to other men. This bewildering phenomenon led West to seek out the works of medical writers on homosexuality—Krafft-Ebing, Ulrichs, Freud—in an effort to learn more about homosexual desire. Some perverse force, some "strange thing" that she did not understand, compelled her to gather this new information and put it into dramatic form. The result was *The Drag*, a work she described as "a realistic play on a modern social problem."[23]

In her autobiography West expatiated on the menace of homosexuality, "a danger to the entire social system of western civilization":

As a private pressure group it could, and has, infected whole nations. The old Arab world rotted away from it. The civilization of Greece and Rome marched their really great ideas, philosophies and arts into being, but both were bisexual to the point where the family unit broke down, and the virility of its great and best breeding lines decayed under attacks from more virile and childbreeding savage tribal orders.[24]

Statements like these have led at least one historian to call *The Drag* a piece of blatant antigay propaganda. In his study of homosexuality in American drama Kaier Curtain argues that West's hostility to gay men led her to fashion a play that aimed to inflame public sentiment against a homosexual "threat."[25]

Curtain takes Mae West seriously when she claims to have written *The Drag* to alert the public to the dangers posed by homosexuality. To me that seems a doubtful conclusion. West wrote her memoirs in 1959, in a time of reaction against all nonconformity, sexual and otherwise. Throughout that decade, suspected homosexuals no less than suspected Communists inspired widespread fears of domestic "subversion." Whatever the truth of West's encounter with "Dupont," the story remains a perfect 1950s fable—a charming, pleasant, attractive man whose facade of normality hides the alien lurking within.

One has only to compare Mae West's statements in the 1950s to those she made nearer the end of her life to question her sincerity as a vigilant social crusader. In 1970, after a decade of sexual liberalism that gave birth to a gay liberation movement, West told interviewer Jack Hamilton of *Look* magazine, "I have always been ahead of my time. I wrote a play about homosexuals in 1927, called *The Drag*, a great evening's entertainment—dramatic, tragic, comic. I glorified them to a certain extent, and treated them very sympathetically."[26] From the late 1960s until her death in 1980 West styled herself a lifelong defender of the rights of homosexuals and pointed to *The Drag* as her pioneering effort to combat social injustice.

Throughout her career Mae West was consistent in one thing: she always aimed to please her audience. In the 1950s she remembered *The Drag* as a clarion call to fight the growing homosexual menace; in the 1970s she spoke of the play as a pathbreaking cry for individual sexual liberty. In reality the play is neither. Mae West did not compose *The Drag* in the 1950s or in the 1970s but in the 1920s, and for a very different audience taste. Then as ever her motives were more pragmatic than political: she wanted to draw a crowd. And if recent Broadway history was anything to go by, a homosexual play could lure them in by the thousands.

On September 29, 1926, four months before *The Drag*'s out-of-town premiere, Broadway had seen the debut of *The Captive*, an American adaptation of French dramatist Edouard Bourdet's *La Prisonniere*. The play created an immediate sensation, packing the houses and drawing the unanimous acclaim of New York's theater critics, who praised its delicacy and "terrific dramatic effect." They chose their words carefully, eager to safeguard a lavish high-quality production that dealt with a highly controversial topic: *The Captive* was Broadway's first full-length, overt treatment of lesbianism.

Bourdet's drama gave homosexuality a cerebral and extremely restrained presentation, and its enormous box office success undoubtedly spurred Mae West to create her own homosexual play. West began casting *The Drag* within ten weeks of *The Captive*'s premiere, and when her show debuted in Bridgeport, Connecticut, she trumpeted it as "A Male *Captive*."[27] But West's play was neither cerebral nor restrained. As she judged her audience's tastes, they were interested in a very different approach.

The Drag told the story of Rolly Kingsbury, the son of a wealthy New York City judge. Rolly is married to the daughter of a Park

Avenue doctor, but the marriage, the audience learns in the first scene, has problems; Claire, his wife, seems inexplicably dissatisfied. By the end of the first act the reason is revealed: Rolly is a homosexual and only married Claire to hide his true nature from his family. For the remainder of the drama the audience watches the consequences of Rolly's deception. Claire is devastated, an innocent young woman trapped in an unconsummated marriage. An unsuspecting male friend falls victim as well—Allen Grayson, a heterosexual engineer in Rolly's employ, becomes the focus of his boss's ardor. In the third act Rolly Kingsbury is murdered, shot to death after holding a party to entertain his flamboyant gay friends. Though Grayson is initially the suspect, Claire's father, Dr. Richmond, reveals the true culprit: David Caldwell, a despondent young homosexual and Rolly's former lover. At the play's conclusion, the conservative Judge Kingsbury, a vehement proponent of the incarceration of homosexuals, is forced to recognize the need for a more compassionate approach. Faced with the fact of his own son's homosexuality, he turns David over to Dr. Richmond for treatment and instructs the police to report Rolly's murder as a suicide.

This slight story could have loaned itself to many treatments, but West chose to clothe it in the trappings of medical authority and sex education. In an era that saw a profusion of popular medical tracts extolling the virtues of sexual candor, she used the familiar figure of the enlightened physician to introduce, explain, and legitimate her discussion of a sexually explosive topic. The presence of Dr. Richmond allowed West to open her play with a clinical view of homosexuality, to present her audience with the symptoms of what medical science categorized as an abnormality, a disease.

If *The Drag* had a message, it lay in these early scenes, in which an anguished David Caldwell seeks treatment from the humane Dr. Richmond. West stressed the compassionate good sense of the medical perspective, contrasting Dr. Richmond with the callous Judge Kingsbury, a representative of a criminal justice system that treated homosexuality as a crime. On the contrary, the doctor argued, if we understand crime as the willful commission of acts known to be unlawful, the "sexual invert" is no criminal. As a biological male with feminine instincts, the invert has no choice but to act as he does; to his diseased brain, his desire for exclusively male sexual relations seems as right and proper as heterosexual desire does to everyone else. Judge Kingsbury was correct on one count, the doctor acknowledged: with more than five million known homosexuals in the United States alone, their unchecked behavior could have a corrupting effect extending to society's very roots. But to brand such men lawbreakers was not only cruel but useless in that it ignored the basis of the problem. The answer, Dr. Richmond stressed, was psychological treatment, carried out in the knowledge that sexual deviance was rarely if ever freely chosen and should elicit not censure but compassion.[28]

Prefaced by these explanatory scenes and culminating in the triumph of the enlightened physician, *The Drag* posed as a vehicle of sex education, a statement of support for modern medical thinking on the problem of homosexuality. Through the story of Rolly Kingsbury and David Caldwell, West ostensibly illustrated the tragic consequences of society's condemnation of what was in reality a curable sickness: two men who must live lives of deceit, ashamed of what they are, afraid to submit themselves for treatment, whose torment finally ends in madness, death, and devastation for their families as well as themselves.

This earnest message, however, was pure pretense, and had next to nothing to do with what *The Drag* was actually up to. West's informational prologue was not exactly inaccurate. The medical profession was indeed engaged in a struggle to wrest authority over homosexuals from the criminal justice system, a struggle that had begun in the late nineteenth century, when doctors first identified "sexual inversion" as a discrete illness.[29] Her etiology of homosexuality bore a loose resemblance to contemporary medical theory, principally in emphasizing that inversion had psychological rather than physiological roots. Even her definition of a homosexual as a male with feminine instincts had its links to medical wisdom. The late nineteenth-century German sexologist Karl Ulrichs had defined homosexuality as the expression of "a feminine soul confined by a male body," a notion that, if something of a hoary chestnut in psychoanalytic circles, still held the allegiance of medical practitioners.[30] Perhaps, as she claimed in 1959, West even read Ulrichs, Krafft-Ebing, and Freud in researching the play, though I tend to doubt it; a grade-school dropout at the age of seven, she reportedly had difficulty reading through Hollywood filmscripts. She may have spoken more truthfully about the source of her information in 1969, moved to greater candor by her desire to prove herself on top of a more recent trend. She told an interviewer:

I'd read Freud, see—not too much, 'cause I don't like to read—
rather have somebody read and tell me—but I found out the female
soul thing from this yogi who'd cured me of this sneaky stomach
pain I'd had. I had him travelling with me. Nowadays they're all
with the yogis—the Beatles have a yogi—and I started that in
[1927].[31]

It was not that West's prologue was misleading by the lights of
the times; but the fact was that whether it was accurate or not
hardly mattered. West dispensed with her "educational" scenes so
hastily that her audience could barely have had a chance to absorb
what was said. With the exit of Dr. Richmond a scant five minutes
into the play, the "pity versus censure" debate disappears, to be resurrected only briefly at the conclusion when David Caldwell returns
to explain his murder of Rolly. And the supposedly leading characters whose actions propel the plot and illustrate the play's "message"—Rolly, Claire, and Allen Grayson—occupy the spotlight for
only half, perhaps less, of the actual running time.

Within the frankly dull narrative of the tragedy of Rolly Kingsbury lay the scenes that formed *The Drag*'s real focus, showcasing a
large supporting cast of flamboyant homosexual men recruited
from New York's burgeoning gay underworld—a part of the play's
history that never made it into Mae West's reminiscences. According
to a writer for *Studio* magazine, late in 1926 West and manager
James Timony paid a nocturnal visit to

> a dimly-lit Village hangout for chorus girls and boys. . . . Word got
> out that she was casting a play about homosexuals . . . and those
> kids really turned it on. . . . She did not stay long and before she left
> borrowed an order book from the waiter and personally wrote
> passes for everyone present, telling them to see her show [*Sex*] the
> following night and then stay for a regular tryout.[32]

From the tryout West and her director, Edward Elsner, assembled
sixty male players and began afternoon rehearsals at Daly's Sixty-
third Street Theater. At that point she was probably working with
only a fragmentary script. To judge by reports that began to surface
in *Variety*, much of what audiences eventually saw in *The Drag*
probably originated in the raunchy ad libs of her very uninhibited
cast:

THE DRAG REHEARSING WITH SIXTY "VILLAGERS"

. . . Rehearsals are being held daily at the 63rd Street, with the chances that a good pre-gross might be rolled up if admission could be charged to watch the Villagers practicing.[33]

At rehearsals Elsner permits the "our sex" members to cavort and carry on as they like. Results are more natural and spontaneous.[34]

Among these natural and spontaneous results were two lengthy scenes that constituted the heart of *The Drag*. In the first, lasting for most of the second act, four male friends of Rolly Kingsbury— Clem, Rosco, Winnie, and "the Duchess"—visit his apartment and discuss a party they are to attend the following night. Assuming (so the stage directions inform us) "artistic" poses, shrieking, giggling, and flourishing powder puffs, the men gather around the piano for a few musical numbers and needle each other with bawdy gibes delivered in affected slang:

DUCHESS: Oh, my goodness. I've got the most gorgeous new drag. Black satin very tight, with a long train of rhinestones.

CLEM: Wait until you see the creation I'm wearing dearie. Virginal white, no back, with oceans of this and oceans of that, trimmed with excitement in front. You know I'm more the flapper type, not so much like a canal boat.

DUCHESS: Creation—ha! That old thing. I knew that three years ago. Oh, Annie.

CLEM (very angry): For Chris' sake sit. This big bitch thinks nobody has anything or looks like anything but her.

DUCHESS: Oh, shut up.

ROLLY: Say, how about a little drink?

CLEM: Yes! How about a little drink?

DUCHESS: I don't mind a little drink once in a while.

CLEM: Why you big Swede. You'd take it through a funnel if anybody would give it to you.

WINNIE: Funnel? That's nothing. I take it through a hose. Whoops![35]

The real high point, however, came in act three, with the scene from which the play took its title. West lavished a full thirty minutes on Rolly Kingsbury's drag ball, an elaborate get-together for his friends. While a jazz orchestra played in the background, the male supporting cast danced onstage, some dressed in women's gowns, some in tuxedos, all "rouged, lip-sticked and liquid-whited to the last degree."[36] Between the group numbers came "specialty" songs ("How Come You Do Me Like You Do," "Goody-Goody-Good") performed by individual cast members, including one man "dressed as an Oriental dancer, bare legs and wearing only what amounts to a brassiere above the waist," who accompanied his singing with a suggestive "muscle dance."[37] At moments the musical numbers halted for snappy, burlesque-style comic bits, insults, and double entendres on the subject of police raids and male lovers:

> WINNIE: My but you're getting thin.
> KATE: I am not. I can at least cling to a man without wearing him out. You're terribly fat.
> WINNIE: Fat! I should say not. I'm the type that men prefer. I can at least go through the navy yard without having the flags drop to half mast.
> KATE: Listen, dearie—pull in your aerial, you're full of static. I'm just the type that men crave. The type that burns 'em up. Why, when I walk up Tenth Avenue, you can smell the meat sizzling in Hell's Kitchen.[38]

To appreciate *The Drag*'s impact, it is important to see that its supporting cast was not a collection of isolated oddities. They were members of an urban subculture that was relatively well-established, if still shadowy and mysterious to most of New York's straight middle class. When the character "Kate" spoke of strolling through Hell's Kitchen, he was referring to only one among many New York City neighborhoods—including Harlem, Greenwich Village, parts of the Lower East Side, and the "Tenderloin" south of Times Square—where a network of gay bars, bathhouses, and other meeting places had been thriving since the final decades of the nineteenth century. New York was not the only American city to see the rise of a gay underworld during those years. As newspaper accounts, medical case histories, and personal correspondence testify, gay men and women had also staked out urban spaces in Washington, Chicago, St. Louis, and San Francisco.[39]

As a working-class woman, Mae West knew that subculture far better than her middle-class counterparts. As historian George Chauncey has shown, "the most visible gay world of the early twentieth century . . . was a working-class world," rooted in the city's Irish, Italian, and African-American neighborhoods—exactly the sort of immigrant neighborhood in which West herself had grown up. There the gay subculture flourished as "a highly visible part of the urban sexual underworld," its institutions part of an array of venues that traded in commercialized vice. By the early twentieth century New York's gay male population had become far more than simply a group of individuals who happened to be drawn to members of their own sex. It was, as one observer wrote in a letter to British sexologist Havelock Ellis, "a community distinctly organized—[with] words, customs, traditions of its own."[40]

The Drag showcased those "words, customs, traditions," bringing them up from the sexual underground to intrigue and titillate Broadway audiences. West's characters laced their dialogue with geographically specific references to their community's distinctive pastimes. The Duchess spoke of "cruising" in Central Park and on Riverside Drive, Clem described sashaying around Times Square, and others made reference to summer excursions to New York coastal resorts. Particular words and phrases, as well, were part of the play's novelty. Addressing each other as "molls," "queers," and "queens" and describing themselves as "gay," the cast exposed audiences to a large and colorful in-group vocabulary organized around gender reversal and rife with sexual overtones. When Clem pursued a burly and presumably straight Brooklyn taxi driver, for example, another character leered knowingly, "Rough trade, dearie," from which the audience could infer that "rough trade" designated a heterosexual working-class male who indulged in homosexual sex for a price.[41] Much of this slang has entered the mainstream in the past decades—so much so, in fact, that we must make an effort to sense its foreignness to 1920s ears. So odd did the jargon appear to contemporaries that reporters covering the out-of-town tryouts felt obliged to act as translators between the gay cast and the public at large, particularly when it came to the play's "mysterious" title. One, explaining a "drag" to his readers as "a party of homosexuals," went on to describe the event at length:

> The party is called, in the esoteric set, a "drag," and to go "in drag" means for a person to appear in women's clothes.
>
>   It is privileged for few to be present at one of these "drags," but to those who have attended them it is a never-to-be-forgotten sight, although it does leave a bad taste in the mouth. People who were,

seemingly, males before they came to the party, suddenly are transformed to shrieking, screaming women. They hurl ribald epithets at
one another, in jocular fashion, drink, and, if it happens to be a
"drag" to which they bring their male sweethearts, then the function becomes the most disgusting orgy imaginable.[42]

West encouraged her cast to play up the novelty and outrageousness of gay life. Characters like Clem, Winnie, and the Duchess
were markedly effeminate. Mincing and posturing suggestively, they
referred to themselves as "women" and "girls" and to their fellows
with feminine pronouns, delivering their lines in shrill, giddy tones
punctuated with hysterical shrieks.

For anyone encountering it several decades after its premiere, this
aspect of *The Drag* can seem rather hard to stomach. Indeed, it is
hard to deny that the play, with its preening homosexual characters,
painted a one-dimensional portrait of New York City gay life.
Depth of characterization was not what West was interested in; nor,
for that matter, was she concerned with the dignity of those she presented. She was unquestionably exploiting them for the fascination
she believed they held for the public. Nevertheless the behavior featured in *The Drag* did play an important part in 1920s gay reality.
As historians are just beginning to document, that early gay community had moments of high visibility in the 1920s, and while drag
queens may not have represented the whole gay subculture, they set
the pace for gay public life far more so then than they do today.

Drag queens and effete though conventionally attired homosexual
men exemplified what historian George Chauncey has called "the
culture of effeminacy," the style and mannerisms that had come to
dominate gay public interaction since the late nineteenth century.
Chauncey's investigation of New York's early gay community suggests that gay men found in affected, "womanish" banter, feminine
nicknames, and female pronouns the clearest means of participating
in the gay social world:

More gay men in the 1920s than today *did* adopt effeminate mannerisms: they provided one of the few sure means of announcing
one's sexuality. But acting like a "fairy" was more than just a code;
it was the dominant role model available to men forming a gay
identity, and one against which every gay man had to measure himself.[43]

The source of that role model lay in the gender dynamics of the nineteenth century, in a cultural system that placed male and female beings at opposite ends of an unbreachable divide. In such a landscape, Chauncey argues, many gay men made sense of same-sex erotic desires by seeing them as one element of a larger gender "inversion." Their desire for men made them like women, and so they adopted feminine nicknames, used female pronouns, and spoke and acted in a brassy female manner.[44] For some the role of the "fairy" became a way of life, a persona both public and private by which they advertised their unorthodox sexual tastes; for others it was a style adopted for the occasion, put on after working hours in preparation for New York's vital homosexual nightlife. There effeminate style set the tone, particularly at what became New York's largest gay social event in the 1920s—a series of drag balls held six or seven times a year at Harlem's Rockland Palace, the old Madison Square Garden, and the Astor Hotel, and often attended by thousands, including a smattering of Vanderbilts and Astors, who regularly took boxes to view the antics below.[45]

Mae West put those drag balls under the Broadway spotlight. Though she presented her play as an exercise in sex education, it was little more than a random assortment of songs, dances, and racy one-liners focusing on her players' "real-life" practices—their slang, their customs, their characteristic style. This was not conventional theater—and most of West's Broadway colleagues refused to dignify it by that name. But in fact there was commercial precedent, however lowly, for the kind of entertainment West offered in *The Drag*. Since the turn of the century gay performers had been a staple of New York's lower-class nightlife, as entertainer Jimmy Durante remembered in a 1931 book. Durante got his first job as a pianist in a gay bar on the Bowery; after the club was raided in 1905 he went to work at Diamond Tony's, a run-down saloon in Coney Island that drew its public with entertainment not unlike that offered in *The Drag*:

At our place, the entertainers were all boys who danced together and lisped. They called themselves Edna May and Leslie Carter and Big Tess and things like that. You know. Just like the first joint I worked in. When they had sung their numbers, they sat at the tables the way hostesses do today, "spinning their web," as they called it.

Some of them were six feet tall and built like Dempsey, so it was never very healthy to make nasty cracks.

Outside of the queer entertainers, our place was no different from most of the others. The usual number of girls hung out there, and the customers were mostly on the level; that is to say, they were not interested in our entertainers any more than they would have been in the freaks that filled the Surf Avenue sidewalks.

It was a tough enough joint, but it didn't bother me, even if I was only fifteen. The Bowery, where I was brought up, isn't any sort of Sunday-school picnic, and I had seen enough to get acclimated to almost anything.[46]

In burlesque too the effeminate and suggestive "nance," as gay men were termed in underground slang, became a fixture of each evening's entertainment, offering patrons ribald amusement in company with cootch dancers and raunchy comedians. By 1910, if not before, "nance humor" of much the sort exhibited in Mae West's play was "a staple of low comedy," in *Variety*'s words.[47]

But an important distinction separated West's endeavor from its forerunners in burlesque and the concert saloon, which flourished in the Bowery and Coney Island, stigmatized neighborhoods that the middle class regarded as debased, corrupting territory where social interaction revolved around alcohol, drugs, and male and female prostitution. Saloons and burlesque halls offered underworld entertainment to underworld audiences, shows where performer and audience shared membership in a world the respectable strictly avoided, and their patronage was very limited—working-class men, a few slumming gentlemen, and virtually no women except prostitutes. Mae West presented this same sexual underworld to a mainstream public in the heart of New York's most celebrated theatrical district, her eyes fixed on the Broadway box office. The sensational success of *The Shanghai Gesture* and *Lulu Belle* had revealed an eager middle-class market for racy tales of prostitution; *The Captive* had proved that this fascination extended to homosexuality. *Sex* and *The Drag* were products of that cultural moment: shrewd pieces of exploitation by a would-be celebrity with an unsubtle sense of theatrical trends. As West allegedly told one of *Sex*'s backers when he expressed hesitation about the play's rawness, Broadway audiences *wanted* "dirt"—and, she added emphatically, "I'll give it to them!"[48]

But with *Sex* and *The Drag* West did more than simply bring "dirt" to Broadway. In addition, she brought a commercial tradition hitherto confined to very different quarters. In January 1927, attempting to legitimate her unusual theatrical style in the midst of a citywide furor, she wrote, "There is one play which we never grow weary of seeing. That is the great show of life as it flows along. *The Drag* is the second of what I am calling 'comedy-dramas of life.' The first is *Sex*, which is playing in New York."[49]

West may well have invented the phrase "comedy-dramas of life" on the spur of the moment, but nonetheless it pinpoints what made her style of theater stand out: the appearance of staging "real life," of unearthing the sexual underworld and its population. *The Drag* did this in quite obvious fashion, offering its audience not actors depicting homosexuals but real homosexuals. As for *Sex*, West as Margy Lamont did all she could to evoke a real woman of the streets. Moreover, the humor in both plays clearly followed the lead of burlesque, where the actresses were occasionally real-life prostitutes and the effeminate comics were gay men, as audiences well knew from vice investigations. Burlesque was not so much a representation of the underworld as a part of the underworld itself, drawing no firm line between the stage and the street, between sexy performances and sexual acts, between the theater and the disorderly house.

Sex and *The Drag* followed in that burlesque tradition, staging "the great show of life as it flows along." By "life" West meant sensational nightlife, the racy experience of individuals enmeshed in the metropolitan vice economy. Her "comedy-dramas of life" simply diverted the "flow" of that experience from the streets to the theater, bringing sexually notorious figures onstage without conventional dramatic mediation.

In retailing "authentic" lower-class notoriety to a broad public *The Drag* resembled nothing so much as the entertainment perfected at Hammerstein's Victoria. Just as Willie Hammerstein had peopled his theater with participants in New York sex scandals, West brought homosexuality to center stage, treating it as a lurid local sensation from which she crafted her own kind of metropolitan "freak act." Like her former employer, she brought a set of infamous New Yorkers onstage as themselves, enticing her public not by the players' skill in interpreting character, but by the air of reality that surrounded them. Some of *The Drag*'s cast already had reputations of a sort before their appearance in the play, as one reporter rather gleefully made clear:

Chief among those reported to have appeared in the last act of *The Drag*, which was the big "camp" scene of homosexuals, was a person known as "The Duchess." . . . She is the arbiter of homo-land. There is no greater authority of manners and etiquette . . . and whenever one of "her" tribe is found guilty of a lapse in the most correct social usage "the Duchess" deals harshly with "her.". . .

Another celebrated homo said to have played in *The Drag* is called "Mother Superior." This character is an indefatigable correspondent. He is said to have studied for the priesthood at one time, but abandoned taking holy orders for the more exciting life of a homosexual in the great city. "Mother Superior" is the confessor and spiritual adviser for a large group of homos and both he and "The Duchess" hold court in a certain eating place on Fifth Avenue in the forties. Whenever a publication takes the queer clan to task, it is always "Mother Superior" or "The Duchess" who [writes] a defense.[50]

Mae West's brand of theater was aimed at a sensation-loving public that could be readily lured by a promised glimpse of New York's criminal and sexual underworld. Its blatantly voyeuristic appeal held particularly low-grade commercial associations, not only with burlesque and the sensational end of vaudeville but with the most excoriated branch of the popular press, the lurid penny dailies that flourished in New York, beginning with Joseph Pulitzer's *New York World* and William Randolph Hearst's *American* in the late nineteenth century and peaking spectacularly with the tabloids of the 1920s, the *Daily News*, the *Daily Mirror* and the *Evening Graphic*. Like the theater of West and Hammerstein, New York's cheap dailies became notorious themselves for relentlessly purveying criminal and sexual scandals—prostitution, drug abuse, adultery, miscegenation, homosexuality—usually as embodied by provocative individuals: chorus girls, murderesses, kept women, drug addicts.[51]

In short, West brought tabloid style to Broadway—and she succeeded beyond anyone's expectations. When *Sex* opened, the critics predicted that at $3 a ticket no audience would be interested in smut. But after an opening week of moderately good business—to be expected, *Variety* opined, once curiosity-seekers got wind of its rawness—*Sex*'s profits began to grow, reaching the phenomenal sum of $16,500 a week by June. By the time it closed in March

1927 *Sex* stood firm in its position as one of the three longest-running shows then on Broadway.[52]

But even more remarkable than the length of its run was the composition of its audience. Within days of the play's premiere, newspapers reported that fans were storming the box office—fans of a very different social stratum from the usual crowd for burlesque. Noted Robert Benchley in *Life* magazine, "The sudden rush to see *Sex* is not confined to the canaille. The agencies are hot after tickets, and each night soft purring limousines roll up with theater parties of gentry, out 'just for a lark.'"[53] Clearly, the respectable were flocking to *Sex*, upper-middle-class women no less than upper-middle-class men—three times *more* women than men, according to one police report.[54] *Sex* became what we would term a "cult" hit, drawing young, self-consciously cynical patrons—*Variety* called them the "jaded weisenheimers"—who were bemused by the novelty of real "dirt" on Broadway.[55] Their enthusiasm made *Sex* into a craze, a Broadway fad, an arena for middle-class theatergoers to parade their adventurousness and daring. Critic Stark Young, writing in the *New Republic* in 1928, recalled the phenomenon: "Who does not know how frequent or chic . . . it was to say that this show was fine, grand, swell, the best in town, I take everybody, etc.?"[56]

The success of *Sex* demonstrated that the "jaded weisenheimers" had become a potent force on Broadway, one that undoubtedly influenced Mae West in her creation of *The Drag*. West composed the play for a *Sex*-style audience that would see homosexuality as amusing, absurd, titillating, and not especially threatening. As it turned out, it was the existence of that audience as much as the play itself that inspired controversy over homosexuality and legitimate performance styles on Broadway.

Chapter 4

SEX ON TRIAL: THE POLITICS OF "LEGIT"

$\mathcal{T}$he curtain had just rung down on the evening's performance on February 9, 1927, when Mae West found herself faced with a novel set of backstage visitors. A phalanx of officers from the municipal vice squad swarmed through Daly's Sixty-third Street Theater, rounding up *Sex*'s cast and crew and herding them into Black Marias. West was the last to be piled into one of the crowded vehicles and was forced to stand for the length of a careening ride through Times Square. By the time they arrived at the police station she was furious.[1]

A few blocks south another raid was under way at the Empire Theater, home of *The Captive*, whose glamorous star, Helen Menken, received somewhat more dignified treatment: she arrived at the precinct station in a police limousine on the arm of a deferential vice squad officer. Once there, however, she was booked with her cast and crew on the same charge brought against *Sex*: staging an obscene production that "tended to corrupt the morals of youth and others."

Some papers reported animosity between West and Menken, and there is little reason to doubt it. Most of Menken's colleagues placed the blame for the theater raids squarely on Mae West's shoulders. Though she was arrested as star and author of *Sex*, all of

Broadway knew her real offense was *The Drag*, which had gone into rehearsal on the heels of *The Captive*'s success. Despite strenuous efforts to prevent it from opening, *The Drag* had had its New York premiere the previous evening, in a surreptitious midnight performance at Daly's.[2]

The introduction of homosexuality to Broadway in the 1926–27 season caused an uproar unmatched in the annals of New York City theater. Police raids were not the only official response. In early 1927 the legitimate stage was threatened with external regulation, in the form of a bill before the New York State Assembly to put Times Square stages under the control of the New York Board of Motion Picture Censorship. The resultant battle not only pitted New York's religious and civic reformers against Broadway professionals but sparked conflict within the theatrical world itself.

When word of West's new play first surfaced in December 1926, theater artists as well as civic reformers quickly sprang into action to condemn it. By the time of the police raids in February 1927, many in the Times Square community had been hard at work on their own solution to the Mae West threat: persuading Broadway managers to boycott her production (a tactic that succeeded until West decided to debut *The Drag* at a theater on which she held the lease) and presenting state legislators with an alternative proposal to reform the stage—the creation of a Theater Supervisory Board, a nine-member panel composed of Broadway's most respected, most self-professedly serious artists, who would scan proposed scripts and oversee rehearsals to ensure that "worthless" productions got nowhere near Broadway.

The hue and cry over Mae West's "comedy-dramas of life" was no straightforward tale of "censorship." Censorship implies a black-and-white division between prudes and progressives, conservatives and liberals—distinctions that are difficult to draw here. It is more useful to look at the 1927 "dirty play" controversy as a struggle for authority over Broadway, a battle about the politics of "legit," fought out among three groups—moral reformers, theatrical modernists, and West's "jaded weisenheimer" fans—that sought to impose conflicting visions of the aim, methods, and audience appropriate to the Broadway stage.

In the disgusting theatrical challenge to decency just revealed at Bridgeport, where the foulest use of sex perversion yet attempted by the theatrical baiters for dirty dollars is being polished for a metropolitan run, we see where the lack of censorship is bringing us.

Here is no pretense to an adventure in the protective name of "art," but a sheer bravado in filth, as starkly vicious as the worst sins in the underworld.[3]

The *New York American*'s tirade against *The Drag* encapsulates the issues at stake for New York's clergy, educators, and social workers, who used the storm over West's play to press for a State Board of Theater Censorship. As they saw it, the problem was not *The Drag* alone. While it was definitely the "foulest" play yet attempted, it was essentially in line with Broadway's penchant for "dirty dollars" and a sign of what New York's citizens could anticipate if the stage remained free from outside control. In attacking Broadway immorality they were in fact addressing a broad spectrum of producers and playwrights, including those who attempted to disassociate themselves from Mae West—a new generation of theater personnel who clothed their dissolute "adventures" in "the protective name of 'art.' "

Before 1920 nothing could have seemed more unlikely than a moral reformist attack on the legitimate stage. From its nineteenth-century beginnings the legitimate stage had been the most respectable of all theatrical arenas, both in its patronage and in its tone, catering to a sentimental and antisensual taste—precisely the sensibility of the moral reformers. They had long been concerned with stage purification, of course, but until the 1920s they directed their campaigns against immoral amusement at the cheap theaters—the small-time vaudeville, burlesque, and movie houses that served the urban poor.

"Vaudeville," wrote investigator Michael Davis in a 1911 survey of New York City entertainments,

may be described as a succession of acts whose stimulus depends usually upon an artificial rather than upon a natural, human and developing interest; these acts having no necessary and as a rule no actual connection. This description, be it noted, also fits the experience afforded by a streetcar ride, or by any active day in a crowded city. . . . Like the succession of city occurrences, vaudeville is stimulating but disintegrating; both excite and claim the mind of the beholder, and interest him transiently; but they do not recuperate or develop him; in the long run, they will cease to amuse him. Both represent hyperstimulus, and lead to neurasthenia, the antithesis of rest or Nirvana.[4]

When Davis or Jane Addams or their fellow reformers decried cheap theater's failure to "develop" its viewers, they were speaking from a quintessential Victorian viewpoint that valued the stage as a vehicle of educational uplift. As with all cultural activity, be it the contemplation of art or the consumption of literature, in Victorian eyes the proper function of the stage was to facilitate spiritual enrichment and detach the audience from corrupting sensual stimuli. Reformers were not hostile to theater per se; in Jane Addams's view it embodied a search for imaginative renewal, for "a conception of life higher than that which the actual world offers.[5] An emotional investment in the theater was potentially a force of great social benefit, especially for young people—if it could be harnessed to a worthy object. Accordingly, the reformers created an alternative network of drama appreciation leagues and municipally sponsored amateur theatricals that replaced the popular theater's "trashy love stories" with spiritually enriching "classics," plays that would teach the principles of genuine drama while instructing in refined manners and the virtues of duty, reverence, thrift, and self-restraint.

Though the reform agenda may sound smug and censorious to modern ears, there was something generous and compassionate behind it, at least originally—a deeply felt impulse to cultural democracy and an incisive critique of commercialized pleasure. If reformers wanted to bring genteel classics to the poor, it was not purely for purposes of inculcation but also because their own lives had been enriched by such writers and they wanted to share that enrichment. They had every confidence that the masses would appreciate great art when they saw it (here they were poles apart from the theater's burgeoning avant-garde, which considered "great art" and the mass audience wholly incompatible), and their hatred of the popular theater was based as much on its commercial as on its sensual nature. As Jane Addams argued:

We see thousands of girls walking up and down the streets on a pleasant evening with no chance to catch a sight of pleasure, even through a lighted window, save as these lurid places provide it.

Apparently the modern city sees in these girls only two possibilities, both of them commercial: first, a chance to utilize by day their new and tender labor power in its factories and shops, and then another chance in the evening to extract from them their petty wages by pandering to their love of pleasure.[6]

But from the beginning there was tension in the reform movement between the desire to democratize and the urge to coerce. At times the reformers spoke as if sheer lack of alternatives led city youth to commercial entertainments—as if the fault lay solely with the "amusement exploiter"—but that conclusion became difficult to sustain as their amateur theatricals and drama leagues languished. Faced with the evidence that young people, with their "modern" spirit of indulgence, remained attached to commercial amusements even when wholesome theater was readily available, reformers redoubled their efforts, this time in a more punitive direction.

In the late 1910s a series of regulations at both state and municipal level brought New York's cheap amusements under government supervision. Moral reformers sought to regulate prior to performance, to institute guidelines and strictures that would ensure a suitable product. By its nature live theater was difficult to control, especially in vaudeville and burlesque, where performers tended to improvise in response to raucous audience interventions. Reformers would doubtless have loved to ban lower-class live performance entirely, and to some extent they succeeded: by 1918 they had closed down the "combination houses," cheap theaters that alternated short motion pictures with live appearances by small-time vaudevillians.[7]

With no possibility of improvisation, motion pictures could be far more easily controlled. In 1921, at the urging of clergymen, social workers, and educators, the state legislature established a motion picture licensing system to be administered by the Department of Education. Modeled on similar panels in Pennsylvania, Maryland, Virginia, and Ohio, the New York State Board of Motion Picture Censorship previewed all films prior to exhibition and had the power to demand cuts before approving them. Such demands, as one might anticipate, reflected the board's roots in the Victorian tradition of policing the cultural activity of the poor. Guidelines were designed with an "impressionable" lower-class audience in mind, to protect from pernicious influences those deemed incapable of protecting themselves. Not surprisingly the chief pernicious influence was sex, and not just its salacious treatment but its use as a theme. Films were to shun prostitution, adultery, underworld romance, any presentation of "illicit love . . . which tends to make virtue odious and vice attractive."[8]

It was one thing to enforce strict regulation on motion pictures, traditionally the preserve of the lower classes. It was quite another to extend it to the legitimate stage. That effort had its beginnings in 1920, when twenty-eight New York religious and social welfare organizations—precisely the same groups that had been battling the cheap theaters—joined forces as the Better Public Shows Movement to lobby for a cleaner legitimate theater.

In the beginning the Better Public Shows Movement assumed a low-key stance, placing its faith in the essential good intentions of the Broadway establishment and its middle-class patrons. Rather than pushing for a state censorship board, the reformers focused on negotiating with producers, playwrights, and Actors Equity spokesmen to create a workable system of regulation that would allow Broadway's majority of right-thinking people to ride herd on the occasional malefactor.

The result was the Citizens' Play Jury, a regulatory body to be convened on order of the district attorney whenever he received a sizable number of complaints against a particular play. At that point twelve jury members would be selected by lot from a pool of three hundred of New York's leading citizens, regular playgoers who enjoyed the drama. Once they had viewed the production they would pass judgment on whether it was objectionable, whether certain scenes should be modified, or whether it should be withdrawn altogether for the sake of the public welfare. At first the reformers wholeheartedly supported the play jury system, but by 1927 they were deeply dissatisfied: the play jury had functioned with unexpected liberality. For one thing, it had been convened only twice. Apparently public complaints against Broadway either were not forthcoming or were not being followed up by the district attorney. More troublesome, on the two occasions when it had been called, its judgments had been distinctly dismaying. Its greatest offense had come in June 1926, when by a narrow margin the jury declared Mae West's *Sex* acceptable Broadway fare.[9]

Exactly how *Sex* managed to satisfy the play jury mystified many observers; no jury, *Variety* implied, could be *that* liberal. It seems likely that West and her producers, James Timony and Clarence Morganstern, had advance notice of the jury's visit and altered the performance accordingly. Like burlesque shows, *Sex* equipped its cast with two separate scripts—one for use when police might be in attendance and the other for use when the coast was clear (in burlesque parlance, "parlor" and "whore" scripts). Percy Hammond of the *New York Herald Tribune* was present at a "parlor" performance:

> I recall that when I went to see Miss West in *Sex*, I was detained for a moment at the box office. It was explained to me the next day that the watchdogs at the gate, fearing I was a spy, rushed their apprehensions backstage to Miss West. So she reformed her entertainment temporarily, and the *Sex* I saw could have been presented at any chapter of the YMCA. Her manager apologized to me later.[10]

No "parlor" version of the script survives, but from what critic George Goldsmith witnessed, we can surmise that West's tailoring included a few sneers at the moralists in the audience:

> It may be worth recording that Mr. James Timony, who with Miss Mae West owns the nursery tale pleasingly entitled *Sex*, has a method of his own for disarming the reformers when they gather to view his production. In the bordello scene, where the sea-faring gentleman, after an elaborate and suggestive explanation, is called upon to bring out an aigrette feather from his bosom, Mr. Timony has arranged a substitute piece of business calculated to inspire emotions of patriotism. . . . Instead of the aigrette, the infatuated mariner pulls out an American flag.[11]

By the time *The Drag* threatened to descend upon Broadway, reformers were adamant: the play jury system had proved unworkable, and the only way to ensure a wholesome legitimate theater was to place Broadway in the hands of a State Board of Theater Censorship that would preview all scripts and performances prior to allowing any production's premiere. By the early months of 1927, according to the *New York Herald Tribune*, the creation of a theater censorship board had become the top priority of New York's social welfare organizations.[12]

In less than a decade an institution that moralists once actively championed had become the target of their strongest condemnation. Reformers still hoped that the theater could serve as a potent vehicle of social amelioration, "one of the noblest and most powerful instruments of education, [with the] power to speak to our hearts, to stir our wills, to renew our devotion to the ideal,"[13] but by the mid-1920s their conception of the purpose of drama was being actively challenged, as the reformers were acutely aware. In dropping their support for the play jury system they demonstrated a newfound conviction that neither the Broadway establishment nor theatergoers were worthy of continued trust. As the reformers saw it, Broadway had been invaded by outsiders, by two groups with no respect for the old values: a new generation of theater professionals and a new generation of fans.

The reformers were correct to see the new theater artists as a threat. Playwrights like Eugene O'Neill were articulating a dramatic standard forged precisely in opposition to the Victorian emphasis on spirituality and uplift. By exploring psychological and sexual experience, they sought to create an aesthetically "authentic" legitimate drama that confronted audiences with the whole of life, the murky and irrational no less than the pleasant and genteel.

From the reformers' perspective, that theatrical philosophy was little more than a sham, a cagey scheme by which "panders and smuthounds" sought to market filth under the cover of art. "Back-fence vulgarity, the indecencies of the corner loafer, the coarseness of criminals, have no place on the stage," wrote Don Seitz in *The Outlook*, a religious journal.[14] To argue that exploring the underside of the psyche was the central mission of art was not only a socially dangerous claim, it was a claim that could expose the reformers to ridicule and deprive them of their place as cultural arbiters. "[It] has become quite the thing to defend something haled into court as offensive on the ground that it is art," wrote an aggrieved John Sumner, head of the New York Society for the Suppression of Vice, "and prosecutors and complainants are lampooned as groundlings incapable of appreciating the things familiar to the intimates of the Muses."[15]

Objectionable as the "panders and smuthounds" were, it was the audience that troubled moral reformers most deeply—an audience composed not of the downtrodden underclass, whose exploitation could be pitied at the same time that its excesses were feared, but of middle-class young people, women as well as men. It was perhaps for that reason that reformers' harangues against the audience took on such a shrill and vituperative tone. The allegiance of the youth of their own class to sexually expressive amusement showed just how embattled moral reformers had become, how rapidly their values of modesty and decorum were being abandoned.

That middle-class young people were patronizing unhealthy entertainments was bad enough, but even worse was the conspicuous presence of women. Reformers waxed particularly vehement on this subject. As far as Elisabeth Marbury was concerned, young women were *responsible* for Broadway's dissolution: playwrights wrote with them in mind, aware that they would flock to anything hinting at sexual extravagance or abnormality:

> The more obnoxious the play, the more one sees the matinees full of young girls from 16 to 20 years of age. . . . They do not buy their tickets either inadvertently or ignorantly, yet there they are in the audience, listening to language that is foul, following a theme which is perverted and revolting, and watching gestures which have but one purpose and one meaning.[16]

Marbury and her colleagues were certainly not imagining this new abundance of female patrons, but their relentless emphasis on it, in such heated terms, points to the broader crisis those patrons seemed to represent. In the Victorian moral landscape women were the mainstays of genteel culture. Indeed, nineteenth-century theater chroniclers had credited the middle-class female audience with the creation of a legitimate stage, their very presence encouraging a bawdy institution to reshape itself into a decent and refined one. For women to shift their patronage to sex and sensationalism was a severe symptom of cultural upheaval, a sign that the world moralists valued was on the verge of extinction.

The "dirty play" controversy was at heart a crisis of cultural authority: not simply the reformers' own authority but the authority of the values that guided them. They had been born into a world mapped out in clearly defined districts of sunlight and shadow: good women separated from bad, the reputable from the dissolute, "nice" neighborhoods from red-light districts, first-class theaters from cheap ones. But by the 1920s such clear distinctions seemed increasingly hard to come by, and all their attempts to contain social decay appeared to have missed the mark. They had closed the red-light districts and the saloons, but that had only complicated matters, driving the sale of sex and liquor underground into night-clubs and speakeasies where prostitutes mixed with crowds of "respectable" women (and where the two were often difficult to tell apart, many women having adopted the prostitute's fashions, her thick dark lipstick, short skirts, silk stockings, cigarettes, and hip flask). The cheap theaters had been policed and regulated, but suddenly they were no longer alone in showcasing provocative themes. As New York minister John Haynes Holmes observed after the theater raids in 1927:

> Right now filth is being presented on no less than 20 New York stages. Most of them are plots displaying the relations between the sexes. From one point of view this is nothing new. Yet from another it is. Years ago such displays were common at another type theater—the burlesque. The difference in those days was that you knew your manager and your theater. You knew what you were going to see when you went to a certain theater, but today you do not.[17]

Reformers saw all around them nothing less than a fundamental shift in New York's cultural and sexual geography, with reputable theaters becoming indistinguishable from havens of vice. More than one observer suggested, as a compromise solution to the crisis, that the municipal government divide Times Square into "red-light" and "lily-white" districts, with the appropriate plays confined to each.[18] Meanwhile, the reformers would keep pressing for a State Board of Theater Censorship as a means of bolstering their own flagging authority and redrawing the old boundaries—reestablishing a world where "you knew your theater."

The impending arrival of *The Drag* on Broadway also galvanized the legitimate theater community. Coming as it did in the wake of *The Captive*, West's play seemed certain to intensify calls for an external board of censorship. Broadway responded in haste, persuading theater owners to close their doors to *The Drag* and countering reformers' legislative proposals with their own plans for a self-regulatory Theater Supervisory Board.

To be sure, these actions were undertaken from a variety of motives. Of the dozens of producers, actors, and writers who denounced *The Drag*, many were doubtless indifferent to West's tactics and were simply afraid that their own work would be censored should reform efforts succeed. But the leaders of the fight had sincere and clearly articulated grounds for opposing external censorship. Those who guided the formation of the Theater Supervisory Board and would have presided over its workings—producer Theresa Helburn of the Theater Guild and Winthrop Ames, director of the Little Theater—were part of a generation of artists and critics who had gained prominence on Broadway in the past decade, bringing a new sense of artistic mission to the legitimate stage. The supervisory board, as they conceived it, would give that mission some practical force by keeping the theater out of the hands of state and civic authorities and reserving the power of judgment to those well-versed in stagecraft.

The new generation's conception of the aim and import of the legitimate stage was antithetical both to the reformers' desire for "uplifting" plays and to Mae West's style of theatrics, which owed more to the slumming excursion and the gutter press than to any cultivated vision of dramatic art. The 1927 theater season brought this conflict to a head with two treatments of homosexuality staged in entirely different spirits. To the reformers, the very subject made both plays equally reprehensible, but Broadway modernists argued that treatment, not subject, was what mattered: *The Captive* did precisely what a quality play should do; *The Drag*, however, threatened to draw exactly the wrong kind of audience. *The Captive* was art, *The Drag* was trash, and the distinction was crucial. Broadway rallied in defense of *The Captive* for reasons that throw the emerging sense of the theater's purpose into high relief.

According to its author, Edouard Bourdet, *The Captive* had its roots in an experience from the Great War. As an infantry officer he had met a young man in the trenches who was deliberately courting death to escape from a miserable home life. Though he was married to a woman he adored, he had discovered that she was incapable of returning his passion—that in fact she was unable to love any man but was aroused only by other women. Haunted by this encounter, Bourdet extracted its emotional core and wove around it a play that explored the anguish engendered by "abnormal" sexual desire.

The Captive tells the story of Irene de Montcel, the twenty-five-year-old daughter of an American diplomat, living with her father and sister in Paris. From the beginning Bourdet shrouds Irene in mystery, presenting her as an edgy, distracted young woman racked by an unnamed torment. As the drama unfolds, the audience gradually learns the source of Irene's pain: throughout the past year she has been pursued by Madame d'Aiguines, an alluring Austrian for whom she has developed a powerful erotic fascination. Over the course of three acts the play depicts the consequences of Irene's attraction: her growing desperation as she comes ever nearer to succumbing to the woman; her attempt to free herself by marrying an old friend, Jacques Virieu, who knows the reason for her torment and sets out to cure her of it; and the collapse of their marriage one year later, as both realize that Irene is incapable of loving a man. In the final scene Madame d'Aiguines returns, in the form of a bunch of violets sent to Irene at the home she shares with Jacques. Irene gazes at the flowers for several moments, mesmerized. Then, her eyes growing "fixed and hard," she leaves the room and walks out on her marriage, the pathetic victim, Bourdet implies, of psychological forces that proved impossible to fight.

One looks in vain in *The Captive* for any of the devices Mae West would deploy in *The Drag*. Bourdet's drama contains no purportedly scientific explanation for homosexuality; for that matter, neither the word "lesbian" nor its more common contemporary synonym, "invert," is ever voiced in the play. Nor did the playwright or the producers draw any obvious connections between the characters of the drama and the reality of lesbianism as it then existed in New York no less than in Paris. They certainly did not recruit an actual lesbian to play Irene de Montcel. The drama's star, Helen Menken, was an established Broadway actress, newly married, as all publicity for the production took pains to note, to a musical-comedy actor named Humphrey Bogart who had urged his wife to put aside her hesitations and take on this controversial part.

More to the point, Bourdet's treatment did everything it could to deflect attention from any physical dimension of lesbianism. In stark contrast to Mae West, he did not present his audience with actively homosexual characters. His drama focused not on Madame d'Aiguines but on Irene, a woman afflicted by lesbian desires she has never acted on. She and her "captor" are never seen to touch, nor do they speak to each other within sight of the audience. In fact, the openly homosexual Madame d'Aiguines, though discussed and described, never appears onstage.

Clearly, this was no Mae Westian showcasing of a sensational sex-

ual subculture. Bourdet was interested not in the sensual manifestations of homosexual desire but in its psychological ramifications—in
the anguish of Jacques and Madame d'Aiguines's husband and the
psychic degradation of Irene de Montcel as she struggles with a terrifying erotic attraction. As embodied in the absent Madame d'Aiguines, lesbianism looms over the play like a kind of vampire's spell.
Irene is gaunt, wraithlike, with a ghostly pallor, and her fascination
with Madame d'Aiguines is presented as a debilitating entrapment
that sucks away her life's blood and drains her of will:

> JACQUES: Why don't you take a train to Rome with Gisele to join
> your father?
> IRENE: I had thought of that. . . . But at the last minute I wouldn't
> go—I wouldn't have the strength—
> JACQUES: Yes, you would! I'll help you if you wish.
> IRENE: (shaking her head) Or else I'd come back.
> JACQUES: No!
> IRENE: You see, there are times in which I can see clearly, such as
> now, when I am sane and free to use my own mind. . . . But there
> are other times when I can't, when I don't know what I'm doing.
> It's like—a prison to which I must return captive, despite myself.[19]

What keeps Irene captive, the play makes clear, is an insidious
erotic passion that draws its overwhelming power from Irene's psychological affinity with her female enchantress. No heterosexual
love, Bourdet suggests, could exert a comparable lure. As Monsieur
d'Aiguines reminds Jacques, a woman can always learn to forget a
man; so great is the psychological distance between them that no
man can ever fully capture a woman in body, soul, and spirit. Lesbianism is the most extreme consequence of that psychological distance, which always exists between men and women; in Irene, Bourdet shows a woman whose psychological makeup—her gentleness,
tenderness, and emotionalism—translate into erotic desires that can
never be satisfied by men. Despite her effort to "cure" herself by
marrying Jacques, she remains physically repulsed by him; when she
sees his face fill with longing as he leans forward to kiss her, she
cannot restrain a shudder of aversion:

> IRENE: I tried my best to love you! You always speak of what *you*
> have done! What about me? What about me? What about my

feelings—did you ever know anything about them? Did you ever give them so much as a thought? You loved me, it's true, but in your way.

JACQUES: Were you expecting platonic love from me?

IRENE: I expected a little more tenderness. Is there no spirit in love? Must it be only—*the body*?[20]

And yet Irene's attraction to Madame d'Aiguines powerfully arouses the body: meeting her after a year's separation, she is breathless, trembling; she caresses her violets and holds them to her face with undisguised sensuality. So close are women from childhood on, so alike in spirit and emotions, that if an erotic attraction arises between them, it goes to the very core of their beings, where no man can ever hope to penetrate, as Monsieur d'Aiguines tells Jacques from bitter experience:

D'AIGUINES: Don't make my mistake. Don't say, as I said in a situation almost like yours, don't say: "Oh, it's nothing but a sort of ardent friendship—an affectionate intimacy . . . nothing very serious . . . we know all about that sort of thing." No! We don't know *anything* about it! We can't begin to know what it is. It's mysterious—terrible! Friendship, yes—that's the mask. Under cover of friendship a woman can enter any household, whenever and however she pleases—at any hour of the day—she can poison and pillage everything before the man whose home she destroys is even aware of what's happening to him. When finally he realizes things it's too late—he is alone! Alone in the face of a secret alliance of two beings who understand one another because they're of the same sex, because they're of a different planet than he, the stranger, the enemy! Ah! if a *man* tries to steal your woman you can defend yourself, you can fight him on even terms, you can smash his face in. But in this case—there's nothing to be done—but *get out* while you still have strength to do it![21]

At the heart of *The Captive* lies this fear expressed by Monsieur d'Aiguines—a terror of lesbianism as a subversive social menace, a "secret alliance" between women, able to "poison" heterosexual love and "pillage" male authority. In this Bourdet's drama is no isolated historical oddity. Certainly in the United States, as historian Christina Simmons has noted, psychologists and social scientists throughout the 1920s feared lesbianism for much the same reasons, as a perverted consequence of modern women's expanding economic and sexual freedom.[22]

Even a cursory scan of *The Captive*'s reviews shows that critics uniformly regarded lesbianism as "loathsome," "revolting," and a "warped infatuation"; without a doubt they were more comfortable with Bourdet's focus on the lesbian threat than with Mae West's sensational exploitation of male homosexual pleasure. Hence it is tempting to ascribe the praise that greeted *The Captive* to what might be called its moral conservatism. But to read the play's reception in that context is to disregard the perspective from which its supporters praised it, and to miss what seemed to them to be at stake when it was raided in February 1927. Indeed, critics lauded *The Captive* precisely for what they saw as its *lack* of moralism, its *refusal* to pander to comfortable moral assumptions.

The Captive was shaped by a distinctly modern theatrical aesthetic, one formed in opposition to the style of playwriting and dramatic criticism that had dominated Broadway prior to the First World War. The critics who championed *The Captive* most ardently—John Anderson of the *New York Evening Post*, Brooks Atkinson of the *New York Times,* and George Jean Nathan of the *American Mercury*—were at the forefront of an energetic group that emerged in the late 1910s and early 1920s, gaining attention through stylish and erudite attacks on the mainstream critical establishment and its "time-honored species of appraisal that confuses morals and art," in Nathan's words.[23] In company with a small number of American playwrights, actors, and producers whose work they praised and publicized, these critics took part in an upsurge of theatrical creativity that augured a new direction for Broadway.

In the early years of the twentieth century many young aspirants to careers in the theater began expressing tremendous dissatisfaction with what they regarded as a staid and unadventurous Broadway stage. Its corruption, they argued, dated back to the late nineteenth century, when massive organizational changes radically altered longstanding methods of American play production. Those years saw the near-total obliteration of the locally based independent stock companies that had constituted the American theater for well over a century. In their place grew a system of temporary production companies organized for one show alone, unattached to any single theater or community, and routed across the country after a New York City run. Increasingly centralized and rationalized in the 1870s and 1880s with the rise of regional circuits and booking exchanges, this system resulted in what could fairly be termed the national marketing of New York drama. By the turn of the century two organizations, the Theater Syndicate and the Shuberts, controlled most of the first-class legitimate theaters across the country, as well as producing many shows themselves.[24]

Critics of the system denounced these changes as the "commercialization" of the American theater, which was now almost exclusively in the hands of a small group of profit-oriented businessmen. But the real issue for these critics was not simply commercialism but the particular commercial nexus within which Broadway operated. Like good businessmen everywhere, Syndicate and Shubert managers worked with their audience in mind. Plays that made it to Broadway were those that theater managers expected their patrons to approve—and that, for young theater critics, was precisely the problem.

During the latter half of the nineteenth century the legitimate theater had catered to a single segment of American society—middle-class men and particularly women. Their patronage encouraged producers and playwrights to fashion decorous plays consistent with middle-class moral imperatives, sentimental comedies, and romantic costume dramas that taught light and entertaining lessons in loyalty, sincerity, and the redemptive value of motherly love. Broadway's critical establishment, headed by the *New York Tribune*'s William Winter, also saw the stage as an arena for the illustration of morality and beauty. Plays that hinted at sensual passion were scorned as morbid and inartistic, as Winter made clear in 1894 when someone had the audacity to stage a production of Henrik Ibsen's *Ghosts*, which dealt with the consequences of congenital syphilis:

A three-act dialogue called "Ghosts"—being one of the most unpleasant of the many unpleasant productions of the Norwegian crank Mr. Ibsen—was obtruded upon the public notice yesterday afternoon at the Garden Theater, where it bored a small audience during several wasted hours. The "Ghosts" in question are the taints of hereditary disease, and reference is made to them for the purpose, apparently, of admonition as to marriage. . . . Physical disease producing moral obliquity is surely inappropriate, not to say obnoxious, as a theme for drama. Persons requiring physiological instruction or medical advice should go to the doctor, not to the theater. Art is for the mind, not for the body, and it should not concern itself with sanitary investigation. The question of sewerage may wisely enough be left to the plumber. . . .

Mr. Ibsen's abominable stuff, which is both dull and dirty, will never prosper in this capital. It may obtain, here and there in a corner, the attention of those uneasy persons, of no sex in particular, who hang limp upon the fringes of nastiness and think that everything is bold and strong ("virile," they commonly call it) which happens to be shameless and impudent; but the health and good sense of the American audience will never accept the nauseous offal of Mr. Ibsen's dissecting table as either literature or drama.[25]

Winter's criticism stemmed from the Victorian vision of the drama, and of all art, as didactic in purpose, its highest aim to illustrate and communicate fixed moral and spiritual truths. To the twentieth-century theatrical rebels, this was an aesthetic of cloying sentimentality, moral propaganda preaching unthreatening lessons to a smug audience that sought no more than a "mental warm bath or emotional chocolate cream.[26] In their view, commercial managers' attentiveness to the taste of their middle-class patrons had doomed Broadway to a succession of trite, saccharine productions marked by vapid subjects, frilly clothes, and happy endings. The legitimate stage, wrote critic Sheldon Cheney, had become not a "temple of art" but simply another outpost of a flourishing middle-class assembly line, generating a product no different from the sentimental novel or the genteel periodical in its appeal to conventional wisdom, prettiness, and romance—"a sort of *Hearst's—Cosmopolitan—Ladies' Home Journal* art."[27]

Denunciations like Cheney's were part of a broader critique of what was seen in many quarters as the prudery and complacency at the heart of American middle-class culture. Like their counterparts in the theater, young novelists, poets, artists, and political activists, gathering in bohemian neighborhoods of Chicago, San Francisco, and New York, launched a revolt against the middle-class gentility that seemed to stultify arts and letters and warp private relations. In subsequent years historians have come to classify all these rebellions under the label "modernism," a term that despite its imprecision remains the best collective description of these restless intellectuals who united to challenge what to them was the dishonesty of Victorian culture—its veneration of the "civilized" and its terror of "animality," of the instincts and passions that threatened self-control.

Modernists drawn to the theater avoided the Broadway establishment to congregate in Greenwich Village. Groups like the Washington Square Players (founded in 1915) and the Provincetown Players (who moved to MacDougal Street in the Village in the late 1910s) attracted members from a variety of avant-garde realms—radical journalism, feminism, the fine arts, and literature. As a result they developed a style of theater colored by the political, social, and personal agendas of the Village milieu.

Like other Village intellectuals, the theatrical rebels decried the sexual repressiveness of mainstream society. From their perspective, the middle-class devotion to beauty and uplift was nothing more than a "superficial seeking of sweetness and light" grounded in a terror of the physical self.[28] That terror forced middle-class men and women along tame and undemanding paths, their private lives governed by a sentimental conception of love that relegated women to an unreal sexlessness, and their cultural lives dominated by pallid commercial products that simply validated easy moral wisdom.[29]

The Young Turks of the theater drew inspiration from the modernist rebellion that had reshaped European theater in the late nineteenth and early twentieth centuries: the social realist dramas of Ibsen and Chekhov, and the art theater companies of Berlin, Moscow, and Dublin, whose productions were staged to enormous critical praise in New York in the 1910s. From the social realists they acquired a taste for plays that challenged bourgeois timidity; and from art theater manifestos they took an aesthetic framework in which to produce and defend them.

What resulted has been described as an American theatrical "renaissance." If the Victorians had valued theater for illustrating timeless moral principles, the modernists championed it for exploring the flow of inner experience, for recording the disturbing workings of individual psychology. As historian Daniel Singal has argued, modernists were "intent on nothing less than recovering an entire aspect of being that their predecessors had tried to banish,"[30] and they undertook this mission in the deepest seriousness, as can be seen from the near-heroic status to which they elevated the "artist/playwright." Hailed for his courage in confronting the "terrors of the inner life," he enjoyed the "unprecedented stature" that came to be invested in all the arts following the advent of modernism, as Susan Sontag has pointed out—a stature rooted in art's newfound imperative of "making forays into and taking up positions on the frontiers of consciousness . . . and reporting what's back there."[31]

These "reports" from the "frontiers of consciousness," however, were not always delivered in a straightforward manner. The dramatist, modernists stressed, was not a classroom lecturer. Aiming to evoke the workings of inner experience, he expressed his artistic vision through the oblique but suggestive language of the stage, through movement, gesture, intonation, lighting, set design, and theatrical symbol. In a play of genuine quality those formal elements worked together to present the creator's vision as a seamless, integrated whole.[32] If the result was not always readily accessible, if the artist's meaning could not be easily discerned, the fault lay with the spectators, not with the playwright. Spoiled for too long by plays that "pandered to the crowd" and delivered simple homilies, audiences would have to learn that a truly artistic drama involved a rigorous intellectual experience. The seriousness of the artist's undertaking demanded equal seriousness on the part of the viewer. As critic Walter Eaton warned, the audience "needs must understand what the art of the theater is, and it is no easier to learn the principles of that art than of any other."[33]

Modernists, in short, disdained didacticism as a falsification of the complexity of experience, championing drama that probed the depths of the human psyche and gave an uncompromising report of its findings. The quality of an individual play was thus to be judged by its "authenticity," by the profundity of the artist's exploration and the skill with which he conveyed it. While the Victorians viewed theater primarily in a social context, valuing it for its educational influence, their twentieth-century challengers saw it as the meeting ground of the playwright and the psyche, a privileged arena of individual creativity.

The Captive fulfilled these new critical criteria to an extent that few other Broadway dramas approached. It was consummately staged by director Gilbert Miller, who orchestrated sets, lighting, and the rhythm of the scenes to realize Bourdet's vision of the destructive power of abnormal desire. "Even before the nature of the malady is defined in the second act," wrote Brooks Atkinson in the *New York Times*, "doom swims over the play like a thick black cloud."[34] No single element was allowed to overshadow the rest and detract from the steadily mounting tension. Under Miller's direction, performances were restrained, austere, and intense, their cerebral tone suggesting that concerted mental effort was required to decipher the psychic turmoil at the heart of the drama.[35]

But Bourdet's "special virtue," as George Jean Nathan described it, lay in his extraordinary "objectivity" in handling a treacherous topic. Despite the horrifying implications of lesbianism, Bourdet was never "guilty of the sin of pleading," and this absence of didacticism sharply distinguished him from an earlier generation of playwrights. As Nathan wrote admiringly:

> There is no hint of propaganda, of lecturing, of pointing a moral. It is easy to surmise what such a fellow countryman as Brieux, say, would have done with the same materials. Act Two would not have gone half its distance before the leading male character would have stepped to the footlights and . . . delivered a statistical speech descanting upon the woe that threatened the world if such conditions were permitted to go on.[36]

The Captive contained no sermons, no tirades against social evil, not even a clear-cut ending warning the audience of the peril of Irene's ways. Irene de Montcel does not repent and abandon her obsession; she does not throw herself in front of a train; she does not wither away from consumption. Instead, she gives in to Madame d'Aiguines. Unable to resist when she receives the final bouquet of violets, she walks out on her marriage, slamming the front door behind her.

Bourdet certainly made a judgment here, but he expressed it in the language of the modern drama, through psychological depth of characterization and the use of theatrical symbols. Though he regarded lesbianism as an insidious menace and felt that women's increasing independence would lead more and more of them to renounce men altogether, he expressed his fears through his nuanced portrait of Irene de Montcel, of the psychic affinities binding her to her female "captor." In the slam of the door that ended his play, Bourdet echoed the final moments of Henrik Ibsen's 1879 *A Doll's House*, in which the oppressed wife Nora walks out on her husband in search of personal liberation. Bourdet used what had become one of the modern drama's classic symbols as an indictment of female independence in a sexualized 1920s world, suggesting that it was linked to sexual "perversion" and might lead to a wholesale rejection of the bonds of "normal" love.

That *The Captive* electrified Broadway in 1926 was a triumph for the art theater movement and inspired hopes for greater victories ahead. Modernists had other reasons for optimism. Already, in the ten years since its beginnings, art theater had shed much of its stigma as a product of fringe intellectuals, gaining greater visibility and status within mainstream theater circles. The Washington Square Players, for example, had left Greenwich Village to relocate on Broadway under the new name of the Theater Guild, attracting a small but growing following that encouraged the founding of other Broadway-based art theater companies. Even more notable was the spectacular success of former Provincetown Player Eugene O'Neill, whose dramas—among them *Anna Christie, The Emperor Jones*, and *Desire Under the Elms*—had garnered international acclaim and two Pulitzer Prizes since 1920. Finally, and perhaps most influentially in the long run, the new generation of drama critics had graduated from small-circulation avant-garde journals and was supporting all these efforts in publications with a larger readership: Atkinson in the *Times*, John Anderson in the *Post*, Nathan in *American Mercury* and *Vanity Fair*.[37]

For modernists the arrival of *The Captive* on Broadway represented the culmination of a decade of progress. Faithfully staged, not by an art theater company (though both the Theater Guild and the Actor's Theater had bid for it) but by a mainstream production company, it was a sign that new principles of dramatic artistry were gaining legitimacy on Broadway. Moreover, its success in packing the Empire Theater with enthusiastic crowds raised the exciting prospect that Broadway had at last captured a large but intellectually discerning public. With the rise of motion pictures as New York's primary vehicle of mass entertainment, Broadway could be a forum for rigorous, challenging art, a medium of genuine cultural distinction, as *The Captive*'s translator, Arthur Hornblow, Jr., argued several weeks after the premiere:

> The moving pictures have left the legitimate stage only the adult portion of the public speaking from an intellectual standpoint. The type of persons who still go to the drama are not the type who would be menaced by subjects of an advanced nature, . . . whereas the moving

picture public covers a much broader mental field and needs to be protected from thoughts it is not qualified to cope with.[38]

The Captive, in other words, initially fed one of the modernists' most cherished hopes: that Broadway had finally risen above the "broader mental field," the panorama of "popular entertainments" for the general public, and could become, as they intended, the province of an intellectual elite.

But if the 1920s brought new possibilities for the modern theater, they brought new difficulties as well, difficulties raised by the question of audience appreciation of *The Captive*. We can sense this in the praise critics lavished on the play's understated intensity. Modernists had always stressed the necessity for restrained staging, which focused attention on the crucial element—the vision of the artist/playwright—and infused the play with a tone appropriate to drama's new elevation to the highest cultural plateau. As Sheldon Cheney wrote in 1917, "For [the modern stage] is to be the temple of the highest art, and high art is always marked by reticence and a reverential rather than a forward spirit."[39] But something more was at work in the critical acclaim for *The Captive*'s austerity. Reviewers hailed its restraint less for fostering artistic integrity than for refusing "truckle or smirk," as Brooks Atkinson put it. Like his fellows, he implied that homosexuality was certain to appeal to the prurience of at least part of the Broadway public. That Bourdet's drama refrained from playing to "low curiosity" formed much of its distinction, making it, in Atkinson's words, "a restrained though uncompromising tragedy" rather than "a commercial exploitation of a revolting theme."[40]

This linking of Broadway commercialism to sexual sensationalism marks a sharp break with the past and points to the changing cultural context in which the modernist agenda was being played out. Modernists' ambitions for revitalizing the drama had taken shape in the early twentieth century, when "Broadway commercialism" meant a genteel sentimentality and "playing to the crowd" meant infusing productions with sweetness and light. Their plans for an alternative "noncommercial" theater turned on the expectation that only a select public would be drawn to in-depth explorations of treacherous sexual matters like venereal disease, prostitution, and homosexuality.

Early modernist critics had scorned middle-class female playgoers for shying away from "unpleasant" topics; by the 1920s those women's daughters were thronging Broadway in search of the very "unpleasantries" their mothers' generation had avoided. "Playing to the crowd" now meant not refraining from sexual topics but embracing them in breezily suggestive style. As critic John van Druten noted in *Theater Arts Monthly*, more and more producers were catering to audiences with "exhibitionistic" plays presenting "the pictorial side of sex . . . whose appeal can only be explained on the assumption that people will . . . go to the theater in the vain hope of witnessing an actual seduction or violation onstage."[41] *The Drag*, to be sure, was a far bolder venture than any established manager had yet attempted, but the very fact that Mae West could expect it to be commercially viable suggested the existence of a vast new public for legitimate theater, one that sought neither uplift nor challenge but sensational and sensually explicit amusement.

For the modernists this public was as great a threat as the reformers. If the drama was to be established as a serious art, it had to cultivate an audience that would approach it with a purely intellectual interest. In the 1920s modernists confronted an audience that approached Broadway as "the Coney Island of America," in producer Winthrop Ames's words, another commercialized arena where inhibitions could be discarded.[42] Suppressing *The Drag*—and ensuring through the Theater Supervisory Board that similar productions stayed out—was essential to keep Broadway from becoming just another nightlife hotspot.

[To] see one of the largest theaters in New York crowded nightly with spectators who strain forward with the tension of their interest to see a play that deals with a woman in love with another woman is a matter to think upon. One thinks of Brieux and Ibsen and their earlier battles over subject matter, when venereal disease and cave men were handled with a directness that raised a storm, and reflects upon this theme which is new to our theater and which might be thought a very strong dose. Then one tries to consider just what happens in this instance of *The Captive*.[43]

In speculating on *The Captive*, critic Stark Young raised the question that came to lie at the heart of debates about the play, especially after *The Drag* began packing theaters in Connecticut and New Jersey. As was obvious from West's advertising of her play as "A Male *Captive*," she had looked at the success of Bourdet's drama and made her own wry assessment of why audiences were there.[44] Parading the gay subculture across the stage with an open appeal to voyeurism, *The Drag* was the final provocation for a citywide crisis over the composition and motives of Broadway audiences who were "strain[ing] forward with the tension of their interest" in same-sex passion.

The crisis was not confined to Broadway. Outside the walls of the legitimate theaters New York's nightlife horizon was changing. Young middle-class men and women had become enthusiastic patrons of openly sensational entertainments organized around the experience of "slumming," of poking into obscure urban corners for the thrill of flouting barriers of class, race, and sexual decorum.

Slumming, of course, was hardly a new phenomenon. Beginning in the early nineteenth century—as soon, in fact, as there were déclassé districts to slum in—daring gentlemen from New York's elite had ventured to lower-class taverns and music halls for potent drinks, rough camaraderie, and bawdy sexual escapades.[45] Even middle-class New Yorkers had been drawn by the same fascination, although they tended to pursue it vicariously through a veritable genre of slumming literature, the array of "lights and shadows" guidebooks whose clergymen authors warned of the dangers of underworld locales while describing them in tantalizing detail. But by the 1920s that moral and physical distance had been defiantly abandoned by a new generation of middle-class amusement patrons for whom the "shadow" areas of New York life, once deemed places of moral contagion, became entertainment hotspots retailing a novel taste of lower-class life.

At times slumming could be fairly innocent. For example, the 1920s saw the beginnings of the transformation of New York's Lower East Side, with its exotic smells, intriguing dialects, and abundance of Eastern European restaurants and coffeehouses, from vital neighborhood to mythologized tourist haunt.[46] More often, however, slumming had a racier aim: prowling the city's vice haunts in search of sexual titillation. In the past adventurous gentlemen had headed for the red-light districts of the Tenderloin, the Bowery, and Chinatown, but by the 1920s New York's "vice map" had changed, with the Bowery and Chinatown home to a stable Asian community and the Tenderloin dispersed by industrial development.

Slummers in the 1920s traveled uptown to Harlem, a locale so heavily visited that, as one observer noted, it occasionally resembled "a white man's house of assignation."[47] Or they stayed in Times Square, in nightclubs and taverns rendered tantalizingly illicit by the coming of Prohibition.

More than any other single factor, Prohibition helped transform the tone of middle-class leisure, turning slumming from an indulgence of the male elite into a recreation of the respectable citizenry. In the 1910s the cabaret had become the focal point for middle-class nightlife; in the 1920s the Volstead Act drove the cabarets underground (or forced them, even if they did not serve liquor, to maintain a discreet tolerance for patrons' flasks), and clubs took on a palpable seaminess.[48]

In part the new ambience stemmed from a change in management. With Prohibition the posh restaurateurs who had backed nightclubs in the 1910s gave way to racketeers with plenty of capital, little concern for elegance, and reputations that a raid by federal agents could not tarnish. Often they had strong gang connections and were directly involved in wider criminal enterprises. Owney Madden, who owned Harlem's Cotton Club, also supplied bootleg liquor to much of the Eastern Seaboard. (In 1928 Madden would extend his activities to Broadway, putting up half the money for Mae West's *Diamond Lil*.)[49] But even the more sedately managed establishments could not help involving their patrons in a new style of nightlife. Gathering in humble surroundings (the threat of raids made ritzy decor too expensive), rubbing shoulders with crooks and prostitutes (the trade in sex had fled underground along with the trade in liquor), prepared to hide their activities at a moment's notice, people intent on drinking had to accustom themselves to a tawdry atmosphere.[50]

Far from dampening patrons' enthusiasm, however, the new lowlife flavor became a big part of the lure. Most clubs made little effort to disguise their underworld links, and many positively flaunted them, or dramatized them in entertainments that offered a firsthand glimpse of underworld thrills.

One such thrill was the campy, effeminate style of New York's gay male subculture. By the mid-1920s the "horticultural young man," in journalist Jack Kofoed's phrase, had become a genuine nightlife phenomenon. At the Rubaiyat, a gay club in Greenwich Village, middle-class couples crowded in to witness the nightly antics of "boys with falsetto voices and girls who sang in basso profundo." Times Square's Club Pansy, as its name suggests, built its reputation on similar fare, and other establishments followed suit. What little evidence survives suggests that gay style in these clubs was little different from that on display in *The Drag*. Kofoed remembered one male performer "trigged up in an evening gown, painting his lips and powdering his face and going on the floor to sing in a mincing, high-pitched voice."[51] Even gay streetlife became a source of entertainment for the after-hours theater crowd, as one tabloid informed its readers jocularly: "The latest gag about two a.m. is to have your picture taken with one or two pansies on Times Square. The queens hang out there for the novel racket."[52]

While this observation may seem free from moralizing, it is also smug and vaguely contemptuous. Indeed, it exemplifies all that is offensive and disturbing about the slumming trend. So much of the human richness that made up the early gay community and the black culture of Harlem was ignored in favor of the exotic elements that intrigued a white middle-class sensibility. Almost by definition slummers were not interested in genuinely *learning* from these urban subcultures; rather, with their pose of hard-boiled sophistication, they objectified them as a source of "thrills," and thus their covert contempt was able to persist.

But the undeniably distasteful aspects of slumming should not blind us to what was challenging about it. Young men and women engaged in slumming as a means of articulating a sexual style, of participating in the turn-of-the-century revolt that saw the rise of recreational sex, sexuality separated from procreation and valued as a source of identity and pleasure. It was the same sexual revolt, in fact, that had given rise to the gay subculture, which had certain affinities with nightlife style. Both involved a playful disruption of conventional gender boundaries: "mannish" women and "womanish" men in the gay subculture, and the "mannish" fashions and social mannerisms of young female nightlifers.

In gearing their nightlife toward underworld adventure, young people elaborated a unique conception of entertainment, one that would prove abhorrent to both reformers and modernists when transported to the legitimate theater. They brought their whole lives to their leisure, including their senses. An evening at a nightclub was no mere diversion; it was a means of asserting a personal style, of expanding sexual experience, however vicariously, and of defining a rebellious modern identity. Entertainment, in short, was not something that slummers passively absorbed but an active, participatory process, a means of discovering and creating a new sexual self.

The Captive and *The Drag* appeared at a time when this new nightlife audience was becoming increasingly visible, and that was in large part why they generated so much controversy. Newspapermen showed as much curiosity about who was attending the plays as about the productions themselves. The tabloid *New York Daily Mirror*, for example, devoted a full front page to a photo of a line stretching across several city blocks of Bayonne, New Jersey, where would-be patrons had gathered hours in advance in their eagerness to gain admission to *The Drag*.[53]

In covering *The Drag*'s Connecticut and New Jersey tryouts, reviewers reported diverse reactions, but on two facts all were agreed. First, the play attracted a large number of young women "who determinedly giggled at the least excuse."[54] And second, in targeting her play at an audience that found homosexuality amusing, West had hit her mark. If spectators occasionally appeared bored, it was because there were not *enough* of the titillating scenes to suit their tastes. In every town in which it played, reviewers noted that *The Drag*'s most flamboyant and suggestive scenes earned the most enthusiastic response. *Variety* wrote of the play's premiere in Bridgeport, Connecticut:

> The body of the audience laughed immoderately. During the "drag" scene they were convulsed with mirth. There could be no question about it, they thought for the moment the scene was uproarious comedy.
>
> ... At the end of the play they seemed to realize that something else was expected of them, for a considerable part of the crowd remained in their seats and applauded.
>
> Bridgeport talked of nothing else. The *Variety* reporter stopped at a one-arm lunch near the station on the way to the train. All the men in the place were discussing the event. Five had tried and failed to get seats and the other man, who had been in the audience, was telling them about the performance with much gusto.[55]

By all accounts, audiences watched *The Drag* in a slumming frame of mind, as a means of satisfying voyeuristic curiosity and of proving their own broad-minded sophistication by "determinedly giggl[ing] at the least excuse." The play threatened to bring that nightlife style to Broadway, and for that reason it was opposed by *everyone*: by moral reformers because it seemed sure to provoke youthful sexual experimentation, by the theatrical mainstream because it seemed sure to provoke censorship, and by modernists because of its "mindless" appeal to prurience.

But what about *The Captive*'s audience? Critics had been certain that the play was entirely without sensationalism and that in consequence it drew a mature, discerning public—an audience, to quote its translator, of adults "from an intellectual standpoint." But by early 1927 *The Captive*'s supporters had been confronted by a startling fact: the play's patrons were overwhelmingly young women. Police reports filed before the February raid showed its audience to be 70 percent female and 60 percent under twenty-five. Many teenage girls, moreover, arrived unescorted by an adult.[56]

This flood of youthful feminine patronage created a crisis for *The Captive*'s modernist champions. Some would continue to insist on the intellectual maturity of the play's viewers, but most found it impossible to do so. That they backtracked publicly attests both to the limits of their ideals—the elitism of their vision of legitimate theater—and to the intense social tension that youthful female sexuality aroused.

Of all the equivocations on the impact of *The Captive*, none was more startling than that of George Jean Nathan, a former editor, with H. L. Mencken, of the sophisticated journal *Smart Set*. Like Mencken, Nathan had made his reputation as an acid-tongued iconoclast who delighted in debunking the sentimental moralism of American arts and letters. Arguing for a bold and probing American drama, Nathan had been the earliest critical champion of Eugene O'Neill, publishing three of his one-act works in *Smart Set* in 1918 and arranging for the professional production of O'Neill's first full-length play, *Beyond the Horizon*, in 1920.[57]

Nathan's original review of *The Captive*, published in *American Mercury*'s December 1926 issue, praised it as exemplary modernist theater: psychologically compelling, dramatically effective, and above all, told with a complete absence of moralizing. With "no hint of propaganda, of lecturing," Bourdet had simply permitted his adeptly fashioned materials to tell their tale. "Unpleasant" that tale definitely was, but it represented nonetheless "the most finely wrought drama of sex" to reach Broadway in years.[58]

Within four months Nathan reconsidered his praise in a column published in *American Mercury* in March 1927 but written before the February theater raids. He maintained that he did not want *The Captive* censored; nor, for that matter, had he changed his mind about its quality. In his first review he had simply done the job of a good critic, who, like the dramatist, need ordinarily pay no heed to questions of public morality. "If a fine piece of work sends ten thousand morons to perdition," Nathan wrote with characteristic acerbity, "it remains nonetheless a fine piece of work, and that is all that the critic has a right to say of it." Yet in the case of *The Captive* he had to make an exception. In its New York production—and more precisely, for its particular New York audience—it was "the most subversive, corruptive and potentially evil-fraught play ever shown in the American theater."[59]

Focusing on the intricacies of individual psychology, *The Captive* gave a straightforward portrait of a woman who, in line with contemporary psychiatric theory, had not inherited her lesbian compulsion but had "freely chosen degeneracy." For an audience composed of individuals like Nathan—mature, rational, and male—it was an absorbing, intellectually exhilarating dramatic experience. But for the audience the play actually drew—young, impressionable, and female—it was a drama that stimulated morbid curiosity, eroded will, and sapped sexual self-control.

When writing his original review shortly after *The Captive*'s premiere Nathan had been unprepared for the huge female patronage that was to greet Bourdet's drama. Explaining to an interviewer what had led him to revise his assessment, he said:

> I had been talking to a man who attended a matinee performance. . . . He told me that he, and apparently a mere handful of males in the house, felt embarrassingly conspicuous amidst such overwhelming feminine assemblance. . . . If all the ladies present were not weakened they were at least made curious.[60]

Women would be "made curious" by Bourdet's drama, Nathan argued, because it did not guide them toward any other response. Precisely the absence of moralizing that distinguished *The Captive* as "sound drama," in other words, made it thoroughly pernicious before this particular audience. By delving into the psyche of Irene de Montcel the play encouraged its feminine viewers to grapple with the emotions of a woman who "deliberately . . . enters upon perversion and intimates her enjoyment of it." Presenting those emotions without preaching, it left women to their own devices in interpreting Irene's experience, and with no dissuading voice to warn them otherwise they were likely to judge Irene's attraction "an adventure of high excitement."[61]

In Nathan's view *The Captive* had become "a document in favor of sexual degeneracy" for its young female audience, tititlating them with what they took to be its thesis: "that a degenerate physical love between women is superior to the normal physical love of the opposite sexes." Their exposure to *The Captive*, he concluded, could only have dire consequences for their personal conduct: "To believe that such stuff does not at least pique curiosity on the part of susceptible young women—and the Empire Theater has been full of them since news of the play first got around the boarding schools—is to believe more than I, for one, am capable of."[62]

Nathan was certainly alone among modernists in his extreme wariness of *The Captive*'s corrupting influence on feminine morals. Other modernists continued to champion the drama, though they often felt compelled to shift their ground. Universally lauded in its opening weeks for its refusal to propagandize, by January 1927 *The Captive* was being praised for its enormous "social value," its effectiveness in "educating" sexually impressionable young women. Far from glamorizing lesbian attachments, the play's defenders now argued, *The Captive* vividly warned against them by plumbing the psychological anguish that followed Irene's infatuation with Madame d'Aiguines. The play's star, Helen Menken, told a reporter, "I believe *The Captive* is the greatest moral lesson Broadway has seen in many years. I think all girls should see it, that they may understand the horrible unhappiness a similar relationship may bring them."[63] Stage manager Percy Shostac explained to the press that many girls in the audience had been sent in detachments from boarding schools and all-female colleges, and that Helen Menken had "received several notes from women educators in the audience, deans of women's colleges and finishing schools, who said they were already concerned with the necessity of impressing the girls in their charge with the dangers of a reprehensible attachment between two women."[64] The play, he argued, filled exactly that need—a view seconded by another supporter in a letter to the *New York Times*:

If the moral in a play is what is to be judged, *The Captive* by no possible standard could be said to fall down, for not a person who saw it can fail to be tremendously moved by pity and a wish to understand and help those so afflicted. If, as a famous neurologist says, woman inverts are more often made than born, those of us who have the training of children in our hands can only be too glad to have brought to our attention the sad results of something we might have prevented. No one goes away from *The Captive* desirous of becoming an Irene, but only more healthily thankful one is not, and more pitifully sorry for the poor mortal.[65]

What an extraordinary reinterpretation this was: from stark, objective modern drama to powerful force for female moral education in only four months. And all because young women rather than mature men filled the seats of the Empire Theater. The modernists may have been motivated by expediency, but it is nonetheless a measure of the discomfort aroused by youthful feminine desire that they made no effort to sustain their earlier defense. Despite their own rebellion against prudery, in the last instance they too accepted the notion that sensuality, at least among the young female "mass," needed to be controlled and guided. Liberation from Victorian constraints was only for those deemed to have the intellectual capacities to handle it.

In so altering their argument the modernists betrayed their own strenuous attempt to separate art from morality, and they may have helped doom *The Captive* in the process. By discarding their insistence that plays be valued solely for promoting concerted intellectual engagement they centered the public debate on the question of *which* moral (whether lesbianism was glamorous or loathsome) the play actually taught. They ceded the central point, agreeing that the young women flocking to *The Captive* were not those adults "from an intellectual standpoint" at whom their high-quality legitimate theater was aimed.

Three weeks after the New York City police raided *The Captive*, New York State Supreme Court Justice Jeremiah Mahoney barred it from ever returning to the Broadway stage. In his decision the judge agreed that mature and intelligent minds ran no risk of being harmed by the play, which he acknowledged had great literary merit. But Broadway was inherently a mass medium, attracting a wide variety of patrons. Advanced artistic intentions were fine for select audiences, but "the young, immature, ignorant, sensually inclined," Justice Mahoney maintained, must be "protected from their very selves."[66]

On March 26, 1927, in response to the turmoil of the previous months, the New York State Legislature passed a measure aimed at combating the spread of "dirty plays" on Broadway. As signed into law by Governor Al Smith, the bill did not, to Broadway's relief, place the stage under the supervision of the New York Board of Motion Picture Censorship, but neither did it recognize the authority of a supervisory board to regulate the theater from within. On the whole it simply reinforced the existing penal code, which empowered the district attorney to shut down productions judged offensive in court, but it did add two new provisions. The first, widely decried in theater circles, allowed the municipal government to "padlock" for one year any theater showing a play convicted of obscenity. The second provision passed largely unnoticed. It banned, flat out, any depiction of homosexuality on the New York stage.[67]

It was a significant piece of legislation. The past several weeks had seen the culmination of a struggle for authority over the legitimate stage, a battle between moral reformers and Broadway intellectuals as the theater was colonized by a youthful nightlife public. Reformers argued that such patronage made Broadway a mass entertainment; thus, like the cheap theaters, it needed policing by governmental authorities. Modernists did not dispute the vulnerability of the "masses," especially when they were young and female, but they still resisted external supervision. In their view no mere civil servant or women's club matron was a fit judge of the drama. As the *New York Herald Tribune* summarized their argument, "Lay persons were not qualified to pass judgement as censors upon plays and things theatrical. . . . it was a difficult enough job for experts, and . . . inexpert meddling would result in chaos."[68]

The New York State Legislature had the unenviable task of resolving this highly contentious dispute. In the end, however, neither reformers nor modernists were able to claim victory. Reformers' hopes of putting Broadway under state regulation came decisively to an end with their bill's defeat in the legislative battle. Modernists, for their part, not only failed to win state recognition for the Theater Supervisory Board, they failed to gain unanimous agreement to their plan within the Broadway community itself. Many producers whose self-interest led them to support the boycott of *The Drag* still balked at allowing their own productions to be judged by a theater board that in its zeal for "quality" might be as censorious as the reformers.[69]

From the beginning the state government was eager to stay out of the fray. On the one hand Al Smith's Democratic administration was officially opposed to government censorship. (Smith favored dismantling the Motion Picture Censorship Board.) On the other hand it was the target of press attacks, led by William Randolph Hearst's *New York American*, accusing it of tolerating "filth" on Broadway. With a presidential bid in the offing, Smith could ill afford charges of encouraging pornography. The result of this pressure was the February theater raids. Press accounts make clear that they had little to do with municipal government outrage and far more to do with the prodding of Governor Smith, who hoped police raids would prove that a theater censorship board was unnecessary and that "dirty plays" could by controlled through the existing legal apparatus.[70]

New York's state government felt compelled to pass some sort of legislation, but it carefully refrained from endorsing the vision of either the moral reformers or the Broadway modernists. As a result, and largely by default, it was the nightlifers' vision of Broadway that triumphed, as can be seen most clearly in the padlocking provision. Padlocking was an evocative symbol in the 1920s: it was the practice employed by federal agents when they closed down speakeasies. As the "Padlock Law" implied, Broadway would henceforth be policed as an adjunct of New York's underworld. And under the graft-ridden administration of Mayor Jimmy Walker, an enthusiastic nightlifer himself, that policing was haphazard, inefficient, and exceedingly sporadic.

The one unquestionable victor in this complex affair, as I read it, was Mae West. The events that surrounded *The Drag* and forced West to close it—her arrest for *Sex*, her trial and conviction on charges of staging an obscene production, and her ten-day jail sentence on Welfare Island—are among the most legendary of her career and were all perfect fodder for the tabloids. Throughout late winter and spring of 1927 photos of West covered the front pages of the *Daily News*, the *Daily Mirror*, and the *Evening Graphic*, and even the more reputable papers carried front-page accounts of her imperturbable demeanor in court, where she listened to former associates give damning testimony about her motives in staging *Sex*—that she had said she was "interested in the box office, that's all"; that she and her manager, James Timony, had hoped for a raid on the preview performance in Waterbury, Connecticut, to stimulate New York ticket sales; that Timony had cornered reviewers before the New York premiere, urging them to "tell the public *Sex* is the dirtiest show in town"[71]—and responded to it all with an enigmatic smile.

Those press accounts made Mae West into a household name throughout New York City. Both moral reformers and theater intellectuals had failed to constrain her and to create an official mechanism for regulating the Broadway stage. West could do whatever she pleased on Broadway, subject only to the interference of the police—and audience tastes.

West's exploits with *Sex* and *The Drag* established her reputation as a kind of underworld impresario and made her a cult heroine to New York's adventurous youth, the "jaded weisenheimers" who were drawn by the novelty of real "dirt" on Broadway. But such a cultish appeal could last only so long. Indeed, *Variety*'s records indicate that attendance at *Sex* had begun to flag by early 1927, before the police raid in February sent it skyrocketing once more.[72]

For Broadway's largely middle-class public, Mae West's plays were the theatrical equivalent of a slumming excursion, and while that indisputably recommended them to some, it scared off many more. Something would have to change for West to be more than a fringe attraction. She made that change in 1928 with her production *Diamond Lil*.

Chapter 5

A LITTLE BIT SPICY:
DIAMOND LIL

*A*fter suffering the twinges of disgrace for a time, Miss Mae West is now enjoying the comforts of respectability. . . . [She] has become an institution in the Broadway Drama since her release from the house of correction. Instead of sullenly reverting to her former iniquities she decided to be a friend rather than an enemy of society, and to join her fellow citizens in obeying the laws. . . .

The result of Miss West's reformation is that the Theater Royale is crowded at each performance of *Diamond Lil* with persons anxious to encourage a conscious-stricken transgressor in her desire to be meritorious. It is one of the "hits" of the waning season and vies in money-making values with the most prosperous output of dramatists who have never been in jail. Miss West, its star and author, recently under lock and key, is now more admired by her public than is Jane Cowl, Lynn Fontanne, Helen Hayes or Eva Le Gallienne.[1]

Theater critic Percy Hammond, writing the above in 1928 in the *New York Herald Tribune*, may have aimed his tongue decidedly toward his cheek, but he nonetheless pointed to a genuine phenomenon. With the premiere of her fourth full-length Broadway play, *Diamond Lil*, on April 9, 1928, Mae West became a full-fledged Broadway star, appealing to a broad range of theater patrons and drawing raves even from many of the very "art theater" advocates who had derided *Sex* and *The Drag*. With critics, with the more staid theater patrons, and with young people alike, *Diamond Lil* was a hit, and its success, in Hammond's eyes, gave Mae West something approaching respectability.

Diamond Lil certainly gave Mae West a more lasting brand of celebrity than she had earned with *Sex*—and that was a change she badly needed. Appearances to the contrary, the pre-1928 Mae West occupied a decidedly precarious place in New York's cultural panorama. Undeniably she was widely known, her name synonymous with sensationalism, scandal, and sex, yet that by no means guaranteed her theatrical future—as West learned seven months after her release from Welfare Island, when she attempted to capitalize on her sudden notoriety by staging a new self-scripted play, *The Wicked Age*. The story of a suburban flapper who flees her puritanical family, wins a rigged beauty contest, and luxuriates in high Manhattan living, *The Wicked Age* attempted to strike an uneasy compromise between the demands of the law and the desires of West's fans. Centered around a flapper, not a prostitute (a tamer if no less topical main character), the play nonetheless took shape onstage with all the trappings of a burlesque show—erotic movement (including a cootch dance by Mae West) and leering double entendre.

Predictably, *The Wicked Age* was reviled by critics, who found as much vulgarity in the "matronly," "pudgy" appearance of the star as in the raunchiness of the script, which was so lewd, according to *Variety*, that even the Mutual Wheel would hesitate to stage it. More surprisingly, audiences seemed uninterested as well. After a decent but unspectacular first week's take, box office receipts quickly dwindled, leaving West unable to pay her cast. With financial difficulties mounting and theater seats empty, *The Wicked Age* closed on November 21, 1927, only seventeen days after its Broadway premiere.[2] The implication seemed clear: West's novelty, though strong enough to keep *Sex* running for nearly a year, was now beginning to wane.

In truth, even in the best circumstances, West's plays had always appealed to a limited audience. Certainly *Sex* drew a larger segment of Broadway's middle-class public than anyone had anticipated; just as certainly its rawness kept many patrons away. Nearly every New Yorker knew Mae West's name, yet relatively few actually sought out her plays. Her trial and jail sentence threatened to turn her into just another "freak" of publicity, alongside such New York tabloid sensations as child bride (and child divorcee) "Peaches" Browning and adulterous murderess Ruth Snyder. In a decade that was never short on lurid sex scandals, West's could readily prove evanescent, fading from popular memory once fresher headlines came along.

It was at that moment, when *The Wicked Age* had revealed the shakiness of her public appeal, that West embarked on *Diamond Lil*. The play had its beginnings in an idea she lifted from somebody else. Late in 1927 she was approached by Mark Linder, a musical-comedy actor and sometime playwright, who wanted to star her in his comedy *Chatham Square*, a tale of New York's Bowery at the turn of the century. Though Linder's play had a male lead, West liked the idea of a Bowery setting. Offering him a share of the royalties, she refitted his script with new dialogue, new situations, and a new title, centering the action around an imperious dance hall madam. It is impossible to determine the extent of her revisions, as no copy of Linder's original script survives. Some skeptics have suggested that he, not West, deserves credit for *Diamond Lil*'s success, but though Linder fought bitterly with West about royalties, he never disputed that she alone had devised the play's content and that his contribution extended only to locale.[3]

West's story was absurd, but essentially simple: a tale of a tough, alluring Bowery queen who falls for the man who is out to reform her. As the mistress of Gus Jordan, ward boss and dance hall owner, Diamond Lil has risen from a shady past to a position of power: a provocative, dazzling entertainer, leader of a team of female shoplifters, and source of cocaine for junkies on the Lower East Side. But her power is threatened when Captain Cummings of the Salvation Army arrives to redeem the Bowery's fallen. Lil initially mocks the man, but when he shows no sign of succumbing to her charms, she is perplexed and increasingly drawn to him. At the play's conclusion Jordan's dance hall is raided by the police, and Lil discovers that Captain Cummings is a cop in disguise. She scornfully denounces him and holds out her hands for arrest, but instead Cummings takes her hands in his. Not only is she not under arrest, he tells her, but *she* has made a conquest of *him*.

Enmeshed in this rather far-fetched story were countless instances of underworld vice, from drugs and petty crime to a dance hall trade in prostitutes to explicit violence. In the second act Diamond Lil stabs a female rival to death when the woman accuses her of stealing a lover; then, with the help of a loyal henchman, she calmly disposes of her victim's body.

Clearly, West may have been seeking to broaden her audience, but not at the price of sensational subject matter. Far more than *The Wicked Age, Diamond Lil* remained an underworld play whose shady heroine outdid even Margy Lamont. In other words, though she sought a wider public, West did not contrive to get it censoring herself or whitewashing the story. It was something other than subject matter that made *Diamond Lil* different.

For different it was, sufficiently so to make it the only truly broad-based triumph of West's pre-Hollywood stage career, winning near-unanimous critical praise and an audience "from avenues as diverse as Park and Tenth."[4] If the social diversity of the *Diamond Lil* public startled many critics, its moral diversity surprised them even more. The play satisfied all the old Mae West fans—the thrill-seeking nightlifers who had flocked to *Sex* and delighted in West's "boldness" and "daring"—at the same time that it attracted more traditional, "comfortable" theatergoers, people who would never have considered attending a West show before. *Diamond Lil*'s popularity even extended beyond New York; alone among West's plays, it enjoyed a successful national tour on the heels of its Broadway run. In addition, under the title of *She Done Him Wrong*, it was made into a motion picture in 1933—the only one of the West's plays to move to the screen (though not without a struggle, as we shall see). To an extent West had never before approached, *Diamond Lil* seemed to offer something for everyone.

"*Diamond Lil* catches exactly the spirit of the Bowery as I first knew it in 1891, with its bosses, thugs, procurers and cops," said British theatrical producer Charles Cochran.[5]

Cochran was not alone. Nearly all the critics testified to the appeal of *Diamond Lil*'s setting: the Bowery, the wide lower Manhattan thoroughfare stretching from Chatham Square to Cooper Union. Even in 1928, when it was little more than a slightly down-at-the-heels commercial avenue, the Bowery remained one of New

York's most intriguing sites, drawing scores of curious tourists who hunted for glimpses of its infamous past, when it was reviled by middle-class New Yorkers as a haven for thievery, political corruption, and all forms of underworld vice.

The Bowery had a long history of notoriety, well predating the 1890s. Beginning in the early nineteenth century, with the departure of well-to-do New Yorkers for plusher accommodations to the north, the streets of lower Manhattan had become the near-exclusive province of the city's immigrant poor—first Germans, then Irish, and finally, toward the end of the century, Italians, Chinese, and Eastern European Jews. The Bowery took shape as their commercial mecca, a noisy, gaudy street of taverns, pawnshops, dance halls, shooting galleries, concert saloons, and variety theaters. In the process genteel observers came to loathe the place, whose flashiness and volatility symbolized all they most feared in working-class culture: its high-spirited excess and sensual unrestraint.[6] One chronicler, writing in 1872, gave his readers a warning that must have been echoed in pulpits throughout New York:

> Respectable people avoid the Bowery as far as possible at night. Every species of vice and crime is abroad at this time watching for its victims. Those who do not wish to fall into trouble should keep out of its way.[7]

But the Bowery's unsavory reputation reached a new peak in the 1890s through the spectacular revelations of two state commissions investigating the links between commercialized vice, the police force, and the New York City municipal government. The Lexow and Mazet committees of 1894 and 1899 unearthed a thriving vice economy operating in and around the Bowery: a network of gambling, drug dealing, and male and female prostitution, all conducted under police protection, often with the financial backing of Tammany Hall politicians. The investigations had their roots in a long-standing crusade by New York evangelical reformers, social workers, and journalists, who in sermons, treatises, and press exposés had painted a grim portrait of the exploitation of the lower Manhattan immigrant poor for political and commercial gain.[8]

The state hearings, widely reported in print, brought the specifics of that portrait into even sharper focus. In their aftermath all New Yorkers knew about the seamy dives that flourished in and around the Bowery, occasionally financed by Bowery ward boss (and later congressman) Tim Sullivan. These places fed on real desperation, as the grim black humor of their names suggests: the Plague; the Hell Hole; the Fleabag; the Bucket of Blood; Paresis Hall, a hangout for male prostitutes, named after a form of paralysis believed to be transmitted by homosexual sex; and most notorious of all, Suicide Hall, established in 1895 at 295 Bowery by veteran saloonkeeper John McGurk. Suicide Hall was one of the neighborhood's many "Raines Law Hotels"—saloons that were able to pose as "hotels" (and thus to serve liquor on Sundays under the 1896 Raines Law) and whose upper rooms were used exclusively for prostitution. Such establishments were legion on the Bowery in the late 1890s, but Suicide Hall was undoubtedly the best known, after a fifteen-year-old prostitute named Emma Hartig attempted suicide on the premises and testified before the Mazet committee in 1899. The saloon had acquired its bleak nickname, according to its boastful owner, because more prostitutes killed themselves within its walls than at any other spot in the world.[9]

Writing in 1928, Mae West deliberately invoked this bleak Bowery past in her *Diamond Lil* plot. West's Bowery seethed with the same activities that had filled the files of the Lexow and Mazet committees: drug use, shoplifting rings, gang crime, male prostitution, and white slave trafficking, based in Gus Jordan's saloon and protected by collusion among the police, the procurers, and the ward boss. And the saloon itself, in which a prostitute attempts suicide in act one, was explicitly modeled on John McGurk's Suicide Hall, as West's script spelled out.

Diamond Lil's Bowery, in short, was an urban underworld. As such, it was familiar terrain for West—the very sort of locale whose "authentic" re-creation had made her scandalous reputation. In *The Drag* she had staged an apparently true-to-life picture of New York's shadowy homosexual subculture; in *Sex*, a vivid depiction of a Montreal brothel—too vivid for most reviewers' tastes: a hostile, uninviting world of tawdry sex, drunkenness, graft, and violence. Both plays gave the impression of reality—of bringing viewers face to face with the hidden world of the criminally and sexually notorious as it really was.

In its advertising and publicity *Diamond Lil* made a claim to "realism" too. But while the realism of *Sex* had appalled critics, the realism of *Diamond Lil* delighted them. Reviewer after reviewer cited as one of the play's major pleasures the "authenticity" of its turn-of-the-century Bowery, from Charles Cochran to the critic for the *New York Evening Post*:

> For those of us few remaining New Yorkers who have a sentimental if somewhat hazy recollection of the Bowery, *Diamond Lil* contains a wealth of entertainment in the lusty and lewd enthusiasm with which it paints the underworld of the '90s. Somebody with a genuine sense of that atmosphere has created those Bowery scenes of ten cent revelry with an authority just as honest as the Moscow Art Theater's studies of Chekhov, and much nearer home.[10]

The contrast between the praiseworthy "honesty" of *Diamond Lil* and the repellent "realism" of *Sex* points to a major shift in West's theatrical style. *Sex* and *The Drag* were disturbingly authentic because they appeared to offer a direct peek at the sexual underworld, unmediated by the conventions of respectable theater. They were "real" precisely as burlesque was real: it did not merely depict the sexual underworld, but was itself an underworld product. In burlesque—as was always suspected and occasionally confirmed—players often were what they portrayed onstage: sexually alluring women really were prostitutes, and effeminate comics really were homosexuals. This was the heart of the offensive authenticity of *Sex* and *The Drag*: they brought to Broadway what seemed to be an insider's experience of the underworld.

The "reality" *Diamond Lil* captured was different: the Bowery not as an 1890s underworld denizen would have seen it, but as the 1920s theatergoing middle class remembered it. As West discovered during rehearsals, the turn-of-the-century Bowery, correctly crafted, held a ready-made commercial appeal for a Broadway public. When the *Evening Post* critic described his recollection of the old Bowery as fond and "sentimental," chances are that he was not thinking of the grim facts reported by the Lexow committee— poverty, drugs, political corruption, prostitution. Rather, his remembrance was most likely colored by another set of Bowery images that built on those facts but significantly reshaped them— images that flourished at the turn of the century and were therefore no less "authentic," though they emanated from a very different source.

Beginning in the late nineteenth century a series of enormously popular melodramas, short stories, and songs had made the notorious Bowery into a staple image of New York commercial culture—a world of amusingly stylized streetlife, carefully pitched to a citywide cross-class public. The memory of that world lingered in the twentieth century, on the border between myth and history, a kind of Bowery folklore sufficiently vivid and particularized to be widely taken for fact. This was the Bowery "reality" *Diamond Lil* brought to mind, from its opening moments.

The curtain rose to the jangling accompaniment of a turn-of-the-century popular song as the audience got its first glimpse of the *Diamond Lil* world: a group of amiable Bowery barflies in a crowded saloon, flashily attired in loud checked suits and gray derby hats. Brandishing foaming schooners of beer, they traded wisecracks and badgered the piano player, who obligingly broke into an 1890s standard that was doubtless familiar to many in the *Diamond Lil* audience:

Oh, the night that I struck New York, I went out for a little walk.
Folks who are onto the city say, better far that I took Broadway.
But I was out to enjoy the sights: there was the Bowery ablaze with
*   lights.*
I had one of the Devil's own nights; I'll never go there any more.

The Bowery, the Bowery! They say such things and they do strange
*   things*
On the Bowery, the Bowery! I'll never go there any more!

I went into an auction store; I never saw any thieves before.
First he sold me a pair of socks. Then he said, "How much for the
*   box?"*
Someone said two dollars and I said three. He emptied the box and
*   gave it to me.*
"I sold you the box, not the socks," said he. I'll never go there any
*   more.*

The Bowery, the Bowery! They say such things and they do strange
*   things*
On the Bowery, the Bowery! I'll never go there any more!

I struck a place that they called a dive. I was lucky to get out alive.
*   When the policeman heard my woes, saw my black eyes and my*
*   battered nose,*

"You've been held up," said the copper fly. "No, sir, but I've been knocked down," said I.
Then he laughed, but I couldn't see why. I'll never go there any more.

The Bowery, the Bowery! They say such things and they do strange things
On the Bowery, the Bowery! I'll never go there any more!

Written in 1892 by Charles M. Hoyt for his nationally touring, popularly priced play *A Trip to Chinatown*, "The Bowery" quickly became the most famous comic song of the decade.[11] In part its appeal rested on the Bowery's notoriety; narrated by a visiting yokel who is rolled by thieves and con men, the song relied for its humor on the contrast between his bewilderment and the listener's knowledge of just what "things" were said and done there. Crucially, however, it presented a much tamer Bowery than the Lexow committee had revealed. While it took its spice from the ill-fame of the New York City underworld, it reshaped it for a wide audience by leaving the unsavory specifics unspoken.

The style of "The Bowery" would be emulated in an outpouring of songs, melodramas, and newspaper short stories that used Bowery streetlife to fashion a humorous world of endearing, eccentric underworld "types." There were, for example, the Bowery Boy, a pugnacious, plucky wisecracker (the wisecrack quickly came to represent distinctively "Bowery" humor) wearing a loud checked suit from Baxter Street, a pinstriped shirt, a flaring box overcoat, and a derby tilted over one ear; and his feisty Bowery Gal, a pleasure-loving "spieler" attired in a tight-fitting jacket, a bedraggled floor-length skirt, and a hat with a broken feather. And there were the neighborhood's "celebrities": real-life Bowery personalities whose exploits and witticisms were lavishly embellished by journalists. Steve Brodie was prominent among them; he was a saloonkeeper who won fame after a highly suspect "leap" from the Brooklyn Bridge. Most popular of all was Chuck Connors, raconteur and self-appointed "Mayor of Chinatown," who enlivened newspaper feature pages throughout the 1890s with his comments (as purveyed by columnists Roy McCardell of the *New York World* and Frank Ward O'Malley of the *New York Sun*) on the trials and tribulations of Bowery life.[12]

Connors's observations, like those of all Bowery characters, derived added humor from his accent, which turned "these," "them," and "those" into "dese," "dem," and "dose," and "pearl," "girl," and "twirl" into "poil," "goil," and "twoil."[13] Such "Bowery talk" was more than simply a style of pronunciation; as transcribed and elaborated by turn-of-the-century playwrights and journalists, it was a full-fledged subcultural dialect with its own words, gestures, and modes of expression. Undoubtedly part of the appeal of Bowery popular culture lay in the manner in which it made this underworld idiom accessible to all, at once translating it for a wide audience and offering it for imitation. With the rise of the Bowery play and short story, such expressions as "come-on" (an invitation, usually with fraudulent intent) and "easy mark" (a sucker) entered the mainstream vocabulary throughout New York and even nationwide. "Conversation everywhere," recalled one reporter, "was punctuated with the supposed Bowery gesture, a lateral slicing motion with the hand held flat, palm down and almost at a right angle to the arm; and spiced with 'youse guys,' 'dead game sport,' 'Hully chee!,' 'Chase yerself!' [and] 'Wot t'ell!' "[14]

This world was by no means wholly a fictive creation, of course. Steve Brodie and Chuck Connors really did exist. So too, as historian Kathy Peiss has shown, did Bowery Boys and Gals: participants in a vital working-class youth culture, these real-life "mugs" and "rags" served as inspiration for newspaper copy and in turn adapted their style to suit their press image.[15] "Dese," "dem," and "dose" were genuine elements of working-class "New Yawk" speech; the Bowery dialect, with its distinctive words and gestures, was the language of the New York streets, not the creation of outsiders. At the same time Bowery images took shape in print and onstage as glossy folklore, closer to myth than reality. The reason for that had everything to do with the commercial vehicles for which those images were produced: the melodramas of the popularly priced circuits, which toured nationwide to mixed-class audiences; and in particular the new mass-circulation newspapers that dominated New York City journalism after the 1880s.

Low-priced and of ever-expanding length, papers like Joseph Pulitzer's *World* and William Randolph Hearst's *Journal* sought a broad market through a range of features designed to offer something for everyone. In practice that meant that many of those features, from comic strips to "local color" columns to short stories, centered on the working-class life of New York—a major selling point in the context of the times. Such papers profited from the contemporary social reality of a city in flux, where longstanding residential segregation by class was suddenly being countered by new urban institutions (vast office buildings and department stores; a developing mass transportation system of elevated trains, streetcars, and, after 1904, subways) that brought people of different classes into frequent and intriguing proximity. Feature stories of Bowery life were one of many means by which newspapers capitalized on these developments, appealing to middle-class curiosity about working-class life, but in such a way that everyone, even working-class New Yorkers, could read them with pleasure.[16] Like Charles Hoyt's "The Bowery," newspaper stories of underworld life traded on the Bowery's unsavory reputation but sanitized the details or left them unspoken. The Bowery of popular culture was to be sure a world of crime, but not the litany of horrors the Lexow and Mazet committees revealed; its criminals were far more tame: pickpockets, con men, small-time crooks who were comically naive and somehow endearing.

If the stories avoided a blunt presentation of vice, which might have offended more fainthearted readers, they also avoided overt mention of class politics, which might have had the same effect. The Bowery of the newspapers was a lower-class world abstracted from any political understanding, any notion that it existed within a larger context, at the bottom of a class system. The characters on this Bowery voiced no political resentments; instead, they were a collection of colorful individuals, their lives a demonstration not of anger or suffering but of sweet eccentricity and innocent arrogance. Insofar as the stories pitted individual against society, any suggestions of class conflict was replaced by the spectacle of a lovable loner confronting the conformist mass—a presentation that doubtless accounted for much of the stories' wide appeal.[17]

Finally, while avoiding explicit mention of vice and class, these stories focused on what historian William Taylor has called "socially prismatic" characters—characters whose behavior had comic significance for a range of readers, whether working class or middle class.[18] Chuck Connors with his gutter dialect, his lofty pronouncements on life, and his garish, pretentious clothes (he reportedly acquired his fondness for derby hats as a sailor, when he saw them on the heads of the "swells" of London), was just such an open-ended figure. Middle-class readers might well laugh *at* him, at his malapropisms, his "gentlemanly" airs, his pompous philosophizing; working-class readers could readily laugh *with* him, in sympathy with his folksy Bowery wisdom and in delight at seeing their own world (or something approximating it, despite the patronizing distortions) lauded in the big-time press.

This turn-of-the-century folklore shrouded the real-life Bowery in a haze of fondly humorous associations and proved a rich resource for Mae West. Her *Diamond Lil* deliberately evoked that Bowery folk world throughout, in its music, costuming, stage effects, performance styles, and comic rhythms. The play clothed its supporting cast of Bowery thugs in the flashy trademark attire of Chuck Connors and Steve Brodie; the female supporting players, a motley assortment of pickpockets and saloon singers, appeared in the garb of the feisty Bowery Gal. Male or female, all the characters packed their lines with slang and delivered them in "Bowery talk." Even many of the jokes were recognizably "Bowery" in the manner popularized by 1890s newspaper columnists: snappy wisecracks about the neighborhood's customs and characters, gently mocking the underworld speaker himself in the "socially prismatic" style of the 1890s originals.

Finally, *Diamond Lil* conjured up this popular vision of the Bowery through its sensational, melodramatic plot. It told the story of a missionary unmasked as a cop and a scarlet woman with a hidden heart of gold in the midst of frenetic action on a jam-packed stage. As many critics pointed out, those elements recalled the turn-of-the-century theatrical forum in which Bowery folklore had first taken shape: the ten-twent'-thirt' blood-and-thunder circuit, specializing in hair-raising melodramas of virtue revealed, rescued, and rewarded, to the accompaniment of lively musical interludes and cheap but spectacular special effects. Many of these plays had underworld settings, often the Bowery itself—a craze evidenced by the array of Bowery melodramas registered for copyright between 1890 and 1917: *The Bowery, The Bowery After Ten, The Bowery Bud, The Bowery Boy* (four of these in the 1890s alone), *The Bowery Boys, The Bowery Girl* (three separate versions), *The Bowery King, The Bowery Caruso, The Bowery of New York, The Bowery Newsgirl, The Bowery Pawnbroker, The Bowery Waif,* and, most famous of all, *The Bowery After Dark,* an implausible tale of lowbrow thugs that was a nationwide sensation in 1900.[19]

Diamond Lil's studied resemblance to the Bowery of turn-of-the-century popular culture was an important factor in its success. That resemblance did not wholly shape the play, since the seamier elements that were suppressed in Bowery popular culture—prostitution, drugs, violent crime—remained prominent in *Diamond Lil's* plot. Yet in contrast to the gritty authenticity of *Sex, Diamond Lil* was elaborately mediated, suffused with suggestions of old-time popular entertainments that gave the middle-class playgoing audience a familiar frame of reference in which to absorb the play's sensationalism, as Stark Young, drama critic for the *New Republic,* made clear:

> *Diamond Lil* is as daring in the end [as *Sex*], the same sexy morsels, embraces, interventions of the law with rank suspenses, frank speeches, underworld and so on. But it is more covered, continuous and studied than the other production, and the crowd of characters, the costuming and vaudevillistic intervals, pull the whole of this later play into a more familiar style, less crudely and sheerly singular than *Sex* appeared to be.[20]

Indeed, so "familiar" did *Diamond Lil* appear that *Variety* maintained it was based on fact: that Diamond Lil had actually existed, like Chuck Connors and Steve Brodie, and had been as colorful and eccentric and mythologized as they. "There was such a Bowery bimbo. The original Lil came from Chicago and became known through having a diamond set in one of her front teeth, among other things."[21] That, in the end, was *Diamond Lil's* "realism": resurrecting the turn-of-the-century Bowery folk world with enough authenticity to be mistaken, in the words of one critic, for "a grand Bowery folk play" itself.[22]

Recycling popular imagery was one of *Diamond Lil's* secrets; another was its calculated use of nostalgia. Consider Gus Jordan's dance hall and saloon, modeled on Suicide Hall, a site many New Yorkers remembered in lurid detail. Writer Herbert Asbury included a description of Suicide Hall in *The Gangs of New York,* an early 1928 best-seller that West could certainly have consulted had she been interested in achieving a degree of historical accuracy. But accuracy, in this instance, was not her aim. Like the original, West's Suicide Hall was a haven for drugs and prostitution; but unlike the original, it was a place where those activities were overshadowed by picturesque musical entertainment, quaint high spirits, and remarkably tame "wildness."

At Jordan's saloon the beer was served by mustachioed singing waiters who entertained the crowd with turn-of-the-century standards in recognizably turn-of-the-century style. Rowdy customers tossed coins and roared their approval at female singers decked out in the high-necked, floor-length, hourglass-shaped gowns that constituted the height of 1890s allure. And scattered throughout the saloon, usually in the hands of avid male readers, were copies of the *Police Gazette,* a nineteenth-century tabloid whose cover portraits of corset-clad temptresses had won it a reputation for raciness.

West's aim here was not to resurrect the real 1890s—if indeed that were possible—but to cast the decade in a particular light, as a time of naiveté, still constrained by Victorianism despite its self-styled daring. The period elements that stood out in *Diamond Lil,* that reviewers praised and audiences seemed to love, were those that provided an amusing contrast with the present by demonstrating the innocence, the sexual timidity, of their predecessors' stabs at nightlife.

Diamond Lil resounded with period melodies, from its opening moments ("The Bowery" and "She Was Poor But She Was Honest") to its final act, much of which was given over to musical performances by the waiters and chorus girls of Gus Jordan's saloon. As reviewers made clear, those barbershop melodies sounded quaint to ears accustomed to jazz, and the accompanying dancing appeared positively circumspect.

The copies of the *Police Gazette* dotting the *Diamond Lil* stage provided another such source of amusement. The *Police Gazette* had amassed a huge readership in the late nineteenth century with lurid exposés of underworld sex and crime—subject matter not so different from *Diamond Lil*'s. But it was primarily the memory of the magazine's covers that *Diamond Lil* played off: portraits of heavyset models encased in tight corsets and thick striped stockings. As racy journalism, this could only have seemed laughable to a 1920s audience, which could have seen far more generous glimpses of legs and breasts on any New York newsstand, or for that matter in Broadway plays and even motion pictures.

In the eyes of the 1920s nothing could have more fully revealed the period's sexual innocence: the clothing that expressed 1890s sensuality obscured exactly those features that constituted 1920s sexual allure. The heavy floor-length skirts hid the wearer's legs; the corset exaggerated her breasts and hips, giving her an "hourglass" shape that seemed fat and matronly in comparison to the slim, short-skirted sexual playmate celebrated by 1920s fashion. So off-putting was such attire to contemporary observers that *Variety*, in the course of an otherwise favorable review, even wondered if West should not have given the play an up-to-date setting:

> You could take the same book and troupe, spot it in a modern cabaret, dress up the frails in modern clothes and it would play just as well and probably have more appeal. The fillies in long skirts would be safe now on double fifth and wouldn't get a tumble at a longshoreman's picnic.[23]

But *Variety* missed the point. *Diamond Lil*'s 1890s costumes appealed precisely *because* of their comical unattractiveness, the tameness of what purported to be provocative. The clothes, along with the period music and the *Police Gazette*, affirmed a developing memory of the period that would come to be dubbed the Gay Nineties.

That phrase, which critics would use consistently when discussing West's *Diamond Lil* revivals in the 1940s, appears nowhere in the reviews of the original Broadway production—from which I assume that in 1928 it either had not been coined or had not entered general circulation.[24] But whenever the phrase itself appeared, the sentiment from which the Gay Nineties myth would grow was widespread in the 1920s, at all points on the ideological spectrum. From progressive marriage counselors celebrating the era's liberation from the Victorian dark ages to disgruntled traditionalists yearning for the days when women were women and men were men, commentators throughout the 1920s were gripped by the certainty—exhilarating to some, troubling to others—that their society had moved headlong into a sexualized modernity marked by sophistication and complexity. The 1920s saw an increasingly intense public debate over what seemed radically nontraditional sexual behavior: a newly aggressive and public middle-class female sexuality, exemplified by women who streamlined their bodies into sleek instruments of pleasure, embracing styles of dress and expression previously associated only with prostitutes; and new forms of specifically sexual identity—male homosexuality and lesbianism—that blatantly detached sex from procreation, and from traditional notions of masculinity and femininity, and made it into a style of life.

In the context of this contemporary debate the turn of the century took on new colors: it was a time of lost sexual innocence. The decade was "gay" not at all in the underground sense—precisely the reverse: it was an innocent era beset by none of the modern world's sexual convolutions. Pleasure was simpler then, at once chaste and lighthearted, an indulgence of high spirits by men and women whose very attempts at daring—in music, in printed matter, and above all in clothes—revealed an essential sexual naiveté.

Too simplistic a view of the past, certainly, but eminently marketable, as *Diamond Lil'*s success made clear. All shades of moral temperament could, and did, love the play's reminiscent appeal. Sexual conservatives could wistfully remember a stabler, "healthier" sexual past and a vision of female sexual style that the modern world had all but obliterated. ("Mae West is gorgeous," wrote one such traditionalist in *Variety*, "and doesn't she remind you of many women of the voluptuous blonde type?"[25]) Ardent devotees of modernity could smile with bemused condescension at the innocent adventures of their grandparents' generation, so tame compared to their own.

*Diamond Lil'*s contrived air of nostalgia thus helped make the play accessible to all. Like the studied links to Bowery folklore, it also helped neutralize the punch of a sensational plot. In the words of a reviewer for the *New York World*, the play "lived and breathed with all the garishness of a lurid lithograph seen under a flaring gas jet, and that is probably just the reason it was such good fun."[26] No less "lurid" in subject matter than its predecessors, in other words, *Diamond Lil* evoked its setting by turning the whole play into an artifact, transforming vice and sex into naughtiness and "gusto"—elements far more easily assimilated than West's initial theatrical style. Stark Young, writing in the *New Republic*, was nearly alone among reviewers in recognizing what West had accomplished:

Putting this play back into the '90s and giving Lil the clothes, the great hats and golden wig of Lillian Russell was a very smart thing to do; it gives the whole affair a kind of irresponsibility, since we grant almost anything to those inferior days and the people in them;

it lets in the indulgence of sentiment; it gives also a picturesqueness amounting to a kind of glamor.[27]

In *Diamond Lil* West manipulated her underworld setting to make it "glamorous," "sentimental," and "picturesque"—three adjectives that would never, by any stretch of imagination, have been applied to *Sex*.

Thus far I have focused on *Diamond Lil*'s surfaces: the elements West added to her Bowery backdrop to make it more marketable than the underworld of *Sex*. But the difference ran deeper than her studied evocation of Bowery folklore and her romanticized memory of Gay Nineties innocence. Underpinning these trappings was a more important shift in the vantage point from which West viewed the underworld, a shift signaled by her presentation of class.

To perceive that shift, one need only compare West's opening night script to her original version: the playscript she hurriedly completed in January 1928 and sent to the Copyright Office of the Library of Congress. Unearthed by researchers five decades later, that first draft provides an illuminating contrast to the jovial period play that premiered on Broadway after four months of revisions. It demonstrates, in fragmentary but unmistakable form, West's first, intuitive sense of how best to make use of her Bowery setting.[28]

In West's original script the period elements that distinguished the staged play were given no special emphasis or were absent altogether. Music, for example, played almost no part in the original *Diamond Lil* world. Aside from a brief musical interlude in act one—consisting of two unspecified songs, one by Lil and one by a nasal-voiced saloon singer—the action was to take place with no musical accompaniment. Nor did the script include other period trappings such as the *Police Gazette* or the wisecracking hijinks from a supporting cast of "Bowery types."

Instead, West's original Bowery came alive through its sheer harshness and nastiness. In this respect it closely resembled the underworld of *Sex*, an insider's underworld where no middle-class person could hope to feel at home. Respectable visitors dropping in for a lark faced not only theft and assault but pitiless abuse from the play's heroine, who was bitterly, vocally aware of her own condemnation at the hands of an unjust social system that decried the "viciousness" of the poor while determinedly keeping them down.

This same perspective on class relations structured the original script of *Diamond Lil*, appearing nowhere more clearly than in the character of Lil herself. In her first conception of her prostitute heroine, West created a character who would alienate, even repel, middle-class viewers, a sharp-tongued, imperious product of a brutal underworld, smoldering with resentment of the privileged classes. She is keenly aware that she and her fellows are a stigmatized social group, condemned and disdained by those with more money, better backgrounds, and an uptown address. The script is studded with moments when that resentment boils over and Lil explodes with rage at the oppressive actions of middle-class intruders, meddlesome hypocrites who condemn the Bowery's downtrodden while blocking their every effort to reform. Nowhere does this hostility come across more clearly than in her initial confrontation with Captain Cummings. As in the staged version of the play, Cummings eventually becomes Lil's love interest; here as later, her attraction to him intensifies the longer he seems impervious to her charms. But in West's first script, that slowly developing love interest is nearly overshadowed by Lil's anger when the Salvation Army preacher first arrives. To Lil, Cummings represents the whole arsenal of weapons the respectable deploy to shame the poor and lowly: exhortations to chastity, temperance, and religious piety. When Cummings visits the saloon in the first act, Lil makes no effort to hide her loathing and attacks him by mocking all those weapons, even the most sacrosanct among them:

> LIL: So! We have the Army here tonight. Nice, clean little boy in a bright new uniform, all ready to steer us to Heaven. . . . I ain't got no conscience, my psalm-singing pirate, . . . and since you came in for the prayer-meeting stuff, I'll give you a Hallelujah you won't forget. (grabs his hat and puts it on her head) Folks, we are now going to pray!
>
> GUS: Lil, don't!
>
> LIL: Shut up. I'm going to put this guy in his place. Let's see how does it start—oh yes our—
>
> CUMMINGS: Stop! I refuse to listen to such blasphemy.
>
> LIL: Folks have to listen to it from you! (mockingly) Be patient, my son, and I—

(As Lil folds her hands in prayer, the Captain grabs them)
CUMMINGS: Don't you dare—you miserable—[29]

At the root of Lil's outburst, the play makes clear, lies a specifically political hostility toward religion. Lil labels Cummings a
"psalm-singing pirate," which makes religion, by implication, a
kind of emotional piracy, a moralistic ambush in which the middle
class trap the poor by convincing them that earthly insubordination
brings eternal retribution. Not, perhaps, the most startling of arguments, at least to our ears, but a jarring one for a middle-class audience in the 1920s, especially when voiced by a prostitute who grabs
a preacher's hat and derisively parrots the Lord's Prayer.

West must have realized how unsettling such a scene would be.
Indeed, it seems clear that to unsettle was precisely her intention. In
Sex, as we have seen, West effectively drew the underclass from the
inside out: she created a hostile and resentful leading character who
felt her class status as an alienating, divisive force. The first *Diamond Lil* employed the same strategy.

By no means, however, should this emphasis on class divisions be
mistaken for an act of political conviction. Mae West was no ideo-
logue. Though herself the product of working-class Brooklyn, she
held, as far as I can make out, no political opinions whatsoever. Her
overwhelming interest in the 1920s—as throughout her life—lay in
the progress of her own career, and to that end she aimed to give
her audience what she thought it wanted. In the 1920s she was convinced it wanted "dirt," and if the resultant scripts stressed class
divisions, it was not for reasons of politics; rather, it was because
her shrewd showman's sense told her that class divisions were part
of what real "dirt" was all about. Both *Sex* and the original *Diamond Lil* aimed to evoke a palpably lower-class feel: they presented
the underworld as an alien, forbidding realm at which the audience
was offered a titillating peek.

It was commercial expediency, not political conviction, that dictated West's initial presentation of class. For that reason, the presentation could easily change if another approach seemed more
promising—which is precisely what happened during the four
months of rehearsals that preceded *Diamond Lil*'s Broadway premiere. The actual rehearsal process must remain a mystery, as no
detailed account survives, but it is clear that West relied heavily on
improvisation by the large cast of veteran New York actors that her

substantial budget enabled her to hire. By her own account the cast members played a crucial part in fleshing out the play's dialogue from the "notes" that made up her sketchy original script:

> When all my notes are put together and typed I have a play. See? I put in the real stuff at rehearsal. Know what I mean? I let the actors write a lot of their own lines. I pick them out for types, and then let 'em talk. You can't tell how lines will go over until you try them out on the stage.[30]

In rehearsals West asked her experienced cast to improvise turn-of-the-century Bowery "types," and we have seen what resulted—a profusion of comic and romanticized images, some drawn from turn-of-the-century urban folklore, others built on contrived nostalgia. West clearly judged those images commercially advantageous, as they became the heart of her staged script. But though she may not have consciously realized it, incorporating those elements and making them "go over" demanded that she alter the focus of her original script.

We can see this shift most clearly in the characterization of Diamond Lil. In place of the cold, off-putting woman of the initial script appears a far more amiable figure: playful, good-humored, with none of the original Lil's seething resentment of the middle class. Indeed, the staged Lil is no longer recognizably working class; certainly she never voices the specifically working-class hostility that informed her predecessor. Her ferocious mockery of Cummings in act one as an intrusive middle-class hypocrite becomes a bemused skepticism directed at him as an individual, at his pose of pious indifference to sensual pleasure. That he is a minister no longer provokes Lil to outrage, for unlike her predecessor, she does not see religion as "piracy" perpetrated on the poor. At most the staged Lil is indifferent to religion; at times she even gives hints of accepting its basic premises. As she explains to Cummings, she never worries about good and evil, but if her earthly conduct dooms her to an eternity in hell, she is perfectly prepared to accept it.

This change in the characterization of Diamond Lil is reflected throughout the play's Bowery setting. The staged *Diamond Lil,* while still populated by prostitutes and petty thieves, presents a Bowery without class antagonisms. Gone are the hostile confrontations that marked the first script, the charged encounters between

Lil and Cummings in which an underworld denizen excoriates an exploitative social system. In their place were encounters of a more amiable sort, as in act three, when a party of middle-class slummers slips in timidly to see the evening performance and finds themselves greeted not by aggression but by humor directed at bourgeois inhibitions. As the slummers struggle to maintain their dignity amid a chorus of teasing wisecracks, the play suggests that beneath the middle-class facade of piety and decorum lies a deep yearning to run wild.

That suggestion is at the core of the staged *Diamond Lil*'s presentation of class. No longer do we see a hostile underclass seething with hatred of the respectable and genteel. Instead, we see the poor as the fortunate ones, objects of wistful middle-class envy. The members of that slumming party may sniff at the Bowery's lack of refinement, but we know that they secretly yearn to adopt its freewheeling style, just as we know that Captain Cummings is no oppressor but a timid puritan whose ascetic pose conceals a deep-seated hedonistic desire.

To be sure, the notion of the middle class as inhibited hypocrites had appeared in West's original script, but there it was surrounded by open expressions of class hatred. That the middle class secretly envied the poor appeared as one more count in the working-class indictment, one more proof of the repressive mean spirits that led the respectable to keep the lower class down. It was, in short, one more factor that *divided* the classes, whereas in the staged *Diamond Lil* it decisively brings them together. In the world of West's staged Bowery the poor give middle-class slummers a bemused and teasing welcome, secure in the knowledge that their visitors envy their high Bowery style. For them the social hierarchy carries no sting: they exhibit no malice, no bitterness, no awareness of oppression.

In this sense the staged *Diamond Lil*, unlike its predecessor, was by no means "realistic" in depicting class relations. It presented an underworld cartoon in which an amiable scarlet woman and colorful Bowery thugs trade wisecracks to the accompaniment of period song, in carefree ignorance of the larger social framework that keeps them in their lowly place. With its links to Bowery folklore, its calculated nostalgia, and its excision of class antagonisms, *Diamond Lil* allowed its audience to enjoy lower-class "color" while ignoring the truth of class relations in which they themselves took daily part. By obliterating any awareness of the larger social order, the play gave even the most staid middle-class patrons a chance to identify with the under-class (or at least with certain romanticized aspects of their lives) while pretending that class as a relation of power did not exist.[31]

Diamond Lil's nostalgic evocation of the Gay Nineties was an important part of its appeal, but for a full explanation of the play's success we must come back, as all the critics did, to Mae West. Reviewers were enchanted with the West of *Diamond Lil.* Within weeks of the opening, the woman they had scorned only a few months earlier as a pornographer and an opportunist became the darling of the New York press—even, and perhaps especially, of its "art theater" advocates. So marked was their enthusiasm that *Variety* (whose own taste for West was decidedly new, but whose hostility to "highbrows" was longstanding) repeatedly dropped derisive comments about "the arty bunch finally 'discovering' Mae as a great dramatic actress."[32]

Given West's previous critical reception, any sort of praise for her would have been novel, but the nature of the new raves is particularly intriguing, focused as they were on West's mannerisms—on her full figure (what one reviewer called her awesome "physical architecture") and her use of it to bring her heroine to life.

It is almost impossible to exaggerate the relish critics took in West's physical style, the descriptive flair they mustered in discussing the movements of her torso, the surliness of her voice, the peculiar deliberation of her gestures. "She plays with a controlled, slow-paced undulation that extends from her head to her hips," wrote John Mason Brown in *Theater Arts Monthly*, "and with a low-toned, casual toughness that seems to spill from only one corner of her mouth."[33] "She is a plump, almost Circassian blonde whose ample figure overflows her girdles in graceful cascades," said Percy Hammond. "She walks with a cunning strut and she talks in a quiet monotone, never disturbing her humorous lips with the noises of elocution."[34] The *New Yorker*'s Charles Brackett admired West's entrance in act one, "pushing hip after hip with defiant languor," and his colleague Thyra Samter Winslow agreed: "She is slow, rhythmic, insinuating. She moves with almost feline intensity, a curious sort of wiggle, inside her corsets of the nineties."[35] But it was the *New Republic*'s Stark Young who most effectively described what his fellow critics found so remarkable:

Nobody, seeing her play, can fail to wonder at that audacity of leisure, motion which becomes almost an intensity of movement by its continuity, but is almost stillness because it is so slow. The whole body—not a beautiful one—is supple, flowing, coolly insinuating, the voice and enunciation only more so.[36]

Young's praise was noteworthy for more than its eloquence. Along with John Mason Brown, Young was among New York's most prominent critical supporters of the art theater movement. Fully aware that his newfound enthusiasm for West might take his readers aback, Young asserted that her performance gave vivid life to a cherished premise of modernist drama. Her "supple, flowing, coolly insinuating" mannerisms, he argued, were modernist theater at its best, a powerful demonstration that the drama, like all art, was distinct from "reality," a pure and abstract realm of its own:

Glamor Miss West herself undoubtedly has, a kind of far-offness, a footlighted difference, an unpredictable something about her that we watch as we do animals in a cage. I delight in this point. It illustrates and rubs in the fact of art's apartness from nature, its parallel character. Here is a stage figure who is not one of those players, however admirable, with whom we can feel at home, knowing that they are the same sort of human beings as we are, save for a desire to imitate or to exhibit themselves, or both. . . . [The] whole result of her presence and her acting is something less usual . . . and more abstract, impressive, ironical and teasing in its unreality, and unforgettable. What is created by Miss West finally is as remote as Sarah Bernhardt's art in *La Tosca*, no more accessible, no more actual, no less purely theatrical, though the plane of it may be, of course, another matter.[37]

This sudden discovery of West as a magnetic, even artistically avant-garde performer was truly extraordinary. Critics assumed, if they did not say outright, that West's mannerisms were a new acquisition, that she had somehow developed them since the time of *Sex*, when they had unanimously reviled her. But of course those mannerisms long predated *Diamond Lil*. The suggestively swaying hips and sullen nasal delivery, honed on the circuits of small-time vaudeville and burlesque, were the very same mannerisms with which West had evoked Margy Lamont, the bitter prostitute of

Sex—a fact that the reviewer for the *Evening Post*, alone among *Diamond Lil*'s critics, was able to see:

> Miss West seems to belong to the single characterization class of actress with trademarks quite as definite as the fluttering of Pauline Lord's hands or the horizontal elevation of Charlotte Greenwood's legs. As Diamond Lil she oozes her way through a rowdy melodrama with the familiar undulation of hips, the porcine manner of gaze and the red plush thickness of accent that kept *Sex* running at Daly's 63rd Street Theater for about a year.[38]

But none of *Sex*'s critics had thought to praise West's mannerisms—and certainly not in Stark Young's terms, for their "apartness from nature," their "unreality." To the contrary: it was precisely the apparent *reality* of West's embodiment of sex that so disturbed, even revolted, the play's reviewers. At their most vituperative, they had suggested that she was not performing at all—that if she was not a genuine prostitute plying her trade onstage, she was at least experiencing genuine sexual pleasure. Recall the critic who fumed, "She undresses before the public, and appears to enjoy doing so."[39] One finds no catalog of West's gestures in *Sex*'s reviews, not because the gestures were absent but because critics could not distinguish them *as gestures*, as "style."

Diamond Lil changed this dramatically. In a remarkably short period of time it made West's mannerisms discernible as a set of distinctively "Mae Westian" affectations. Audiences, no less than critics, apparently shared this new perception. Within a few months of the premiere, Mae West imitations made their first appearance in Broadway revues (beginning in the summer of 1928 with *Grand Street Follies*, in which West was imitated by actress Dorothy Sands)[40]—an indication not simply that West was assumed to be widely known (the theater raids, after all, had accomplished that) but that she was assumed, like Eva Tanguay, Eddie Cantor, and other widely imitated performers, to be immediately recognizable by a set of trademark gestures.

What made West's once-repellent "realism" suddenly perceptible as an abstract, intriguing, and imitable "style"? In part it was the changed context in which she performed, all the shifts I have described in the presentation of the Bowery as a fantasy underworld of high spirits and good times, where everyone lives freely and no one feels oppressed. And as we have seen, a vital element of that presentation was the 1890s attire, which was particularly important in reshaping the impact of West's physical style. As *Sex*'s Margy Lamont, she had clothed her fleshy body in skimpy modern sheath dresses that barely covered her thighs. But as Diamond Lil, she was decked out in the "racy" clothing of the Gay Nineties.

One can imagine the effect when she took the stage: an actress notorious for her lurid theatricals, playing a woman lauded for her sexiness—and suddenly materializing in an hourglass dress and a huge picture hat, clothes that to 1920s eyes looked almost grotesquely *un*sexual. As West oozed across the stage in a series of increasingly ludicrous outfits, her slow, insinuating wriggles and low murmurings lost their sleazy air. Instead, within the rigid confines of a turn-of-the-century corset (what *Variety* dubbed an "armor-plated body gripper"), those seductive mannerisms appeared newly incongruous—at once innocent and comic, even vaguely tongue-in-cheek, as if West were mocking the very notion of "sexiness" itself.

Was she? One might well suspect so. Up to now I have argued that the unprecedented appeal of the *Diamond Lil* Mae West stemmed from a new context that defused the unnerving "realism" of her subject matter and physical style. But that is only part of the answer. Though West's gestures and delivery were certainly not new, it seems indisputable that she was injecting them with a new spirit. More than West herself may have recognized, and certainly more than she originally intended, Diamond Lil was a different kind of character with a new perspective on sexuality, as a quick glance back at Margy Lamont reveals.

Margy Lamont was a working prostitute who took money for sex. Diamond Lil may live in a brothel, she may have a "past," but unlike Margy she does not work at sex for a living. While Margy's customers pay her for services rendered, sometimes giving her checks, and bad ones at that, Lil's lovers ply her with diamonds in hopes of keeping her interested—a very different transaction. It puts Lil in a position of power. She has a choice of lovers, and her wealth represents not payment but "gifts," which makes her oddly class-less: part of the Bowery underworld yet dripping with diamonds and somehow exalted above it.

Lil is a far more assimilable figure than Margy Lamont could ever have been—and a far more familiar one, at least in a theatrical context. Since the late nineteenth century, beginning with Alexandre Dumas's *La Dame aux Camélias*, prostitution had been represented onstage in much this same manner, embodied in a beautiful, desirable, enigmatic woman—the "courtesan" whose luxuriant lifestyle and power of choice gave her the appearance of classlessness. As art historian T. J. Clark has noted, the mythical courtesan provided a means of representing prostitution comfortably in art no less than onstage: in her beauty, her wealth, her autonomy, she obscured her real-life counterpart's status as a sexual commodity, a sex worker who traded her body for cash.[41]

Lil was no sexual commodity, and that fact carried enormous weight. In Diamond Lil the audience had a figure they could recognize, a woman who paraded an abstract sexuality divorced from uncomfortable social realities that might scare the timid away. In Lil sex was detached from the ties to underclass economics that Margy Lamont had flaunted and that gave it the power to disturb. Thus presented, sex was more legitimately taken as comedy—an interpretation that the play overtly encouraged.

Consider Lil's bedroom. Within the walls of the brothel, Lil reclines on a huge golden creation molded in the shape of an enormous swan, a very significant detail of staging. If Margy Lamont's jokes about bounced checks forced one to confront the reality of prostitution, the meeting of bodies and the exchange of cash, Lil's swan bed obscures that reality altogether. So outlandish is it, so inherently comic, that one cannot imagine it as the site of genuine wickedness. It caricatures a sexual setting rather than evoking the real thing.

In the same way Diamond Lil herself is not a flesh-and-blood prostitute but a cartoon of desirability: the woman all the men want, whose merest look overwhelms them. So, at least, we are told, over and over again, by nearly every character in the play short of Lil. Indeed, the habitués of Gus Jordan's saloon cannot seem to extol her enough: she is gorgeous, dynamic, irresistible, and so sizzling a performer that even Tony Pastor, the city's most eminent variety producer, has asked her to appear at his Fourteenth Street showplace. We are left with the impression that all of New York is talking, speculating, enthusing about Lil. So relentless is this avalanche of praise that it more than does its job of establishing Lil's character. Before long it begins to strain credibility, to verge on bombast, to sound just the tiniest bit funny.

And into the midst of all this hyperbole walks Diamond Lil herself, treating her vaunted allure with ironic good humor. If her suitors have inflated her charms beyond all proportion, have made her into a fantasy figure of sexual desirability, Lil seems aware of that fact and even amused. She makes her entrance fresh from a photo studio, distributing pictures of herself that she has had taken for her admirers, and commenting on each with a mix of self-love and self-mockery suggesting that her sexiness is a good-natured pose, that she is keenly aware of the impression she makes and vastly entertained by it:

> LIL: There, I had them taken with all my rocks. Here, this one is great, isn't it? And this one is a pip—full length, see? Gives me style and dignity. This is my best; this is for the bedroom; you'll get one. You can have that, Flynn; a little bit spicy but not too raw.[42]

It is impossible, I think, to recite the above without slipping into an imitation of the movie Mae West: seemingly of their own accord, one's lips curl into an ironic smile, one's body begins to sway, one's voice takes on an exaggerated toughness. This is indeed Mae West as we now remember her, her words dripping with barely concealed amusement, hinting that she is not simply playing a sexy woman but parodying one. Familiar as this persona may sound to us, however, in 1928 it was new indeed. Margy Lamont had never spoken like this. West had enacted Margy's sexiness straightforwardly—indeed, far too straightforwardly for most critics' tastes. There was nothing posed about Margy's sexuality, and that was why it shocked: it seemed to arrive on the Broadway stage straight from the burlesque halls and the underworld streets.

In creating Diamond Lil, West's initial impulse had been to convey Lil's sexual prowess in that same fashion. Her first draft of the playscript contained none of the final version's hints of humor and irony. In the original script Lil bursts onstage in the first act, sullen, bitter, imperiously erotic—and without the too insistent chorus of praise that predisposes us to find her sexuality amusing. Lil herself in no way does so; she takes her sexuality seriously, uses it ruthlessly to vanquish the Bowery's middle-class intruders. When Captain Cummings first enters the saloon and is roused to a fury by Lil's contempt for religion, it is her formidable sexual powers that give her the final, victorious word:

LIL: You know, I always liked a man in a uniform, and that one fits you marvelous. (goes closer) In fact, I have the feeling that you and me is going to be friends. (The woman grabs him quickly to her, and presses his mouth savagely to her own, to the amusement of the crowd.)

(Captain Cummings, startled, ashamed, taken back, breaks away from her and rushes madly from the room, followed by the ringing laughter of Lil and the rest.)[43]

The scene is played for laughs, to be sure, but Cummings is the object of our amusement, while Lil's sexual prowess is presented with a straight face. Lil humiliates her adversary by arousing him against his will. Startled by her aggression and shamed by his response to it, Cummings feels compelled to flee from her presence, making himself ridiculous in the process.

One only need contrast this scene with its revision in the final script to see how sharply West's presentation of sexuality had changed. As I noted earlier, the class-based rancor of the original scene had been considerably toned down by opening night. The staged Lil, far more amiable than her predecessor, does not berate Cummings as a "psalm-singing pirate," steal his hat, or mock him in prayer. And just as dramatic was the complete restyling of Lil's sexual aggression. In the final script the scene West originally envisioned as Lil's triumph over middle-class hypocrisy becomes a playfully sardonic flirtation ending in *Diamond Lil*'s best-known line:

LIL: I always liked a man in a uniform, and that one fits you grand. Say, why don't you drop in and see me some time? Home every evening you know.

CUMMINGS: I'm sorry, but I have a previous engagement. I'm busy every evening.

LIL: Previous engagement! . . . You don't fool me pretendin' to be so good. I've met your goody-goody kind before. Why don't you come up some time? You needn't be afraid, I won't tell—oh, you can be had![44]

In place of a "savage" kiss, a vivid demonstration of sexual power to which Cummings unwillingly responds, the staged script presents an arch, innuendo-laden invitation to "drop in and see me" and a good-humored, confident prediction that the missionary, despite his pretense of indifference, "can be had." It substitutes, in short, a teasing proclamation of sexual allure for a physical display of it, and a very different type of humor results. While in the first instance we laugh at Cummings, at his helpless submission to Lil's sexual powers, in the second we laugh at those powers themselves. We laugh at Lil's bemused sexual arrogance and her exaggerated seductiveness, visually reinforced by her overblown hourglass physique and affected gestures.

Sex, in short, became the joke—or rather, a caricatured enactment of sex that could be taken as an elaborate put-on. In isolation on the printed page or in the hands of another actress such a scene would not have been particularly amusing. That it worked as humor, and with spectacular success, had everything to do with Mae West. Every person in the *Diamond Lil* audience would have known—could not have failed to know—that West had created a reputedly pornographic play, that she had prepared another judged too shocking to open in New York, and that she had gone to jail. When Lil is threatened with jail at the end of the play and dismisses her antagonists with a wisecrack, who could help but remember West's own disdainful treatment of her jailers and her pithy remarks (she was widely quoted on her release as saying that the only thing that had bothered her about prison was the cotton underwear) that had filled the tabloids only a year earlier?

Thus West presented her audience not only with "Diamond Lil, queen of the turn-of-the-century Bowery," but with "Mae West, infamous tabloid headliner"—and played both with a slight detachment, with a hint of irony that allowed viewers to suspect, if they so desired, that the purported pornographer had been kidding all along. Of course, that was only one possible interpretation among many. West certainly seemed to be laughing at *something* by investing her Diamond Lil portrayal with irony, but the precise content of the joke (was she laughing at her puritanical critics? her gullible fans? sex itself?) was left up to the audience to decide.

As Eva Tanguay had done in vaudeville, West in *Diamond Lil* reenacted her own scandal with each night's performance; and like Tanguay, she invested that scandal with an ambiguity that allowed the public to interpret her meaning in a variety of ways. It brought her, as it had brought Tanguay, a large and diverse audience; most important, it won her fans of a type that had studiously avoided her so far. Traditional middle-class theatergoers—people who had avidly followed

West's tabloid misadventures but had been put off by the alleged raw-ness of *Sex*—flocked to *Diamond Lil* in droves. Seeing and liking the notorious Mae West was testimony to their modernity and sophistica-tion; yet West herself, with her ironic detachment, allowed them to enjoy her notoriety in comfort. Critic William Bolitho, reviewing *Dia-mond Lil* on its national tour in 1930, shrewdly assessed West's rela-tion to that segment of her audience, which thought it liked her because she was "sinful," though that was not the case at all:

> To be really sinful you must have a strain of genuine piety in the character. If you cannot feel wicked you cannot charge the atmo-sphere of your acts, whatever they may be, with the heady and stealthy vapor of hell. A Sunday school teacher can put more sinful-ness into wearing a new pair of silk stockings than Diamond Lil does in a murder. Her deeds are simply naughty.
>
> There is, in fact, some absurd reminder of a naughty little girl behaving grown-up in mother's dress when mother has gone out in Miss West's most famous gestures. That sudden jerk of the hips, that sideways smile with the half-closed eyes, instead of rousing your worst instincts in the least, irresistibly causes [a] smile. . . . It was a comfortable audience that filled every seat to hear her, all with money in the savings bank, and they smiled exactly like that every time she did it. Sometimes she smiled back at them the same way, and gave another twitch.[45]

The *Diamond Lil* Mae West, with her "famous gestures," created a playacted sexuality that neither threatened nor unnerved. No wonder, then, that "comfortable" fans now thronged the theaters to see her, for she offered them what amounted to an immensely flat-tering in-joke: the suggestion that more was going on than lay on the surface, that her "sinfulness" was a bit of a put-on, and that they—unlike the police and the jurors of 1927—had been smart enough to catch on.

"Go slumming with *Diamond Lil*—it's the smart thing to do," urged an advertisement for the play's 1929 national tour:

> See the Good Bad Girl—Mae West—in the Sizzling Drama of the Gay Nineties *Diamond Lil*. Miss anything else but don't miss the Most Talked Of Star in the World.

Mae West as Diamond Lil will present to you a vivid picture of the famous Old Bowery—in the Gay Nineties—when the Bowery was looked upon as the most wicked street in the world—where only a brave few dared enter. You will meet the real living characters of this famous street, just as they existed thirty years ago. *Diamond Lil* will thrill and entertain you as you have never been thrilled and entertained before.[46]

This titillating promise pinpoints the paradox at the heart of *Diamond Lil*'s appeal. West's play sold itself, and was praised by many critics, not as a parody but as the real thing: a "sizzling" slice of underworld life, a walk back in time down the street that "only a brave few dared enter." It offered its patrons a genuine slumming excursion, in the company of a notorious scarlet woman, but it gave them an underworld fantasy, a sentimentalized Bowery whose "real living characters" stepped straight from the pages of popular culture. *Sex* and *The Drag* had likewise promised underworld reality, but their realism had rung too true. Critics hated them—and not only the intellectual supporters of art theater but second-string reviewers who were often only a step removed from press agents and who asked little more of the theater than that it provide a rollicking good time.

Many theatergoers would doubtless no more have gone to *Sex* and *The Drag* than they would have ventured into the back alleys of Harlem to seek out rough blues alongside a black clientele. But those same theatergoers might have gone to other nightlife amusements that drew a large middle-class public in the 1920s. They might have gone, for example, to the Cotton Club, where black patrons were banned, lyrics were relatively circumspect, and black performers were "classed up" in glamorous costumes. Or they might have gone to one of Texas Guinan's nightclubs, which unmistakably suggested brothels through their dim lighting, velvet-draped ceilings, and fourteen-year-old chorus girls, but that tempered those associations through their hostess's folksy personality and their carnival atmosphere, as a press release for Guinan's Century Club makes clear:

The entrance is a dream of cartoons and after descending the pillowed stairs you will scream irrepressibly in front of a series of messed-up mirrors that make you look like a fat man on one side and the world's thinnest on the other. . . . Texas, her gang, her dad, ma, et al. will meet you beyond the telephone booths and houses of comfort for ladies and gentlemen. The head waiter with whip in hand will address you and announce you, if you are a celebrity or notorious or somebody, just like the ringmaster of a circus. The orchestra will greet you in clown suits and a special selection suited to your temperament.[47]

At a place like the Century Club, New York's middle-class nightlifers could indulge a taste for the risqué in a safe setting, where they could let loose among their own kind while thornier matters of sex and class were glossed over or unspoken. This is a pattern historians have found repeatedly in the successful commercial amusements of 1920s New York. Those that drew a broad audience, across class, gender, and moral persuasion, developed from disreputable roots to present a synthetic underworld, tantalizing enough to draw the adventurous but sanitized enough to reassure the more reticent—precisely the commercial strategy Mae West pursued with *Diamond Lil*.[48]

If my analysis has a danger, it lies in suggesting that this was a deliberate and calculated change, that West surveyed the Broadway public with the analytical acumen of a market researcher to determine what would attract the biggest crowd. On the contrary: I think the changes that went into making *Diamond Lil* such a different play and Mae West in it so new a performer were largely the result of experimentation and chance: inspired improvisation by her experienced cast and West's own acute but unreflective theatrical instincts.

Those instincts enabled her to sense the value of irony while still believing—as I am convinced she did—that she was indeed unsettlingly sexy and that her public was there for "dirt." West was a vaudevillian at heart, and she aimed to give her customers what they wanted; if inflecting her dialogue and gestures with irony seemed to make them happy, she was more than willing to do so. But that didn't mean she had lost her faith in the appeal of "dirt." For proof of that, one need only look at the play she staged only months after *Diamond Lil*'s opening, which would bring the vice squad back out in full force.

Chapter 6

"I'M THE QUEEN OF THE BITCHES"

"Stop where you are! The show is over!" With those words, on October 3, 1928, detectives from the New York City vice squad leaped to the stage of the Biltmore Theater and clapped their hands over the actors' mouths. The offensive production was *Pleasure Man*, written and directed by Mae West. Its crime: "endangering the morals of youth and others" through the "degenerate" antics of its supporting cast, the very men the police had silenced—a troupe of female impersonators.

Pleasure Man was far and away the most controversial play of West's career, in sheer shock value surpassing even *The Drag* and provoking her second arrest. The October 3 raid, which closed the show down, was the second to hit it in only three days. The play's premiere on October 1 had ended in what one newspaper described as "the most sensational raid in New York theatrical history," with cast and crew dragged into Forty-seventh Street and shoved into Black Marias in front of a jeering crowd of three thousand.[1] Critics, to a man, endorsed the police action: the play was "unspeakably slimy," "perverted," "revolting." Concluded one: "They don't come any dirtier."[2]

Mae West, for her part, claimed total incomprehension of what all the fuss was about. Hauled in from the Royale Theater, still in full Diamond Lil costume, she told reporters indignantly, "Some people seem to have the idea that if a play is written by Mae West it must be a dirty play."[3] But *Pleasure Man* was simply a backstage melodrama set in the world of small-time vaudeville, centered on a compulsive Lothario—the "pleasure man"—whose relentless philandering leads to his murder. There was, she insisted, "nothing dirty" about it—a claim she would make until the end of her life.

Indeed, until two weeks before the play's Broadway opening, few reporters suspected anything different, since *Variety*'s accounts of the rehearsals made it all seem harmless enough. Originally entitled *Back Stage*, then *Five-a-Day*, the play was touted as a satirical look at the failed performers who populated the small-time "coffee and cake circuit."[4] Critics prepared themselves for a kaleidoscopic comedy in the best *Diamond Lil* style.

Exactly what West was really planning became evident only in mid-September, when *Pleasure Man* opened in preview performances at the Bronx Opera House. *Variety* responded with a satirical notice penned by columnist Jack Conway, an expert mimic of subcultural slang, who unveiled the show's secret under the headline, "MY DEAR, HERE'S MAE WEST'S NEW SHOW—GET A LOAD OF IT AND WEEP":

Oh, my dear, you must throw on a shawl and run over to the Biltmore in two weeks to see Mae West's *Pleasure Man*. . . . It's the queerest show you've ever seen. All of the Queens are in it.

You haven't seen anything like it since the gendarmes put the "curse of the seven witches" on *The Drag*.

Must give you a vein full of that last act. One of the Queens who used to be in show business throws a party for all the performers on the bill. The female impersonators, four strong, and some other queens all go in drag. Are you screaming? . . .

The party is the pay off. If you see those hussies being introduced to do their specialties you'd pass out. One, Sylvan Repetti, was just too adorable as a snake dancer, and stopped the show. The host sang a couple of parodies, one going "When I Go Out And Look for the Moon," now I ask you. Another guest very appropriately sang "Balls, Parties, and Banquets," and I ask you again.

That West girl knows her box office, and this one is in right now. It can't miss, and if you think it can, hope you get henna in your tooth brush.

But don't miss it, because you must see it to appreciate the strides we girls are making.[5]

With its sardonic use of gay argot, Conway's review made clear to its readers that, under the guise of a backstage melodrama, West had restaged *The Drag*. The new play repeated some of *The Drag*'s wisecracks; it climaxed in a drag ball; it even employed the same gay performers (who, the *New York Times* reported, were not at all abashed by their prior arrest and "seemed to glory in their opportunities for exhibitionism").[6] This time, however, West cast the gay men not as overt homosexuals but as female impersonators in a vaudeville show. It was a shrewd—and explosive—maneuver. For those who saw it, female impersonation would never be the same again.

I have some lady impersonators in the play? In fact I have five of them. But what of it? If they are going to close up the play and prevent these people from making a living because they take the part of female impersonators then they should stop other female impersonators from appearing on the Keith Circuit.[7]

Mae West's defense of her play, while clearly self-serving, made a point that none of her contemporaries denied. Up to the time of the *Pleasure Man* raid, female impersonation had been a mainstay of the most spotless of showbiz arenas: the Keith Circuit, which presented "big-time" vaudeville to America's genteel middle class.

That fact may seem inconceivable now. For the final two-thirds of the twentieth century, professional female impersonators have been viewed with suspicion, consigned largely to the margins of show business, to a netherworld of bars and nightclubs far removed from the entertainment mainstream. At the heart of that stigmatization lies the perception of female impersonation as a homosexual practice. As a theatrical specialty it is consequently regarded as "extreme, bizarre and morally questionable," an illicit parading of sexual deviance, as anthropologist Esther Newton has argued. "The work is defined as 'queer' in itself. The assumption upon which both performers and audiences operate is that no one but a 'queer' would want to perform as a woman."[8]

Yet the presumption of female impersonation's inherent "queerness" was far from universal when *Pleasure Man* was raided in 1928. In the early twentieth century, on the contrary, it was one of the most popular of theatrical specialties. Several impersonators boasted nationwide followings. The best known—Francis Leon in the 1870s, Julian Eltinge in the 1910s—were among the most renowned entertainers of their day. Even as late as the 1920s this mode of performance had lost none of its appeal. "There are more female impersonators in vaudeville this season than ever before," noted *Variety* in 1923. "Three impersonators in one bill at a split house recently is viewed as a record."[9]

At the heart of female impersonation's broad-based popularity lay its unimpeachable respectability, as its very prominence in vaudeville makes clear. Vaudeville, after all, spotlighted "wholesome amusement," "entertainment for the masses, children and adults, to be given without bringing a blush or a shiver," as one manager put it.[10] Female impersonation fit that demand perfectly. Indeed, so esteemed for wholesomeness was it that simply labeling it "respectable" does not do it justice. At the turn of the century female impersonation was deemed *particularly* suited to middle-class taste, *particularly* fit for women and children. Emerging as a theatrical specialty in minstrel shows in the late 1860s, it was created with precisely that public in mind.

While to an 1860s American audience cross-dressed male performers were nothing new, professional female impersonators decidedly were. The distinction is important. In the minstrel show before 1860 male comics had occasionally performed as women, usually in the service of bawdy satire, as in the stock character of the "Funny Old Gal," a caricature of an aging woman played by a burly comedian in frumpy clothes. But in the late 1860s and 1870s the minstrel show began catering to a growing middle-class, female entertainment market, and that meant respecting its concern with gentility and decorum. Out went the raunchy humor; in its place came a new phenomenon: specialist female impersonators who built their careers solely on that ability. For late nineteenth-century theater managers seeking to pull in "respectable" crowds, those performers proved an unbeatable draw.[11]

In part the impersonators' appeal can be traced to the content of their performances, which validated some cherished cultural norms. Unlike the actors who portrayed the "Funny Old Gal," female impersonators did not lampoon femininity. Their performances were serious, even reverential; they celebrated femaleness rather than mocking it. And crucially, they celebrated a construction of femininity that gave them a built-in attraction for the middle class. From Francis Leon, who impersonated lovely ladies of fashion, to Julian Eltinge, who presented a demure ringletted child and a "dainty young miss in a pink party dress," the best-loved impersonators embodied the Victorian feminine ideal.[12] Their performances exalted those qualities deemed essential to respectable womanhood: delicacy, gentility, modesty, and grace.

Yet the fact that female impersonation upheld feminine norms does not fully explain its astounding popularity. It does not explain the career of Julian Eltinge, whose thirty-year reign as one of vaudeville's top performers brought him his own fan magazine, his own line of cosmetics, and a theater named after him in the heart of Times Square. Nor does it explain the tremendous enjoyment the respectable derived from these performances, the thrill that kept them on the edges of their seats for each of Eltinge's female sketches.

What thrilled and astonished fans about female impersonators was the apparent truth of the illusion. "I'll never forget the first time I saw him," recalled a vaudeville prop man of an Eltinge performance. "I couldn't believe it was a man. He was the most beautiful woman I ever saw on Keith's stage and that includes Lillian Russell and Ethel Barrymore and all the rest."[13]

Though the prop man marveled at Eltinge's beauty, his real wonder was directed elsewhere: at this male performer's ability to project convincing femininity, replicated down to the most minute detail. It was a feat that inspired endless awestruck comment. "There is not, from the time of his entrance until he quits the stage, the slightest suggestiveness of a disguised member of the sterner sex," rhapsodized a Leon admirer in the 1870s, praise that Eltinge's fans echoed forty years later:[14]

> He does not . . . force his voice to an unnatural soprano pitch, but maintains a natural tone, speaking very deliberately, so that it is a low contralto. There is, therefore, no incongruity between the woman's appearance and the spoken word. He walks with the short steps of a woman, but with the recognized gait required by the slightly hobbled dress.[15]

Altogether lacking in "incongruity," Eltinge unerringly re-created feminine nuances, even capturing the peculiar gait demanded by a lady's high-fashion attire.

To turn-of-the-century middle-class audiences, this was nothing less than an incredible feat. It confounded one of their most basic assumptions: that men and women were fundamentally different, separated in habits of thought, feeling, and action by a deep and unbridgeable divide. Men were aggressive, competitive, active; women were gentle, spiritual, passive; and no common ground existed between these polarized positions. To nineteenth-century middle-class Americans, these were indisputable biological facts.

In this context the impersonators' popularity may seem perplexing, since the very ease with which they crossed gender boundaries appears to challenge these rigid assumptions. But in fact their performances did precisely the opposite. Billing themselves as "female illusionists," impersonators were lauded as magicians, able to conjure themselves across gender boundaries that their audience believed to be fixed and immutable. Their middle-class appeal turned on that most awe-inspiring of theatrical skills, the ability to perform an act of magic. Done successfully, *Variety* noted, it constituted a "thing of wonderment."[16] Audiences marveled at Julian Eltinge as they did at the likes of Harry Houdini: at the conjurer's skill by which he went from man to woman, transgressing the boundaries of nature itself.

It was that set of associations that rendered *Pleasure Man* so appalling. While vaudeville hailed impersonators as virile men transforming themselves through magical skills of performance, Mae West suggested a far more sensational reading: that female impersonators were homosexuals engaged in an act of self-expression, a flamboyant display of their "womanly" sexual selves.

The aim of *Pleasure Man*, as municipal authorities saw, was to convey to the audience "that these men were not mere female impersonators, but degenerates, who, even offstage, when not performing, adopted the mannerisms of women."[17] To that end, West structured the play as a behind-the-scenes look at a vaudeville troupe, presenting five female impersonators—the Bird of Paradise and his four "Manlykins"—before and after their evening performance. Even when dressed in male attire, joking with their fellow actors, the men minced and sashayed with their hands on their hips. The police officers who raided the show described their behavior as befitting a group of "proud young girls": in one scene a male character threw open a door to find a female impersonator changing clothes; the impersonator pulled a kimono around himself and screamed "like a frightened woman."[18]

The impersonators, in short, were biological males who lived out a feminine social identity. Some, like "Bunny" and "Peaches," went by female names; all employed feminine pronouns and described themselves as "women" and "girls." Above all, their effeminacy extended to their taste in sexual partners. Like women, they slept with men, a fact made unmistakably clear in countless instances of acid-tongued banter: in Peaches's complaint about a clumsy ex-lover ("Men are such uncouth things"),[19] and in bawdy exchanges scattered throughout the play, full of leering allusions to male anatomy:

STAGEHAND: Have you had your cream-puff this morning?
PARADISE: Oh, I always eat early—you know it's the early bird that catches the worm, dearie.[20]

BUNNY: Peaches dear, did you see that glorious Adonis directing traffic at Broad and Main Street?
PEACHES: Do you mean the one on the horse, dearie? You know that's the statue of some General.
BUNNY: Oh, perhaps it's General Coxey.[21]

Finally, *Pleasure Man*'s female impersonators displayed the quintessential badge of 1920s "degenerates": they diverted themselves after hours by attending an outrageous drag ball. That spectacle, taking up most of act three, was lifted, occasionally word for word, from *The Drag*. At the post-performance extravaganza, a dozen impersonators cavorted in women's clothes, singing musical numbers rife with gay slang ("I'm the Queen of the Bitches") and speaking "an unparalleled argot unrivalled in theatrical history":[22]

1ST BOY: I hear you're working in a millinery shop.
2ND BOY: Yes, I trim rough sailors.
3RD BOY: My, what a low-cut gown you've got.
4TH BOY: Why, Beulah, a woman with a back like mine can be as low as she wants to be.

3RD BOY: Oh, look, I can almost do the splits.
4TH BOY: Be careful, dearie, you'll wear out your welcome.[23]

In *Pleasure Man* Mae West sensationally redefined female imper-sonation, linking onstage cross-dressing with offstage effeminacy and equating the latter with homosexuality. Given the style that predominated in 1920s gay culture, that linkage was clearly there to be made. In the "culture of effeminacy" described by George Chauncey, gay men did emulate women. As one vice investigator put it, "although they represent and are dressed as one sex they act and impersonate the opposite sex ... by gesture, voice inflection, manner or mode of speech, or walk, and in general [they] imperson-ate all of the other characteristics of a female that they can possibly assume."[24]

Like *The Drag, Pleasure Man* was a deliberately titillating pro-duction that unearthed the social style of New York's gay subcul-ture. But to that it added a second offense—it impugned female impersonators in the process. Broadway performers and critics were outraged. "It is a libelous and treacherous portrayal of show peo-ple, and one that demands retraction to the thousands it so falsely paints and so grossly insults," fulminated the trade magazine *Bill-board*.[25] West was deemed nothing less than a crass pornographer exploiting a time-honored theatrical tradition as a pretext for "degenerate antics," usurping the artistic terrain of Broadway with something that belonged in the streets. "There was no trace of play-writing in it," protested drama critic George Jean Nathan indig-nantly in the *American Mercury*. "The thing was a mere lifting over to a theatre stage of the kind of Harlem 'drag' that the police peremptorily raid."[26]

In some ways the theater community was right. West had long specialized in raunchy plays that retailed "dirt" to the Broadway public, and her interest in female impersonators was clearly exploitative: they provided a brilliant pretext under which she could flaunt censorable stage content. In 1927, in the wake of *The Drag*, New York State had banned the open stage depiction of homosexu-ality. Yet West managed to portray gay culture's most sensational elements, and to deny any sensational intent, by exploiting the link between mainstream vaudeville tradition and the female imperson-ation at the heart of gay style.

But though West's lurid intentions are undeniable, she was hardly as inventive as her detractors made out. Critics accused her of sin-glehandedly perverting female impersonation: of fabricating a con-nection between the sexual underworld and the world of the the-atrical female impersonator, thus opening the stage to sexual deviants whose performances were foreign to dramatic tradition. In *Pleasure Man*'s obscenity trial, the district attorney echoed that charge. "They were not doing any female impersonation," James Wallace maintained of Mae West's gay cast. "They were acting in an effeminate manner, walking like and talking like women, they were depicting fairies or degenerates."[27]

But though West obviously capitalized on the link between stage tradition and New York's gay style, she didn't invent it out of whole cloth. The fact was that there did exist female impersonators who were unabashedly "fairies"—impersonators who'd long been con-signed to the dives of the underworld but were beginning to make themselves known above ground.

For information about them, one need only return to Jimmy Durante, who encountered them in his early years as a pianist in concert saloons. Recall his description of Edna May and Big Tess, the "boys who danced together and lisped." The impersonators he witnessed were not just performers—they were (in Durante's phrase) "queer entertainers," men who adopted female dress and mannerisms to suggest an illicit sexual identity. That identity per-sisted when they stepped off the stage. Sitting at the tables, "spin-ning their web," they mimicked the actions of "the usual girls who hung out there," prostitutes who mingled with patrons soliciting for drinks and sex.[28]

What Durante witnessed was the underground tradition of the "fairy impersonator," a fixture in concert saloons and other work-ing-class theaters since the late nineteenth century. Not surprisingly, vice investigators loathed the whole spectacle, and well into the 1920s the fairy impersonator remained a decidedly lowlife phe-nomenon. Nonetheless, he occasionally popped up in more respectable venues, even making it—once—onto Broadway, in the person of Bert Savoy, an overt fairy who specialized in raunchy female mimicry that delighted a cult following of urban sophisti-cates. (Savoy's career came to a premature end in 1923, when he was struck by a bolt of lightning while walking on the beach at Fire Island.[29])

Clearly, fairy impersonators and vaudeville impersonators offered

very different forms of amusement. For one thing, they impersonated different women. While vaudevillians like Julian Eltinge posed
as lovely ladies of fashion, fairy impersonators, most decidedly, did
not emulate ladies. The impersonators described by Jimmy Durante
resembled the brassy tarts of working-class street culture. So did the
figure embodied by Bert Savoy, whom Edmund Wilson remembered
as "a gigantic red-haired harlot, swaying her enormous hat, reeking
with corrosive cocktails of the West Fifties."[30]

More fundamentally, the two traditions differed in the thrill that
each offered its audience. The thrill of an Eltinge, billed as a
"female illusionist," lay quite explicitly in his skills of performance—his ability to conjure himself across what spectators
believed to be an immutable gender divide. The thrill of the fairy
impersonator, in contrast, lay in the fact that he was not, techni-
cally, performing at all. Like the burlesque dancer whose raunchy
presence suggested an offstage identity as a prostitute, he blurred
the boundary between stage life and street life and displayed his
authentic self—as a "third sexer," an "invert" who straddled the
gender divide.

Yet even though he was essentially performing his self, the fairy
impersonator developed a set of stage conventions, a "code" that by
the turn of the century was instantly recognizable to underworld
spectators. So powerful was that code, one vice investigator argued,
that it rendered the whole practice of impersonation pernicious,
whether it was performed in the slums or on the most reputable
vaudeville stage. As she explained in 1895:

> If you want to understand the full measure of the harm that can be
> done by masqueraders of this sort, you should go, as I have gone, to
> some of the concert halls on the Bowery, and see in what fashion
> they make their appeal to the boys and men who constitute almost
> their entire audience, and with what evil intelligence the audience
> responds to their insinuations of word and action. These denizens
> of the slums know too well the awful horror which the masquer-
> ades may be made to suggest.[31]

What was most appalling to the investigator was the sheer familiarity of these spectacles to lower-class patrons, who readily
decoded "the awful horror" the performances so clearly suggested.
Imbued with "evil intelligence," the audience knew that these

impersonations did not in the least connote acts of magic, but the "horror" of an invert's identity, the impersonator's feminine sexual self.

As long as that knowledge was familiar only to "denizens of the slums," vaudeville female impersonation could continue to flourish, with the middle class reading it as thrilling yet wholesome theatrical magic. Yet it seems clear that well prior to *Pleasure Man* this traditional reading had come under strain. While the most renowned vaudeville impersonators remained as popular as ever, they were framing their performances to cope with new challenges—rumors circulating among middle-class spectators about their performances' "deviant" meanings.

Take Julian Eltinge. In the 1910s he remained one of the most popular performers in vaudeville, but his publicity took on a defensive new slant, carefully framed to alleviate doubts about the nature of his private life. "JULIAN ELTINGE ISN'T EFFEMINATE WHEN HE GETS HIS CORSETS OFF," trumpeted one press notice:

> This is Julian D. Eltinge, a handsome, healthy young man, filled with the joy of life, bubbling over with spirits, a strong young athlete who covered right garden for the Harvard baseball team, and who has every appearance on the stage of a charming young woman, who sings divinely and dances as lightly and gracefully as a ballroom belle.
>
> There is nothing feminine about Julian, for when off the stage he will get into a game of poker, can beat Bob Hilliard playing pinochle, can row in a varsity eight, or can eat chop suey with the sticks and talk nonsense with the ladies. Julian is certainly all right.[32]

He was "all right," the article insisted, because he was a genuinely masculine male: an athlete, a gambler, an adventurous rake, able only by sheer skill of performance to transform himself into a convincing woman. Clearly, it is only necessary to insist that "there is nothing feminine about Julian" if one fears that one's readers suspect precisely the opposite. In stark contrast to earlier vaudeville impersonators, Eltinge felt compelled to surround his performances with assurances of his offstage masculinity. Only those assurances could counter a growing awareness among his middle-class fans that female impersonation could hold a sensational meaning: it could imply a sexually inverted offstage self.

That such an awareness existed seems indisputable; where it came from is more difficult to pin down. Certainly, it must have stemmed at least in part from the growing visibility of New York's gay community. By the 1910s vice investigations, police raids, and press exposés—to say nothing of what could be seen on the streets—were familiarizing middle-class New Yorkers with the city's homosexual subculture. That familiarization may well have brought with it a sense that gay men "impersonated women" as a means of expressing a gay identity and participating in underworld theater and nightlife.

The turn-of-the-century medical profession played a key role as well. In a voluminous body of literature describing and classifying sexual abnormality, it brought cross-dressing under scientific scrutiny, deeming it a prime symptom of "sexual inversion." As conceptualized by European sexologists Richard von Krafft-Ebing and Havelock Ellis, "sexual inversion" defined gay men and women as victims of a medical disorder, a dysfunction compelling them to adopt not just the sexual preferences but the appearance and behavior of the opposite sex. Through theories of inversion, cross-dressing reentered the culture as a symptom of pathology. Indeed, according to some medical theorists, cross-dressing constituted a pathology unto itself; by 1910, studied and analyzed, it had acquired its own name: "transvestism."[33]

Gay streetlife and medical literature were exposing middle-class audiences to new ideas and influences; but just as crucially, the most basic middle-class beliefs and values were themselves in the process of change. The early years of the twentieth century saw the decline of Victorian "separate spheres" ideology, the belief that men and women were mentally, emotionally, and psychologically different. By the 1910s scientific studies were undermining that belief, and young middle-class women were actively flouting it, adopting male habits (smoking, drinking) and male vocations (college attendance, professional careers) to express a new middle-class conviction of the basic similarity of the sexes' talents and temperaments.

All performance traditions, in order to flourish, must bear some relation to social reality. Yet the traditional reading of vaudeville impersonation suited a world that was rapidly fading, a world where men and women were deemed to be fundamentally distinct species. Only there could a convincing female impersonation seem as baffling and as thrilling as an act of pure magic. For the two decades preceding *Pleasure Man*'s premiere, female impersonation had been losing its capacity to provoke audiences to "wonderment" and may well have been provoking their prurient curiosity. Mae West addressed that curiosity far more baldly and sensationally than anyone else had dared.

In March 1930, after repeated delays, Mae West stood trial for *Pleasure Man*. From the beginning the cards were stacked in her favor. The prosecution faced the near-impossible task of convicting her for a production staged eighteen months previously—a production for which they had no script (West claimed none had ever existed) and whose crucial actors were conspicuously absent (all the female impersonators, West reported, had joined the navy).[34]

In addition, the state had to do battle with West's attorney, the suave, shrewd Nathan Burkan, who, to the delight of the New York press, proved brilliantly adept at making police witnesses look ridiculous. Cross-examining one police complainant, the unfortunately named Lieutenant James Coy, Burkan forced him to demonstrate the play's alleged obscenity, a demand "that brought the big officer to his feet with kittenish manner and fingertip to chin to mimic a man actor saying 'Whoops, my dear.' "[35] At Burkan's urging, West denied everything: all the sexual double entendres, all the connotations of homosexuality. The *Pleasure Man* cast members backed her up. Burkan called to the stand only those who were unimpeachably straight, like actor Alan Brooks, who swaggered through his testimony "all vigor and masculinity," blankly denying any knowledge of alleged improprieties. As the *New York World* reported:

> He rode the witness chair as if on horseback. . . . Nor did he understand what police contend were words of double meaning, referring to sex perversion, in the play. That was "absolutely news to me," he said. Mr. Brooks said he understood the word commonly applied to male degenerates as meaning "a being endowed with supernatural powers, generally invisible to the eye."[36]

As Margy Lamont in *Sex*, 1926, sporting the infamous ostrich feather. *(The Shubert Archive)*

Hitting the tabloid headlines: the *New York Daily Mirror* on the *Sex* raid, February 1927.

"You can be had": with Curtis Cooksy as Captain Cummings in the 1928 Broadway production of *Diamond Lil*. *(The Billy Rose Theatre Collection, The New York Public Library for the Performing Arts, Astor, Lenox, and Tilden Foundation)*

In the golden swan bed, *Diamond Lil*, 1928. *(The Billy Rose Theatre Collection, The New York Public Library for the Performing Arts, Astor, Lenox, and Tilden Foundation)*

"Flaming Mae" makes the front page of the *New York Evening Graphic* after the first *Pleasure Man* raid, October 1928.

Two days later: the *New York Daily News* on the second *Pleasure Man* raid. Female impersonators sashay into police van (*upper left photo*).

Glamorous publicity portraits
for *The Constant Sinner*, **1931.**
(The Shubert Archive)

Publicity portraits for *The Constant Sinner* with West's black lover nowhere in sight.
(The Billy Rose Theatre Collection, The New York Public Library for the Performing Arts, Astor, Lenox, and Tilden Foundation)

The Constant Sinner's
supporting cast.
(The Billy Rose Theatre Collection, The New York Public Library for the Performing Arts, Astor, Lenox, and Tilden Foundation)

"Goodness had nothing to do with it": newly arrived in Hollywood for *Night After Night*, 1932.

"Diamonds is my career": with Cary Grant as Captain Cummings in *She Done Him Wrong.* *(Paramount, courtesy The Kobal Collection)*

"The finest woman who ever walked the streets," with Gilbert Roland in *She Done Him Wrong*. *(Paramount, courtesy The Kobal Collection)*

As Tira, the "dancing, singing marvel," in *I'm No Angel*, 1933. *(Paramount, courtesy The Kobal Collection)*

With W. C. Fields in a film she detested, *My Little Chickadee*, 1940. *(Universal, courtesy The Kobal Collection)*

"Is that a pistol in your pocket. . . .": in the locker room in *Sextette*, 1977. West is eighty-four.

Given this strategy, the trial swiftly descended into a tangle of cross-accusations. The state charged West with "parading degeneracy" but lacked supporting evidence. The defense, for its part, claimed municipal harassment, a police campaign to "get Mae West." The conflicting testimony made balanced judgment impossible, and on April 3, 1930, the jury broke down in a seven-to-five deadlock.

More or less by default, Mae West was cleared, but female impersonation decidedly was not. As the 1930s went on, it became increasingly stigmatized, pushed from the stages of respectable theaters. There was no more eloquent testimony to this process than the fate of Julian Eltinge. Still a vaudeville headliner in the 1920s, he migrated to Hollywood at the end of the decade but found his entry to movies effectively barred by a new city ordinance outlawing male cross-dressing onstage. For a 1931 comeback bid, the only forum open to Eltinge was the stage of a cheap Hollywood nightclub. Prevented from appearing in women's clothes, he attempted to compensate by displaying his costumes on a rack and gesturing alongside them. As one might expect, he performed to a virtually empty house, and his "comeback" collapsed within a week.[37]

As Eltinge's story indicates, within an astonishingly short period of time female impersonation's past connotations had vanished. By the late 1930s it held only one meaning: it was purely and simply an act of "degeneracy." Interpreted as a vehicle of homosexual nightlife, it was banned by municipal and state authorities as part of a larger crackdown on gay male culture that swept the nation during the Depression.[38] Professional impersonators were excoriated in the press as deviant, perverse, and potentially dangerous. "BAN ON FEMME IMPERSONATORS, SAYS DETROIT MD, ONE WAY TO STOP SEX MURDERS" was by no means an exceptional *Variety* headline.[39]

"How many thousand female impersonators do you think there are in the country?" Mae West had demanded after the *Pleasure Man* raid. "Are they going to put them all out of business?"[40] West's words proved prophetic. By the end of the decade female impersonation was held in thorough contempt. Impersonators were no longer seen as performers—they were performing homosexuals. In a culture that demonized homosexuality, that was enough to exclude them from the mainstream, to put them out of business once and for all.

*   *   *

In many ways *Pleasure Man* marked the end of an era in Mae West's career, her final foray as an underworld impresario lifting the veil on New York City's gay men. Over the next two years West would become more and more wedded to her Diamond Lil persona—and to her new reputability, as her next play, *The Constant Sinner*, would show.

At the same time it would be misleading to see *Pleasure Man* as a simple anomaly, the last gasp of Mae-West-the-sensationalist as she moved into the entertainment mainstream. While the play was West's most disreputable enterprise, it was also one of her most fruitful and did more to influence *Diamond Lil* than might at first appear.

Diamond Lil owed its success to the new tone West displayed as a performer—she handled her sexuality with a faint trace of mockery, a teasing suggestion of hidden meanings. As one reviewer put it, "She seems to recoil with an almost gun-like precision after each of her more tawdry speeches, and make her own comment upon them, even while she continues to play them seriously."[41] Critics adored it but were bewildered: the new tone seemed to come out of nowhere. But it came, in fact, from the *Pleasure Man* rehearsals, as West learned from her fairy impersonators, from their stylized injection of double meanings into even the most innocuous lines. ("The early bird catches the worm, dearie.") As film historian Pamela Robertson has noted, the tone employed by those impersonators sounds like nothing so much as Mae West herself.[42]

Whether deliberately or not, by mid-1928 Mae West had absorbed the fairy's style and echoed it in her own performance. That it appealed should not be surprising. As a working-class woman, she knew fairies intimately and shared their theatrical roots. West's stage style, like the fairy's, was anchored in raunchy underworld theater; as he had done in the dives of the Bowery, she swaggered in the guise of a brassy working-class woman. But the fairy added a touch of irony, hinting at a submerged layer of meaning, at the put-on's hidden truth: the impersonator's "womanly" sexual self.

When West employed that same touch of gay irony, removing it from its real-life referent, she enraptured the very critics who found *Pleasure Man* "revolting," prompting them to extravagant efforts to capture her style in words. Their difficulty is understandable, for

West's style was exceedingly hard to pin down. She performed an impersonation at several removes: an authentic tough girl mimicking fairy impersonators mimicking the flamboyance of working-class women. What resulted was a baffling hall of mirrors that fascinated and bewildered nearly all who saw it, providing West with an enduring foundation on which she would build her career.

There is, of course, a word for West's style: even in the 1920s it was called camp. West had learned both the word and the concept from her friends in New York's gay underground. She used it often in *Pleasure Man*, in stage directions and in dialogue to denote an extravagant form of behavior that the play presented as characteristically gay. When *Pleasure Man*'s "boys" were instructed to "camp," they screamed and preened, took up piles of knitting, and flounced about the stage with their hands on their hips, flaunting a feminine social identity in acid-laced, brazen, and blowsy remarks. To camp, in short, was to enact a playful gender inversion as a means of expressing a "third sex" identity. Its hallmark was a sly, teasing tone that conveyed an ironic distance from social convention, mocking it through the deployment of artifice, humor, and theatricality.[43]

By injecting camp into her performances, West crossed over to a mass audience, but at the same time she charged her theatrics with special meaning for gay men. In the 1930s in Hollywood West in a sense took the place of the drag queens and other overt manifestations of gay culture that were rapidly being pushed underground. Her films subtly but unmistakably acknowledged gay viewers and invited their appreciation. Not only did her delivery echo drag humor, but her scripts were dotted with homosexual in-jokes. In *I'm No Angel* (1933), bantering with a debonair suitor, she toyed with the words "out" and "sophisticated," both of which had double meanings in gay male culture—the former meaning, then as now, out of the closet, the latter a slang term applied to a man who was "apparently straight, but open to suggestion":[44]

WEST: I like a sophisticated man to take me out.
SUITOR: Well, I'm not really sophisticated.
WEST: Well, but you're not really out, either.[45]

Beyond this, it's probably also worth mentioning West's frequent use of what the rumor mill labeled gay actors: Cary Grant, Randolph Scott, and in bit parts in nearly all her films, Edward Hearn, an ex-vaudevillian and silent film actor who played prominent roles in both *Pleasure Man* and *The Drag*.

The evidence from filmgoers is admittedly minuscule, but it suggests that gay men in the 1930s enjoyed West precisely as a skillful camp agent. The novelist and critic Parker Tyler recalled that "when I was very, very young [in the 1920s and 1930s] Mae West was an acknowledged camp."[46] To see West as "a camp" was to savor her ironic detachment, her skill in *doing an act*. The journalist George Davis made exactly that point, in exactly those words, in *Vanity Fair* in 1934, becoming the first person ever to link West in print to a tradition of gay performance:

> I can pay you no greater tribute, dear lady, than to say that [my love for you] has healed the wound in my heart caused by the death of the one and only Bert Savoy. I love you, Miss West, because YOU are the greatest female impersonator of all time.[47]

Chapter 7

THE HONOR OF WHITE WOMANHOOD

From the beginning of time it has mystified, misled and maddened men. Today, in New York's feverish nightworld, it turns hardened men into weaklings; it drags the rich and the well-born into the depths.

Sex! In some women it exists as a superhuman power, an irresistable [*sic*] lure, a consuming destruction.

No woman has hitherto dared to tell the truth about her. Mae West tells it. She minces no words. As she herself built her plays, crude but powerful and full blooded creations which the critics came to mock, but stayed to cheer, so in this book she builds a powerful, vigorous, big-framed book that glows with reality.[1]

Published on November 5, 1930, by the New York firm Macaulay's, *Babe Gordon* was touted as "Mae West's novel of the New York underworld." West wrote the novel rapidly after *Diamond Lil*'s national tour, shaping it as a sensational advertisement to whet audience appetite for the play that would follow. The book appeared in a blaze of publicity, much of it centered on the title. In their haste to get West's tale into print, Macaulay's named the story after its central character while piquing interest with a title competition: a hundred dollars to be paid to the reader who devised the spiciest one. At the end of the year the contest's judge, Walter Winchell, announced the winner: *The Constant Sinner*. That title appeared on all subsequent editions, and West went on to employ it for her Broadway play.

Macaulay's was renowned for publishing sex novels, and Mae West's tale was no exception. It tells the story of Babe Gordon, an eighteen-year-old hooker who turns to prostitution simply for pleasure. Absolutely without morals, she's on the prowl for the utmost in sexual sensation, a search that ultimately takes her to Harlem. There, in New York's prime erotic haven, she finds the sexual underworld's savage, pulsating heart. She dallies with a string of lovers, marrying a prizefighter, Bearcat Delaney, and leaving him for a wealthy department store magnate, Wayne Baldwin, who whisks her off to Paris at the story's conclusion. But it is midway through the novel that Babe encounters her most sensational conquest: the "magnificent animal" Money Johnson, a black Harlem racketeer.

Babe Gordon's original title was *Black and White*, and for good reason. The excitement of the tale is enhanced by its Harlem setting, and Babe's involvement with a black lover demonstrates how far into savage thrill-seeking she goes. Attention-getting material at any time, perhaps, but never more marketable than in 1930. That year saw the peak of white fascination with black Harlem, a fascination accommodated throughout the late 1920s by a new brand of Harlem nightclub, as well as novels, plays, and press exposés that claimed to unveil the district's primitive core.

With *Babe Gordon*, Mae West jumped on the Harlem bandwagon, attempting to show her own mastery of a locale mythologized as the sexual underworld's barbaric heart. At least initially she was successful. Within weeks booksellers as far away as Los Angeles ranked *Babe Gordon* one of their top-selling titles. But transferring *Babe Gordon* to the stage as *The Constant Sinner* got Mae West into trouble—although not, this time, trouble with the law. The problem now was Mae West herself: enamored of her new reputability, she proved uneasy with her material. As she soon discovered, dallying with black savagery might look enticing on paper, but it could be much more problematic in the flesh.

The old, old story of civilization's lusts was being retold in Harlem. The lusts that ancient Rome and Athens could not purge from their proud and disciplined cultures—the flesh cry that has persisted through all time—found expression and release in New York's black belt.

Harlem is the Paris of the Western Hemisphere—a museum of occult sex, a sensual oasis in the sterile desert of white civilization, where conventional people can indulge in unconventional excesses.[2]

The Harlem of *Babe Gordon* is an exotic world of dance halls, speakeasies, dope dens, and gin flats, where all the repressed lusts of white civilization find exhilarating and ecstatic release. Though the novel presented it as a hidden world, in fact West's Harlem was no more hidden, no more unfamiliar to consumers of popular culture, than the amiable haunts of her Gay Nineties Bowery. Look anywhere in New York's commercial culture of the late 1920s, and you'll find Harlem as West drew it: barbaric, uninhibited, seething with sensual savagery. By 1930, through Broadway, fiction, and the popular press, Harlem had emerged as an immensely tantalizing draw for nightlifers, surrounded by a lurid yet standardized commercial mystique. It was sold as a voyage of exploration, the ultimate dare, a trip past the packaged hijinks of other New York amusements into the underworld's throbbing heart.

Like all commercial fantasies, that of raw, savage Harlem bore some relation to social reality. A real-life black Harlem of course did exist, stretching from 120th Street to 155th Street and from Eighth Avenue to the Harlem River. As a community it took root around 1900, when black New Yorkers, drawn by a real-estate surplus, abandoned their crammed quarters in the Tenderloin district, braved hostility from resident Germans, and moved into Harlem's spacious brownstones. They were soon joined by a flood of black migrants who had pulled up stakes from the American South, and by others from the West Indies, Africa, and Latin America. By 1930, with over two hundred thousand inhabitants, Harlem had become the center of Afro-America, synonymous, wrote one contemporary journalist, "with black life and black style in Manhattan."[3]

It was also increasingly synonymous with vice. From the beginning Harlem housed a vibrant indigenous nightlife, clubs like Basement Brownie's and the Bucket of Blood, raucous rent parties ("jumps," "shouts" or "struts," pianist Willie "The Lion" Smith called them) where a quarter would leave you "howling and stomping sometimes well into dawn in a miasma of smoke, booze, collard greens and hot music."[4] The scene grew even wilder with Prohibition, when Harlem became a haven for illegal liquor, and for the racketeering that inevitably followed. By the late 1920s you could buy liquor virtually anywhere in Harlem—at drugstores, newsstands, soda fountains, shoe shops. Brothels abounded; so did "buffet flats," makeshift operations offering a smorgasbord of drugs, music, liquor, and sex. Such places catered to tastes to all sorts, for Harlem was also home to a sizable (and integrated) gay underworld.

Yet New York had a lot of poor neighborhoods whose residents supplemented their incomes by trading in what outsiders called vice. Harlem's particular lure stemmed less from such associations than from the contours of white fantasy. The new commercial ventures that took off in the 1920s, marketing Harlem to a white audience— Owney Madden's Cotton Club; the 1926 Broadway hit *Lulu Belle*, Charles MacArthur and Edward Shelton's high-voltage melodrama of Harlem streetlife; the 1926 best-seller *Nigger Heaven*, Carl Van Vechten's sensational survey of Harlem highlife and lowlife; and the multitude of plays, novels, and press exposés that followed—titillated white audiences by shrouding Harlem in an aura of barbaric sexual exoticism and purporting to offer a confrontation—a candid face-to-face glimpse of the primitive truth of the black race.

One of *Babe Gordon*'s immediate predecessors, Wallace Thurman and William Rapp's Broadway hit *Harlem*, spelled out the nature of that confrontation. Premiering in March 1929 and heralded as "the most unretouched and, therefore, the most accurate of the photographs made at Seventh Avenue and 132nd Street,[5] *Harlem* created a sensation with its supposedly authentic re-creation of this "strange exotic island in the heart of New York."[6] Not surprisingly, it was strange exotica that the production stressed. The playwrights, a black Harlem novelist and a white tabloid journalist, claimed to be uncovering phenomena "peculiar to Harlem alone, phenomena which are inherently expressions of the Negro character before it was conditioned by the white world that now surrounds him."[7] Just what that unassimilated "Negro character" consisted of was nowhere more evident than at a Harlem rent party:

When the party reaches a climax it is the piano player alone who controls its emotional and physical destiny. Some inkling of this seemingly permeates his being, and a strange barbaric ecstasy emanates from his perspiring body. The dim lighted rooms will surge with strange rhythms and barbaric quarter-tone beats.[8]

That the playwrights repeated the words "strange" and "barbaric" twice in two sentences suggests the limited, predictable, and thoroughly conventionalized images that resulted when Harlem nightlife was commercially "unveiled." Thurman and Rapp knew what their white spectators expected to find in this exotic heart of darkness: bodies swaying to tribal rhythms with untamed sensuality, an utterly uncivilized state of being where passion reigned unfettered, beyond the control of the rational mind.

By 1930 this unadulterated Negro primitivism had become one of the most salable commodities in the commercial culture of Prohibition-era New York. Like so much of New York's 1920s nightlife, it was popular in part because it enabled its consumers to thumb their noses at the fears of the late Victorian middle class. Harlem spectacles proved thrilling precisely because they would have horrified turn-of-the-century genteel Americans. At once convinced of and terrified by black people's innate savagery and barbarism, they had decried the increased visibility of "alien" races as perhaps the nation's most ominous threat.

Racial fears had rarely been as intense, or as intensely politicized, as in the 1910s and 1920s, when eminent custodians of genteel culture issued virulent warnings about America's looming racial destruction. In highly influential diatribes like Madison Grant's *The Passing of the Great Race* (1915) and Lothrop Stoddard's *The Rising Tide of Color Against White World-Supremacy* (1920), the authors, both reputable scholars, warned of the country's imminent "mongrelization": the dire possibility that "old stock" Americans (i.e., Northern Europeans or "Nordics")—a "highly evolved" race with "specialized capacities"—would be swamped and ultimately obliterated by racially inferior stock.[9] That strident insistence on a racial heritage in crisis dominated American politics in the early 1920s, spurring Congress to curtail immigration with the 1924 Johnson-Reed Act. Intensifying a climate of white middle-class fear, it also helped reinvigorate the Ku Klux Klan, which reemerged in the 1920s as a nationwide movement, with the explicit aim of protecting "Nordic civilization" against nonwhite enemies within.

At heart the racial purity panic represented a crisis of cultural values, the protest of an embattled elite against an American landscape in the process of change. At the turn of the century the nation was becoming visibly different as it absorbed a new wave of immigrants—from Asia and Southern and Eastern Europe—and a newly mobile population of African-Americans, freed from slavery and moving away from the American South in increasing numbers. In genteel eyes all these "alien races" were threats, and a multiracial nation dominated by multiracial cities portended nothing less than disaster. Racial purists deemed the new foreigners *intractably* foreign, shaped by inherited character traits that outweighed any effects of environment. They were incapable of imbibing the "highly evolved" traits of Nordics: the purity and modesty of white women, the discipline and purposefulness of white men, the ethic of self-restraint and self-improvement that had guided the Victorian middle class.

Racial purity campaigners feared all non-Nordics but considered none more frighteningly alien than blacks. "Sharply differentiated from the other branches of mankind," according to Lothrop Stoddard, black men and women simply could not be guided by the genteel ethic: their ferocious, uncontrollable physical animalism marked them as the lowest and most primitive in the hierarchy of races.[10] This inherent baseness, racialists argued, had only been exacerbated by the abolition of slavery. "Everybody knows," wrote the *Charleston News and Courier* in 1898, "that when freed from the compelling influence of the white man he reverts by a law of nature to the natural barbarism in which he was created in the jungles of Africa"[11]—a belief as widely accepted in the North as in the South, voiced by America's most prominent: religious leaders, politicians, and academic social scientists. At its most extreme it led to calls for black disfranchisement or deportation. More commonly, racialists urged that future immigration be restricted to white people and that within America, by law or by practice, blacks be segregated from whites.

At the heart of racialist fears lay what Lothrop Stoddard called "the lurking spectre of miscegenation": Nordic civilization overwhelmed by the raging force of black animalism, obliterated in a catastrophic "mingling of the blood." For Stoddard and other self-proclaimed guardians of white culture, interracial sex would inevitably result in a disastrous degeneration: the disciplined morality evolved by Nordics could only be "vanquished by the invincible prepotency of the more primitive, generalized and lower Negro blood."[12]

In the early years of the twentieth century blacks loomed in the genteel mind as a sexual menace, terrifying harbingers of social destruction. It was this sheer weight of dread surrounding black sexuality that led nightlifers to seek it out. To delight in a firsthand glimpse of black barbarism was to prove their modernity and adventurous daring. By demonstrating their unshockability, their pleasure, in the presence of what their elders had most feared, nightlifers could flaunt their flamboyant rejection of what they derided as a sexually repressive American past.

For her part Mae West was determined to prove herself the most fearless enthusiast of all with a full-scale attempt to capitalize on the white vogue for Harlem. Under the tagline "Mae West Can Tell!!," ads for *Babe Gordon* promised a guided tour of New York's wickedest underworld led by an acknowledged expert, and the text itself did not disappoint. As the novel's tough, jaded narrator, West conducts her readers through a primitive Harlem full of writhing black bodies and savage jazz music, where the color line has simply ceased to exist: it is a "pool of sex, where all colors are blended, all bloods mingled."[13] And no "bloods" mingle more luridly than those of the white Babe Gordon and the black Money Johnson. Spotlighting Stoddard's "lurking spectre," West turns it into sensational spectacle, allowing her readers to indulge their fascination with the Victorians' most horrific nightmare of all.

West never lets her readers forget how much Babe's affair would shock the prudish. It even appalls the worldly Wayne Baldwin. A department store magnate and descendant of "Puritan ancestors," he becomes Babe's suitor and ultimately her avenger after a slumming excursion to a Harlem nightclub, where he gazes across the room and is revolted by what he sees:

> The arm of the colored Apollo was over the back of Babe's chair, and his large bronze hand rested on her ermine shoulders, the finger tips caressing her cream-white throat. The saxophones crooned a low barbaric jungle moan. Baldwin looked on fascinated, unable to take his eyes off the monstrous sight that held him spellbound.[14]

Baldwin is shocked by this spectacle, this "public exhibition of sensual pleasure"; Mae West, however, as the book's narrator, most definitely is not. "Yes, Babe Gordon had a nigger lover. Why not?" she asks airily. "Other white women had them."[15] This is a woman who knows the turf, who has experienced Harlem and has seen it all. As her contemptuous dismissal indicates, she is shocked by nothing that she sees.

In many ways this was an audacious text. Quite obviously it mocked Victorian pride in white modesty and self-discipline—particularly Victorian pride in the purity of white women. Babe Gordon is an unashamed aggressor who seeks out the hot-blooded, lynx-eyed Money Johnson expressly to satisfy her lusts. West's treatment abounds in salacious detail, lingering on Babe's excitement as she glides her eyes appraisingly over Johnson's naked body, and on her arousal as she watches their lovemaking in the mirror over Johnson's bed. West's point is clear: while Johnson may be an "animal," a sexual "primitive," Babe is as animalistic and primitive as he.

Such a portrayal was anathema to the genteel sensibility. While all interracial sex was deemed an abomination, sex between a black man and a white woman was so explosive as to be virtually unthinkable. Indeed, Victorians simply could not envision it happening freely; the only way they could conceive of it in (relative) comfort was as an act of rape. In that guise, as the brutal assault of black male savagery on virtuous white femininity, interracial sex haunted late Victorian life, a potent cocktail of racial and sexual terror. In the South the vision of the "Big African Brute . . . molesting our God-like pure snowwhite angelic American Woman" served as justification for lynching.[16] In the North no less than the South, it loomed over the era's popular culture, appearing most memorably in Thomas Dixon's 1905 novel *The Clansman* and in its film adaptation, D. W. Griffith's 1915 *The Birth of a Nation*, as the tale's melodramatic climax: the attempted rape of chaste Little Flora by a ferocious black attacker.

Babe Gordon is no Little Flora. As if to emphasize that point, West subjects *The Clansman*'s black-on-white rape scenario to deliberate mockery. When Wayne Baldwin shoots Johnson in a jealous rage (after a two-day tryst Babe has avidly courted), Babe turns the loaded stereotype to her own advantage: she convinces her husband, Bearcat Delaney, to claim responsibility for the shooting and engineers his exoneration by claiming that Johnson had been trying to rape her. Her husband, a white man, alerted by her cries, shot the black man to protect her honor. The jury unblinkingly accepts this as truth.

Here the novel's intention is clearly satirical. Its account of the trial mocks the old-fashioned mentality that so readily takes Babe at her word. Masquerading as rape victim makes Babe a celebrity, held up by the press as an innocent flower woefully abused by a savage black villain. The agents of the court are even more emphatic. In a chapter entitled "The Wheels of Justice," West chronicles the defense attorney's plea to the jury to redress the assault on Babe and free the man "who has upheld one of the finest traditions of the white race, the honor of its womanhood," by heroically slaying her attacker, who after all was nothing more than a "low, lustful black beast":

> This was the criminal who dared affront the whole white world by luring to his hideaway this beautiful woman to gratify his lusts. There he kept her an unwitting prisoner, forced his brute attentions upon her, tore the clothes from her body, and threatened her with a fate far worse than death to a sensitive highstrung soul. And thus her husband found them. Think what must have passed through his mind, when he burst into that room to find the wife he loved and adored naked and helpless in the cage of that black gorilla.[17]

With its racial imagery so raw, it may at first be hard to see that this speech was intended to be ironic and funny. (When enacted onstage it vastly amused the New York critics, who lavished praise on its "sly irony.") The irony stems from the fact that the lawyer's scenario so ill-fits the truth. Babe was not an "unwitting prisoner," and Johnson did not "force his brute attentions upon her"; on the contrary, it was Babe who surveyed Johnson's naked torso and tore off her black lace dress, in a state of feverish arousal. As the audience would have recognized, the defense attorney reshapes their encounter in terms lifted straight from Victorian melodrama: black male lust assaults white feminine virtue. But Babe by no means embodies "the honor of white womanhood"—nor would the audience have wanted her to. The humor drew on the nightlifer's modern, rebellious conviction that pride in white modesty is old-fashioned and false.

With that humor at its center, *Babe Gordon* determinedly refuted the Victorian vision of white sexuality as radically different from black. In the process it deflated the most hyped of Victorian sexual nightmares: it refused to demonize black men and women as sinister sexual threats. All the same, one wouldn't want to claim too much for West's novel—or for the white enthusiasm for Harlem from which it sprang. Nightlifers' passion for black "barbarism" simply placed a positive cast on Victorian racial mythology; it never disputed that mythology itself. Where Victorians had feared black "hypersexuality," nightlifers adored it: they paraded their *lack* of fear, their ability to enjoy it as a titillating spectacle. But in so doing they turned black men and women into little more than objects— exotic and alluring objects to be sure, but objects nonetheless.

In objectifying its black characters, *Babe Gordon* was no doubt a product of its time. Yet even in that context, West's excursion into "primitive Harlem" leaves a peculiarly unpleasant taste. In her zeal to flaunt her unshockability in the face of black sexuality, West comments on it with a worldly familiarity that more than occasionally slips into contempt. Money Johnson, for example, labeled Babe's "nigger lover," is at once sensationalized and derided: in the eyes of the press he's a vicious rapist, but to Babe he becomes simply a buffoon and a bore. "She had become quite used to Baldwin's more sophisticated brand of passion," West coolly states when Johnson begs Babe to return to him. "And she had lost her interest in this big dinge."[18] West is certainly no moralist, no Victorian— she's not recoiling from the danger blacks allegedly represented; instead, she's parading herself as a worldly woman, a sexual connoisseur who is far too experienced to succumb to black primitivism and indeed finds it faintly grotesque.

Distasteful as this is, it may be understandable. Mae West had based her career on her reputation as New York's premier underworld expert. By 1930 her position could be challenged by no one—except, perhaps, by the people of Harlem. Their muchvaunted "barbarism" made them, in a sense, her professional rivals. *Babe Gordon* was Mae West's attempt to retain her preeminence. To prove herself the underworld's master, she had to prove her mastery of *them*.

In the late summer of 1931 West returned to the site of her *Diamond Lil* triumph, Broadway's Royale Theater, to prepare her new production, *The Constant Sinner*. To judge by the talk, her page-to-

stage strategy looked certain to pay off. Critics were widely predict-
ing that West's new comedy-drama would be one of the smashes of
the forthcoming season. West's backers, the Shuberts, agreed: they
seized on West's play as the new season's salvation and rushed it
into a September debut.

Despite the high hopes, West found herself faced with a vexing
dilemma: how to stage her high-voltage novel in a style that
retained her new mass appeal. *Diamond Lil* had pointed the way
with its fortuitous blend of the lurid and the fantastical, setting its
pornographer star against an overblown, sentimentalized underworld backdrop. *The Constant Sinner*, with its focus on interracial
sex, had more than its share of the lurid; what it needed was a suit-
ably comfortable underworld that would surround the star with an
aura of fantasy, titillating audiences while not scaring them off—a
challenge given the materials of West's novel.

While "primitive Harlem" was on widespread display in the commercial culture of Prohibition-era New York, it offered a controversial brand of pleasure, particularly in live performance. Harlem
plays and nightclubs that sought broad middle-class patronage took
care to prune out its most troublesome elements. As most nightlife
entrepreneurs sensed, no primitive extravaganza could be commercially viable if it made white patrons uneasy—if, in other words, it
threatened the psychological underpinnings of basic structures of
power. Precisely that threat would have been posed by an erotic celebration of black men, one suggesting that black males were
endowed with a degree of virility that white men, by comparison,
lacked.[19]

Accordingly, New York's most successful primitivist spectacles
channeled Harlem's allure through black female bodies. Thurman
and Rapp's *Harlem*, for example, revolved around the exploits of
an insatiable black adventuress and ran advertisements that showed
a naked black woman presiding over a panoply of nightlife amusements. Barron's Exclusive Club on West 134th Street drew hordes
of white patrons with its chorus of "colored girls . . . clad only in
brassieres and trunks . . . [who perform] a very wild and suggestive
dance, imitating the act of sexual intercourse, in which each one in
turn tries to outdo the other."[20] In both New York and Chicago,
black female singers of provocative blues won an avid white following in clubs and on records—unlike most of their male counterparts. As would remain the case for the next several decades, black

women singing sensual blues-based material could get engagements in white-oriented nightclubs; black men singing similar material could not.[21]

Race mixing posed a more immediate problem: undoubtedly titillating on paper, it drew municipal ire in practice. During the late 1920s the rise of Harlem as a white nightlife center caught the attention of civic reform groups, who focused much of their crusading energy on race mixing in nightclubs. By 1926 their protests had generated sufficient heat that Police Commissioner McLaughlin told Harlem club managers to observe racial proprieties—an order with which many chose to comply. The Cotton Club solved the problem by refusing to admit any black patrons at all; others, like Happy Rhone's at 143rd and Lenox, admitted black customers but forbade interracial socializing within. Many club owners acted out of sheer self-interest, not only to cultivate friends in high places but to avoid possible offense to their white patrons. These were expensive, high-profile clubs: they ran advertisements in the *New Yorker* and catered to a well-heeled upper-middle-class crowd. Though "black savagery" was the big attraction, club managers kept it at a safe distance; it was unclear how close to actual black people their thrill-seeking customers wanted to be.

But while some clubs complied with McLaughlin's orders, others did not. Race mixing was the rule, not the exception, at Harlem dives frequented by more adventurous whites in search of ever more "authentic" sensation (as well as cheaper prices after the Wall Street crash). At Edmond's, the Oriental, and the Capitol Palace, "the nightlifers," noted Jimmy Durante, "don't know there is such a thing as a color line."[22] Those clubs, and the vice trade they harbored, aroused fierce opposition from both middle-class blacks and reform-minded whites, who combined forces in an undercover investigation of Harlem clubs mounted in 1928 by the Committee of Fourteen.

That context of municipal unease shaped West's staging of *The Constant Sinner*. As she clearly realized, it would require great care to convert the book's interracial plot into a comfortable fantasy. Accordingly, her press releases barely mentioned Harlem; instead, they focused on West's now-patented spectacle: "The swaggering walk, drawling voice and impudent bearing so familiar to theatergoers are again manifested in her latest sensation."[23] The play itself picked selectively from West's novel in a hesitant, not to say timid, way, as was most evident in its treatment of Money Johnson, the black racketeer and onetime pimp whose liaison with Babe forms the novel's sensational core. West's book depicted Johnson as "a huge, lordly lion" with "hot burning eyes," "a magnificent animal" who has no hesitation in expressing his appetites and loves Babe with a passion nearly beyond his control:

> His hand started moving down her arms, fingering her black lace dress.
> "Take dis here thing off," he cried. "Ah jus' can't stand it. Ah'm jus' goin' to lose mah mind, that's all!"[24]

Onstage, however, the savage Money Johnson was rendered almost entirely mute.[25] Though a commanding figure in the Harlem underworld, he never gave voice to his sexual desires. He certainly did not finger Babe's dress and urge her to rip off her clothes. In only one scene did he appear with her alone, sitting in a chair while Babe leaned against a bureau at the opposite end of the stage. In the course of the play the pair never embraced; they barely even touched. Finally, if all that weren't caution enough, the actor who played Johnson was white.

West hired George Givot, an ex-vaudevillian, to act the part of Money Johnson in blackface. "We hit on an old-time make-up," Givot told West's biographer George Eells, "Warrenson's Number Four. Under the lights I looked fine, even alongside the twenty blacks Mae made J. J. Shubert hire for small roles and atmosphere."[26] But that he should look *too* convincing was not the idea. Though presumably the sight of a white man in blackface was familiar to anyone who'd ever stepped inside a theater, West had Givot unmask himself, doffing his wig at the curtain call to reveal a strip of white skin beneath.

Casting a black actor to play a white woman's black lover on Broadway in 1931 would have caused an uproar, perhaps even provoking police intervention, but hot municipal issue or no, it would not have been unprecedented. The interracial liaison enacted by an interracial cast had been introduced in 1924, when the Provincetown Players staged Eugene O'Neill's *All God's Chillun Got Wings*, a dramatic study of a mixed marriage starring Paul Robeson and Mary Blair.

Penned by the pioneer of American modernist drama, *All God's*

Chillun had the mantle of avant-garde art to protect it. (Even so, it occasioned much public outrage, with some papers calling for a vice squad raid.) No such protection awaited Mae West. Had she followed its lead and cast a black actor, *The Constant Sinner* would undoubtedly have created an even more intense furor. Yet that had never dissuaded West in the past. On the contrary, raiding the high-minded terrain of art theater was precisely the sort of activity she relished. Now, however, the woman who had boasted to Noël Coward of staging *Pleasure Man* with "seventeen real live fairies onstage"[27] shied away from casting one real live black man on the grounds that it was simply too risky.

It seems clear that West wanted to disabuse her audience of the slightest suspicion that her play was more than pure fantasy. To some extent, she may have been spurred by the Shuberts' misgivings, eager producers though they were. Yet the blame cannot be placed on the Shuberts alone, for even staged in such timid fashion, *The Constant Sinner* evidently made West herself nervous. It certainly prompted her to resort to decidedly atypical behavior: a highly unusual curtain speech in which she disclaimed all connection between herself and her character, stressing that the sensational antics of Babe Gordon bore no resemblance to the private life of Mae West. That message reappeared, in expanded form, in a press release West issued after the play's premiere, which the *New York Times* printed with the wry note that "Mae West, it appears, is just a misunderstood woman":

> As a corollary to the success of my latest play, reports come to me that there is a great deal of idle gossip going around New York reflecting upon my personal character. . . . I do a play like *The Constant Sinner*—depicting a phase of life which every civic-minded person must understand if there is to be any improvement in the moral tone of the city—and I hear that I am retailing dirt out of my private experiences, and doing it for the effect on the box office.
>
> But nobody ever saw me in the dives which I am supposed to know so intimately and which I have put on the stage in *The Constant Sinner*. The reason is, I was never in one. Nobody ever sees me in nightclubs and cabarets, anywhere, whatever their reputation. Even if I cared for night life, which I don't, I wouldn't have time to indulge myself in it.
>
> People who know their Broadway will bear me out that there is

no star on the stage today who is less of an exhibitionist or who shows herself less in public places than myself.

I am, in fact, retiring by nature, in my private life, to the point of shyness. I even do all my shopping by telephone, because I cannot stand all the attention other shoppers give me in a store. I am not upstage or conceited or anything like that, as anyone who knows me will agree, but it is averse to my nature to feel myself being pointed out in public as a celebrity.

For that same reason, perhaps, I live very quietly on Long Island when I have no theatrical engagement, and in an apartment on Park Avenue when I am playing, as at present. On the stage I may dress vividly; but off it I am usually attired in black. I do not drink, I do not smoke. I have my books, my writing, my friends—that is my private life.

And otherwise, I could not have experienced what I show on the stage, for I never have had time. Since the age of six I have been a professional actress, with scarcely an interval in that time when I was not playing or—as in recent years—writing at some novel or play.

The public wants Mae West, as the success of my current play shows once more, just as it wants an end to prohibition. I intend on my part to keep faith with the public.[28]

Coming from a woman who had made her name by parading her intimacy with New York's "feverish nightworld," this was an extraordinary statement. In the strictest sense, it was probably more or less true. West visited nightclubs, but only occasionally, her devotion to her career being so consuming that it ate up most of her scant leisure time. But what's intriguing here is less the statement's validity than the fact that West felt compelled to make it. That what provoked her was a play about interracial sex in Harlem was surely no coincidence. West was wary of being mistaken for Babe Gordon, and extremely disturbed by the prospect that her audience might believe she'd had sex with a black man.

As the play's run continued, West's nervousness mounted and even tempered her customary flamboyance. Backstage one evening West approached Adele Gilbert, a supporting actress in *The Constant Sinner* cast, and a predictable West target, with her slight build, demure appearance, and paid-up membership in the Daughters of the American Revolution. At first West retailed her voluminous sexual experience, but at one crucial point she felt obliged to retreat. She had "done everything," West announced—"except," she added hastily, "cross the color line."[29]

If West seemed unusually eager to disclaim any intimacy with the black men of Harlem, it may well have been because she *had* taken black lovers. In the mid-1950s the scandal sheet *Confidential* alleged precisely that, and an infuriated West hit them with a lawsuit. But in the more liberal 1960s she occasionally spoke fondly of a black boyfriend she'd had as a teenager in Brooklyn—though even then she entrusted such recollections only to a few interviewers.[30]

But just as crucial here as West's personal passions was her reputation as a performer. As she may well have realized, her own theatrics and those of black culture had been judged uneasily similar in the past. The pre–*Diamond Lil* Mae West had defied convention and achieved a kind of stardom as, in essence, a primitive, an unvarnished exemplar of sexual realism—much the same aura as surrounded black men and women, as did not escape some of West's contemporaries. One actress remembered that West's early Broadway exploits earned her the title "World's Wickedest White Woman," a phrase that suggested an excess of lewdness rivaled only by legions of lascivious blacks.[31] Critic George Jean Nathan, in a scathing attack on *Pleasure Man* and "the West woman" as an artless vulgarian "usurping the theatre to her nasty purposes," reached for a comparison that was explicitly racial: she knew "absolutely no more about playwriting than the colored piano professor in a bawdy house."[32]

Although Nathan wrote with his usual flippant elitism, in fact West's early performances bore clear debts to black culture and particularly the black bawdy house, as the African-American folklorist and novelist Zora Neale Hurston attested. In 1926, while studying anthropology at Barnard College, Hurston had followed the crowds to Daly's Sixty-third Street Theater to see Mae West in *Sex*. In her eyes the play was not in the least shocking; on the contrary she found it rather amusing, largely because it borrowed so heavily from the pleasure houses of the black underworld, establishments Hurston called by their slang name, "jooks." As she remembered eight years later:

I noted that Mae West in *Sex* had much more flavor of the turpentine quarters than she did of the white bawd. I know that the piece she played on the piano is a very old jook composition. "Honey Let

Yo' Drawers Hang Low" had been played and sung in every jook in the South for at least 35 years. It has always puzzled me why she thought it likely to be played in a Canadian bawdy house.[33]

What Hurston found puzzling many whites found disturbing, even if they didn't recognize or couldn't articulate just how direct West's racial borrowings were. What they did recognize was a seemingly unmediated, fully fleshed physicality, an aggressive sexuality that they readily associated with black women but that they linked to white women of only the most debased sort. Since the turn of the century middle-class discourse had jointly stigmatized black women and working-class "tough girls" as "hypersexuals," who were mentally unstable, even moronic, and driven by rapacious desire. As literary critic Sander Gilman has shown, that vision found its way into art, literature, and public health tracts, which conflated black females and white prostitutes as symbols of pathological erotic excess.[34]

Mae West was a white woman offering sexual entertainment in a profoundly race-conscious world. In a sense her performances had always been about race. Part of their thrill lay in seeing a white woman daring to be bad, bad in a way an earlier generation associated most strongly with blacks. The product of an immigrant neighborhood, West grew up in what Lothrop Stoddard would have deemed a racially alien subculture. In vaudeville she had highlighted a "tough girl" style that borrowed heavily from black culture: she performed "rag" and "turkey" dances, the sensual steps featured in underworld amusement dives and rooted in African dance. At times she borrowed even more directly, particularly when she wanted to give her act extra fire, though in later years she would not always acknowledge her source. On a vaudeville tour in 1914, observing black dancers on the South Side of Chicago, West learned the wriggling pelvic dance called the shimmy and incorporated it into her act forthwith. Four years later she created a minor sensation in *Sometime* with what *Variety* labeled the rawest shimmy in New York. (In the program for *The Constant Sinner*, West's capsule biography claimed that she was the dance's originator.) In her most transgressive moments the Broadway Mae West was linked to black culture and derided for her raw vulgarity.

Yet West, unlike African-Americans, had a way out. Black performers working in New York in her era simply could not escape from their "primitive" aura—that, not their artistry, remained the source of their appeal even for their most ardent and erudite fans. Critic and novelist Carl Van Vechten, for example, lauded Bessie Smith in essence not for performing but for exuding savage emotion like some "conjure woman" whose voice had its source at the heart of the Nile.[35] Mae West, in contrast, was able to silence charges of primitivism by changing her style in *Diamond Lil,* where she veiled her seeming rawness in irony and won praise as a proficient performer, an artist.

Having risen above primitivism, West was determined to stay there, and she was leery of any association that threatened to drag her back down. *The Constant Sinner* revealed how deep her wariness ran. It showcased a new Mae West, conscious of herself as a public presence, concerned to retain her mainstream fans' approval, and exuding narcissistic delight as never before.

For some critics this proved less than enchanting. Robert Benchley, a *Diamond Lil* fan, thoroughly loathed *The Constant Sinner.* Where it might have provided "a certain tough entertainment value," instead it tottered under "the heavy personality tax it has to bear." Benchley continued:

> Those serious-minded critics who hailed her in *Diamond Lil* as the great American actress-playwright did both her and her public a disservice, for Miss West evidently believes it and has fed upon it until she has reached an almost insupportable satisfaction with her own powers and personality. Duse herself could not have filled the stage with such an aura of complete success and confidence as that which Miss West gives off.[36]

Wilella Waldorf of the *New York Evening Post* agreed: "It's impossible to regard *The Constant Sinner* as anything more than an excuse for Mae West to show off." More distressing, West was not even showing off—"fling[ing] herself into the business of being Mae West"—with the same gusto she had shown in the past. While in *Diamond Lil* West had writhed and wriggled her way through the rowdy whorehouse ballad "Frankie and Johnny," in *The Constant Sinner* "not a song was forthcoming." Instead, in a Harlem nightclub scene, West sat "sedately" at a ringside table, "swathed in pure white . . . while a hired entertainer did an 'African Strut.' It was a bit sad," Waldorf concluded, "though perhaps a bit more dignified than 'Frankie and Johnny.' "[37]

One can hardly conjure up a more evocative image: Mae West wrapped in ermine, whiter than white, in "dignified" repose, observing torrid gyrations against a black backdrop. What Waldorf describes is in fact a fitting emblem for the whole of *The Constant Sinner*. West felt obliged to safeguard her reputation when working with black performers and enacting an interracial liaison between a white hooker and a black ex-pimp. Her "dignity" (shorthand for racial privilege and social reputability) demanded that she distance herself, more explicitly than ever, from the sexual spectacle her play exploited. For all its apparent daring, *The Constant Sinner* reveals a newly cautious Mae West, eager to capitalize on the lure of black Harlem but afraid of being besmirched by its taint. For the first time in her career, Mae West was worried about her reputation.

To be fair, it should be noted that West's new decorum had definite limits, as the events of subsequent months would show. *The Constant Sinner* drew mixed reviews in New York City but not nearly the anticipated wealth of attention; some critics found it amusing, a few found it offensive, but most found it a bit of a bore. Audiences, too, seemed indifferent. Clearly, West had fallen short of both the crowd pleaser of *Diamond Lil* and the shocker of *Sex*, *Pleasure Man*, and *The Drag*. In contrast to *Lil*'s ten-month first run, *The Constant Sinner* closed after a mere seven weeks.

By mid-November West had apparently come to blame the play's failure on an excess of caution. As she prepared for a national tour, she abandoned most of the hesitations that had constrained her before. Despite strong opposition from the Shuberts she determined to open in Chicago with a black actor as Money Johnson. That plan, however, soon came to nothing. Before West had a chance to put it into action, *The Constant Sinner* opened for a week's engagement in Washington, D.C., where two performances earned it more press notoriety than it had achieved in seven weeks in New York. Deemed "obscene and indecent" by the local district attorney, the play was threatened with a raid from the vice squad, and the Shuberts closed it down after the second performance. At that, West's frustration with the project was strained beyond endurance, and she abandoned all plans for a national tour.

If nothing else, this episode must have emphasized for West the difference between New York and the national market, at least when it came to commercial fantasies of crossing boundaries of race and of class. *The Constant Sinner* provoked only yawns in New York, but it threatened to provoke the vice squad in Washington. Clearly, this was one fantasy whose very outlines proved too transgressive for the national market, particularly below the Mason-Dixon line. In the 1930s the Prohibition craze for "primitive Harlem" would be one component of New York commercial culture that Hollywood emphatically refused to touch. African-Americans ceased being enticing savages and became support staff to white exotics, as they would be to Mae West.

Chapter 8

MAE WEST MANIA

*O*n October 19, 1932, Harry Warner, head of Warner Brothers, sent an urgent telegram to Will Hays, head of the Motion Picture Producers and Distributors of America (MPPDA):

> Please wire immediately whether I can believe my ears that Paramount has arranged to make *Diamond Lil* with Mae West.
> . . . Recollect that it was absolutely definite that *Diamond Lil*
> . . . was not to be produced stop I am not sending this wire as a protest but I want to know how to run our business in the future.[1]

Paramount's decision to sign Mae West and produce her Broadway play *Diamond Lil* sent not just Warner but the whole film industry into turmoil. Until the fall of 1932 it had indeed seemed "absolutely definite" that *Diamond Lil* would never be filmed. Since 1930, when Universal Pictures had briefly considered it for purchase, it had remained firmly on the industry "banned list," a roster of theatrical and literary properties reviewed and judged unsuitable for the screen by the MPPDA, the film companies' self-regulatory body, popularly known as the Hays Office.

Diamond Lil may have been reasonably uncontroversial on

Broadway, but that did not make it uncontroversial in Hollywood—or, as some industry strategists might have put it, on the
"Main Streets" of the American heartland. Like *The Shanghai Gesture* and *Lulu Belle*, which the MPPDA resolution of October
1930 also banned from "picturization," *Diamond Lil* had gained
nationwide renown as a ribald example of New York's Prohibition
nightlife.[2] West came to Hollywood from a Broadway that had
built its reputation on the style of theatrics she had helped to make
famous, marked by a "realism" that blurred the boundaries
between theater, nightlife, and vice.

As a potential source of actors, writers, and screenplays, that
entertainment culture posed no end of problems for the MPPDA.
Established in 1922 in the wake of a series of Hollywood scandals,
and headed by former postmaster general Will Hays, the MPPDA
aimed to protect the industry's economic and political interests, in
part by forestalling controversies that would threaten its power and
profits, and that inevitably loomed whenever the movies tried to
replicate the appeal of Broadway.

An urban amusement turned mass entertainment, the movies had
long provoked suspicion and fear. Their early popularity in city
slums and the prominence of immigrant Jews among the film
moguls made the new industry anathema to many Americans, particularly those outside the big cities, members of a provincial Protestant middle class who feared encroachment by an alien metropolitan world. As historian Richard Maltby has written, "With the road
house and the dance hall, the movie theater was one site at which
they felt their values and their children endangered by a newer,
urban, immigrant, largely Jewish and Catholic culture."[3] Their
sense of embattlement increased with the coming of sound, which
threatened to transplant Broadway's much-publicized "realism"
directly to Main Street. By the end of the 1920s seven states had
established censorship boards, and many congressmen had begun to
call for a centralized federal censorship.[4]

In Hays's view the film industry, like it or not, had to take this
hostility seriously. While Broadway could afford to revel in its reputation for serving up metropolitan wickedness, filmmakers could
not: they had to sell their product around the country, in small
towns as well as big cities, under the scrutiny of state regulators.
That would be impossible if they alienated opinion shapers in
churches, reform groups, and local government. Not only did such

individuals fill the ranks of the state censorship boards; even more worryingly, as their success in implementing Prohibition had shown, they could exert a powerful influence in Washington.

To counter the threat, Hays set out to unite the industry behind a clear public relations strategy: selling movies as a brand of entertainment that was quintessentially mainstream, detached from the worlds of theater and publishing and in line with the values of the American heartland. Beginning in the mid-1920s the MPPDA issued a series of resolutions pledging its commitment to wholesome features and endorsing the distaste of civic and religious groups for New York commercial culture. Over the next several years the campaign intensified, and at the end of the decade, with great fanfare, the MPPDA adopted the Production Code, a statement of industry policy that spurned "immoral" films and affirmed responsibility for the moral well-being of the viewer. Additionally, through a procedure known as "the Formula," the industry promised strict scrutiny of all potential film projects drawn from publishing and the theater. It was this procedure that gave rise to the "banned list" and the presence on it of *Diamond Lil*. On the surface, at least, the film industry stood in opposition to the very theatrical milieu from which Mae West sprang, its resources mobilized, as Hays put it, behind a "special effort to prevent the prevalent type of book and play from becoming the prevalent type of picture."[5]

Under the circumstances, what was remarkable was not that it took Hollywood so long to court West but that she got a film contract at all. To be sure, she didn't get it without a struggle—as well as some assistance from an old flame. Rising matinee idol George Raft helped to engineer West's screen debut in what was essentially a novelty role. A former henchman of *Diamond Lil*'s financier, New York racketeer Owney Madden, Raft had met West during the play's run when he paid regular backstage visits to collect Madden's share of the box office receipts. Four years later, when Paramount needed a character player for Raft's nightclub melodrama *Night After Night*, he urged the studio to pass up its first choice, Texas Guinan, in favor of "a woman who'd be terrific. Mae West." On the advice of Raft and the film's producer, William Le Baron, Paramount offered West a two-month contract at $5,000 a week. On June 16, 1932, contract in hand, she boarded a train for Hollywood.[6]

No one—not Raft, not Le Baron, not Paramount head Adolph

Zukor—expected anything more to come of West's appearance. For one thing, West herself—"fat, fair and I don't know how near forty," columnist Louella Parsons caustically observed—was clearly no conventional Hollywood siren.[7] More to the point was the notoriety she'd built through her exploits on Broadway. As Zukor would later recall, filmmakers considered her a raw New York novelty—and not even a timely one at that.[8] Her last Broadway play, *The Constant Sinner,* had closed after a matter of weeks, and to some that seemed emblematic of both West's decline and the collapse of the New York nightlife culture that bred her. The stock market crash in 1929 had drastically eroded the Times Square economy: by 1932 cabaret patronage had dwindled, playhouses stood empty, and the Shubert chain of theaters had gone into receivership. Perhaps it was the case, as one critic speculated, that American audiences had lost their taste for sensationalism, that West's raucous theatrics were not "in a Depression tune."[9]

Yet with all odds against her, West's debut convinced a skeptical Paramount that she could prove a worthwhile investment. Cast as Maudie Triplett, Raft's blowsy ex-mistress, she did wonders with a small role, a performance all the more remarkable for being her first in front of a camera. If nothing else, she showed Paramount that they were dealing with an expert scene stealer. Mortified on reading the original script to find hers a slight and colorless part, she insisted on rewriting all her lines and virtually directing all her scenes, forcing a standoff with her director until Le Baron intervened in her favor. As a result, and as was clearly her aim, she succeeded in upstaging everyone around her. The sheer pace of her delivery made her stand out. Reversing the choreography she'd deployed onstage (the "supple, flowing, coolly insinuating" style that would become a hallmark of her films), West sped up her movements and banter, lending an air of boisterous exuberance to her tart one-liners: "Goodness, what beautiful diamonds!" "Goodness had nothing to do with it, dearie." Her alterations won her the studio's respect as a skilled actress who could shape her own material. In addition, they won her plaudits from critics, warm letters from fans, and praise from theater owners, fifty-five hundred of whom rebooked the film on the strength of audience enthusiasm for her performance.[10]

Night After Night helped spur a hesitant Paramount to take a chance on *Diamond Lil,* but it wasn't decisive in itself. While the studio now had proof of West's talents and her ability to amuse a film audience, weighing against those factors was the emphatic sentiment that *Lil* could only do the film industry harm. That sentiment had not only placed it on the banned list but had guided the decisions of studio heads: it had led Universal to reject West's play back in 1930, and it still colored the thinking of Harry Warner, as his shocked telegram to Will Hays demonstrates. What ultimately tipped the balance was a shift in Paramount's Hollywood management that took the studio in a new direction, a sensational foray into a controversial filmmaking trend.

Until 1932 Paramount had been among the most cooperative of studios in putting Will Hays's ideas into action. Under its production head, B. P. Schulberg, it hewed to the guidelines dictated by Hays and the Studio Relations Committee (SRC), his office's West Coast representative charged with administering the Production Code in detail. However, Schulberg wasn't alone among the film moguls in believing in the wisdom of Hays's commercial approach. Though lampooned in most histories as a hapless prude unable to rein in an unruly industry, Hays had much more success than is commonly recognized. Research into the MPPDA files makes clear that well before 1934 (when the Hays Office was reconstituted in a blaze of publicity and the Production Code supposedly fitted with teeth), Hays had united much of filmdom behind his effort to restrict and regulate controversial content.[11]

Nonetheless, difficulties remained—moments when the industry moved in a direction the Hays Office abhorred. While all company heads endorsed the wisdom of Hays's long-term strategy, at least on the surface, individual producers sometimes risked alienating moralists in the service of short-term profits. When their films cleaned up at the box office, all of the studios would follow suit, in line with their "crude but reliable market mechanism" of imitating recent screen hits.[12] This penchant and the periodic film cycles it spawned caused the Hays Office no end of worry. In 1930 and 1931 it generated a spate of gangster films that sent reform groups into an uproar and necessitated special action by Hays's board of directors, which issued a public declaration that the studios would "voluntarily" cease production of such films. By late 1931 the locus of the problem had shifted, as Hays lieutenant Jason Joy noted: "With crime practically denied them, with box office figures down, with high-pressure methods being employed back home to spur the studios to get in a little more cash," filmmakers turned to another "sure-fire" crowd-pleaser: sex.[13]

The years 1931 and 1932 saw the release by all major studios of a cycle of what the Hays Office dubbed "sex films": *Back Street*, *Possessed*, and *Blonde Venus*, among others, tales of the sexual transgressions of beautiful and willfully modern young women. Their tone melodramatic, their conclusions moralistic, they drew their novelty—and to the censors, their danger—from the aura of glamor with which they surrounded the heroine. Inverting the formula of nineteenth-century melodrama, in which fallen women descended into privation and squalor, the new narratives rewarded loose-living women with luxury (though depriving them again in the final reel). As an alarmed Will Hays noted, these films laid the industry open to charges of glamorizing illicit sex—charges that intensified in June 1932 when MGM released *Red-Headed Woman*. Starring Jean Harlow as a gleeful gold digger sleeping her way up the social ladder, *Red-Headed Woman* constituted an all-time screen low, the moralists railed: its ending left Harlow unrepentant and unpunished, luxuriating in Parisian riches, and, throughout, the film invested her waywardness with humor and scrapped the conventional melodramatics. By July 1932 the Hays Office was wringing its hands over the extremes to which the film might press other studios. "Probably right now," wrote Joy, "half the other companies are trying to figure out ways of topping this picture."[14]

That definitely applied to Paramount. In 1932, burdened by falling revenues and mounting debts and tottering on the brink of receivership, the studio that had long been a model of caution and one of Hays's favorites set off on an abrupt new course. Under the stewardship of Emanuel Cohen, its new chief of production, Paramount broke with its longstanding conservatism and cashed in on the proven market for *Red-Headed Woman* by buying properties other studios wouldn't touch. Over the next twelve months Paramount would produce Ernest Hemingway's *A Farewell to Arms*, buy the screen rights to William Faulkner's *Sanctuary*, and announce plans for a film entitled *Virgins in Cellophane*.[15] Most troublesome from Hays's perspective were rumors that surfaced late in October: that the studio had given the go-ahead for *Diamond Lil*.

For Paramount this decision made commercial sense. For the Hays Office it promised disaster, and not only because of the prospect of a big-screen Mae West. More ominous still was

Paramount's modus operandi—its failure to consult the Hays Office. According to the 1930 agreement signed by all the major film companies, potentially troublesome Broadway properties were subject to review by the MPPDA board of directors, which would determine whether they could be filmed at all and what restrictions should apply. Clearly defined and scrupulously observed thus far, this process was intended to provide demonstrable proof of the industry's sense of social responsibility, its "special effort to prevent the prevalent type of book and play from becoming the prevalent type of picture."

But in late 1932, as it readied *Diamond Lil* for production, Paramount took no notice of the MPPDA board. By mid-November three versions of a script had been drafted, cast and crew hired, and players rehearsed, all in blithe defiance of a flurry of letters, phone calls, and personal visits from Dr. James Wingate, the head of the Studio Relations Committee and the Hays Office's chief West Coast official. On November 23, when Wingate learned that filming was to start in two days, the MPPDA flew into a panic. An aggrieved Will Hays informed Adolph Zukor:

> The serious element, of course, is that they start to shoot the picture on Friday. By all means this ought to be stopped as it is a direct violation by Paramount of its most solemn agreement. You realize, as I do, the serious effect this will have on the other companies.[16]

"Serious effect" was putting it mildly. What Hays foresaw was nothing less than an end to even a pretense of self-regulation, an intensified outcry from reform groups, and federal legislation that could restrict not just movie content but lucrative monopoly trade practices. Up to that moment Hays had kept government regulators at bay through his much-heralded system of internal control; but Paramount, by flouting MPPDA procedures entirely, threatened to strain the system to the breaking point.

At the eleventh hour that threat was averted, at least for the time being. Hays managed to win the ear of Adolph Zukor, who issued last-minute orders to halt production until Monday, November 28, when he took West's play before the MPPDA board of directors. By the end of the meeting his studio had secured the requisite permission: *Diamond Lil* could be filmed, though only under the strict supervision of the Studio Relations Committee, and only with i stage origins muffled. Accordingly, the title was changed to *She Done Him Wrong*, West's character became "Lady Lou," and publicity stressed West's most famous (if misquoted) catchphrase, "Come up and see me sometime," instead of the play's best-known line, "You can be had."[17] With this compromise both Paramount and the Hays Office could claim victory: Paramount could proceed with its plans, and the Hays Office could proclaim the integrity of self-regulation, its control mechanisms bruised but not shattered. Nonetheless, Will Hays's troubles were by no means over. An even more onerous task lay ahead: averting a massive public relations problem as Paramount "picturized" a stage property that the industry had promised would never be filmed.

While the Hays Office worried about a moralist protest, Mae West faced different but no less vexing pressures. In bringing *Diamond Lil* to the screen as an employee of Paramount, she came face to face with filmmaking bureaucracy that radically diminished her accustomed control. Always suspicious of outside interference, West was compelled to turn her playscript over to Paramount's John Bright, who was hired to do the screen adaptation. West hated Bright nearly from the beginning; through skilled bargaining she won the right to approve any changes he made in the original script.[18] Other changes, however, were not so easily dealt with—the changes advised by the Studio Relations Committee.

In later years and in her autobiography West minimized the importance of the negotiations with the censors. To judge by her reminiscences, the Hays Office was but a trivial annoyance that she deflected with a canny deployment of subterfuge:

> When I knew that the censors were after my films and they had to come and okay everything, I wrote scenes for them to cut! Those scenes were so rough that I'd never have used them. But they worked as a decoy. They cut them and left the stuff I wanted. I had these scenes in there about a man's fly and all that, and the censors would be sittin' in the projection room laughing themselves silly. Then they'd say "cut it" and not notice the rest. Then when the film came out and people laughed at it and the bluenoses were outraged, they came and said, "Mae, you didn't show us that." But I'd show them the scripts they had okayed themselves![19]

There is no doubt that scriptwriters did employ such strategies, submitting "decoy" material that was sure to be cut in hopes of retaining what mattered, but West's account obscures more than it clarifies of both the method and scope of the censorship process. Her assertions to the contrary, Hays Office regulation did not involve men in projection booths demanding deletions from completed films. While state censor boards could and did demand cuts from films to be exhibited within their jurisdiction, such demands represented failures of the industry's own regulatory process, which got under way on every Hollywood production well before the cameras began to roll. This was no less true of West's first starring feature than it was of any other studio film. Within twenty-four hours of the emergency board meeting, the SRC's Dr. Wingate wrote to Paramount's Harold Hurley to comment at length on the first proposed script; over the next few weeks Wingate scrutinized every aspect of the film's production—each successive script draft, all the song lyrics, and the finishing touches for the release print.

For its part, Paramount cooperated fully, forwarding scripts, requesting suggestions, and in most cases acting on them. Despite its previous indifference to Hays Office approval, here it acted willingly, out of pure self-interest. Unhappy as Hays and his officials might be about sex films in general and *Diamond Lil* in particular, they aimed to assist, not impede, once the studio prepared for production. Their suggestions dealt far more in pragmatics than morals. Through advice on dialogue, characterization, setting, and "atmosphere," they guided Paramount in shaping controversial material so as to safeguard its investment and protect the film against costly deletions by state censor boards.

As a consequence, in taking *Diamond Lil* from stage to screen, West had to contend with a censorship procedure much more systematic and comprehensive than she was ever willing to admit. At the same time, however, she can perhaps be excused a bit of gloating: despite weeks of Hays Office tinkering, the fact is that *Diamond Lil* emerged unscathed from the negotiations, arriving onscreen as *She Done Him Wrong*, the new alterations largely unnoticeable. Certainly they were unnoticeable to critics who had adored the original play. "Nothing much changed except the title, but don't tell that to Will Hays," was *Variety*'s verdict on the film version.[20]

Diamond Lil's apparent success in eluding regulation demands some explaining, since even a glance at film and playscript makes clear that there were indeed changes. Certain elements of the play were scrapped without argument in John Bright's first draft, before any intervention by the Hays Office, including references to homosexuality, drug use, and white slavery, which any experienced scriptwriter knew were forbidden. Accordingly, Bright deleted the play's occasional suggestions that one minor character was homosexual, dropped an exchange in which Lil supplies a dope fiend with cocaine, and altered a subplot in which saloon owner Gus Jordan and an accomplice ship young women to Rio as prostitutes.[21] (This last change did prove problematic: while acknowledging that white slavery had to go, the studio proved much less decisive about what sort of racket to put in its place, and in the film it remains unclear.)

Yet such incidents, despite West's undoubted reluctance to lose them, were largely incidental to the play's focus, which lay full force upon Lil and her sexual exploits in pursuit of protection, diamonds, and pleasure. Here *Diamond Lil* had its greatest success in outwitting the censors, for its brand of sensationalism proved impervious to the controls the Hays Office tried to impose.

The Hays Office's approach to *Diamond Lil* stemmed from its experience with other sex films, most of them tales of ambitious women who used love affairs to move up the social and material ladder. In vetting such stories, the censors had a clear aim: to get them onscreen in a form that could turn a profit without causing trouble for the film industry. That did not mean deleting sexual material entirely. As in Keith Circuit vaudeville, the mass-market precursor of motion pictures, the censors sought to walk a fine line: to avoid offending the traditional without boring the adventurous. This goal demanded strategies of screen representation in which sexual content was not overt but suggested, "from which conclusions might be drawn by the sophisticated mind, but which would mean nothing to the unsophisticated and inexperienced," as James Wingate's precursor Jason Joy put it.[22]

In practice, this meant infusing sex films with a high degree of ambiguity. The SRC urged that wherever possible, the heroine's sexual encounters be shown indirectly, through vague verbal or visual allusions, leaving it an open question when (or whether) they took place. Just as important, the SRC insisted, the film should not seem to endorse her conduct. If only for the purpose of disarming critics, it had to condemn her, whether through scenes in which she is denounced by others, or through the woman's own repentance, or (as the SRC urged for *Red-Headed Woman*) through humor: making the heroine so farcical that it ought to be impossible to take her conduct seriously.[23]

From the beginning the SRC's James Wingate approached *Diamond Lil* with an eye to the last strategy. Clearly, it needed some sort of revision, given its reputation as a ribald slumming excursion, a sensational example of the new Broadway realism. As Wingate commented to Hays, "The basic elements of the original story and its Bowery background must of necessity bring it within the category of low-tone pictures."[24] The solution they found to the problem of tone struck them as foolproof: veiling the story in nostalgia and comedy. The Hays Office, in other words, would out-West Mae West by employing precisely the devices that made *Diamond Lil* such a departure from her other Broadway forays.

Wingate's first letter to the filmmakers laid out that strategy, urging them to "develop the comedy elements, so that the treatment will invest the picture with such exaggerated qualities as automatically to take care of possible offensiveness." Over the next several weeks he worked with Paramount to put that plan into action, to ensure "that the whole picture be directed and played with sufficient emphasis on the comedy values and exaggeration of the manners and customs of the period as to remove it as far as possible from any feeling of sordid realism."[25]

Avoiding "sordid realism" demanded new material and treatment. To address Wingate's concerns about the potentially dissolute setting, the filmmakers thickened the air of nostalgia. The transition to film in itself facilitated this: the movie employed period music not just within the narrative (that is, performed in the saloon) but as background accompaniment throughout, echoing behind the opening credits and heralding the appearances of Lady Lou. Those jangling melodies and barbershop harmonies helped to defuse the proceedings, lending both the Bowery and Lou's exploits an even quainter sentimentality than in the stage version. The atmosphere was established in a lighthearted montage that followed the opening credits. Introducing the Bowery setting through an organ grinder and monkey, two elegant women on bicycles, and an aggravated street sweeper cleaning up after a horse, it stressed the sexual innocence of this picturesque Gay Nineties, a time "when there were handlebars on lip and wheel—and legs were confidential!" as an explanatory caption put it.

The Hays Office's main worry, however, was Lady Lou herself. Wingate bemoaned her "low-toned" characteristics, her seeming rootedness in the underworld, and sought to downplay her realism and make her a creature of fantasy. At Wingate's request, Paramount made several script changes that muted Lou's past transgressions, "soft-pedalling the many references to the number of Lady Lou's previous affairs" and leaving the nature of the relationships "open to debate."[26] In practice this meant channeling most mentions of Lou's history through comic repartee with her black maid, a wholly new character who (in the words of the first script draft, titled *Ruby Red*) "knows everything about Lou," and whose sly familiarity with her mistress allowed viewers to infer what the film could not directly state.[27] It also meant replacing blunt references to the heroine's predatory passions with allusive one-liners. Gone, for instance, was Lil's recital of her encounters with fiery lovers; in its place was Lou's memorable description of herself as "the finest woman who ever walked the streets."

In the end Wingate's attempt to tame *Diamond Lil* resulted in a substantial number of changes, but onscreen hardly anyone noticed them: they fit with uncanny neatness into the trajectory of the original script. More fully than the SRC ever realized, its strategy of investing the narrative with ambiguity and replacing sexual aggression with comedy and nostalgia had been part of the original play. Ironically, then, the more Paramount worked to implement SRC suggestions, the more like the play the film became. Successive drafts of the script make clear that West was able to use the Hays Office's insistence on comedy to her advantage in overturning many of John Bright's alterations. Bright, who had made a name for himself with *The Public Enemy*, a violent gang tale, initially sought to recast the script as a more conventional underworld drama, dropping wisecracks and inserting moments in which Lou sees the error of her ways. By the time the cameras rolled, West had reinstated many of her one-liners and cut the new emphasis on melodramatic repentance, which disrupted the desired tone of humor and fantasy.[28]

As a consequence, the film Paramount released in early 1933 struck *Variety* and most other observers as a carbon copy of *Dia-*

mond Lil. By all appearances it seemed to have a near-identical impact on audiences. The film, like the play, came across as a trip to a genial urban underworld; and despite the Hays Office's eagerness to avoid Broadway realism, reviewers brought up that word again and again. To the Hays Office's certain chagrin, nearly all noted the screenplay's stage origins—and how little it had changed in transition. Still exuding "that lusty quality which made the play indigenous to both its star and to Broadway," the film altered little except the names and the title, "to deceive Will Hays, who seems easy to deceive."[29] The script and the backgrounds may have been toned down, but juxtaposed against them were sensational elements whose power made the completed film much less safely fantastical than its regulators had hoped.

Foremost among them, of course, was Mae West herself. Neither Wingate nor Hays nor anyone else had anticipated the nature of her performance, how completely it would prove resistant to external control. One look at the completed film convinced Wingate that West's acting style subverted all his efforts to veil Lou and her surroundings in comedy. He wrote to Will Hays with obvious dismay, "Miss West gives a performance of strong realism."[30]

What Wingate saw as "realism" was West's highly conventionalized performance style, the oozing walk, the hard-boiled speech that lent unexpected saltiness to seemingly innocent lines. However familiar it may have become on Broadway, on film it shone forth as altogether novel, not least because the camera served it up as spectacle, West's body an eroticized feast for the eye. While a stage audience might have elected to watch West alone, the screen audience was given no choice. As *Variety* noted, supporting characters are "never permitted to be anything more than just background. Miss West gets all the lens gravy and full figure most of the time."[31]

In reading her sexual style as "realism," Wingate was most likely joined by much of the film's audience. Studio publicity for *She Done Him Wrong* touted its authenticity and sexual frankness, attributing them to West's real-life links to the urban underworld. Newspaper stories and fan magazine interviews generated by Paramount lavished attention on her Broadway arrests ("Welfare Island Fails to Tame the Wild West!"), on her friendship with "the Killer of Tenth Avenue," jailed racketeer Owney Madden, and even on the fact that she "freely admits she has been the patron big sister of the afflicted of what Broadway calls Fairyland."[32] This was no ordinary actress, and certainly no purveyor of fantasy, but a convicted sex offender who used the screen to display her true self. "Mae West actually courts gossip," studio publicity emphasized, "and your worst innuendoes are music to her ears."[33]

Such blatant appeals to sensationalism appalled the Hays Office—not least because they proved so effective. By early March it was apparent that with this five-year-old play by a purported has-been, Paramount had produced a sensation. Released in February around the time of Roosevelt's Bank Holiday, *She Done Him Wrong* defied the trend of declining attendance, raking in huge box office receipts even in areas where West was previously unknown, none particularly renowned for urban sophistication. Evidently good-natured slumming excursions appealed nationwide, in Mississippi no less than in Manhattan. In Birmingham, Alabama, West's film became the biggest draw in town. In Lincoln, Nebraska, it played three week-long engagements, drawing larger and more boisterous audiences each time. Return engagements, in fact, became the rule for West's picture. In a time when most movies had only a single week's run and were lucky to fill a theater for all seven days, *She Done Him Wrong* after six months of release had been called back for six thousand return engagements, surpassing the all-time record set by *The Birth of a Nation*.[34] For their part the critics adored it. Greeting the film as "astonishing entertainment," "slangy, gaudy, naively coarse and frankly ribald," reviewers across the country extolled the sheer bawdiness of West's "really brilliant" performance.[35]

Back at the Hays Office, the reviews only made matters worse. As Wingate must have realized, the gibes about West's triumph over the ineffectual Will Hays only added fuel to the reformist fire, lending new justification to the contention that the industry was unfit to control its own products. Wingate was not alone in his worries. Sidney Kent, the head of Fox Film Company, saw *She Done Him Wrong* shortly after its release and wrote an aggrieved letter to Will Hays in New York:

> In my opinion it is the worst picture I have seen. It was the real story of Diamond Lil and they got away with it. They promised that that story would not be made. I believe it is worse than *Red-Headed Woman* from the standpoint of the industry—it is far more suggestive in word and what is not said is suggested in action.

I cannot understand how your people on the Coast could let this get by. There is very little that any of us can do now.[36]

Kent's letter was a sign of forces brewing that would compel Mae West to change, despite her box office success. *She Done Him Wrong* infuriated reform groups already distressed by the onslaught of sex films and now horrified to discover that a convicted pornographer was parading onscreen for all the world to see. As their protests intensified in the spring of 1933, Will Hays became increasingly nervous. With Hollywood receiving so much bad press, and with government intervention in business an apparent trend, Washington might well decide to subject the film industry to heavy-handed federal controls. The only way to quash the threat was to tighten the self-regulatory process. By April Hays was in Hollywood haranguing filmmakers in person. More ribald productions, he warned, more Broadway sensationalism, and they could be certain of punitive government action, for they would have provided their critics with precisely the ammunition they needed.[37]

By late spring, as West prepared to begin filming a followup, she found her employers at Paramount under new pressure to proceed with care. In truth they might well have acted more prudently even without the Hays Office. *She Done Him Wrong* may have made a mint, but it also caused the studio more than a few headaches: much bad feeling within the industry, a profusion of deletions by the state censors, and an expensive last-minute cut demanded by a panicky Hays Office. One week before the premiere, and after all the prints had been sent to exhibitors, MPPDA official Vincent Hart saw the film and was shocked by West's performance, particularly her rendition of "A Guy What Takes His Time" (or "Slow Motion Man"), on paper a mild love lyric, but in West's hands a graphic celebration of languorous sex. At the insistence of Hart and Hays, Paramount recalled the prints and deleted all but the song's first and last verses. Compounding the studio's embarrassment, James Wingate wrote to the heads of all the major film companies to inform them of the Hays Office's action.[38]

This time around Paramount was determined to avoid any such wrangles and to keep West's creative influence within bounds. Though she received a full screenwriting credit for the feature that took shape over the summer and probably did contribute a skeletal narrative,[39] the final product was almost certainly fleshed out by

Paramount scriptwriter Harlan Thompson. "Harlan *wrote* the script," his widow insisted, and it seems indisputable that hands other than West's were involved.[40] At least on the surface the new vehicle, *I'm No Angel*, was more circumspect than anything she had ever created alone.

The most obvious change was in the film's setting. The tale of a circus dancer turned lion tamer who wins the heart of a society man, *I'm No Angel* extricated West from the New York City underworld on which she had built her Broadway career. Gone was even a romanticized trace of a milieu like the Bowery, whose unsavory associations had so dismayed the Hays Office. Instead, the new film was rooted more securely in fantasy, following Tira, the "dancing, singing marvel," from a carnival sideshow to a penthouse apartment and the unreal luxury of the movieland rich.

Tira too represented a bow to caution. No queen of the underworld, she is a wisecracking gold digger, shrewd and ambitious, out less explicitly for sex than for money. "Somewhere there's a guy with a million waitin' for a dame like me," Tira says, and her eagerness to find him impels the narrative, leading her from a circus tent to the lap of luxury and the seductions of orchids, diamonds, and furs.[41] At the same time there is a conspicuous if formulaic display of atonement. Unlike Lady Lou, seemingly an unashamed carouser to the final credits, Tira is reformed by love. "I never knew I could go for anyone like I have for him," she announces of her wealthy suitor Jack Clayton, and the film goes out of its way to show that she means it. When Clayton believes her unfaithful and breaks their engagement, she is genuinely shattered. "I ain't never seen nobody so broken-hearted as you was when you and Mr. Clayton done bust up," testifies her maid, Beulah. "He's made me feel like a different dame," Tira agrees. "I ain't just a Sister Honky-Tonk no more."

Clearly, Will Hays's admonitions had had some effect. Even Paramount's publicists got into the act, as *Variety* reported shortly before *I'm No Angel*'s release:

> To offset any possible backfire from women's club groups and hinterland censors, Paramount executives have given orders to the studio publicity department to change its policy on the type of publicity going out on Mae West, . . . with a soft pedaling on any attempt to present her as the spectacular and bizarre character she is on the screen.[42]

The results put an end to fan magazine profiles of West as an authentic sexual outlaw. "The difference between her and her characterizations amazed me," one colleague asserted in a press release. "Despite the lurid publicity her sensational stage plays and jousts with the law have earned for her, she has never had her name blemished by any personal scandal."[43] Quiet, generous, deeply religious, this was a woman who cared for her craft and served her jail sentence as a "sacrifice to her principle that honest views of love, life, and sex were less harmful than dishonest and glossed-over implication."[44] Certainly the prison officials were never misled:

> How seriously the authorities regarded the sentence may be gathered from the fact that she spent none of that time in a detention cell with the real offenders against public decency.
>
> The warden saw in her a superior woman of charm and intelligence. For that ten days she was the guest in his house. His children loved the beautiful lady who taught them songs and dances. He is still one of her staunchest admirers.
>
> And many of the less fortunate inmates are grateful to Mae West for acts of kindness and charity.[45]

But it would be wrong to give the impression that *I'm No Angel* set out to purify West entirely. After all, her ribald performance in *She Done Him Wrong* had made her Paramount's hottest commodity. The challenge was to repackage West more acceptably within a contentious mass medium, not by deleting all sexual references, but by burying them more subtly beneath the film's surface. This *I'm No Angel* accomplished, to the Hays Office's evident relief. "While many of the gags border on questionable dialogue . . . most of the suggestions are left to the imagination," Vincent Hart noted approvingly.[46]

The chief food for the imagination was Mae West's persona. On paper Tira was an ambitious dancer, with a craving for money. On the screen she exuded earthier desires. West's swiveling hips, knowing laugh, and appraising gaze injected a bawdiness that the script had carefully eschewed. Her one-liners were vague but allusive, and her delivery conveyed a full-fledged sexual history that the film did not otherwise avow:

FORTUNE-TELLER: You are very wise.

TIRA: Oh, I profit by my experiences. (Chuckles.) Now, listen, honey—uh—you just tell me about my future. You see, I know all about my past.

As Joseph Furnas of the *New York Herald Tribune* observed, while the plot

seems to be trying to lace Miss West's pungency into the stiffly-boned confines of the screen formula for heroines, however reckless, . . . Miss West bursts gloriously forth from these restraining influences, much the same overblown, gaudy and zestful lady as before. The scenarist may insist that she is the customary hard-boiled heroine with the heart of gold, but through means best handled by herself, she keeps the audience profitably reminded that her hard confidence and carnal humor are something new on the screen.[47]

With its circus narrative so patently absurd, *I'm No Angel*'s true subject matter was West's performance. To that extent, the film made a lasting change in what she herself would come to call the Mae West character. On Broadway and in *She Done Him Wrong* she had plugged herself into the lore of the urban underworld, offering herself up as a genial scandal. This Mae West was different: stripped of her New York associations, she became more iconic, a universal figure larger than life. The only lore at work was Mae West's—her style, her wisecracks, her famous spectacle. As one critic put it, "The show, this time, is entirely the Mae West personality."[48] West became an enigmatic plot in herself.

At the heart of the enigma lay the issue of the "real" Mae West. Who was she? Why did she specialize in sexual roles? What did she *intend* by her enactments? *I'm No Angel* heightened the debate. At the same time that Paramount's publicity department, in an abrupt about-face, was claiming that the offscreen West bore no relation to her film persona, the script subtly but persistently hinted the opposite, encouraging viewers to conflate actress and character through suggestively autobiographical details. Tira's birthdate, August 17, is the same as West's; her cootch dancing in the circus recalls West's shimmy dancing in vaudeville; her appearance in court near the end of the film, rebutting Jack Clayton's slurs on her character, evokes West's notorious courtroom battles on Broadway.[49]

Throughout the film, viewers are encouraged to watch and wonder at West's flamboyant style. Often they can do little else as the action comes to a halt, or rather hangs suspended, while the camera focuses on West simply doing her stuff. To musical accompaniment, she banters with her maids and her admirers, parrying their compliments with ironic comebacks to a chorus of appreciative laughter. At times her encounters with suitors seem almost surreal in their scrupulous avoidance of physical contact. The one kiss in *I'm No Angel*, between Tira and Jack Clayton (Cary Grant), is filmed from behind with Clayton's head filling the screen, completely obscuring our view. Clearly, West's much-vaunted sexual frankness, as presented by Paramount, had little to do with fleshly passion. Instead, the film offered her style as a treat in itself: the arched eyebrows and pelvic gyrations accentuating wisecrack after quotable wisecrack, many bandied about in press releases even before the premiere:

CLAYTON: Ah, you were wonderful tonight!
TIRA: Ummm. I'm always wonderful at night. (Laughs.)
CLAYTON (laughs): Yes, but tonight you were especially good.
TIRA: Well, when I'm good I'm very good, but when I'm bad, I'm better. (Laughs.)
CLAYTON (laughs): . . . Of course, if I could only trust you.
TIRA: Oh, you can. Hundreds have. (Laughs.)
CLAYTON (laughs): Don't you know I'm mad about you?
TIRA: I could tell you'd be the first time I saw you. (Laughs.)
CLAYTON (laughs): Say, I must be transparent.
TIRA: Honey, you're just wrapped in cellophane. (Laughs.)

It's difficult to exaggerate the sheer peculiarity of such exchanges; almost ostentatious in their physical reticence, they amuse but they also bewilder. They push West's artifice and secret bemusement to the foreground while leaving their meaning entirely unclear. Consciously or not, West had achieved a similar effect with *Diamond Lil*, her irony suggesting some private joke that she seemed to be savoring but never revealed. Now, thanks to the censors, audiences had even more cause to wonder exactly what she was laughing at. On that score the film remained stubbornly open-ended, leaving the task of interpretation to the viewer.

And one need only examine the critical raves showered on West from the most unlikely quarters to see how varied the interpretations could be. In the wake of *I'm No Angel* she was praised by a diverse collection of writers who united in adoring her performance style while holding flatly contradictory opinions about what it actually meant. To the French novelist Colette, West's manipulation of her heavyset body (the "powerful" breast, the "well-fleshed thighs," "the short neck, the round cheek of a young blonde butcher") signaled her defiant and explicitly feminist rejection of the demure, compliant Hollywood heroine.[50] To West's onetime detractor George Jean Nathan, she was the embodiment of old-fashioned womanliness, in stark contrast to the "endless succession of imported lesbians and flat-chested flappers" foisted upon filmgoers before.[51] Gilbert Seldes saw West's air of good-humored mockery as a joyous affirmation of healthy heterosexuality and a populist rejection of the "infertile . . . and moribund" inversion of high culture artists like Marcel Proust,[52] while George Davis and Parker Tyler read her irony as a homosexual style directly inspired by the theatricality of the gay male subculture.[53]

That Mae West could sustain all these interpretations and more was the secret of her Hollywood success. *I'm No Angel* was West's biggest hit, with good reason: male traditionalists could delight in a full-figured sex bomb, feminists in an unabashedly autonomous heroine, homosexual men in seemingly intentional camp, and the Hays Office in seemingly intentional restraint. "On the whole much better than we expected," wrote a relieved James Wingate. "In fact, the film contained nothing which we considered basically questionable or liable to cause trouble, and though it contained the expected number of wisecracks and Mae Westisms, we believe it will meet with no real difficulty."[54] Even some of West's harshest critics within the Hays Office found the picture delightful—not least the official who had been most outraged by *She Done Him Wrong*. Paramount, declared Vincent Hart, "is to be congratulated. This picture will be box office to the nth degree. . . . It is a knockout all the way through, and . . . I'm for it, irrespective!"[55]

His enthusiasm was shared by the public. *I'm No Angel* was West's biggest screen triumph, drawing fans nationwide, women and men, young and old, highbrows and lowbrows. No one was prepared for the frenzied reaction to its release. On opening day in New York City four mounted policemen and twenty-eight patrolmen were needed to keep the massive crowds in check. In the end the Paramount Theater could only accommodate the clamoring fans by instituting round-the-clock screenings for a full four weeks.[56] Elsewhere in the country the reaction was similar. *I'm No Angel* set all-time attendance records in St. Louis, Kansas City, San Francisco, and Boston. New Jersey's Newark Theater called out the fire department to keep the milling throngs in order; Cincinnati introduced midnight performances; Birmingham took "the dust off some of the unpopular seats"; and Washington, D.C., filed this report:

> Town is gaga. Midnight opening of *I'm No Angel* sold out and Loew office rushed extra print through and opened Fox simultaneously to take care of overflow. Result was attendance at both spots of over 5,000. And the usual turn-out for local preview on off nights is around 1500![57]

I'm No Angel and *She Done Him Wrong* made Mae West the most famous woman in America, her persona a hot topic of controversy, her name a byword for sex. In the months that followed she could be found everywhere: in the lyrics of Cole Porter's "Anything Goes"; in a WPA mural in San Francisco's Coit Tower; in *She Wronged Him Right*, a Betty Boop cartoon; in *My Dress Hangs Here*, a painting by Mexican artist Frida Kahlo. Kahlo's husband, Diego Rivera, paid his own tribute: West was "the most wonderful machine for living I have ever known—unfortunately on the screen only."[58] To F. Scott Fitzgerald, she was a rare treat: "the only Hollywood actress with an ironic edge and a comic spark."[59] By all indications West was on top of the world. As *Variety* put it, her two films had made her "the biggest conversation-provoker, free space grabber and all-around box-office bet in the country. She's as hot an issue as Hitler."[60]

Chapter 9

IT AIN'T NO SIN

$\mathcal{I}$n the late autumn of 1933, her popularity at its peak, Mae West began work on her third starring picture. *Variety* first mentioned it on November 28, reporting that it was "written around the old New Orleans red light district" and that its title was *It Ain't No Sin.*[1]

That title must have seemed a deliberate provocation to a new protest movement that would become a powerful force over the next eight months. In November 1933 the annual conference of Catholic bishops announced a national campaign to combat the spread of immoral movies. Under the bishops' leadership, an estimated five million to nine million American Catholics proclaimed themselves part of the "Legion of Decency," pledging within their local dioceses to boycott "salacious" and "criminal" films. Jewish and Protestant organizations followed the Catholic lead. The Federal Council of Churches of Christ in America reportedly distributed "hundreds of thousands" of pledges, and representatives of the Knights of Columbus, B'nai B'rith, the Elks, the Masons, and the Oddfellows formed an Emergency Council of Fraternal Organizations to assist in the pledge drive.[2]

By July 1934 local movie exhibitors were being bombarded with letters from Legion of Decency supporters demanding that their anger be made known to the industry and that Hollywood stop producing indecent movies and concentrate on wholesome, family-oriented themes. In Philadelphia the protest went well beyond letter writing: at the urging of the local bishop, Catholics boycotted movies altogether, causing theater attendance to drop by 40 percent.[3]

This moralist crusade has since become the most famous episode of Mae West's career. As her fans described it, and as West herself mythologized it, the protest movement would never have erupted had it not been for West and her freewheeling, rowdy, uninhibited heroines. That argument is questionable, to say the least: organized Catholic opposition to film immorality dated back at least to 1929, when Father Daniel Lord, a Jesuit, drafted the Production Code, and civic leaders, educators, and clerics of all denominations had been attacking the movies since the industry began.

But the protest did reach new levels of intensity in 1934, and for that West was at least partly responsible. The Legion campaign began in 1933, the year she became a box office sensation; the campaign itself was announced only weeks after the wildly enthusiastic reception accorded *I'm No Angel*. Contemporary chroniclers deemed this no coincidence. As New York rabbi Sidney Goldstein, a Legion crusader, remembered in 1935, "The Mae West pictures were rated as successes and yielded a large return upon the investment. No pictures, however, did more to arouse the indignation of the country as a whole."[4] If not "the country as a whole," vocal segments within it did indisputably object to Mae West. In contemporary accounts of the Legion crusade, West was mentioned more often than any other performer, until her name became virtually synonymous with Hollywood immorality.

The crusade waged by the Legion of Decency is one of the legendary moments of West's career: the last word in puritanical foolishness, led by a group of humorless bluenoses who recoiled in horror from the sight of Mae West's swiveling hips. The legend does contain a measure of truth: the moral reformers of the Legion of Decency undeniably distrusted the sensual life, as New York City cleric John Haynes Holmes made clear in 1935 when he described Hollywood's films of the early 1930s as "pornographic" and excoriated those who made them:

There seemed to be nothing too sacred, too beautiful, to be wantonly defiled by the gang of clowns and perverts who were in control at Hollywood. . . . Adultery was depicted not as a crime, but as an amusement for the rich, a game for the idle and luxurious, and a joke for everybody. Passion was presented not as poetry and romance and beauty, but simply as an incentive to lust and an excuse for the fleshy appetites of the body. And love, the noblest inspiration of music and poetry, the comfort and solace of the inmost hearts of men, was seldom revealed in its basic spiritual integrity, but almost invariably degraded to the level of mere animal sensationalism.[5]

Inveighing against films that dealt in "the fleshy appetites," Holmes demonstrated his allegiance to a Victorian vision of social order that stressed the control of sensual instincts and expected "culture" to elevate one from their pull. It was the same vision that had animated leisure reformers in the 1910s and 1920s in their efforts to abolish or sanitize urban amusements and keep "dirty plays" off Broadway.

Yet, as with earlier reform campaigns, this one involved a complex set of issues; its opponents were not uniformly "progressive" and its supporters were not simply "prudes." Take, for example, the Reverend Holmes: undeniably Victorian in sexual attitudes, he was a well-known political liberal and a supporter of the American Civil Liberties Union. In his view the "real devil" imperiling the movies was not immorality but commercialization; the only sure cure for the movies' ills was to drive the money-makers out. "Until the movies are rescued from the hands of ignorant, coarse, vulgar, greedy men, who have no knowledge of literature, no understanding of human nature, no standards and ideals, and are in this business simply because they can use it for profit-making, and passed over into the hands of informed and high-minded men, who can make of this business a great art, it is certain we shall get nowhere."[6]

At the heart of Holmes's critique lay the intense suspicion of commercially motivated "amusement exploiters" that had fueled leisure reform campaigns since the turn of the century. Reformers believed that the new amusement industries were too important to be left to private business alone. Guided by a clear cultural elitism (and in some cases, though not Holmes's, by a rank anti-Semitism), they assailed movie moguls and other merchants of leisure as unprincipled hucksters incapable of exercising social responsibility and willing to lure paying customers by any base means.

It was those customers and their moral welfare that formed the focus of the Legion's concern. Like cheap theater and other popular entertainments before them, but to an even greater extent, movies attracted the poor, adolescents, and women (especially young women), groups seemingly uninterested in more "demanding" art forms, unpredictable in their responses to cultural expression, and ill-equipped (so reformers believed) to exercise moral discernment.[7] Though all forms of popular culture excited that criticism, it gained particular force when applied to the movies, for not only did the low admission price invite the poorest spectators, but the ease of reproduction and distribution enabled films to penetrate every locale.

In addition, and in contrast to their view of the theater, reformers deemed movies to be *inherently* a mass medium: they drew a broad audience because they were fundamentally simplistic. While literature and drama "appeal to the mature," demanding a "keenness of imagination," a "capacity for understanding," if one were to grasp their full meaning, movies required no such mental acumen. Composed of two basic and direct elements—"looking at a picture and listening to a story"—they could be watched and appreciated by toddlers.[8] And indeed, said the *Literary Digest*, it was "children and the child-minded, . . . almost everyone will agree, [who] form the bulk of the movie audience."[9]

Tracts like the Production Code had that childish mass in mind: one cannot read them without being struck by the literal and even prescriptive manner in which the audience was believed to interpret what it saw on the screen. "It cannot be denied," wrote Martin Quigley, Catholic publisher of the *Motion Picture Herald*, "that . . . the motion picture readily and effectively conveys impressions which are formulative as to character and directive as to conduct."[10] Movies, in other words, did not simply influence viewers; they shaped moral ideas and imposed behavioral standards.

Movies could exert so profound an effect because they reached an audience incapable of distinguishing fantasy from fact. To the average moviegoer, Father Lord contended, filmed events came across "with apparent reality of life."[11] In part this was put down to cultural illiteracy, since moviegoers were assumed to lack the "keenness of imagination" to negotiate the fictional world of the novel. In addition, however, the very technology of the cinema invested the screen world with the look of reality. Movies brought the audience physically close to their stories, into far greater intimacy than literature or drama. Presenting their stories not "on a cold page" but through "apparently living people," movies enlivened their presentation with cinematic devices—above all, the closeup—that brought viewers and screen characters into seemingly intimate proximity.[12]

In addition to this simulated physical intimacy, movies conveyed emotional intimacy through the star system—to the reformers, the most insidious danger. The fascination with screen actors, "developed beyond anything of the sort in history," could only endanger an audience whose powers of discrimination were weak to begin with.[13] Movie fans lacked the intellectual know-how to distinguish an act of performance; when they admired stars, they admired their screen characters and even took them as role models because they believed star and character to be one and the same. As Lord put it:

> The enthusiasm for and interest in the film actors and actresses . . . makes the audience largely sympathetic toward the characters they portray and the stories in which they figure. Hence the audience is more ready to confuse actor and actress and the characters they portray, and it is most receptive of the emotions and ideals presented by their favorite stars.[14]

Those assumptions about movie spectatorship, which had fueled film reform efforts since the 1910s, were in fact broadly shared in the early twentieth century, reaching far beyond the reformers' own ranks. They were even shared by the defiantly unprudish: supporters of the modernist avant-garde, who mixed contempt for Hollywood's assembly-line methods with disdain for its viewers' mental powers. Many agreed with *The Captive*'s translator, playwright Arthur Hornblow, when he argued that movies, unlike the theater, drew the mentally stunted and morally vulnerable. Though Hornblow did not support censorship, he believed that special care of some sort was necessary, for the movie audience "needs to be protected from thoughts it is not qualified to cope with."[15]

And, as their response to *The Captive* showed, even in the case of the theater, modernists conceded that young female patrons required more protection than anyone else. Many others agreed. Since the turn of the century, concern about young women's vulnerability and irresponsibility as consumers of popular culture had spurred calls for the regulation of dance halls, amusement parks, and other entertainments noted for drawing a large female crowd. The movies were no exception, particularly in the early 1930s when Hollywood embarked on its cycle of "sex films." None of the Hays Office's strategies for defusing their content had put a halt to allegations that such movies tempted suggestible girls to experiment with vice.

Proof of that allegation, for many, was supplied in early 1933 with the serialization of Henry James Forman's *Our Movie-Made Children*. Summarizing a series of investigations carried out from 1929 to 1932 into the influence of movies on American youth, the study lent reformers' assertions about young women an aura of scientific legitimacy, which was certainly the intent.

Forman's study was commissioned by the Motion Picture Research Council, a social welfare lobby bent on producing a report that would intensify calls for federal movie censorship. The MPRC had commissioned the original studies too but had apparently been dismayed by their rather nuanced conclusions. Researchers had found that movies, far from exerting a uniformly bad influence, had effects that varied from one child to the next—which was not what the MPRC's director, Reverend W. H. Short, wanted to hear. ("That man," remembered one researcher, "was really out to damn the movies straight away to hell!") Forman, a journalist, was brought in at that point to "summarize" the findings in a suitable fashion.[16] His study offered a one-sided analysis engineered to exploit public anxieties about the corruption motion pictures could bring in their wake.

The most widely quoted portion of Forman's book was the section devoted to young women, in whose hands sex films became potent agents of moral decay. Swayed by the glamorous stars and by the luxuries that surrounded them, girls read the films as virtual lessons in using their bodies for material gain. Even simple imitation was dangerous. In mimicking the behavior of provocative actresses—"learning to handle a cigarette like Nazimova, to smile like Norma Shearer, to use [their] eyes like Joan Crawford"—girls fell victim to sexual impulses they were too weak to control.[17] Forman supported that contention with quotes from reformatory inmates, girls who had obviously deduced what their questioners were after and blamed their downfall squarely and solely on the movies. His solemn presentation gave their responses the weight of fact:

> [From a fourteen-year-old]: After I have seen a romantic love scene, I feel as though I couldn't have just one fellow to love me, but I would like about five.
>
> [From a sixteen-year-old]: When I was on the outside I went to the movies almost every night, but only about twice in two months to a dance. I don't like dances as well as I do movies. A movie would get me so passionate after it was over that I just had to have relief. You know what I mean.[18]

Forman hammered home his point, most memorably with what he called a "graphic description of [one girl's] thrills and stirrings under the impact of sex movies":

> When I see movies that excite me I always want to go home and do the same things I saw them do. . . . One night I went to a movie with a fellow of mine. . . . In the movie he sat with his arms around me, and every time the fellow would kiss the girl, he would look at me lovingly and squeeze my hand; after the movie we went to my girlfriend's house and got her and her fellow. Then we all went for a moonlight spooning ride and had sexual relations.[19]

Widely excerpted after its initial publication in the spring of 1933 and eventually published in hardcover, Forman's book created an uproar, intensifying provincial middle-class fears of movies as a catalyst for social decay. In the midst of that uproar came *I'm No Angel*, with its high-profile promotion of West's "PERSONALITY—swinging hips—bedroom eyes—and the throaty growl of an amorous cat."[20] Though the Hays Office's James Wingate expected the film to provoke "no undue criticism," he could not have been more mistaken.[21] For those seeking proof of Forman's conclusions, West's new film seemed to supply it in spades.

For one thing, *I'm No Angel* made abundantly clear that Mae West's most ardent fans were young women. That fact flew in the face of all predictions; given her burlesquian curves and ribald reputation, most had assumed she'd prove a limited stag draw. On the contrary—*I'm No Angel* drew such a large female audience that an Omaha theater owner held women-only screenings, complete with complimentary coffee and rolls, so that women could savor West among themselves.[22]

But it was the manner in which they responded as viewers that prompted the greatest anxiety, for to educators and clerics it seemed undeniable that young women were taking West as a role model. "There must be tens of thousands of high school girls all over the United States reading, hearing and seeing all they can of this particular star and her wanton heroines, imitating them so far as they can," lamented Presbyterian educator Harmon Stephens in the *Literary Digest*:

> On a "character day" in one high school, nine girls came in imitation of her. "She," according to the billboard, "is the kind of girl who can lose her reputation and never miss it." Virtue lies prostrate.[23]

To reformers, as Stephens's words indicate, imitating Mae West was no laughing matter. She embodied the threat of the whole cycle of sex films as a glamorous and all-too-enticing gold digger. In a decade short on material luxuries she showed girls the wealth that was theirs for the taking should they only make use of their bodies to follow her character's lead.[24]

Yet West was always more than a run-of-the-mill gold digger, more than an ordinary sexual object; to that extent the upheaval she provoked was unique. One has only to read her (largely male) detractors to sense that they found her peculiarly unsettling, an unease provoked less by West's immorality than by her unabashed pleasure in calling the shots. That was what fueled the outrage of industry critic Martin Quigley, who damned *I'm No Angel* by thundering, "There is no more pretense here of romance than there is on a stud farm."[25] West was a singularly disturbing sex symbol because her agency was too apparent. She too obviously relished her sexual power and her independence from male control.

In an era when men's status as breadwinners was so precarious, male control was a sensitive issue. One has only to look at oral histories of the Great Depression to see how often families were broken by sexual tension and by men's flagging sense of authority.[26] In that context West's popularity with women endangered the industry by making it vulnerable to male resentment, for even men who enjoyed West themselves may have bristled at her influence over young women, as the Hays Office's Ray Norr cautioned Will Hays: "The very man who will guffaw at Mae West's performance as a reminder of the ribald days of his past will resent her effect upon the young, when his daughter imitates the Mae West wiggle before her boyfriends and mouths 'Come up and see me sometime.' "[27]

As historian Nancy Woloch reminds us, the Depression was not a feminist era. However ambiguously, popular amusements of the 1920s had celebrated female sexual expressiveness; in the 1930s that may well have stirred growing unease. The evidence from social history is largely speculative, but it does seem probable, as some historians have suggested, that Depression-inspired fears of family instability were accompanied by a reaction against sexual liberalism, even by a sense that past moral profligacy was to blame for the present crisis.[28] It made sense that those tensions would center on girls: 1920s moral transformations had been most visibly embodied by aggressive young women, by the revealing fashions and risqué tastes of the flapper. Insofar as she reached precisely that audience and seemed likely to inspire emulation, Mae West could indeed be seen as a threat.

In carefully shaping *I'm No Angel* the Hays Office had tried to avert that prospect; not only did the effort fail, but in some ways, ironically, it made matters worse. Though no longer billed as an outright sensationalist, West became a larger-than-life sexual puzzle, an endlessly debatable erotic enigma who was more intriguing to viewers than ever before. One hostile critic argued that while in *She Done Him Wrong* she had been "amusing in a flamboyant way and different," *I'm No Angel* turned her into a "goddess, . . . an example and a model for the girlhood of the world."[29] By encouraging speculation about her intentions and leaving conclusions "to the imagination," the film openly provoked imaginations that could not be trusted. As one outraged reformer put it, the Hays Office's strategy "compelled [the audience] to do its own dirty thinking on inferences that it cannot escape."[30]

The uproar over *I'm No Angel* helped intensify divisions within the Hays Office, consolidating the power of those officials who had been hostile to West from the beginning. Central among them was Joseph Breen, an adviser to the Studio Relations Committee and a longtime campaigner to reform the industry, who replaced James Wingate as the SRC head in January 1934.[31]

Breen approached his job in the fervent belief that the film industry was in imminent danger not simply from the Legion of Decency but, more critically, from the federal government. By the early 1930s Congress was threatening legislation that would regulate movie content and ban the practices of block booking and blind selling, both means of compelling exhibitors to buy movies in bulk, sight unseen, rather than just the one or two films they actually wanted. Moral reformers deemed these iniquitous practices whereby the industry saddled helpless exhibitors with immoral material. But for the "Big Five" film corporations, block booking and blind selling cemented their control of the movie market, guaranteeing exhibitors for even their most mediocre films and closing the doors to independent and foreign competitors.[32]

The prospect of federal regulation to destroy the Big Five's monopoly drove Breen into a wholesale effort to implement change. From the beginning of his tenure at the Studio Relations Committee he established policies of regulation that imposed the Production Code on sex films with a new stringency.[33] At the same time, to win over the dubious, Breen sought something even more dramatic: a spectacular act of public repentance in which the industry would renounce immoral film content. As *Variety* explained, he set out "to make an example of any persistent Hays Code offender," which would prove Hollywood's concern for the vulnerable masses and silence its critics once and for all.[34]

Perhaps inevitably, given her public profile, that act of repentance centered on Mae West. Breen set it in motion in February 1934, when he turned his attention to *It Ain't No Sin*. He was determined to turn the film into an inoffensive narrative, and he would not hesitate to get tough if he had to. As it happened, he faced a struggle, for West had ideas of her own.

Mae West wrote the script of *It Ain't No Sin* at a time when her studio influence was at its height. With two enormous film successes to her credit, no one at Paramount was about to question her vision of the proper setting and story for "the Mae West character." As a result, as originally conceived, *It Ain't No Sin* was thoroughly Mae West's creation, assembled through a partial (if unacknowledged) adaptation of her final Broadway play, *The Constant Sinner*.

West's direct borrowings were few: some of the play's plot, but little else (though one line of dialogue made its way into the film nearly unchanged from the play, when the West character tells the manager of her prizefighter lover, "You may not know it but I'm a lady, and take off your hat in my presence you half-washed heel!").[35] She made no attempt to tell the original story of Babe Gordon, Harlem streetwalker and drug dealer. Instead, in well-established Westian style, she recreated the pivotal characters in a far more fantastical setting. Like *She Done Him Wrong*, which it resembled in many ways, *It Ain't No Sin* was infused with a haze of nostalgia, set not in contemporary Harlem but in a picturesque turn-of-the-century New Orleans red-light district. The heroine, Ruby Carter, was no longer explicitly a prostitute. Rather, like Lady Lou, she was more loosely defined as a "scarlet woman," a stage entertainer famous for her scandalous sexual past. Both films did occasionally hint that the West character had been a prostitute at some time in the past. West's opening boast in *She Done Him Wrong*, for example, that she was "the finest woman that ever walked the streets," was matched in *It Ain't No Sin* by her crack to a bevy of male suitors, "No souvenirs, boys. I never give anything away."[36] But in both films those remained hints alone, left to viewers to read as they pleased. They could, if they chose, dwell on elements in West's performance that worked to defuse her sexual roughness—her faintly grotesque Gay Nineties attire or her trademark mannerisms.

West made similar alterations in revising *The Constant Sinner*'s underworld plot. She deleted altogether its most lurid situations, miscegenation and drug peddling, and inserted less incendiary (if no less criminal) exploits. Ruby Carter is a notorious entertainer who attracts a string of ardent admirers, from Tiger Kid, a petty thief and ambitious prizefighter, to Brooks Claybourne, a naive young millionaire, to Ace Lamont, the owner of the Sensation House, the gambling club where Ruby works. When Ruby refuses Ace's advances, he hires Tiger Kid to steal her jewels, only to have Ruby unravel their plot and stage a spectacular revenge. She drugs Tiger so he loses a championship fight, and then convinces him that Ace was responsible, which drives Tiger to kill Ace, exactly as Ruby had hoped. But when Tiger explains that he does truly love her, she decides to reward his devotion, setting fire to the Sensation House and sending evidence of the murder up in flames. At the script's conclusion, Ruby and Tiger flee New Orleans, reunited in love, and Tiger chides her for her immorality. "My morals are all right," she responds, adding her words of wisdom: "Take it easy, you'll last longer."[37]

I have described the plot in some detail because its specifics were of great concern to the Hays Office, as we shall see; at the same time, its far-fetched complexity is significant in itself. Like *She Done Him Wrong*, *It Ain't No Sin* was potentially a sensationalistic tale, a story of a flatly amoral underworld woman who schemes, thieves, murders, and emerges triumphant. Yet its very exaggeration, its convoluted, fast-paced plot, gave it the feel of "blood-and-thunder" melodrama, thus turning the whole story into something of an artifact. While the audience could still find sensational thrills, it could as easily find exaggeration and comedy—an underworld bearing "little or no relation to life," full of exaggerated events that held "the heightened unreality of a waterfront ballad."[38]

On the whole, *It Ain't No Sin* followed the lead of *She Done Him Wrong* in lacing sensationalism with humor, nostalgia, and fantasy. But it marked a departure in one crucial respect: its treatment of the West character's sexuality. In both *She Done Him Wrong* and *I'm No Angel*, verbal innuendo deflected and replaced physical encounters. West's heroine remained untouched and untouchable, surrounded, to quote Gerald Weales, with "metaphorical bars."[39] *It Ain't No Sin* dissolved those metaphorical bars. According to Paramount's draft screenplays and Hays Office reports on the original film, shots of West in the arms of various men were "spread pretty heavily throughout the picture."[40] One such scene occurred midway when Ruby entertains a new acquaintance, Brooks Claybourne. After some suggestive banter, she feels his muscles, then reclines with him on a sofa, at which point they kiss "passionately," "lustfully," and "not only does Brooks fondle her body, but she, likewise, fondles his."[41] (Their tryst is interrupted when Ace Lamont enters and Ruby hastily whispers to Claybourne, "What's your name?")

But the most explicit scenes occurred early on during Ruby's seduction of Tiger Kid. Within minutes of having met him, Ruby convinces Tiger to take her home to her apartment. At first we see only the empty living room. Tiger and Ruby are audible but hidden from view, and what they are doing is left to the imagination. Tiger says that he is nervous, never having done "this" before, to which Ruby replies, "You're doin' all right for the first time." Then they move into the living room within range of the camera, and we see that Tiger has apparently helped Ruby undress.[42]

What followed was described by the Hays Office as a series of shots of "violent and lustful kissing," initially with Ruby and Tiger standing in the living room, and then with Ruby seated on Tiger's lap. Between kisses, Ruby glances "slyly" at her bed, and the camera focuses on the empty bed in closeup:

> TIGER: I've got a lot of your pictures . . . I used to cut them out of the *Police Gazette*. I was always stuck on your shape. But now that I've met you it's more than that.
> RUBY: (feels his muscles) You're in pretty good shape yourself. . . .
> TIGER: After I knock off this next fight, you and me is goin' to have a swell time.
> RUBY: Hmmm . . . Well, honey, if you're lookin' for a good time . . . I'm familiar with all the ways.
> TIGER: It ain't just havin' a good time I want . . . It's you . . .
> RUBY: Well, if you're a nice boy, I'll letcha have both.
> TIGER: Honey, you're makin' me break one of the Ten Commandments.
> RUBY: Well, there's still nine more left.

At this point Ruby, still in Tiger's lap, remarks, "You're not comfortable"; in the next shot, the pair are lying on the bed. At first only their entwined legs are shown, then full-length views of the couple in each other's arms and "several shots of passionate kissing and hugging." The film cuts to the clock on Ruby's wall, the hands whirling, and back to Ruby and Tiger, still lying on the bed but now half in shadow, possibly undressed. Tiger looks out the window at the heavy rain and says that he will stay until the weather improves, at which the film cuts to the exterior of Ruby's apartment for "several shots showing five days of intensive rain with fadeout on a room."

To be sure, these were only a few among many scenes, but they differed dramatically from the sexual style of West's first two films, where sexual wisecracks substituted for physical interaction. Here they complemented and provoked it. I have no definite explanation for this change, but it seems almost certain that it was not imposed on West but was her own idea. *Why* she altered her sexual style is the more perplexing question. One hint may lie in the script itself, in Ruby's description of the changes she needs to make within her stage act: "I guess I'll have to show more skin in the next one. The public's demandin' it. You know, when they ask for meat you can't give 'em vegetables."[43] Perhaps West's reasoning was much like Ruby's and her physical aggression in *It Ain't No Sin* was a response to what she too perceived as public demand. While West understood audience diversity and took care to maintain elements of humor and fantasy, as in the past she never doubted her sensational allure. She may well have shared the belief of her reformist critics that most of her fans responded to her straightforwardly and came in search of voyeuristic thrills, and thus the way to keep them happy was to give them "more meat."

Whatever West's motives, the key point is her producers' willingness to allow that greater sensationalism—and this at the height of the Legion of Decency protest. It was precisely as protest intensified over the late spring of 1934 that *It Ain't No Sin* took on much of its overt physicality. Ruby's encounter with Brooks Claybourne, for example, was initially written to emphasize his slavish adoration. (He kisses her hand devotedly and calls her an angel; she responds wryly, "Well, don't try to get to heaven in one night."[44]) It wasn't until the scene was filmed that it became more explicit, with Brooks fondling Ruby's body "and she, likewise, fondl[ing] his."

For West and her producers, their huge success with sex films in the past had fortified their resolve to provide more of the same, if need be with even more punch on offer—an attitude that ensured trouble with the Hays Office, whose longstanding worries about the movie industry's social and economic profile came to a head in 1934 with the growing threat of federal regulation. For Joseph Breen, West's new endeavor was not just a single objectionable picture but an exemplar of an objectionable trend, a politically loaded property made by the woman who incarnated film immorality.

One might expect that what most exercised Breen was the more explicit physicality of *It Ain't No Sin*, West's newly demonstrated eagerness to do more than simply talk about sex. But in fact, though Breen was repelled by those scenes, they were not the focus of his attack. He targeted not what made this film different from West's others but what made it similar: the outlines of its gold digger plot. He told Paramount:

> The story, as we read it, is a vulgar and highly offensive yarn which is quite patently a glorification of a prostitute and violent crime without any compensating moral values of any kind. From the out-

set, the leading character is definitely established as a person with a long and violent criminal record who displays all the habits and practices of the prostitute, aids in the operation of a dishonest gambling house, drugs a prizefighter, robs her employer, deliberately sets fire to his premises, and, in the end, goes off scot free in company with her illicit lover who is a self-confessed criminal, a thief and a murderer.

This script suggest[s] the kind of picture which is certain to violate the provisions of our Production Code for any one—or all—of the following reasons: (A) Vulgarity and obscenity (B) Glorification of crime and criminals (C) Glorification of a prostitute (D) The general theme of the story which is definitely "on the side of evil and crime" and "*against* goodness, decency and law." The treatment of this story is certain to "throw the sympathy of the audience with sin, crime, wrong-doing and evil." A picture based on this script would be rejected *in toto*.[45]

A different observer, of course, might well have argued that *It Ain't No Sin* was not "patently a glorification" of crime and prostitution at all. Compared to its progenitor, *The Constant Sinner*, the story was positively a caricature in its outlandish depiction of crime, and West's character was no two dollar tart but an amorphously delineated woman with a past. The suggestion of vice was undeniably present, but the film remained carefully ambivalent about actual facts. Moreover, if earlier "Mae Westerns" were any guide, the film would be suffused with humor and nostalgia, as the producers tried to explain to Breen in a stormy conference held at Paramount on March 7:

The company officials, especially Mr. Botsford and Mr. Hammell, sought to persuade us that we were unnecessarily alarmed. They agreed that the reading of the script suggested a very difficult picture but argued that deft treatment, which they proposed to give the script, and their proposal to play the whole story in a light, humorous vein would result in an inoffensive picture of high entertainment quality.[46]

As Breen described Paramount's strategy to Will Hays, it "would soften—if it did not actually remove—the definite antisocial factors with which much of the script is crowded."[47] But any strategy that did not "actually remove" those factors was unacceptable to Breen. It would create a film like West's others—slyly, dangerously enigmatic, the "light humorous treatment" allowing the studio to disclaim any sensationalist reading while doing nothing to prevent it.

It is worth remembering that the Hays Office had never before reacted to a West film with such flat condemnation. It had never been happy about West's move to the screen, of course, but under James Wingate the office had helped shape a strategy of mediating West's sensationalism with humor. Breen might have taken a harder line in any case—his correspondence reveals a true moralist—but his response was also colored by his acute awareness of external threats to the industry. As he told Paramount's John Hammell, *It Ain't No Sin* was "all the more dangerous with reference to our present position with the public and its many critics."[48] Breen's judgments on *It Ain't No Sin* were guided by the moral reformist insistence that filmmakers gear their products to an immature, impressionable mass audience. For such an audience, Breen implied, West's movie was flatly inflammatory. The masses might not catch its subtlety, and even if they did, there was no guarantee it would have the proper effect. Indeed, as Martin Quigley had argued in a review of *I'm No Angel*, West's "sportive wisecracking tends to create tolerance if not acceptance of things essentially evil."[49]

A far blunter strategy was demanded to prevent West's audience from sympathizing with vice. As Breen told Paramount, the script would have to highlight "compensating moral values." For every moment of wrongdoing, in other words, the story must make it unmistakably clear that such behavior was in fact wrong. "The Code," Breen wrote to Will Hays in 1936,

> demands "that in the end the audience feels that evil is wrong and good is right." To satisfy this requirement of the Code, stories must contain, at least, sufficient good to compensate for the evil they relate. The compensating moral values are: good characters, the voice of morality, a lesson, regeneration of the transgressor, suffering and punishment.[50]

"Compensating moral values" were a means of leading the viewers through the story by the hand to ensure that they did not get the wrong idea. In the case of *It Ain't No Sin*, these devices would eliminate all ambiguity about the interpretation of West's behavior.

Paramount could achieve the desired effect by various means: by sprinkling the film with "good" (read respectable and middle-class) characters who would arouse audience sympathy and provide a countervailing "voice of morality," or by subjecting the West character to some significant transformation—a descent into misery or a conversion to "decency" that would show her past sins in their true light.

Mae West, of course, would have none of this, and neither would her producers. For West it was crucial to hang on to sensationalism: sufficiently mediated, it could accommodate all varieties of taste and temperament. *Variety* noted that all "major filmmen" felt the need to "get in just one scene to appeal to the morons," but the hallmark of West's style was precisely her eagerness to bring in all types of viewers, *including* "the morons" (the young, the adventurous, the sensation-seekers).[51] It was a style that acknowledged a diversity of opinion on sexual and social issues. It recognized, in short, that there was no national moral consensus—that definitions of "goodness" and "morality," which the Legion of Decency took as self-evident, were in fact very much up for grabs. In that context the Hays Office's strategy amounted to an expressly political choice: filmmakers were expected to cater to a fictive consensus about "traditional," "mainstream" social values. In effect the Hays Office demanded that filmmakers direct their product to a more limited market, which didn't, on the surface, make economic sense. But that particular market, the respectable family trade, not only was more prestigious than the mass audience but also was presumed to have a more stable income, no small consideration during the Depression.[52]

By the end of May 1934 Breen and Paramount were at a standoff over *It Ain't No Sin*. His strongest admonitions had no effect on the studio, which pretended to welcome his advice while taking no notice of it whatsoever. "We are quite aware," wrote Paramount's William Botsford to Breen, "that this script contains many lines which are censorably dangerous and it is our intention to correct these danger points."[53] Reaffirming that intention in another letter, he said, "We realize there are still some lines in the white [draft] script which are censorable, and which we definitely plan to take out."[54] But most of those lines remained, and far from eradicating the early script's "danger points," subsequent revisions added new ones. Clearly, neither Breen nor moralists' attacks in themselves were sufficient to convince West's producers to abandon their course.

What finally made the difference and prompted a wholesale revision of *It Ain't No Sin* was another factor altogether: a change in Paramount's top-level management. Breen and the SRC negotiated with Paramount's West Coast staff, producer William Le Baron and Emanuel Cohen, the studio's Hollywood-based head of production. Both had to answer to Adolph Zukor and his board of directors, who made final decisions on Paramount's production, distribution, and exhibition of motion pictures from the head office in New York.

At first Zukor apparently supported his studio's tilt toward sensationalist themes, and certainly turned a blind eye to its flouting of the Hays Office in the decision to film *Diamond Lil*.[55] But Zukor's power grew increasingly unstable as Paramount's financial difficulties mounted. In January 1933 the corporation had filed for bankruptcy and had been placed in equity receivership, and in subsequent months, as the studio faced complex financial reversals, Zukor's control over his company gradually eroded as Paramount brought in new financial advisers. By 1935, when the corporation emerged from receivership, the former Lower East Side garment dealer wielded only a fraction of his former power in the nominal post of "chairman of the board." Real control was in the hands of financiers who had spent the past two years consolidating their position: the Lehman Brothers (Wall Street bankers) and the Atlas Corporation (an investment trust linked to the firms of J. P. Morgan).[56]

The changes in process at Paramount's top level created new insecurities for its West Coast producers. As the Hays Office soon became aware, Cohen and Le Baron were more and more eager to evade their superiors' scrutiny. In late May, when Breen threatened to withhold MPPDA approval from *It Ain't No Sin*, Cohen came to him with a sudden request: when he made his final judgment on the film, would he please refrain from notifying Cohen in writing? Breen, it seems, had recently inaugurated a new policy: copies of all such final decisions would be sent not only to the Hollywood studios but to executives in the New York offices.[57]

Breen was not surprised by Cohen's request. He had recently received an identical one from Louis B. Mayer, head of production for Metro-Goldwyn-Mayer, which was undergoing a restructuring similar to Paramount's. Breen told Will Hays:

I am considerably concerned about the turn of events in the past week or ten days. There is much "under cover" work going on that smacks to me of a desire on the part of the studios definitely to out-smart and outwit the machinery of the Code, and to fly a lone kite in the matter of production, without any counsel, guidance or refer-ence to New York offices.

The situation initially put Breen in a quandary. If the Hays Office was to succeed in its negotiations with the studios, it had to main-tain a cordial relationship with West Coast officials. As a conse-quence, on the morning of June 2, after attending a screening of *It Ain't No Sin*, he initially decided to comply with Cohen's request. Not to do so would create too much "unpleasantness"—though he refrained at a price, he added to Hays: "it is certain to complicate matters later on if we are not in a position to produce documentary evidence, in the case of troublesome pictures, that we warned the studio of the danger."[58] But in the end Breen was too shrewd, and regarded the situation as too dire, to pass up a chance to turn Paramount's top-level changes to his own advantage. Within hours of writing to Hays he had reversed his decision. On the afternoon of June 2 he sent Paramount's West Coast office a lengthy letter deny-ing MPPDA approval for *It Ain't No Sin* because of its violations of the Production Code. A copy of the letter, preceded by a telegram, was sent to Adolph Zukor and his colleagues in New York.

As subsequent events would demonstrate, the Wall Street financiers who were coming to dominate the film industry were responsible for the triumph of Joseph Breen's strategy. The Legion of Decency certainly recognized these new executives as a more sympathetic force. By mid-June the reformers had abandoned nego-tiations with West Coast producers and had gone over their heads to New York. As *Variety* reported it, "Switch of all moral problems from the West to the East is revealed to have been motivated by an understanding that the crusaders have lost patience with studio heads, but still believe in the judgement and good intentions of the East Coast execs."[59]

It should come as no surprise that these new executives were dis-posed to cooperate with the Hays Office. They were men of a cau-tious, conservative temperament, and from their perspective, appealing to the family trade made economic sense. For one thing, an effective Production Code might help to standardize content, streamlining and rationalizing production in a financially troubled industry that badly needed to control expenditures.[60] (That expectation proved accurate, as *Variety* reported in August 1934: "The newly strengthened Hollywood purging mill, a direct outgrowth of the clean-up campaign, is not adding to major production costs, but on the contrary, is proving a medium of budget saving greater than anything existent in the past."[61]) In addition, neutralizing film content along moral reformist lines would lend motion pictures a new respectability. Not only would they appeal to a more prestigious and economically stable market, but moviemaking itself would become a more reputable business, shedding the last traces of the sensationalist style that marked its lower-class urban origins. To the industry's new brand of financier, that must have been a crucial consideration.

With the summer of 1934 came two events that provided concrete evidence of the new industry climate. On July 1 the major film companies agreed to the creation of the Production Code Administration, which promised to tame recalcitrant filmmakers by fitting the Production Code with teeth. Under Breen's leadership the PCA performed the same functions as had the old Studio Relations Committee: reviewing script drafts, noting censorable "danger points," advising on revisions, and passing judgment on the final film. But the PCA, unlike the SRC, had the power to enforce its judgments. A film released without a PCA seal of approval would be banned from all MPPDA-controlled theaters—which meant, in practice, virtually every theater in America. In addition, noncompliance with the Production Code's provisions would subject the offending studio to a $25,000 fine.[62]

In mid-September, after repeated delays, Paramount released its new Mae West picture: *Belle of the Nineties*. The change in title was an index of just how radically the film had been altered: little of the original "sin" remained. West's film had been cleaned up not once but twice to earn its PCA seal of approval: first after Breen rejected it in June, and then after the New York State Board of Motion Picture Censorship rejected it in early July. In turning down a picture sufficiently whitewashed to satisfy Joseph Breen, who had approved the first revision, New York's board seems to have been motivated by pressure from the state's moral reformers, who wanted to make it crystal clear to the industry that they were serious about change.[63]

The film that resulted was a far cry from *It Ain't No Sin*, Mae West's rowdy comedy of the New Orleans red-light district. The story was thoroughly revamped through a long series of excisions and retakes, so that it could no longer be accused of allowing its audience to sympathize with vice. Its criminal adventures were broadly curtailed—this was not to be a story of colorful amorality. Tiger Kid was redrawn as simply an ambitious fighter, not an experienced thug; he kills Ace Lamont accidentally, stands trial on charges of murder, and is acquitted on grounds of self-defense. Similarly, Ruby Carter no longer destroys the Sensation House deliberately. The fire starts when she inadvertently drops a lit match; immediately thereafter she bats at the flames with a pillow in a futile effort to put them out.

But prostitution, not arson, was the crime that really worried the Hays Office. Paramount's main duty, as Will Hays saw it, was "to negative the inference that [Ruby Carter] was a successful prostitute"—in other words, to remove the least possibility that viewers might read the character in that light. Neither the original film's "light, humorous" treatment nor Mae West's air of ironic detachment was deemed sufficient to accomplish this. Stronger measures were demanded; as Hays put it, the film must "show affirmatively that she was boisterous, robust, tough, indeed, but not a prostitute and that she was very good at heart."[64]

From the notorious Ruby Carter, Paramount had to create a good-hearted character, a woman who subscribed to traditional morality—no easy task, given the footage they had to build on. Nevertheless, the studio did its best. It deleted all references to Ruby's scandalous history, no matter how vaguely worded, making her a famous entertainer instead of a "woman with a past." Predictably, it cut all sexual encounters, but beyond that it attempted to expunge the vaguest suggestion of them. Tiger Kid no longer lingers in Ruby's apartment but leaves her at the door with a sweet "Good night, dear." Brooks Claybourne still showers her with diamonds, but Ruby is careful to remark that she barely knows him and that she must give the jewels back because "people will talk." Finally, the studio took no chances with the ending. Ruby and Tiger's romance had already been rendered thoroughly chaste, but lest anyone get the wrong idea when they were reunited after Tiger's acquittal, the revised film rushed them before a justice of the peace.

Such changes had dire consequences for the picture as a whole. What had been a farfetched but coherent story became virtually unintelligible. In its zeal to eliminate any possible offensiveness, Paramount largely abandoned plot continuity. Determined to avoid the charge of "romanticizing" the underworld, the studio hustled the audience through it, excising all moments when the film could be seen to linger on its setting with any semblance of affection. As the *New York Herald Tribune*'s Richard Watts observed:

> All through the picture you will find evidence of the clumsy way in which the picture has been cut into shreds. Of course, the plot of a Mae West picture is not necessarily the important point. I fear, though, that there is far less of the dashing gayety and good, hearty laughter of one of the star's best chosen satires on sex than there should have been, and probably than there was originally. . . . On the whole, *Belle of the Nineties* is lacking in flavor, comedy richness and shrewdness of plot manipulation.[65]

It was no wonder that the finished film lacked the "flavor" that had distinguished West's films in the past. It had been stripped of the very elements that had helped give West her broad and varied appeal. The resultant film was not only confused but pallid, with West herself looking distinctly listless. As critic William Troy noted, "The obvious delight and amusement with herself which she used to show are no longer there."[66]

Paramount's experience with *Belle of the Nineties* had one definite consequence: the studio would never risk such controversy again. From then on West's films would be built around very different settings and characters. *Belle of the Nineties* was the last to have an underworld setting and a "slumming excursion" plot—a change that carried huge implications for the nature and style of Mae West's performances. Whether appreciated for thrills or for ironic amusement, West's links to the urban sensationalist tradition lay at the heart of her entertainment appeal. After 1934, under PCA guidance, Paramount set out to eradicate those links, and derailed Mae West's career in the process.

Paramount's handling of West reflected the industrywide triumph of the reformist argument that sensationalism would corrupt the impressionable masses. Very few voices disputed that argument—

not even West's critical champions, for the most part. Her most erudite supporters defended her films not by making a case for the
legitimate place of sensationalism in popular entertainment but by
arguing that West was not sensationalistic at all. Theater critic John
Mason Brown, assessing West's sexual style in *She Done Him
Wrong*, was typical: "She seems to recoil with an almost gun-like
precision after each of her more tawdry speeches, and make her
own comment (which is the comment of modernity) upon them,
even while she continues to play them seriously." With that ironic
detachment, West signaled her intention to "burlesque" sex, to
"date it," to put it "in the museum class."[67] By these lights, her
style was sharply at odds with vulgar movie treatments that *did*
seek to provoke sexual feeling; in contrast, her air of detachment
spoofed the whole subject and revealed heavy-breathing passion as
a ludicrous farce. Thus, some critics maintained, her films could
even be said to act as agents of education, countering Hollywood's
usual message that romantic passion constituted life's sole interest.
"Mae West's version of sex was far more decent than anything the
screen had shown for years," wrote the *Nation*'s James Rorty at the
height of the Legion of Decency protest,[68] an opinion with which
Richard Watts agreed: By "burlesqu[ing], with a satirical hilar-
ity, . . . all of the slinking, determinedly seductive amorousness of
the customary cinema sex heroine," West's films exerted "probably
something of a moral influence."[69]

In asserting Mae West's beneficent "moral influence," critics
essentially endorsed the reformists' contention that the purpose of
entertainment was to educate and uplift its audience. Many of those
who rallied to West were New York intellectuals who had their
roots in modernist thought and championed treatments of sex that
exhibited psychological depth or sophistication. In their own way
they were as contemptuous as the moralists both of the mental
powers of the mass audience and of "low" forms of art appealing to
"mindless" prurience. In their hands West's enigmatic style became
a mirror for their own tastes and values: not straightforward sensationalism but a witty, ironic parody of sex.

Such a defense proved hard to sustain, given the evidence provided by the woman herself. Mae West had her roots in sensationalism and prurience, in art aimed at provoking the body, and while
she may have learned how to mediate raw sexuality, she never
entirely lost faith in its appeal. No sooner had she completed *I'm*

No Angel, with its conspicuous physical reticence, than she embarked on a straightforward attempt at voyeuristic titillation in *It Ain't No Sin.* Though critics read her "irony" as a self-conscious statement that mocked rather than exploited the lure of sex, West's intentions were clearly far less cerebral: she understood her irony simply as a suggestive inflection, a means of hinting that more was going on than met the eye, a vague something whose exact substance she never defined.

In championing Mae West as they did, critics steered clear of the one argument that would have given her genuine support. What was missing from the debate on movie morality was a defense of performance that *did* cater to the senses, and a defense of the audience's right to enjoy it. In its absence, *It Ain't No Sin* was altered beyond recognition, and Mae West's performance style thoroughly transformed. It is worth noting, however, that this reshaping of the film in line with "mainstream" values was overwhelmingly unpopular with "mainstream" audiences. Although *Belle of the Nineties* turned a profit, it was far less successful than the two films that preceded it—largely because of its well-publicized "scissoring," according to exhibitors. (The film did earn a near-record gross in New Haven, Connecticut, thanks to the ingenuity of a local theater manager who implied he was showing the original *It Ain't No Sin* by posting signs that proclaimed, "Presented exactly as produced."[70])

The lukewarm reaction to *Belle of the Nineties* foreshadowed Mae West's fate under the Production Code Administration. West was a performer who had spent her whole career searching for ways to mediate her rough urban style in order to draw in progressively broader audiences. She succeeded by adding humor and irony, smoothing out the rough edges. But there were limits to that process of "smoothing out," a point beyond which it became counterproductive. Under too many layers of detachment and irony, the "thrills" they were mediating disappeared, and West's style, severed from its origins, came to seem increasingly artificial.

Chapter 10

MAE WEST IN EXILE

*I*n early 1936 the Production Code Administration filed a scathing critique of the latest Mae West release, *Klondike Annie*, written by "a liberal minded and intelligent social worker about thirty years of age [who] is not connected with the motion picture industry":

> Mae is like a cartoon. She's all veneer and trappings. . . . She has leered so long that she now leers all her best lines—and one feels that even her love and desire are not genuine emotions.
>
> Mae seems to be losing ground. This picture may make money but she cannot hope to remain popular much longer. I have talked to a few people who saw the present picture and they said it bored them. This boredom will increase and many people will not know why. It seems to [me] the reason is that she is too UNREAL.[1]

Even Mae West might have savored the irony: a social worker, the embodiment of moral reform, complaining that she had lost her authenticity, that she had become a creature of fantasy who was altogether "too UNREAL." A mere two years earlier, such moralist critics had lambasted her excessive "realism," her swaggering pleasure in sexual autonomy, but in the wake of *Belle of the Nineties* that Westian realism became a thing of the past. Under heavy pressure from the Hays Office, Paramount set out to reform West's screen image. The four films that resulted—*Goin' to Town* (1935), *Klondike Annie* (1935), *Go West, Young Man* (1937), and *Every Day's a Holiday* (1938)—expunged the last traces of her native roughness, wrapped her ever more thickly in artifice, and turned West, as charged, into "veneer and trappings," a caricature of her former self.

To reduce Mae West to self-caricature was not, of course, Paramount's direct intention. She remained the studio's most reliable investment, its hottest box office draw. But the trouble-fraught production of *Belle of the Nineties* had convinced Paramount that some change was necessary. As the emblem of the dirty film crisis and the embodiment of the threat to impressionable viewers, West's image demanded concerted revamping if problems were not to erupt again.

No attempt to reform West's persona was more carefully thought out than *Klondike Annie*. From the beginning the studio aimed to place West in a new type of narrative that (as Paramount's John Hammell explained to Will Hays) would "take full advantage of those qualities which have endeared Mae West to millions of theatergoers" but would prove inoffensive to all the rest. West was cast as the Frisco Doll, a dance hall singer who is implicated in a murder and flees on a ship to Alaska, only to be transformed by her cabinmate, a Salvation Army missionary out to save souls among the Klondike miners. When the young woman dies before reaching port, the Doll disguises herself in her uniform, but finds herself drawn by her calling and morally reborn. As Hammell explained it:

> In their close contact on board ship, we have the contrast and clash of the two characters—the earnest devout mission worker and the flippant product of a hard, cruel upbringing—West.
>
> During the voyage, we see the gradual impression the mission worker makes on West. She tells stories of her work among the unfortunates in the slum district of San Francisco and the good work she hopes to do in her new field. She tells the story of her life of service and sacrifice. West becomes, little by little, deeply impressed with it all. . . . We have many scenes connected with this

work in which West is shown as helping the unfortunates, lifting the fallen, etc.[2]

Klondike Annie took West's scarlet woman through a transformative encounter with "service and sacrifice" and showed her experiencing a conversion to decency that no viewer could possibly miss. The film could not have been more different from *She Done Him Wrong*, and Will Hays could not have been more delighted. He wrote to Hammell as *Klondike Annie* went into production:

> I am constrained to take this opportunity to compliment Miss West, the studio, and all of you who have a part in the development of this [project]. I think it is splendid from every standpoint and if it is carried out with the high integrity and completeness as planned it will involve elements of real industry service as well as the creation of new and, I think, lasting substantial values for all.[3]

Still, the Hays Office knew that creating "new values" for Mae West would not be easy, no matter how carefully Paramount crafted the plot. Given her famously ironic delivery, even the most heartfelt "regeneration" could remain open to question. In this regard, Hammell anticipated Hays's worries and attempted to quell them in advance:

> At no time in our picture will West play the religious character with her tongue in her cheek. At no time will religious services be held by West which will have any indication of levity or burlesque ... [and] the laughs that come from our picture will never be at the expense of religion, religious people, or earnest workers in the missionary field.
>
> The ending of our story will be a romance between West and one of the characters in our picture, and it will indicate for the future a normal life and nothing that will bring condemnation from the most scrupulous.[4]

Hays, however, was not persuaded, and neither was Joseph Breen, who'd had far too much trouble with West in the past ever to trust her again. Over the next five months he pored over the script in search of the least trace of ambiguity, the faintest encouragement of a sensational reading, the remotest hint of "a suggestion that has a flavor of sex."[5] Out went the reformed Frisco Doll's statement of her philosophy of salvation: "You can't save a man's soul if you don't get close to him. It's the personal touch that counts. That's my experience."[6] In memo after memo Breen bombarded Paramount with suggestions for additional scenes that would make the Doll's conversion even more convincing. How about, he proposed, a scene of West doing "settlement-type activities" with the debauched miners—cutting out paper dolls, for example, or playing charades? How about turning the Frisco Doll into a Carrie Nation–style crusader who would clear out the saloons? Or even better, endowing the Doll with a large sum of money that she's determined never to give up but ultimately spends on some good cause—"an airplane to pick up serum for a dying child, or steamship fare home for some poor devil anxious to start life anew"?[7] Breen's enthusiasm for these changes fairly carried him away; he wrote to Hammell exuberantly:

> It seems to me that you might be able to get a lot of fun out of this kind of an incident. I can imagine how Mae would put on a thing like this.
> Yours for bigger and better films![8]

Even for Breen this was an extraordinary degree of interference, but West was extraordinarily hard to control. Reforming her meant suppressing her trademark style, with its layers of ambiguity, its sly suggestions of hidden meanings, and stowing her safely within straightforward narratives from which all ambiguity had been removed. If *Klondike Annie* were to mark a departure, Breen stressed, it should "depend for entertainment less on her wisecracks and more on a legitimate story and sincere characterizations."[9] In other words, it should downplay what *I'm No Angel* had spotlighted, the enigmatic Mae West spectacle, in favor of a clearcut tale full of "compensating moral values" that would defuse West's incendiary presence and prevent viewers from getting the wrong idea.

With that aim in mind, Breen maintained a sharp scrutiny and forced repeated rewrites and retakes, finally granting *Klondike Annie* a Production Code Administration seal of approval in December 1935. Despite the hassles involved, he felt confident that the film successfully revamped West's image with "a new type of characterization" that would make her respectable at last.[10] But never had his confidence proved so misguided. Within days of its release *Klondike Annie* engendered an uproar, fast becoming the most controversial picture of West's career.

The first attacks came from an unlikely source: the sensational newspapers owned by press baron and would-be film mogul William Randolph Hearst. Shortly after *Klondike Annie*'s premiere, Hearst directed his staff to go on the offensive in a private memo sent to his papers all over the country:

> The Mae West picture, *Klondike Annie*, is a filthy picture.
>
> I think we should have editorials roasting the picture and Mae West and the Paramount company for producing such a picture— the producer-director and everyone involved.
>
> We should say it is an affront to the decency of the public and to the interests of the motion picture profession. . . .
>
> After you have had a couple of good editorials regarding the indecency of this picture, then DO NOT MENTION MAE WEST IN OUR PAPERS AGAIN WHILE SHE IS ON THE SCREEN AND DO NOT ACCEPT ANY ADVERTISING OF THIS PIC-TURE.[11]

Even at the height of the dirty film crisis, Hearst had never been especially troubled by West, and it seems clear that this sudden vendetta had little to do with *Klondike Annie* itself. *Variety* speculated that the real cause lay with Hearst's role as director of Cosmopolitan Pictures and his resentment of Hays Office demands for cuts in an upcoming Cosmopolitan release.[12] Others suggested that West had provoked him by making a slighting remark about Hearst's mistress, actress Marion Davies.[13] But whatever its origins, Hearst's attack reinvigorated West's image as a sexual outlaw, precisely the image that Paramount and the Hays Office had gone to such efforts to change. "In 1927 [actually 1926], Mae West wrote and produced a play called *Sex*," Hearst's *Los Angeles Examiner* reminded its readers in an editorial entitled "THE SCREEN MUST NOT RELAPSE TO LEWDNESS":

> In March 1927 the play was raided as obscene by the New York police. . . . With this record of police raids, of indictment, conviction, a fine and term in the workhouse on Welfare Island for a criminal offense, Mae West was approached by the moving picture

business as a fit subject to introduce into the wholesome homes of the country and present to the young people of clean moral families. . . .

It was Miss Mae West's screenplays which were largely responsible for the uprising of the churches and the moral elements of the community against the filth in moving pictures, and which resulted in a temporary improvement in moving picture morals.

The attention of the churches, women's clubs, the various state censors, the state legislatures and the Congress of the United States is called to the fact that Mae West has produced another screenplay, which she wrote herself, as she wrote the play called *Sex*, which was raided as obscene in New York City and for which she was indicted, convicted, and served her sentence. . . .

The play was produced by Paramount.

The Hearst papers have refused its advertising.[14]

In the end, Hearst's press boycott did not damage West's new release at the box office. On the contrary, *Variety* maintained that it doubled its gross, since its "chief effect was to stir up interest in the film, cancelling attempts of non-Hearst critics to label it merely mediocre."[15] Exhibitors reached the same conclusion. A theater manager in Boston, reporting that *Klondike Annie* was performing well above expectations, attributed its drawing power to Hearst's claims that the picture was "lewd and libidinous": "It's not often that Boston gets a hot tip like that."[16]

But to the Hays Office, and even to Paramount, box office takings were not the point. As long as West was labeled "lewd and libidinous," she posed a danger to the film industry. That fact was made abundantly clear by government hearings into the major film companies that, with supremely bad timing, coincided with *Klondike Annie*'s release. In February and March 1936 Congress reopened debate on the industry practices of block booking and blind selling, which reform groups claimed forced local exhibitors to show dirty pictures, as they phrased it, of the "Mae West type." So often did West's name recur as shorthand for Hollywood immorality that, reported the *Motion Picture Herald*, she overshadowed block booking as the hearings' "real star."[17]

But while the congressional hearings and the Hearst boycott helped doom the effort to reform West's persona, it was sabotaged far more spectacularly by the actions of Mae West herself. West's resistance to the studio's plans turned the set of *Klondike Annie* into a war zone as she waged fierce battles with Ernst Lubitsch, the new Paramount chief of production. Lubitsch attempted to persuade West to strengthen the part of the ship's captain, Bull Brackett, and turn him into a full-blown love interest. "Why can't you write a script with two major roles instead of just one?" Lubitsch demanded. "Don't forget that Shakespeare wrote a play called *Romeo and Juliet*." West shrugged and replied disdainfully, "Shakespeare had his style, and I have mine."[18]

West's refusal, as Lubitsch charged, was indisputably bound up with egotism, with the stubborn unwillingness to share the spotlight that she displayed throughout her career. But that very stubbornness also reflected her determination to protect her style, which, she sensed, was being assailed on all fronts. While *Klondike Annie*'s script was taking her character through a conversion experience, Lubitsch was trying to submerge her in a conventional romance. Both strategies would have diverted viewers from West's performance to the film narrative—and in the process, as Joseph Breen recognized, would have kept their imaginations safely in line.

West would have none of this. She spent the five months of *Klondike Annie*'s production vetoing Lubitsch's proposed script changes and charging her performance with enough innuendo to undermine the Doll's "reformation" wherever she could. The finished film was not at all what Joseph Breen had envisioned, as several critics were quick to point out. While the plot may have posed her as a "soul saving sister," West's performance declared her "the insinuatin' Mae West of old, . . . looking her men up and down and reading startling meanings into [the] most innocent speeches."[19] Religious groups, uniformly, were outraged. With West at the helm, one critic fumed, the picture was "at the lowest possible level," "laud[ing] disreputable living and glorif[ying] vice." The spectacle of the sardonic Mae West preaching the benefits of virtuous living reeked of lampooning religion and made it West's most offensive film yet.[20]

And if all that weren't dismaying enough, Breen barely avoided an even bigger furor when he discovered, just days prior to opening, that West was trying to smuggle out an uncensored copy of the film. The *Klondike Annie* she exhibited in previews was not the version approved by the Hays Office—it was chock full of "questionable details" that stressed West's pleasure in sexual power. One such scene showed the Doll wiggling her body to inflame Bull Brackett, and moved on to show the pair entwined on a couch, the Doll on Bull's lap and Bull "with his hair dissheveled [*sic*], his uniform mussed, his shirt and tie open at the top."[21] Though Breen caught the print before West could release it, he was furious at the deception. As he made clear in a private memo, the episode was the last straw:

> Just so long as we have Mae West on our hands with the particular kind of a story which she goes in for, we are going to have trouble.
>
> Difficulty is inherent with a Mae West picture. Lines and pieces of business, which in the script seem to be thoroughly innocuous, turn out when shown on the screen to be questionable at best, when they are not definitely offensive. A special memorandum should be prepared on this matter for presentation to Mr. Hays.[22]

Whether Breen ever wrote that special memorandum or not, the *Klondike Annie* debacle convinced the Hays Office that Mae West could not be cleaned up. A systematic attempt to reform her had failed in large part because she refused to cooperate. Without question, she was more trouble than she was worth. For its part Paramount was beginning to reach the same conclusion. West may have brought the company short-term profits, but she also brought volumes of bad publicity, expensive production delays, and multitudinous hassles with the Hays Office. In the wake of *Klondike Annie* the studio began to put her at a distance. Refusing to renew her contract, it forced her to work as an independent agent on a two-picture deal with ex-Paramount production chief Emanuel Cohen. Paramount served as distributor for the films that resulted, *Go West, Young Man* and *Every Day's a Holiday*, but that was as close to Mae West as they were willing to get.

Paramount's decision to break with Mae West may not have been that hard to make. West had always remained an outsider in Hollywood, even at her box office peak. Widely resented for her success, she was also ridiculed for her working-class habits—the regular attendance at boxing matches, the garishly decorated apartment, the phalanx of thugs and other disreputables who followed her from New York. "Mae was considered low-class," recalled one acquaintance, "because it was rumored she hung around with blacks, wrestlers, and fags."[23] On top of all that was her sexual life. West, like her screen character, was an adventuress, and her unabashed pleasure in male sex objects riled more than a few one-time paramours who were summoned to her mirrored bedroom and dismissed without a glance. Said one: "With her it came through loud and clear that you could be a combination of Einstein and Cary Grant but you would mean nothing if a well-built fighter with a crooked nose, cauliflower ears, and the IQ of an ape appeared."[24]

To make matters harder for West, critics had also come to detest her, reacting to her performances with relentless derision—and with anger, as if at betrayal. She was not the ironic delight they had championed: her style had grown coarse, tedious, vulgar, her characterization was "less ribald than ludicrous," and her films were marred by her "overstuffed ego," by smug self-parody.[25]

That criticism did have some basis in fact, as anyone who has watched *Goin' to Town* can testify: West had become more self-conscious and mannered than she had ever been in the past. But the blame for that change lies with the Hays Office, whose pressures pushed West into scripts that buried all echoes of her raucous history and tipped her finely tuned balance of sensationalism and fantasy, forcing her to rely on fantasy alone. In the wake of *Belle of the Nineties* West sashayed through ever more far-fetched narratives set in the Klondike, the Wild West, the "high society" of Buenos Aires and New York. The films replaced the potentially corrupting thrill of slumming with the far more innocuous diversion of novelty, a substitution that was quite deliberate. In 1938, when West attempted to insert a brief Bowery saloon scene into *Every Day's a Holiday*, Joseph Breen sternly vetoed it, telling the producers: "You will improve the tone of your picture very much if you keep Miss West away from any scenes showing groups of low-toned, undesirable people."[26]

Severed from that "low-toned" sensationalist tradition, barred from employing double entendres, West responded by exaggerating her already fantastical mannerisms, "leer[ing] all her best lines" in a last-ditch effort to get something of the old West across. Instead, and inevitably, she came across as a caricature, a creature of little more than "veneer and trappings," a grotesque parody of her former self. Reviewers, nearly to a man, came to loathe her. From America's number one critical darling, West became its number one figure of ridicule, deemed "a cinematic freak," "archaic," "monotonous." Only the most perceptive critics saw how that monotony had been forced upon her. "Since Miss Mae West insists on writing her own stories for the screen, and since somebody is equally insistent on taking the characteristic quality of Miss Mae West out of them, there is really nothing left in a Mae West picture these days but a series of undulations," noted the *London Observer*. "A graph, really, is the only review."[27]

But even a graph, as it happened, had the potential to unhinge the Hays Office. Reduced to self-caricature though she was, West remained a source of unending problems, capable of subverting the most innocuous narrative with her wriggling hips, rolling eyes, and delivery straight out of a bawdy burlesque. Simply put, she could not be reformed, and her unregenerate presence left the industry vulnerable to charges that it was corrupting its viewers. After *Klondike Annie*, West would find herself increasingly marginalized in Hollywood, and the interpretive variety her films had allowed would be gradually weeded out too.

Mae West's declining fortunes at Paramount signaled a larger transformation in the film industry, one with which the Westian style was thoroughly out of sync. Her films, at their best, had been participatory amusements, presenting a deliberately enigmatic spectacle and leaving viewers to read it however they pleased. The result made room for a range of patrons with varied opinions on questions of sex, including the audience West had attracted on Broadway: young women who frequented sensational nightlife as part of a sexual rebellion, a means of defining a modern sexual self.

That female audience had surrounded Broadway with controversy, a state of affairs that the film industry sought to avoid at all costs. As Lea Jacobs observes, the PCA introduced new forms of censorship affecting not just Mae West but the whole genre of sex films and eliminating "the double meanings, the calculated ambiguities, and the narrative disjunctures which gave the films of the early thirties their zest."[28] With those changes came films that gave an upfront endorsement to female passivity and premarital chastity, packaged as "romance," as "harmless amusement"—a package into which Mae West simply could not fit.

If West's decline needed confirmation, it came late in January 1938 with the release of *Every Day's a Holiday*. The film received withering reviews ("Sex ain't what it used to be, or maybe Miss West isn't"[29]) and inspired little enthusiasm among fans. Even a pre-release scandal—West's banning from NBC radio after she traded ribald jokes with ventriloquist Edgar Bergen—stirred up only minimal audience interest. Most theaters showed the picture for a single week, in sharp contrast to the month-long runs accorded *She Done Him Wrong*. By the end of its release the film had lost money, West's first out-and-out box office failure. For Paramount its fate confirmed that West, too long a source of Hays Office difficulties, was now an embarrassment and a liability. *Every Day's a Holiday* ended West's association with Paramount once and for all.

The film itself was sad testimony to the constraints under which West had to operate. Though she attempted to recapture her early success by setting the film in 1890s New York City, the script lacked the rowdy good humor and sly double meanings she had been able to employ in the past. West's adventures as con woman Peaches O'Day were carefully confined to high society, and her criminality consisted of nothing more inflammatory than convincing a small-town yokel to buy the Brooklyn Bridge.

But the world premiere at the Paramount Theater in New York was a thrilling evening nonetheless. The police department turned out in force, and uniformed officers swarmed through the theater. The *New York Times* reported:

> It was like old times yesterday, with a new Mae West show opening and a squad of patrolmen marching down the aisles. The joker is that the police weren't after Miss West, but had been called in to restore order when a personal appearance by Benny Goodman and his band threatened to turn the Paramount into a playground for the intellectually suspect (we hesitate to call them mentally retarded). What with the adolescent exhibitionists dancing in the aisles, clawing their way upon the stage or swaying animalistically in their seats, Miss West's *Every Day's A Holiday* just couldn't escape being the second feature on the bill. And if there had been a Popeye or a Betty Boop on the program, she would have run third.[30]

By the end of the 1930s the "adolescent exhibitionists" had abandoned not just Mae West but the movies in general. Young women's desire to be thrilled, to use leisure to forge a sexual identity, was now played out not in the theater, but in music—in swing, in jazz, and eventually in rock and roll. These arenas were no less stigmatized than movies as a "playground for the intellectually suspect," but for the moment, at least, they were free from the heavy hand of "protective" control.

*   *   *

Mae West's rejection by Paramount was the beginning of the end for her as a film actress—only two more parts came her way over the next five years. In 1939 Universal Pictures offered her a co-starring role in a comedy with W. C. Fields tentatively titled *My Little Chickadee*. Despite appearances, this was far from a triumph. A relatively low-budget company, Universal relied on faded film talent, onetime big names available cheaply. It did occasionally resuscitate flagging careers—Marlene Dietrich in *Destry Rides Again*— but for a star of West's former caliber, it held an undeniable stigma. Still, West signed the contract; she had no other offers. Her salary was a mere $50,000, $100,000 less than was offered to Fields and a fraction of what she'd earned in her prime, but given her much-publicized PCA wrangles, she was lucky to find work at all.[31]

From the beginning West loathed the experience. It proved nearly as difficult for everyone else. The script uneasily balanced two separate stories—one focusing on con man Cuthbert J. Twillie, the other on scarlet woman Flower Belle Lee—and the two stars, cagey strategists both, forced repeated delays through their maneuvering for onscreen advantage. In the end their harassed director, Edward Cline, found it simplest to reduce their joint scenes to a minimum. Even that concession did not satisfy West, who felt she'd been used as a mere comic foil. She hated the finished product and detested Fields. In later years she often told reporters, "I sorta stepped off my pedestal when I made that movie."[32]

Whether West "stepped off her pedestal" or not, she indisputably steered clear of controversy. The production of *My Little Chickadee* provoked barely a ripple from the Hays Office: the script studiously avoided the double entendres and suggestive settings that had doomed West's films in the past. A far-fetched Western tale of a shyster, a hussy, and a "kissing bandit," the film spotlighted its principals as quaint comic legends and set them in motion strutting their (distinctly tamed) stuff. *Chickadee*, in other words, presented West as an artifact; yet the result did not win over anyone—audiences yawned, and so did critics. Precisely what would delight the film's later admirers—the extremes of its stars' flamboyant self-parody—struck its original viewers as predictable, dull, and in West's case, rather sad. "Miss West's humor, like Miss West herself, appears to be growing broader with the years and begins to turn upon the lady," wrote Frank S. Nugent in the *New York Times*. "It's one thing to burlesque sex and quite another to be burlesqued by it."[33] In the eyes of most critics, the film cemented West's decline into a grotesque, an egocentric fat lady whose alluring poses were rather pathetic.

My Little Chickadee left Mae West stranded. Although her contract held out the possibility of two more films with Universal, the studio declined to exercise the option. For three years she made no films whatsoever, only to return in Columbia's *The Heat's On*, the story of an aspiring musical-comedy star. It was an unmitigated disaster. "The heat is off, but definitely," stated the *New York Times*, a line that proved prophetic: *The Heat's On* would be Mae West's last screen appearance for the next twenty-six years.[34]

As West had shaped her, the Mae West character was an indomitable, irresistible, all-conquering temptress, a shrewd, resourceful, powerful siren who triumphed in every encounter. But by the early 1940s her real-life counterpart found herself confronting colossal failure: the complete collapse of her film career, with no change for the better in sight.

West never admitted even the smallest setback, to say nothing of something as catastrophic as this. In her autobiography she maintained that her absence from film work resulted from her own free choice. "I made up my mind that I would never do another picture unless everything, but everything, was to my satisfaction," she stated in 1959. "If I'm not convinced that what I do is great entertainment, I would rather do nothing at all but sit home and polish my diamonds."[35] Yet her account of this period, read between the lines, reveals much about how she struggled to come to terms with the crisis that brought her career—for West, her life—to an abrupt and inglorious halt.

In the early 1940s, as West told it, she experienced what can only be called a spiritual crisis. In previous years she had occasionally toyed with Eastern religion, but now, moved by a deep curiosity, she turned to the metaphysical world with a vengeance. Her search led her to the Reverend Thomas J. Kelly, head of the Spiritualist Church of Life in Buffalo, New York, who was visiting Los Angeles for a psychics' convention. After Kelly stunned her with his supernatural powers (he predicted, among other things, the attack on

Pearl Harbor), West became a passionate spiritualist. She spent the rest of her life surrounded by psychics, exploring her extrasensory powers, in thrall to "the Forces around us in a world where Time and Space as we know them don't exist," as she put it.[36]

West's conversion to spiritualism, though she never admitted it, reshaped her sense of herself as a performer, bolstering her belief in her own importance at the time when she needed it most. In its wake it became increasingly hard to distinguish between the "public" and the "private" Mae West. As Hollywood's interest in the West character waned, the attention of "the Forces" more than made up for it, and West threw herself into the role with a passion, identifying with it more closely than ever before. Looking back on her career, she saw the determining hand of supernatural spirits, who had told her "what will play" to audiences at every step.[37] Above all, she saw the Forces at work in the creation of the Mae West persona, and what they had wrought was no mere screen character. It was nothing less than her cosmic destiny, the equal of history's greatest sex goddesses, a modern-day Cleopatra or Catherine the Great.

Just how deeply West believed this was never more apparent than when she actually played the Russian empress on Broadway in a 1944 play of her own composition entitled *Catherine Was Great*. The play was staged by her old friends the Shuberts, who backed the production in large part out of loyalty, though they anticipated that West's turn as the randy ruler of Russia would make for a reasonably profitable run. To give it a properly extravagant treatment, they hired Broadway impresario Mike Todd, who set out to create an overblown satire, expecting West to burlesque the central character in Hollywood's classic Mae Westian style.

Todd's vision of the play was not shared by Mae West. The only sources for West's production of *Catherine* are theater reviews and her autobiography—alone among West's plays, the script for this one has been lost—but it's clear that she conceived it both as an homage to Catherine, of whom she believed herself the reincarnation, and as a celebration of Mae West, a revelation of the West's character's own regal essence. "I saw the Empress as a warm, gay, very sensual woman, and yet a monarch who was a skillful politician and master statesman," she explained. "After my years of surviving studio politics, I saw Catherine was really a portrait of myself."[38]

West, in short, intended the play as both a tribute and an act of self-vindication. She did not, at least initially, intend it as comedy or farce. Theater critics simply could not believe it. Arriving prepared for a comic Mae Western, they found "a solemn historical document," with West plying her Diamond Lil wriggles with a straight-faced grandeur, "apparently under the serious impression that she is Empress of all the Russias." To that spectacle, they responded with hoots of derision and not a little astonishment. The old Mae West may have been tiresome, but at least she was reliable for a few laughs. The new one was simply (to quote one critic) "batty," presenting herself as "one of the great female lovers of history" in a manner "both baffling and rather pathetic."[39]

Such criticism stung West badly, and in the weeks following *Catherine*'s Broadway opening, she detached herself a bit from the main character, even satirizing the empress with some ribald one-liners to provide her detractors with the comedy they anticipated.[40] In the end the play proved a modest success, but it still left her with long-lasting bruises, and after the close of its Broadway run West never really tried to revive it. Above all, she took care to strike a clearer pose of detachment and would never reveal her emotional investment in her persona so nakedly again.

Nonetheless, for the rest of West's life Catherine remained an important touchstone. She never stopped believing that they were kindred spirits, and she may well have modeled herself upon Catherine: so regal was the glow in which she saw her persona that she considered titling her autobiography *The Empress of Sex*.[41] She may even have stolen some of Catherine's jokes, like this bit of doggerel dating from the empress's lifetime:

COURTIER: How many [men] a day do you desire?
CATHERINE: I am tired from the road—three will be sufficient.[42]

Compare that to West's quip in her 1970 comeback film, *Myra Breckinridge*, as she surveys a lineup of virile young men:

WEST: I'm pretty tired tonight. One of these guys'll have to go.

It's tempting here to speculate that West turned to Catherine and spiritualism for deeply personal reasons, in an effort to cope with her advancing age. That argument certainly has some plausibility. West staged *Catherine Was Great* one year after her fiftieth birthday and after the deaths of several friends and family members. Her passion for Catherine, at some level, reflected an awareness of herself as an aging sex symbol. In contrast to films about Catherine the Great made in the 1930s, which focused on the empress as a young woman, West identified with the imperious stateswoman, the aging ruler who retained her sensual dignity, surrounding herself with adoring young lovers whom she ruled with an iron hand.

Yet we ought to be wary of taking this too far. West never, in any conventional sense, "coped" with aging. In most respects she chose to ignore it, just as she ignored all frailties and setbacks that contradicted the West character's all-conquering image. Identifying with Catherine was part of that process: it kept her rooted in the world of the Forces, where "Time as we know it" doesn't exist. West certainly believed that communing with spirits enabled her to slow the aging process; she may well have believed that she could halt it entirely. While she never tried to hide the year of her birth, she would always insist that she looked twenty-six (the age, as she conceived it, of the Mae West character). Reporters were never altogether sure whether she was putting them on.

Indeed, there was really no way to tell. West never stopped delighting in exaggeration, but no one could miss the undercurrent of seriousness, the ability at once to kid her persona and to hold on to it with a fierce conviction. *Life* magazine's Richard Meryman certainly saw it when he interviewed her in 1969. While at some moments she was "Mae West A," who kept her persona at a satirical distance, in a split second she could become "Mae West B," who believed in "that sexiest-woman-in-the-world role" completely.[43] It was Mae West B who communed with the Forces, who bristled at any slight on her dignity, and who saw herself with an absolute certainty as one of the *grandes amoureuses* of history.

It would be easy to treat this phase of West's life as one long descent into delusion and pathos. More than a few journalists saw it that way. Observing West in the 1940s and 1950s cocooned in her cream-and-gold Hollywood apartment, some deemed her a flesh-and-blood Norma Desmond, the tragicomic heroine of Billy Wilder's 1950 film *Sunset Boulevard*, a faded film queen lost in a dream world and feeding on her memories of the Hollywood past. Not only journalists drew that parallel—Billy Wilder seems to have drawn it himself. The German-born Wilder apparently nursed a long fascination with Mae West's screen image—her "superb vulgarity and fleshiness . . . reminded him of Viennese and Berlin prostitutes," according to his biographer—and in the late 1940s he sought West out and attempted to persuade her to play the part.[44]

But Billy Wilder's vision of Mae West was a far cry from how West saw herself. She rejected his offer without hesitation and with something approaching out-and-out horror. To accept the role of a pathetic has-been would have been a betrayal of her cosmic destiny. She had always refused to play the victim, and she wasn't about to start now.

West's feisty insistence on her dignity ought to spur us to wonder, not pity—under the circumstances, bemoaning her "delusions" seems somehow beside the point. By the early 1940s, with her film career in ruins, the life that lay before her was the stuff of bad melodrama: the international film star rejected by Hollywood, tossed aside by the vagaries of audience taste. By consorting with the Forces, West rewrote her story. So what if the world labeled Mae West a has-been? The Forces made up for that flesh-and-blood audience—they knew she had the soul of a queen.

In her grandiose self-assertion in the face of disaster, West followed the lead of a long line of prima donnas, the self-mythologizing, supremely confident divas celebrated by Wayne Koestenbaum in his book *The Queen's Throat*.[45] Not for nothing did she reportedly develop a great affinity for opera singer Grace Moore, calling her often to her seances after Moore's death in a plane crash in 1946.[46] Moore had personified the tempestuous diva, regal and unflappable throughout every setback. When her brief film career collapsed in the 1930s she responded with an imperious memoir assailing Hollywood's crass vulgarity. Her departure she portrayed as an unalloyed triumph. "Like the queen in the story who ate too many tarts," she loftily noted, "I had had my fill of canned goodies."[47]

Mae West was no opera singer, but she shared Moore's taste for defiant grandeur, for what Koestenbaum calls "retaliatory self-invention—pretending, inside, to *be* divine—in order to help the stigmatized self imagine that it is received, believed, and adored." In response to the film world's hostility, West drew herself up with a haughty indifference, "gathering a self, like rustling skirts, around her."[48] The opinion of the world need no longer matter. Mae West had become a legend unto herself.

Chapter 11

THE QUEEN OF CAMP

In December 1970 a low-budget American film company, Page International, released an X-rated feature called *Dinah East*. The film told the story of a legendary Hollywood icon, a sex symbol who enchanted generations of filmgoers, but who did so through a sensational act of deception. Dinah East was actually a gay man in drag.

As the film's title none too subtly suggested, the model for Dinah East was Mae West. It hinted that West's ample curves hid a homosexual man, and it was by no means the first film to make that point. It had been made six months earlier, even more spectacularly, with the release of *Myra Breckinridge*, the story of a gay male transsexual film buff starring none other than Mae West herself. Though West did not personally play Myra, it was impossible not to make the connection, given the director's much-publicized comment that he was using her as a "drag queen." Michael Sarne told *Interview* magazine that he *meant* for the viewer to see Mae West as Myra. In his words, "That's what the film is *about*."[1]

Myra Breckinridge brought the perception of Mae West as drag queen out of the closet once and for all. West would be compared to a female impersonator in virtually everything written about her thereafter—reviews of *Myra Breckinridge*, interviews with journalists, and articles about her last film, *Sextette*, which she made in 1977 at age eighty-four, three years before her death. Alongside that perception came an awareness, if not an understanding, of West's iconic stature within gay male culture and in the tradition of drag performance that began to find an audience outside the gay world.

Today nearly everyone remembers West's longstanding popularity as a gay male icon. What has been forgotten is that, in the mid-1960s, her image gained followers in a range of new contexts. The film *Myra Breckinridge* came on the heels of a minor but notable Mae West revival, notable because it followed three decades of public indifference. West had made her last film, *The Heat's On*, in 1943, and despite a few stage appearances, in the late 1940s and 1950s she had been largely forgotten. But the late 1960s gave a new life to West's image: it appeared on buttons, pin-ups, posters, and other memorabilia; it was featured in works of pop art, like the collage of cultural icons designed by British artist Peter Blake that adorned the Beatles' 1967 album *Sergeant Pepper's Lonely Hearts Club Band*. Decca Records released an album of West's screen witticisms, interspersed with snatches of groovy rock music and packaged with psychedelic, Peter Max–style graphics. Above all, West's image was resurrected in revival theaters, new independent film houses that showcased "cult" classics—and that screened West's films on a regular basis, heralding her as "the queen of camp."[2]

Camp, of course, was behind all this. It became *the* buzzword for Mae West's 1960s revival and a term that would dog her until the end of her life. As a word, of course, it was by no means new: in common use in gay New York in the 1920s, the term was known to West herself. But in the 1960s it acquired new meanings and found a new audience outside the gay world.

In the process it brought Mae West back to the spotlight—or so, at least, it seemed. In truth, the impact of 1960s camp on West's image was much more ambiguous.

It took a decade of experimentation, of "cultural risk-taking," to shape the striking shift at work in the 1960s, in which the trademark sensibility of the gay subculture was adopted as "hip" by the culture at large.[3] The breakthrough year in this process was 1964, when Susan Sontag's essay "Notes on Camp" appeared. Originally published in *Partisan Review* and almost immediately excerpted in *Time*, it gave camp an air of intellectual legitimacy by effectively detaching it from its gay roots. For Sontag camp's importance lay not in illuminating gay history but in providing a liberating intellectual style. It was a "way of seeing the world . . . in terms of the degree of artifice, of stylization, . . . of failed seriousness."[4]

In Sontag's wake, camp became the trendiest of bohemian playthings, "the favorite parlor game of New York's intellectual set."[5] By 1965 the *New York Times* saw it everywhere: in the revival house taste for "cult movies"; in the new wave of underground films, particularly Andy Warhol's, starring the likes of Candy Darling, Holly Woodlawn, and Mario Montez, drag "Superstars" whose seedy stage names flamboyantly parodied Hollywood glamor; and in phenomena with no obvious links to gay male culture, like Soupy Sales's television series *Hollywood A Go Go* or the boom in nostalgia shops selling "camp merchandise"—old movie posters, old Superman comics, giant black-and-white photos of W. C. Fields, the Marx Brothers, and Laurel and Hardy.[6]

What held these diverse phenomena together was more than (as the *Times* put it) their common "outrageousness." Camp in the 1960s was a process of cultural recycling, as artifacts reclaimed from popular culture's back annals were invested with iconoclastic new meanings. It took hold in a decade of media change, when motion pictures had lost their mass audience and the old Hollywood studios, now outstripped by television, teetered on the verge of financial collapse. As critic Andrew Ross argues, the "camp effect" as we know it is created when a much earlier mode of cultural production loses its power to dominate cultural meanings, and its artifacts are freed for redefinition, made available to be put to new uses according to contemporary codes of taste.[7]

Camp as the 1960s defined it, in short, was a hip new form of cultural connoisseurship, an impish discernment of hidden value in artifacts others disdained. Part of its appeal lay in its snob value, its cognoscenti's codes of appreciation. As Susan Sontag put it, camp solved "the problem: how to be a dandy in an age of mass culture." Its enthusiasts could prove themselves to be rare patrons of mass-market products, for they showed themselves able "to possess [those products] in a rare way."[8]

Camp aficionados prized the garish, the tasteless, the tacky and artificial. Above all, they prized the outmoded—relics of popular culture that had become obsolete. That alone pushed Mae West to the foreground, made her ripe for the plucking as a camp object. Not only was she the product of an obsolete industry, an icon of faded Hollywood glamor, but her long-running act as the Mae West character had been deemed obsolescent since the Second World War.

As early as the first years of the 1940s, in the dying days of West's employment by Hollywood, critics had slammed her last screen performances as painfully old-fashioned and out of date. A decade later, nothing had changed. West's infrequent stage appearances occasionally gained positive critical notice, but even the warmest treated her as an irrelevant remnant of a distant past. When West briefly returned to Broadway with a *Diamond Lil* revival in the late 1940s, she found herself labeled an "American institution," "as beloved and indestructible as Donald Duck." She had become, in essence, a historical monument. As one critic put it, "Like Chinatown and Grant's Tomb, Mae West should be seen at least once."[9]

The reasons for that sentiment are not hard to find. In part they rested upon simple critical boredom. The constraints placed on West's screen characterization and her own refusal to vary the formula lent her last film appearances an ever-mounting air of monotony. Adding to the tedium, though few critics mentioned it, was the delicate matter of West's age. By the late 1940s she was well over fifty in a profession never kind to aging actresses, and aging sex symbols least of all.

Yet intermingled with this was a sense that the West character itself was somehow outmoded, a sentiment that could have only intensified in the conservative social climate that followed the war. As a predatory, independent, aggressive temptress, West evoked the sex role disruptions of the 1920s and 1930s, when women flaunted their bodies on the streets and the dance floors—and could be assertive in the workplace too. The postwar years firmly rejected those changes, defining "modernity" as a move to the suburbs and a return to a passive, maternal feminine ideal. In that context a comic vamp who insisted on calling the shots seemed an archaic relic of an unmourned past.[10]

There was one exception to this widespread indifference, one moment when West did return to the spotlight, but it seems to have depended on decidedly marginal patronage—on an audience of gay men. On July 27, 1954, West opened at the Congo Room in Las Vegas with a nightclub revue she would take to cities across the country over the next several years. Highlighting familiar Westian trademarks (the swagger, the wisecracks, "Frankie and Johnny"), it added an attention-getting gimmick: a lineup of musclemen, eight beefy weightlifters dressed only in loincloths.

The pattern of the shows remained largely the same, with minor variations, until the end of the decade. Opening with a song from tuxedo-clad dancers who extolled West's unsurpassed allure, the spotlight shifted to West herself, resplendent in feathers and sequins, reclining on a chaise longue carried onstage by the eight musclemen, who returned after West's first number. Seemingly naked beneath thigh-length capes, they turned their backs to the audience, faced the leading lady, and threw the capes open, as West strolled down the line, surveying each man from head to toe, her eyes lingering appreciatively at his crotch. "I'm glad to meet you— face to face," she told one. "I feel like a million tonight. But one at a time." Introducing the lineup's star, the current holder of the Mr. America title, she intoned, "Mr. America has my special warranty. If there are any defective parts, send them back to me. Because he's got my ninety-day factory guarantee." For the final number, "What a Night," she passed out keys to her hotel suite to the eight weightlifters. "Don't crowd me, boys," she told them. "There's enough for everybody."[11]

To be sure, you didn't have to be gay to appreciate this. In all her publicity West carefully specified her show's heterosexual appeal. She claimed, in fact, to have targeted women, producing "the first bare-chest act for lady customers in history," and the show got tremendous attention from that angle, as a lighthearted parody of the standard topless revue.[12] And by all accounts women did flock to see it—laughing, screaming, and perhaps playacting an escape from the decade's stultifying skittishness about female desire.

But if you didn't have to be gay to enjoy West's show, it helped. West embellished her act with moves and gimmicks that only intensified its underground appeal. She borrowed her flamboyant entrance on a divan from a female impersonator she had seen once on Broadway, a performer who wore lavish Cleopatra drag and made a parodically majestic entrance on a litter borne by several muscle-bound blacks.[13] The weightlifters themselves were a camp stroke of genius: make-believe men to match West's make-believe woman. Not only that, bulky musclemen held a prominent place as cultural icons in 1950s gay iconography. They were ubiquitous figures in the era's gay porn—in journals like *Vim* and *Physique Pictorials* that provided covert titillation for a growing gay readership under the banner of "physical culture."

Add in the fact of West's age, and the revue became a camp spectacle par excellence. From *Diamond Lil* onward West's gay fans had prized her detached, ironic role playing, but by the 1950s her advanced age made that detachment more obvious than ever before. A clearly sixty-plus woman, West played a twentyish sex bomb, reenacting key scenes from her films to the musclemen's Greek chorus of hypermasculine cheers. To put it bluntly, and whether she knew it or not, she looked more like a drag queen than ever.

This is no loose or offhand comparison. West and her musclemen replicated the tone of the "comic drag" central to the era's gay bars and nightclubs, in which an aging but defiantly glamorous queen parades her conviction that she is still gorgeous, directing her most pointed and salacious barbs at the room's youngest and most beautiful men.[14] So clear were the parallels between West's act and drag that not only gay "insiders" caught on. At least one audience member I've met, a straight man who saw West's act in Los Angeles in the late 1950s, remembers being struck by its obvious gay overtones. He came away convinced that the musclemen were homosexual, that West's siren posturing made her look like a drag queen, and that the show's racy humor rested on the unwitting perversity of West's enactment of her former self.

The muscleman act marked a turning point: it brought West's camp appeal to the foreground, and whether the audience was laughing with her or at her remained altogether unclear. Nonetheless, as a nightclub revue its appeal was limited to closeted gays and casino high rollers, and in the conformist 1950s it could not have gone much further than that. Most Americans barely knew the revue existed. "Mae West?" remarked one astonished cab driver to a journalist who set out to interview West in the early 1960s. "I thought she was dead!!"[15]

By the end of the 1950s West had spent two decades consigned to the dustheap in pop culture oblivion. For that reason, from her standpoint, the changes the late 1960s wrought were dramatic. With buttons, pin-ups, posters, and works of pop art lavishing attention on her hourglass figure, West found herself suddenly hip.

Yet this would prove a decidedly uneasy development, for what impelled her camp revival was not veneration in any straightforward sense. As was the case with the muscleman act, 1960s camp fed on its objects' outdatedness; it prized them, in consequence, with a knife-edged ambivalence, a mix of celebration and derision, affection and mockery.

It's hard not to see derision at work in much of what made up the Mae West revival. Certainly, it thrived upon a singularly flattened view of her image. Throughout the 1960s West's most popular film was *My Little Chickadee*, made at the nadir of West's career and the height of censorial power, with West at her most pallid, her one-liners at their most muted, and the West character a faint echo of its rowdier self. Pop consumers of the 1960s took pleasure, in short, in Mae West at her least incendiary. In itself, that fact suggests an attitude of bemused condescension. Like her *Chickadee* co-star W. C. Fields, West was "campy" in being more cartoon than human, a caricature drawn in very broad strokes. In the words of one 1960s camp enthusiast, she was "dated and ridiculous": an overblown sex symbol from the dark ages before the sexual revolution, the tones of her humor a quaint relic of a naive and innocent past.[16]

Clearly, the sexual revolution in itself fed West's new appeal to the young and the hip. Its impact may not have been wholly unflattering; to some extent, it may have made young people admire her. That seems to have been true of the UCLA students who in 1971 voted West "Woman of the Century" in honor of her pioneering influence on sexual mores. To them, West had gained a new relevance: she was a pathbreaking advocate of sexual frankness, a courageous crusader against censorship.

At the same time, however, the sexual revolution may have led some to laugh *at* Mae West rather than with her. Certainly the new freedoms exhibited by the decade's youth films would have cast her rowdy wisecracks in a rather tame light. Under pressure to draw a young audience, in the late 1960s Hollywood had scrapped the Production Code, bringing nudity, profanity, and (more or less) explicit sex to the mainstream American screen. West, in contrast, had built her career on innuendo that slid past the censors. She could hardly have helped appearing an artifact of a more fettered screen past.

But beyond this, and perhaps even more crucially, the contours of West's body may have made her a laughingstock for a generation that prided itself on its unconventional vision of sexual desire.

West's hourglass figure placed her in the company of the decade's array of unwitting sex parodies, comic sex bombs whose figures were too overblown to be believed—Raquel Welch, Ursula Andress, Jane Fonda in *Barbarella*, all objects, not agents, of audience laughter.

The entertainment value of those pneumatic women had its roots in the nature of 1960s sex radicalism—its utopian vision of the liberated libido, of bodies set free from all social constraints. A reaction against the 1950s strict sexual norms and sharply demarcated gender identities, that vision celebrated "natural" desire: free-flowing, genderless, "polymorphously perverse."[17] To a generation that eroticized unisex fashions and sylphlike bodies for both men and women, obvious markers of sexual difference could only seem ludicrous, and West, perhaps, unwittingly comic as an exemplar of outdated allure.

In any event West's newfound fans rarely noted her skills of performance. She became a silhouette, an inflection, a string of one-liners, a reusable, disposable pop art icon. Such interest as there was in Mae West the woman posed her as a bizarre curiosity: a septuagenarian convinced she was sexy, an embodiment of campy "failed seriousness."[18]

That was the case, at least, in the more mainstream ("pop-camp") reuse of West's image.[19] In the camp employed within gay male culture, the use of West's image was more complex. Undeniably, there was derision there too. The gay camp pantheon placed West and other faded screen divas alongside Carmen Miranda and Maria Montez, performers savored, as one critic put it, "expressly because they are terrible."[20] Gay camp, like pop camp, prized "failed seriousness," and to that it could add a heavy dollop of misogyny. As feminists charged, drag show parodies of Hollywood legends often mocked the women they claimed to venerate, exaggerating the mannishness of their aging features and turning them into ghoulish grotesques.[21]

But that condemnation, for all its validity, neglects the tenderness, the sincere affection, expressed for West by many gay men, including a Canadian-born drag queen called Craig Hurst. In the mid-1960s Hurst was a lonely gay teenager who developed a fascination for Mae West's screen image, and after he founded the Mae West International Fan Club, he wrote to West to tell her about it. They struck up a correspondence, she invited him to come visit her, and he journeyed by bus from Toronto to West's Santa Monica beach house and took up residence as her private secretary.

In the late 1960s Hurst returned to Toronto and began performing in gay bars as a female impersonator. He specialized in Hollywood movie queens; the highlight of his act was his impersonation of West. But he chose to impersonate the aging Mae West and the aging Marlene Dietrich. In a 1978 interview he was very clear about why:

> The sensuality of these women is mostly reminiscent. Dietrich's attempt in concert to recreate the naughty Lola . . . goes to the point of self-parody, and this is what I show with my self-mocking thing on stage. But I also show the tremendous strength that replaces youth, sex appeal, flesh appeal. When that goes, their personality comes in, their sense of showmanship.[22]

What Hurst praised as West's "showmanship" might be called defiant theatricality, an extravagant, willful act of sustaining a persona in the face of the passage of time. Hurst wasn't laughing at this—he admired it. So, more recently, has critic Wayne Koestenbaum in his praise for "retaliatory self-invention": the bravura theatrics of an aging diva combating public derision with her flamboyant projection of style.[23]

For Mae West herself, however, in many ways, whether she was venerated or derided did not really matter. In either case the camp revival depleted her power to create cultural meanings. Under its sway she became a camp object, an artifact for the hip to revive and rejuvenate—and that was true not just in the pop-camp of youth culture but in the more complex camp of gay men. In essence, the camp popularized in the 1960s and that we know today was all about empowering cultural consumers—turning them into cultural producers with the power to confer new cultural meanings. To that extent, it was a radically democratic phenomenon, as Wayne Koestenbaum maintains:

> Susan Sontag defined "camp" as the anarchic jolt we experience in the face of artistic artifacts that try to be serious and fail. But it is not the object's or the artist's failure that makes the artifact campy: the camp sensation is produced by our own joy in having discovered the object, in having been *chosen*, solicited, by it. Experiencing

the camp glow is a way of reversing one's abjection, and, by wit-nessing the depletion of cultural monuments, experiencing one's own power to fill degraded artifacts to the brim with meanings.

When we experience the camp rush, the delight, the savor, we are making a private airlift of lost cultural matter, fragments held hostage by everyone else's indifference. No one else lived for this gesture, this pattern, this figure, before; only I know that it is sub-lime.[24]

Yet Koestenbaum's stress on camp empowerment shouldn't obscure how it constrained Mae West: it fixed her as a "degraded artifact" that others could fill "to the brim with meanings." By defi-nition an object can't speak for itself; an artifact is bereft of all cul-tural power, as West discovered in the 1970s when she tried to chal-lenge her artifact status with her first screen appearances in more than two decades. At worst she would find herself ridiculed; at best ignored.

While in the 1960s the craze for camp had put Mae West's image to a wealth of new uses, by the mid-1970s the gay camp revision proved powerful enough to drown out all the rest. During those years West was compared to a drag queen by virtually every jour-nalist who described her—but by then that comparison targeted not West's iconic image but the alleged grotesquerie of the woman her-self. These were the years when, with *Myra Breckinridge* and *Sex-tette*, West capitalized on her camp revival, returning to the screen opposite much younger actors as the same irresistible siren she'd played in her prime. The film critic who described the result as a horror-movie monster and "a drag queen gone bananas" was mock-ing what West resembled as an elderly woman who persisted in playing her much younger persona, saying those same ribald lines, making those same overblown gestures, seemingly oblivious to the passage of time.[25]

This is the part of Mae West's career that even her biggest fans prefer to ignore. It's hard not to sympathize with that desire; there is something embarrassing, even painful, about it. In part, it's painful simply because it subjected West to such virulent ridicule. Playacting aggression at age seventy-plus, West was deemed no less than revolting by critics—mostly men—who found her not just less than female, but less than human. Rex Reed, West's co-star in *Myra Breckinridge*, was among the most cruel in his review of *Sextette*: "She looks like something they found in the basement of a pyramid."[26]

Feminists, for their part, were no less harsh, if somewhat less misogynistic. Many saw West as simply pathetic—a onetime model of female independence transformed into a "one-dimensional misogynist joke."[27] Blame for that joke fell on West's camp revival and on her iconic stature for many gay men. As the critic Molly Haskell put it, not only was West "much too old" when she made her last films, but "her gay constituency had become more explicit and obtrusive."[28] By these lights West was an elderly, perhaps senile woman, and gay men exploited her vulnerability. They egged her on to pervert her own image, to turn herself into a campy grotesque.

One needn't accept that view to acknowledge that in one respect West's critics were right. In the decades since her rejection by Hollywood, she had indeed become a different performer. Once shrewd and resourceful, attuned to her audiences, West had become remote and defensive, passionately invested in the cosmic importance of her creation, Mae West. By the time of her 1970s comeback she had spent three decades immersed in her own public myths. The "private" Mae West, for all practical purposes, had virtually ceased to exist. Even West's closest friends couldn't discern her. As critic Kevin Thomas would put it in a eulogy delivered at the actress's funeral, in the years since West created the West character "the woman and the legend had long since become one."[29]

That West had changed since the 1930s was undeniable, yet traces of the savvy stage artist remained, even if they emerged only in flashes, as *Life*'s Richard Meryman saw. By the 1970s there were really two Mae Wests: Mae West B, who believed in her legend wholeheartedly, and Mae West A, who was "calculating, shrewd," and tuned in to market demand.[30] It was Mae West A who engineered the 1970s comeback (even if it was Mae West B who performed in the films): a perceptive reader of modern audiences, she discerned the new craze for camp. She even recognized its historical journey, the fact that while "in the twenties and thirties the gay crowd was usin' it," camp had "finally got out to the public."[31] Yet in that very resemblance to the Mae West of old lies the genuine pathos of her comeback attempt. While she was astute enough to sense the camp craze and shrewd enough to tailor her new films around it, West badly misread her new admirers' signals. She misunderstood what they meant by camp.

In 1971, when *Playboy* magazine asked West to set out her definition of camp, she replied without hesitation: "Camp is the kinda comedy where they imitate me." By "they," West explained, she meant gay men, whom she counted among her most loyal fans. As West saw it, her appeal to those particular fans was intimately related to her skills as a camp:

> Camp is bein' funny and dishy and outrageous and sayin' sexy and clever things. I'm always sayin' somethin' sexy and campy and they like to sound that way too. That's one way they feel they *can*, since they feel they're not, you know, naturally sexy. . . . They're crazy about me 'cause I give 'em a chance to play.[32]

What's striking about West's definition is not just what she said, but what she neglected: virtually all the buzzwords by which 1960s cognoscenti defined and enthused about camp. She made no mention of "failed seriousness," of a taste for the garish, the artificial, the outmoded. Instead, she pointed to a psychology of sexuality and gender. To West, camp denoted a comic behavior by which gay men imitated a flamboyant woman. They did so, as she saw it, in a spirit of play, but with an undercurrent of seriousness: to make up for what they experienced as a personal lack of "natural sexiness." ("They like to sound that way, too.")

That contrast illuminates how dramatically West's understanding of camp was itself obsolete. The camp she described was what she had known in the 1920s among "the gay crowd" of New York. It was a playful but purposeful gender inversion, a gay man's expression of a "third sex" identity through his adoption of a brassy, effeminate public self. That brand of camp had mattered to West: she showcased it in *Pleasure Man* and *The Drag* and won national notoriety, and she adopted it herself in *Diamond Lil* and won mass-market popularity. West had borrowed heavily from 1920s camp to create her suggestively swaggering temptress. The links had been readily apparent to the era's gay men, like Parker Tyler, who recalled that in homosexual circles in the 1930s, "Mae West was an acknowledged camp."[33]

To see West in that context as an "acknowledged camp" was not, clearly, to see her as an artifact. It was to admire her finely honed skills as a performer, her abilities less in acting than in "*doing an act.*"[34] West had appropriated camp's ironic detachment, its teasing suggestion of hidden meanings. Like gay men, she impersonated a flamboyant woman with a sly, tongue-in-cheek extravagance.

It was in that sense, as an "acknowledged camp," that West attempted a comeback forty years later. Once she heard herself labeled the "queen of camp," she naturally believed that she knew what that meant. Camp was an ironic, teasing inflection that she had appropriated and learned how to wield. She expected to be appreciated as a camp agent, for her skill in "doing an act."

But that wasn't what happened. What West couldn't perceive was the difference between the camp she'd learned to use in the 1920s and the air of camp that surrounded her in the 1960s. As the "queen of camp," West was no longer being praised as an agent— she was being revived as an object; an obsolete, outmoded object that consumers could revitalize in all sorts of new ways.

That misapprehension set the stage for West's disastrous 1970s comeback. Attempting to re-create herself as a camp agent, she found herself mocked or, just as painfully, ignored. *Myra Breckin-ridge* was a colossal critical and box office failure. *Sextette*'s fate was even worse. Slammed by critics in previews, it then sat on the shelf, with no distributor coming forward at all.

By any objective standard, both films are dreadful: clumsily writ-ten, badly directed, with that lumbering air of ersatz hip that afflicts so many film attempts at deliberate camp. Cast in *Myra* as a lascivi-ous Hollywood agent, in *Sextette* as a much-married screen legend, try as she might, West still comes across as a faint, sad echo of her former self.

So painful are both films to watch that it's hard to credit West's judgment, or even sanity, in making them. Yet their lure from her perspective was eminently rational: they gave her unprecedented freedom to reenact "Mae West." For both films she received full script approval to re-create the West character as she saw it. To her mind, it must have made market sense. She knew modern audiences wanted camp; she believed she and camp were one and the same thing. She was camp, in other words, simply by doing her stuff: "Camp is the kinda comedy where they imitate me."

In essence, the films offered West an unparalleled chance to reclaim her centrality as Mae West's creator. With everyone from drag queens to pop artists appropriating her image, she was determined to step in herself. She was sure she could outstrip any competitor: "I'll be giving them the bust and curves that they always want to see—and the moves, and the things I say."[35] To that end, she filled both scripts with Westian wisecracks resurrected from films she'd made forty years previously. She even, in *Sextette*, resurrected the golden swan bed from *Diamond Lil*.

The response was indifference from audiences and some of the most vicious reviews ever penned, utterly dashing West's expectation that the camp revival would return her to the spotlight. The very same audiences who loved Mae West the icon found Mae West the performer tiresome and repellent. To some, she resembled nothing so much as a second-rate homosexual caricature. As Vincent Canby of the *New York Times* put it, she looked like "a plump sheep that's been stood on its hind legs," "bewigged and smeared with pink plaster" and "dressed in a drag queen's idea of chic."[36]

Over time such attacks took their toll, even on a spirit as indomitable as West's. By the late 1970s, with both films a failure, she was a disappointed, deeply frustrated woman. She hid that frustration as much as possible—it violated the essence of "Mae West, the All-Conqueror"—but it occasionally flashed out in a striking form: in expressions of rivalry with gay men.

At the same time that West watched her comeback collapse she witnessed another cultural phenomenon: gay artists enjoying high-profile success with plays and films on homosexual themes. The audience for those works was not just gay men—it was heterosexuals from the urban mainstream, their traditional notions of gender and sex unsettled by women's and gay liberation. West considered this to be her audience—*and* her material, in a literal sense. She was convinced, for instance, that some anonymous adversary had smuggled a copy of *The Drag* to playwright Mart Crowley, who had simply "changed a few things" to create *The Boys in the Band*.[37]

Behind West's seeming paranoia lay a sharp sense of injustice: gay men's creations were deemed exciting and relevant, hers were quaint relics of an innocent past. That her past was *not* innocent was something she stressed in interview after interview throughout the 1970s. "I was always ahead of my time," West insisted; the public was only now catching up. She had brought to Broadway "screamin' gay great lookin' guys flauntin' it all over the place"; in defiance of the police, she had been gay men's patron and a pioneering champion of gay rights.[38]

But no one was listening. The press treated West's claims with skeptical bemusement; Hollywood, for its part, once more ignored her, showing no interest in West's proposal for a film version of *The Drag*. To West, this was a double blow. Not only were gay men getting all the attention; she feared that they stood to gain all the credit for camp, for the style she saw as uniquely her own.

The truth was, of course, it wasn't her own. She had borrowed that style from gay men in the 1920s—an unpalatable fact for someone so invested in believing that she had created herself. Perhaps that uneasy knowledge was what impelled West to make one last, futile stab at rewriting her past. In 1975, with the help of her secretary, she published a novelized version of her still unpublished play *Pleasure Man*, which replicated the original in all essentials— except that it dropped the gay female impersonators. In their place was a new character, Helen Webster, a sexy, flamboyant singer-dancer, who comments on the proceedings with sharp-tongued, suggestive wisecracks.

The substance of West's revision was to drop the drag queens and throw in Mae West. It was an extraordinary change, wholly baffling on first glance. In the face of West's zeal to prove her past wildness, she threw away the most relevant evidence—the raunchy, scatological homosexual passages that had provoked the 1928 vice squad raid. As to why West did it, one can only guess. Perhaps she considered the play incriminating evidence, its flamboyant gay characters dramatically showing that her style was not as original as she made out. Or perhaps the answer is simpler. West wanted to prove that her past had been lively, but not at the price of sharing the spotlight. *Pleasure Man*'s gay men, quite possibly, could steal her thunder, just as they were doing in real life.

It may well have been exactly that sentiment that doomed West's friendship with the drag queen Craig Hurst. Out of all these instances of West's new sense of rivalry, this one seems the saddest of all. The mid-1970s brought a dramatic change in Hurst's fortunes: he moved to New York, changed his name to Craig Russell, and gained widespread renown as a female impersonator. In 1977 he made a film called *Outrageous!*, a tale of a drag queen's coming of age, featuring Russell in street clothes and in drag incarnations, culminating in his impersonation of West. *Outrageous!* became a substantial cult hit in the United States and Canada, and Russell's performance won several awards: the Berlin Film Festival named him the year's best actor; the Virgin Islands Film Festival named him best actor and best actress too.

In 1978, at the same time that audiences were flocking to *Outrageous!*, West was trying to find a theater willing to showcase *Sextette*. She finally found one, in Los Angeles, but it premiered the film only on the condition that *Outrageous!* was featured on the same bill. West's film was essentially second-billed to Russell's, and she did not take to it kindly. At the post-premiere party she told her escorts to keep Russell away from her table, and she never spoke to him again.

One has to empathize with West's sense of bitterness. She had lost control of her own creation. The imitation had outstripped the original (who was herself, ironically, an imitation). By the late 1970s Mae West the drag queen had more of an audience than Mae West herself.

Epilogue

Although Mae West's friends among the Forces had predicted that she would live to be over one hundred, by the late 1970s even her staunchest admirers recognized her intensifying physical weakness. Superficially buoyant, West had in fact suffered from precarious health since the mid-1960s, when she experienced a mild stroke and developed diabetes. By the 1970s her mental powers were fading and her short-term memory came and went. She was able to perform in *Sextette* only by having her lines broadcast to her through a shortwave radio receiver hidden in her wig.

In August 1980, one week before her eighty-seventh birthday, West suffered a stroke and fell out of bed. Even then she stayed in character, issuing a press release stating that she'd fallen out of bed during a dream and that it hadn't been an unpleasant experience: "How bad can a dream about Burt Reynolds be?"[1] But jokes couldn't disguise the growing seriousness of West's condition. She was hospitalized for the next three months and never really rallied. On November 22, three weeks after returning home to her Hollywood apartment, Mae West died.

*   *   *

In the years since her death, Mae West has occupied an amorphous place in the pantheon of American pop culture legends: though her silhouette and witticisms remain ubiquitous, as an actress she is barely present at all. West is remembered "more as a figure of speech—in both senses of the word—than a beloved movie memory," noted critic Molly Haskell in a centennial tribute. "Unlike other stars, whom we think of in the context of specific films, her image, complete with body language and voice, lifts buoyantly out of celluloid into space like the inflatable life preserver named after her in World War II."[2] We remember, in short, West's curves and her wisecracks, the latter sometimes disconnected from the woman herself. "Or are you just glad to see me?" taunts a buxom model in a 1994 lingerie ad. "Come up and see me sometime baby!" booms the master of ceremonies in the drag ball documentary *Paris Is Burning.*

While bits of West's image have become free-floating shorthand for a campily brazen sexual come-on, the woman herself, what she did, who she was, has all but disappeared from our view. As a film actress West seems to have lost even the limited drawing power that accrued to her during her 1960s revival. While two biographies have appeared since her death, neither elicited the tantalized curiosity that greeted the life stories of Marlene Dietrich (or that, as I write, promises to surround the forthcoming biographies of Greta Garbo). Indeed, the assumption I've encountered in writing this book is that West's life story has nothing to tell us. If Garbo and Dietrich seem faintly contemporary, their androgyny marking a subversive sophistication, West remains a bit of a relic, her image a holdover from a more innocent past.

At least some of the blame for that air of lifelessness must be laid at the feet of Mae West herself, for her expurgated version of her own life story unwittingly cast it in precisely that light. In interviews given throughout her career and in two separate editions of her autobiography, West presented herself as an amiable satirist who stunned a nation of Victorian prudes. The story was appealing in its simplicity: she was "the first to bring sex out into the open and make fun of it," a pathbreaking voice of good-humored candor in a culture of near-total sexual reticence.[3] "In 1926 when my play *Sex* opened they would not allow me to even print the word in the newspapers," she insisted.[4] It was a tale she told reporters as early as 1929.

Yet by radically simplifying both the past and her part in it, that story ultimately did West more harm than good. It lent her stage and screen work an air of innocuousness and, over time, triviality; it made West little more than a quaint artifact of a distant, puritanical past. Placed against an ersatz Victorian backdrop West was reduced in significance even by those who set out to praise her. Even the organizers of a 1982 tribute to West as "writer, impresario, superstar" couldn't help noting that she was "celebrated more for shattering mid-Victorian film taboos with double entendres that would be regarded as pablum by critics of contemporary film erotica."[5]

Seen in that light, as a sexual icon West seems to have little to tell us. As an exemplar of Hollywood history she seems to have even less. Since her death West's life story has held little interest for writers of "serious" film biography, be they feminists or cultural critics, who have celebrated the lives of pop culture dissidents. Louise Brooks, Frances Farmer, Marilyn Monroe—all have been valorized as heroic victims, rebels struggling to preserve their integrity against the corrupting mass-culture machine. West's life simply does not fit that narrative. She always refused to play the victim, and would never badmouth the studio bosses no matter how badly they treated her. She bristled when musician John Phillips, who wrote some of her music for *Myra Breckinridge*, presented her with a number entitled "Hollywood Was Always a Honky Tonk Town." She was a Hollywood legend, she reminded him, and loyal to the institution. Phillips dutifully changed the title to "Hollywood Was Never a Honky Tonk Town."[6]

Intellectuals love "authentic" performers who fight typecasting and commercialization. Mae West, in contrast, claimed to love every typecast minute. "I got fun outta bein' an institution," she insisted, and no one who knew her could possibly doubt it.[7] She embraced her persona as the "Empress of Sex" with a passion that even some fans found embarrassing, and spent her last years replicating the fantastical glamor purveyed during Hollywood's Golden Age. If her own life story contained elements of struggle, if her native roughness had been defused by the star system, she refused to see it that way.

The story that Mae West didn't want told is the one that I have set out in this book: her beginnings as a sensationalist showwoman, an impresario of the sexual underworld, deemed "raw," "crude," and "ugly" not simply by prudes but by critics of acknowledged cultivation and taste. It was the story of her working-class roots and her links to traditions of underworld theater. West denied those links for the rest of her life. She was furious when writer Jon Tuska suggested that she had performed in burlesque; she depicted *Sex* as a lighthearted comedy, suppressing evidence of the grittier truth. The occasional fan who asked her to autograph a photo from the *Sex* stage production found that a truculent West would first attempt to buy it; failing that, she would return it without her signature, claiming that the woman depicted was not her at all.[8]

West rewrote her past in the service of her marketability and reputation. To my mind, however, knowing its true outlines allows us to appreciate her image anew. It was a jumble of disreputable performance traditions drawn from immigrant dives and the gay underground, crafted and recrafted by a shrewd judge of audiences who knew what she was doing at every step. Her sheer inventiveness with her materials makes her a precursor of the likes of Madonna and a forerunner of comic performers like Bette Midler and Sandra Bernhardt, women who deliberately manipulate camp humor rather than remaining naive objects of it.

Out of the hidden corners of working-class culture West created something eminently enduring, a persona that entranced and bewildered millions of spectators, all mesmerized by that delectable secret that West seemed to be savoring but never revealed. To the end of her life, even as West's allure faded, those spectators kept trying to unmask her, to pull back the veil from her unreadable pleasure and expose its genuine source. What was West's "oft-hinted-at secret"? Was she a lesbian? a nymphomaniac? a transvestite? Did she have (a hypothesis advanced by film buff John Kobal) "a touch of color in her blood"?[9]

It was Mae West's genius, as well as her downfall, to keep the answer forever hidden, responding only with an enigmatic smile and hanging tantalizingly out of reach.

Chapter One: Tough Girl

1. *New York Herald*, August 5, 1913, p. 11.

2. Michael Macdonald Mooney, *Evelyn Nesbit and Stanford White: Love and Death in the Gilded Age* (New York, 1976).

3. Abel Green and Joe Laurie, Jr., *Show Biz: From Vaude to Video* (New York, 1951), p. 19.

4. Ibid., pp. 21–22.

5. *Variety*, quoted in George Eells and Stanley Musgrove, *Mae West: A Biography* (London, 1984), p. 33. For more on Willard see Ricky Jay, *Learned Pigs and Fireproof Women* (New York, 1986).

6. *New York American*, September 28, 1913, section CE, p. 5.

7. *Variety*, February 7, 1913, p. 22.

8. Green and Laurie, *Show Biz*, p. 18.

9. *New York World*, December 13, 1911, p. 1; *Variety*, July 22, 1911, p. 23, and December 30, 1911, p. 19; Green and Laurie, *Show Biz*, p. 18.

10. Green and Laurie, *Show Biz*, p. 18.

11. Anthony Slide, *The Vaudevillians* (Westport, Conn., 1981), p. 149.

12. Accounts of the performance can be found in the *New York Herald*, August 5, 1913, p. 11; *New York World*, August 5, 1913, p. 7; *New York Tribune*, August 5, 1913, p. 7; *Variety*, August 8, 1913, pp. 5, 19.

13. *New York Tribune*, August 5, 1913, p. 7.

14. *Variety*, August 8, 1913, pp. 5, 19.

15. Mae West, *Goodness Had Nothing to Do With It* (Englewood Cliffs, N.J., 1959), pp. 9–10.

16. The year of West's birth has long been a source of confusion. In her autobiography she gave the date that I have cited, but others have claimed differently, placing her birth in any number of years from 1888 to 1900. Primary documents, however, back up West's account. While no birth records exist for Mary Jane West in the New York City Municipal Archives, she does turn up in the 1900 United States census, recorded before West's birthday on August 17, which lists three children in the West household: John, aged three months; Mildred, aged three; and Mary Jane, aged six. See Eells and Musgrove, *Mae West*, p. 20.

17. On Greenpoint see Eugene L. Armbruster, *Brooklyn's Eastern District* (Brooklyn, 1992, originally published 1928); William L. Felter, *Historic Greenpoint* (Brooklyn, 1918); and clippings in Greenpoint file, Brooklyn History Collection, Brooklyn Public Library, Brooklyn, N.Y. For reminiscences of Mae West in Greenpoint see *New York Daily News* (Brooklyn section), November 26, 1980, held in Mae West file, also in Brooklyn History Collection.

18. Eells and Musgrove, *Mae West*, p. 21; Maurice Leonard, *Mae West: Empress of Sex* (London, 1991), p. 7.

19. Maurice Leonard in his biography *Mae West: Empress of Sex* argues that Tillie was Jewish. To my mind, her religion remains a mystery. West herself was never consistent on the subject, describing her mother variously as Catholic, Jewish, or Protestant to match the faith of the listener. For more on this point see Eells and Musgrove, *Mae West*, pp. 21–22.

20. West, *Goodness*, p. 3; Eells and Musgrove, *Mae West*, pp. 20–21.

21. Leonard, *Mae West: Empress of Sex*, pp. 8–14.

22. Eells and Musgrove, *Mae West*, p. 24.

23. On the ten-twent'-thirt' circuit see Frank Rahill, *The World of Melodrama* (University Park, Pa., 1960), pp. 271–272.

24. West, *Goodness*, p. 15.

25. Owen Davis, *I'd Like To Do It Again* (New York, 1931), p. 85, quoted in Rahill, *The World of Melodrama*, p. 281.

26 Jane Addams, *The Spirit of Youth and the City Streets* (New York, 1912), p. 88. Published by Macmillan in 1912, Addams's account was first serialized in *Survey* in 1909.

27 Robert O. Bartholomew, *Report of Censorship of Motion Pictures* (Chicago, 1913), p. 14, quoted in Daniel Czitrom, *Media and the American Mind: From Morse to McLuhan* (Chapel Hill, N.C., 1982), p. 46.

28. On the Victorian emphasis on culture as "self-tillage" see Czitrom, *Media and the American Mind*, pp. 31–32.

29. Addams, *The Spirit of Youth*, pp. 16, 27–28.

30. Quoted in Karl Fleming and Anne Taylor Fleming, *The First Time* (New York, 1975), p. 316.

31. Eells and Musgrove, *Mae West*, p. 26.

32. See Kathy Peiss, *Cheap Amusements: Working Women and Leisure in*

Turn-of-the-Century New York (Philadelphia, 1986), for an incisive study of the tough-girl phenomenon.

33. Quoted in Investigator's report on Peter's Tavern, 178 Broadway, Brooklyn, 1916, in Box 30, Committee of Fourteen Papers, Manuscript Division, New York Public Library, New York City.

34. Quoted in ibid., p. 66.

35. Richard Henry Edwards, *Popular Amusements* (New York, 1915), p. 140.

36. Elizabeth Lunbeck, "'A New Generation of Women': Progressive Psychiatrists and the Hypersexual Female," *Feminist Studies* 13 (Fall 1987): 513–543.

37. My account of West's marriage is taken from Eells and Musgrove, *Mae West*, pp. 27–32.

38. Ibid., p. 31.

39. Ibid., p. 40.

40. Ibid., p. 46.

Chapter Two: "That Touch of Class"

1. *Variety*, July 26, 1912, p. 5.

2. Abel Green and Joe Laurie, Jr., *Show Biz: From Vaude to Video* (New York, 1951), p. 27; *Variety*, March 9, 1912, p. 18.

3. *Variety*, May 25, 1912, p. 6.

4. *Variety*, October 3, 1913, p. 22.

5. Robert W. Snyder, *The Voice of the City: Vaudeville and Popular Culture in New York* (New York, 1989), pp. 61–62, 95–100.

6. Mae West, *Goodness Had Nothing to Do With It* (Englewood Cliffs, N.J., 1959), p. 50.

7. Ibid., p. 51.

8. *Variety*, March 23, 1912, p. 26.

9. *Variety*, July 7, 1916, p. 12.

10. On the history of burlesque, see Peter G. Buckley, "The Culture of Leg Work: The Transformation of Burlesque After the Civil War," paper presented to the American Historical Association, December 1986; Irving Zeidman, *The American Burlesque Show* (New York, 1967); and Robert C. Allen, *Horrible Prettiness: Burlesque and American Culture* (Chapel Hill, N.C., 1991).

11. Rollin Lynde Hartt, *The People at Play* (Boston, 1909), p. 7.

12. *Variety*, March 5, 1915, p. 16; Zeidman, *American Burlesque Show*, p. 17; Bernard Sobel, *Burleyque: An Underground History of Burlesque Days* (New York, 1931), pp. 127, 227, 259–261; Hartt, *People at Play*, p. 7.

13. Quoted in Richard Henry Edwards, *Popular Amusements* (New York, 1915), p. 46.

14. Sobel, *Burleyque*, pp. 162–164; Zeidman, *American Burlesque Show*, p. 69.

15. Uncited clipping, dated 1915, in Walter Johnson Burlesque Scrapbook, Billy Rose Theatre Collection of the Performing Arts Research Center, New York Public Library at Lincoln Center, New York City.

16. Quoted in Zeidman, *American Burlesque Show*, p. 11.

17. Sander Gilman, "Black Bodies, White Bodies: Toward an Iconography of Female Sexuality in Late Nineteenth Century Art, Medicine, and Literature," in Henry Louis Gates, Jr., ed., *"Race," Writing, and Difference* (Chicago, 1985), p. 242.

18. Quoted in John F. Kasson, *Amusing the Million: Coney Island at the Turn of the Century* (New York, 1978), p. 26.

19. Quoted in Zeidman, *American Burlesque Show*, pp. 15–16.

20. *New York Times*, January 4, 1912, quoted in Elisabeth I. Perry, "'The General Motherhood of the Commonwealth': Dance Hall Reform in the Progressive Era," *American Quarterly* 37 (Fall 1985):728.

21. *Variety*, April 20, 1912, p. 16.

22. West, *Goodness*, p. 64.

23. *Variety*, March 9, 1912, p. 18.

24. George Eells and Stanley Musgrove, *Mae West: A Biography* (London, 1984), pp. 38–39.

25. *New York Times*, June 11, 1914, p. 11

26. Marion Spitzer, *The Palace* (New York, 1950), p. 4.

27. Green and Laurie, *Show Biz*, p. 17.

28. Douglas Gilbert, *American Vaudeville* (New York, 1963, originally published 1940), pp. 246–247.

29. *Variety*, November 7, 1913, p. 13.

30. Caroline Caffin, *Vaudeville* (New York, 1914), p. 220.

31. Gilbert, *American Vaudeville*, p. 247; Shirley Staples, *Male-Female Comedy Teams in American Vaudeville, 1865–1932* (Ann Arbor, Mich., 1984), p. 152.

32. Green and Laurie, *Show Biz*, pp. 20–21.

33. *Variety*, May 25, 1912, p. 16.

34. Sophie Tucker, *Some of These Days* (Garden City, N.Y., 1945), p. 27.

35. *Variety*, quoted in Staples, *Male-Female Comedy Teams*, p. 119; on stage slang see Marion Spitzer, "The People of Vaudeville," in Charles W. Stein, *American Vaudeville As Seen by Its Contemporaries* (New York, 1984), p. 226.

36. *Variety*, November 28, 1908, p. 13.

37. Julian Street, "Oh, You Babylon!" *Everybody's Magazine* 27 (August 1912):177.

38. William Taylor, *In Pursuit of Gotham: Culture and Commerce in New York* (New York, 1992), p. 80.

39. Ibid., p. 7.

40. *Variety*, March 28, 1913, p. 5.

41. Spitzer, *The Palace*, pp. 12–13.

42. *Variety*, May 21, 1915, p. 3.

43. *Variety*, July 3, 1914, p. 5; Green and Laurie, *Show Biz*, pp. 155–157.

44. Snyder, *The Voice of the City*, pp. 26–41, 64–81.

45. On the transition from concert saloon to vaudeville see Snyder, *The Voice of the City*, pp. 3–25.

46. Quoted in Edwin Milton Royle, "The Vaudeville Theatre," *Scribner's Magazine* 26 (October 1899), in Stein, *American Vaudeville*, p. 24.

47. Peter G. Buckley, "To the Opera House: New York Theatre and Culture, 1820–1860" (Ph.D. thesis, State University of New York at Stony Brook, 1985), chapter 4.

48. Quoted in Royle, "The Vaudeville Theater," p. 25.

49. Quoted in Gilbert, *American Vaudeville*, p. 205.

50. "The Profits in Clean Vaudeville," *Literary Digest* 43 (October 7, 1911):603–605.

51. Snyder, *The Voice of the City*, pp. 141–142.

52. Hartley Davis, "In Vaudeville," *Everybody's Magazine* 13 (August 1905), reprinted in Stein, *American Vaudeville*, p. 100.

53. *Variety*, October 27, 1916, p. 3.

54. Caffin, *Vaudeville*, p. 18.

55. Anthony Slide, *The Vaudevillians* (Westport, Conn., 1981), pp. 146–148.

56. Uncited, undated clipping in Robinson Locke Collection of Dramatic Scrapbooks, Scrapbook #450 (Eva Tanguay), p. 67, Billy Rose Theatre Collection.

57. *Spokane Review*, October 25, 1908, in Robinson Locke Collection of Dramatic Scrapbooks, Scrapbook #450 (Eva Tanguay), p. 88, Billy Rose Theatre Collection; Robert C. Toll, *On With the Show* (New York, 1976), p. 279.

58. Zeidman, *American Burlesque Show*, p. 62.

59. *New York Telegraph*, February 13, 1908, in Robinson Locke Collection of Dramatic Scrapbooks, Scrapbook #450 (Eva Tanguay), Billy Rose Theatre Collection.

60. For more on this point and its importance to early mass culture see Peter Bailey, "Ally Sloper's Half-Holiday: Comic Art in the 1880s," *History Workshop* 16 (Autumn 1983):4–31; and Taylor, *In Pursuit of Gotham*, pp. 69–91.

61. Kasson, *Amusing the Million*, pp. 96–101.

62. Quoted in Toll, *On With the Show*, p. 280.

63. *New York Dramatic Mirror*, October 6, 1915, quoted in Slide, *The Vaudevillians*, p. 146.

64. Ashton Stevens, "Tanguay a Quivering, Shrieking, Undeniable Nerve," *New York Telegraph*, July 26, 1908, in Robinson Locke Collection of Dramatic Scrapbooks, Scrapbook #450 (Eva Tanguay), p. 77, Billy Rose Theatre Collection.

65. *Syracuse Journal*, March 9, 1915, reprinted in *Variety*, March 12, 1915, p. 2.

66. Quoted in Stevens, "Tanguay a Quivering, Shrieking, Undeniable Nerve."

67. Uncited clipping in Robinson Locke Collection of Dramatic Scrapbooks, Scrapbook #450 (Eva Tanguay), Billy Rose Theatre Collection.

68. *New York Telegraph*, December 24, 1907, in Robinson Locke Collection of Dramatic Scrapbooks, Scrapbook #450 (Eva Tanguay), Billy Rose Theatre Collection.

69. Quoted in Slide, *The Vaudevillians*, pp. 146–147.

70. Brian Duryea, "Vaudeville: Where the Acts Come From," *Green Book Magazine* (September 1915):545.

71. *New York Telegraph*, January 21, 1908, in Robinson Locke Collection of Dramatic Scrapbooks, Scrapbook #450 (Eva Tanguay), Billy Rose Theatre Collection.

72. *Chicago Examiner*, March 28, 1911, in Robinson Locke Collection of Dramatic Scrapbooks, Scrapbook #450 (Eva Tanguay), Billy Rose Theatre Collection.

73. *New York Telegraph*, April 5, 1907, in Robinson Locke Collection of Dramatic Scrapbooks, Scrapbook #450 (Eva Tanguay), Billy Rose Theatre Collection.

74. *Boston Transcript*, February 9, 1909, in Robinson Locke Collection of Dramatic Scrapbooks, Scrapbook #450 (Eva Tanguay), Billy Rose Theatre Collection.

75. Quoted in Toll, *On With the Show*, p. 280.

76. *Philadelphia Times*, November 11, 1913, in Robinson Locke Collection of Dramatic Scrapbooks, Envelope #2541 (Mae West), Billy Rose Theater Collection.

77. *Columbus Journal*, November 4, 1913, in Robinson Locke Collection of Dramatic Scrapbooks, Envelope #2541 (Mae West), Billy Rose Theatre Collection.

78. *Variety*, October 11, 1918, pp. 15, 19. West appeared in a Broadway musical comedy, *Sometime,* Sime Silverman recalled "the rough hand-on-the-hip character portrayer that [West] first conceived as the ideal type of a woman single in vaudeville."

79. *Detroit News*, August 26, 1914, in Robinson Locke Collection of Dramatic Scrapbooks, Envelope #2541 (Mae West), Billy Rose Theatre Collection.

80. *Variety*, July 7, 1916, p. 12.

Chapter Three: Sex, The Drag, *and the Comedy-Drama of Life*

1. Jon Tuska, *The Films of Mae West* (Secaucus, N.J., 1973), pp. 30–31.

2. Irving Zeidman, *The American Burlesque Show* (New York, 1967), pp. 92–98.

3. *Variety*, October 11, 1918, pp. 15, 19.

4. Kenneth MacGowan, "The Crisis on Broadway," *Harpers Magazine* 158 (December 1928):112–118; see also Mary C. Henderson, *The City and the Theatre: New York Playhouses From Bowling Green to Times Square* (Clifton, N.J., 1973), pp. 177–199.

5. *New York Daily Mirror*, April 30, 1926, in *Sex* clipping file, Billy Rose Theatre Collection of the Performing Arts Research Center, New York Public Library at Lincoln Center, New York City.

6. *New Yorker*, May 8, 1926, in *Sex* clipping file, Billy Rose Theatre Collection.

7. Uncited, undated clipping in *Sex* clipping file, Billy Rose Theatre Collection.

8. *New York Herald Tribune*, April 27, 1926, in *Sex* clipping file, Billy Rose Theatre Collection.

9. Mae West, *Goodness Had Nothing to Do With It* (Englewood Cliffs, N.J., 1959), pp. 90–91; George Eells and Stanley Musgrove, *Mae West: A Biography* (London, 1984), p. 62.

10. Peter G. Buckley, "To the Opera House: New York Theatre and Culture, 1820–1860" (Ph.D. thesis, State University of New York at Stony Brook, 1985), chapter 3.

11. *Variety*, April 28, 1926, p. 79.

12. Mae West, *Sex*, p. 15, manuscript held in the Mae West Collection, Manuscript Division, Library of Congress, Washington, D.C.

13. George Jean Nathan, *Art of the Night* (Rutherford, N.J., 1972; originally published 1928), p. 90.

14. Testimony of Police Sergeant Patrick Keneally quoted in *New York World*, March 30, 1927, p. 9. "While he was doing it," Keneally added, "people around me were saying 'Oh, my God!' "

15. Zeidman, *The American Burlesque Show*, pp. 92–98.

16. West, *Sex*, Act 1, p. 12.

17. *New York Herald Tribune*, January 23, 1927, in *Sex* clipping file, Billy Rose Theatre Collection.

18. Robert C. Toll, *On With the Show* (New York, 1976), pp. 317–319.

19. Statement of Inspector James Bolan in Case #168495, *New York v. C. William Morganstern et al.*, District Attorney Case Files, Municipal Archives, New York City.

20. Sander Gilman, "Black Bodies, White Bodies: Toward an Iconography of Female Sexuality in Late Nineteenth Century Art, Medicine, and Literature," in Henry Louis Gates, Jr., ed., *"Race," Writing, and Difference* (Chicago, 1985), pp. 223–261.

21. *New York Daily Mirror*, December 31, 1926, p. 3.

22. West, *Goodness*, pp. 91–92.

23. Ibid., p. 95.

24. Ibid., p. 94.

25. Kaier Curtain, *"We Can Always Call Them Bulgarians": The Emergence of Lesbians and Gay Men on the American Stage* (Boston, 1987), chapter 3.

26. Jack Hamilton, "Raquel Welch, Mae West Talk About Men, Morals and *Myra Breckinridge,*" *Look* 34 (March 24, 1970):47.

27. *Variety*, February 2, 1927, p. 39.

28. Mae West, *The Drag*, Act 1, pp. 13–14, manuscript held in the Mae West Collection, Manuscript Division, Library of Congress, Washington, D.C.

29. See John D'Emilio, *Sexual Politics, Sexual Communities: The Making of a Homosexual Minority in the U.S., 1940–1970* (Chicago, 1983), chapter 1; and George Chauncey, "From Sexual Inversion to Homosexuality: The Changing Medicine Conceptualization of Female 'Deviance,' " in Kathy Peiss and Christina Simmons, eds., *Passion and Power: Sexuality in History* (Philadelphia, 1989), pp. 87–117.

30. Hubert C. Kennedy, "The 'Third Sex' Theory of Karl Heinrich Ulrichs," in Salvatore J. Licata and Robert P. Peterson, *Historical Perspectives on Homosexuality* (New York, 1981), pp. 103–112.

31. Richard Meryman, "Mae West: A Cherished, Bemusing Masterpiece of Self-Preservation," *Life* 66 (April 18, 1969):72.

32. Quoted in Eells and Musgrove, *Mae West*, p. 65.

33. *Variety*, January 12, 1927, p. 37.

34. *Variety*, January 26, 1927, p. 49.

35. West, *The Drag*, Act 2, p. 4.

36. *Variety*, February 2, 1927, p. 49.

37. Ibid.

38. West, *The Drag*, Act 3, pp. 2–3.

39. On New York's gay neighborhoods see George Chauncey, "The Way We Were: Gay Male Society in the Jazz Age," *Village Voice*, July 1, 1986, pp. 29–30, 34, and his brilliant book *Gay New York: Gender, Urban Culture, and the Making of the Gay Male World, 1890–1940* (New York, 1994); on the rise of America's gay underworld see D'Emilio, *Sexual Politics, Sexual Communities*, chapter 1, and documents in Jonathan Katz, *Gay American History: Lesbians and Gay Men in the USA* (New York, 1976).

40. Quoted in Katz, *Gay American History*, p. 52. On the working-class roots of New York's gay subculture see Chauncey, *Gay New York*, pp. 10, 33–45.

41. Chauncey, *Gay New York* p. 16.

42. *Zit's Theatrical Newspaper*, February 5, 1927, quoted in Curtain, "We Can Always Call Them Bulgarians," p. 81.

43. Chauncey, "The Way We Were," pp. 29–30.

44. George Chauncey, "Christian Brotherhood or Sexual Perversion? Homosexual Identities and the Construction of Sexual Boundaries in the World War I Era," in Martin Duberman et al., *Hidden From History: Reclaiming the Gay and Lesbian Past* (New York, 1989), pp. 294–317; see also Chauncey, *Gay New York*, pp. 47–63.

45. Chauncey, *Gay New York*, pp. 47–63.

46. Jimmy Durante and Jack Kofoed, *Nightclubs* (New York, 1931), pp. 54–55.

47. *Variety*, February 2, 1927, p. 39; see also Zeidman, *The American Burlesque Show*.

48. *New York World*, March 31, 1927, section 2, p. 1.

49. *New York Morning Telegraph*, February 1, 1927, p. 1.

50. Uncited clipping of February 11, 1927, quoted in Curtain, "We Can Always Call Them Bulgarians," pp. 97–98.

51. On tabloids see Simon Michael Bessie, *Jazz Journalism* (New York, 1938).

52. *Variety*, May 5, 1926, p. 44; May 19, 1926, p. 42: May 26, 1926, p. 42; June 9, 1926, p. 39; and *New York Times*, March 21, 1927, p. 21.

53. *Life*, May 20, 1926, in *Sex* clipping file, Billy Rose Theatre Collection.

54. Statement of Inspector James Bolan, *New York v. Morganstern.*

55. *Variety,* December 22, 1926, p. 33.

56. Stark Young, "Diamond Lil," *New Republic* 55 (June 27, 1928):145–146.

Chapter Four: Sex on Trial: The Politics of "Legit"

1. George Eells and Stanley Musgrove, *Mae West: A Biography* (London, 1984), p. 70.

2. *Variety,* February 9, 1927, p. 1.

3. *New York American,* February 2, 1927, p. 29.

4. Michael M. Davis, *The Exploitation of Pleasure: A Study of Commercialized Recreations in New York City* (New York, 1911), pp. 32–33.

5. Jane Addams, *The Spirit of Youth and the City Streets* (New York, 1912), p. 76.

6. Ibid., p. 99.

7. Daniel J. Czitrom, *Media and the American Mind: From Morse to McLuhan* (Chapel Hill, N.C., 1982), pp. 46–47.

8. "The Thirteen Points of the National Motion Picture Industry—1921," reprinted in Garth Jowett, *Film, the Democratic Art: A Social History of American Film* (Boston, 1976), p. 465. The Thirteen Points were the movie industry's first attempt at self-regulation and listed the screen representations to which state censor boards most often objected.

9. *New York Times,* June 8, 1926, pp. 1, 16.

10. *New York Herald Tribune,* October 4, 1931, in *The Constant Sinner* clipping file, Billy Rose Theatre Collection of the Performing Arts Research Center, New York Public Library at Lincoln Center, New York City.

11. *New York Herald Tribune,* January 30, 1927, section 6, p. 1.

12. *New York Herald Tribune,* March 4, 1927, p. 14.

13. Bishop William T. Manning, "Power of the Theater for Good," *Theater Magazine* 47 (March 1928):15.

14. Don Seitz, "Selling Sin," *The Outlook* (February 23, 1927):241.

15. John S. Sumner, "Padlock Drama," *Theater Magazine* 47 (May 1928):11–12, 62.

16. *New York Herald Tribune,* March 20, 1927, p. 19.

17. *New York Times,* March 21, 1927, p. 21.

18. See, for example, *Theater Magazine* 48 (July 1928):12, 56.

19. Edouard Bourdet, *The Captive,* translated by Arthur Hornblow, Jr. (New York, 1926), pp. 170–171.

20. Ibid., p. 251.

21. Ibid., pp. 149–150.

22. Christina Simmons, "Companionate Marriage and the Lesbian Threat," *Frontiers* 4 (Fall 1979):54–59.

23. *American Mercury* 9 (December 1926):502–503.

24. Alfred A. Bernheim, *The Business of the Theatre* (New York, 1932), pp. 2–74.

25. *New York Tribune*, January 26, 1894, quoted in Barnard Hewitt, *Theater USA: 1665–1957* (New York, 1959), pp. 261–263. On turn-of-the-century Broadway see also Garff B. Wilson, *Three Hundred Years of American Drama and Theater* (Englewood Cliffs, N.J., 1973).

26. Walter Prichard Eaton, *At the New Theater and Others* (Boston, 1910), pp. 311–312.

27. Sheldon Cheney, *The Art Theatre* (New York, 1917), p. 15.

28. Eaton, *At the New Theater*, pp. 316–317.

29. On Village sexual radicalism see Ellen Kay Trimberger, "Feminism, Men and Modern Love: Greenwich Village, 1900–1925," in Ann Snitow, Christine Stansell, and Sharon Thompson, eds., *Powers of Desire: The Politics of Sexuality* (New York, 1983), pp. 131–152.

30. Daniel Joseph Singal, "Towards a Definition of American Modernism," *American Quarterly* 39 (Spring 1987):7–26.

31. Susan Sontag, *Styles of Radical Will* (New York, 1969), p. 45.

32. Cheney, *The Art Theatre*, pp.83–88.

33. Eaton, *At the New Theater*, p. 312.

34. Brooks Atkinson, introduction to *The Captive*, p. viii.

35. Ibid.; see Brooks Atkinson in the *New York Times*, September 30, 1926, p. 23; and John Anderson in *New York Evening Post*, September 30, 1926, p. 14.

36. *American Mercury* 9 (December 1926):502–503.

37. On these developments see Wilson, *Three Hundred Years of American Drama*, pp. 238–261.

38. *New York Times*, November 16, 1926, p. 11.

39. Cheney, *The Art Theatre*, pp. 107–108.

40. Atkinson, introduction to *The Captive*, p. vii, and *New York Times*, September 30, 1926, p. 23.

41. John van Druten, "The Sex Play," *Theater Arts Monthly* 11 (June 1927):25–26.

42. Winthrop Ames, "Censorship of the Stage: A Counter-Proposal," *Review of Reviews* 75 (April 1927):399.

43. *New Republic* 48 (November 10, 1926):324.

44. *Variety*, February 2, 1927, p. 39.

45. Christine Stansell, *City of Women: Sex and Class in New York, 1789–1860* (New York, 1986), p. 95.

46. *Variety*, February 2, 1927, p. 35, and October 3, 1928, p. 1.

47. Eric Walrond, "The Black City," *The Messenger* 6 (January 1924), quoted in David Levering Lewis, *When Harlem Was in Vogue* (New York, 1982), p. 165.

48. Lewis Erenberg, *Steppin' Out: New York Nightlife and the Transformation of American Culture, 1890–1930* (Westport, Conn., 1981), p. 248.

49. Ibid. See also Stanley Walker, *The Nightclub Era* (New York, 1938), pp. 103–127, and Eells and Musgrove, *Mae West*, pp. 76–77.

50. George Chauncey, "The Way We Were: Gay Male Society in the Jazz Age," *Village Voice*, July 1, 1986, p. 34.

51. Jimmy Durante and Jack Kofoed, *Nightclubs* (New York, 1931), p. 34.

52. Quoted in Chauncey, "The Way We Were," p. 29.

53. *New York Daily Mirror*, February 11, 1927, p. 1.

54. *New York Evening Post*, February 4, 1927, p. 8.

55. *Variety*, February 4, 1927, p. 8.

56. *New York Times*, March 9, 1927, p. 27.

57. Tice Miller, "George Jean Nathan and the 'New Criticism,' " *Theatre History Studies* 3 (1983):99–107.

58. *American Mercury* 9 (December 1926):502–503.

59. *American Mercury* 10 (March 1927):373–375.

60. Undated clipping, folder #MWEZ n.c. 6901, Billy Rose Theatre Collection of the Performing Arts Research Center, New York Public Library at Lincoln Center, New York City, quoted in Kaier Curtain, *"We Can Always Call Them Bulgarians": The Emergence of Lesbians and Gay Men on the American Stage* (Boston, 1987), pp. 62–63.

61. *American Mercury* 10 (March 1927):373–375,

62. Ibid.

63. *New York Morning Telegraph*, January 16, 1927, quoted in Curtain, *"We Can Always Call Them Bulgarians,"* p. 64.

64. *New York Herald Tribune*, February 21, 1927, p. 15.

65. *New York Herald Tribune*, February 12, 1927, p. 14.

66. *New York Times*, March 9, 1927, p. 27.

67. *New York Times*, March 18, 1927, p. 1, and March 26, 1927, p. 6.

68. *New York Herald Tribune*, January 29, 1927, p. 1.

69. *New York Herald Tribune*, February 28, 1927, p. 13.

70. Curtain, *"We Can Always Call Them Bulgarians,"* pp. 84–86.

71. *New York World*, March 31, 1927, section 2, p. 1, and April 1, 1927, p. 15.

72. *Variety*, March 16, 1927, pp. 1, 40.

Chapter Five: A Little Bit Spicy: Diamond Lil

1. *New York Herald Tribune*, April 29, 1928, section 7, p. 1.

2. *Variety*, November 9, 1927, pp. 49–50; November 16, 1927, pp. 48, 50; November 23, 1927, p. 48.

3. George Eells and Stanley Musgrove, *Mae West: A Biography* (London, 1984), p. 76; see also *Variety*, July 4, 1928, pp. 1, 3.

4. Uncited newspaper clipping dated June 23, 1928, *Diamond Lil* clipping file, Billy Rose Theatre Collection of the Performing Arts Research Center, New York Public Library at Lincoln Center, New York City.

5. Quoted in ad for *Diamond Lil* in *Variety*, August 22, 1928, p. 71.

6. Christine Stansell, *City of Women: Sex and Class in New York, 1789–1860* (New York, 1986), pp. 89–101; and Peter Buckley, "To the Opera House: New York Theatre and Culture, 1820–1860" (Ph.D. thesis, State University of New York at Stony Brook, 1985), chapter 4.

7. James D. McCabe, Jr., *Lights and Shadows of New York Life; or, The Sights and Sensations of a Great City* (Philadelphia, 1872), p. 193.

8. See Alvin Harlow, *Old Bowery Days: The Chronicles of a Famous Street* (New York, 1931); and Herbert Asbury, *The Gangs of New York: An Informal History of the Underworld* (New York, 1928). For excerpts from the committee hearings see Jonathan Katz, *Gay American History: Lesbians and Gay Men in the USA* (New York, 1976), pp. 44–47.

9. Harlow, *Old Bowery Days.*

10. *New York Evening Post*, April 10, 1928, p. 18.

11. Harlow, *Old Bowery Days*, pp. 422–423.

12. Ibid., pp. 423–434.

13. Ibid.

14. Ibid., p. 427.

15. Kathy Peiss, *Cheap Amusements: Working Women and Leisure in Turn-of-the-Century New York* (Philadelphia, 1986).

16. William Taylor, *In Pursuit of Gotham: Culture and Commerce in New York* (New York, 1992), pp. 69–91.

17. I owe this point to William Taylor's analysis of turn-of-the-century newspaper comic strips. See Taylor, *In Pursuit of Gotham*, p. 84.

18. Ibid., p. 83.

19. Play titles listed in the index of the Copyright Office, Library of Congress, Washington, D.C. Unfortunately, the playscripts themselves, though originally deposited with the Copyright Office, have been destroyed. On the blood-and-thunder circuit see Marion Spitzer, "Ten-Twenty-Thirty: The Passing of the Popular-Priced Circuit," *Saturday Evening Post* (August 22, 1925):40, 42, 48.

20. *New Republic* 55 (June 27, 1928):145–146.

21. *Variety*, April 11, 1928, p. 51.

22. *New York Evening Telegram*, undated review, quoted in *Variety*, August 22, 1928, p. 71.

23. *Variety*, May 9, 1928, p. 69.

24. The earliest usage I have found of the phrase "Gay Nineties," in *any* connection, is in the 1929 advertisement for *Diamond Lil's* national tour quoted at the end of this chapter.

25. *Variety*, May 23, 1928, p. 50.

26. *New York World*, April 10, 1928, in *Diamond Lil* clipping file, Billy Rose Theatre Collection.

27. *New Republic* 55 (June 27, 1928):145.

28. The original script of *Diamond Lil*, received by the Copyright Office on February 9, 1928, is now in the Mae West Collection, Manuscript Division, Library of Congress, Washington D.C. The script West used on opening night in April 1928 can be found in the Shubert Archives, New York City.

29. West, *Diamond Lil* (Library of Congress script), Act 1, pp. 26–28.

30. Thyra Samter Winslow, "Profiles: Diamond Mae," *New Yorker* (November 10, 1928):28.

31. My thinking on this point owes a great deal to T. J. Clark, *The Painting of Modern Life: Paris in the Art of Manet and His Followers* (New York, 1984), chapter 4, "A Bar at the Folies-Bergere."

32. *Variety*, June 27, 1928, p. 55.

33. *Theatre Arts Monthly* 12 (June 1928):394.

34. *New York Herald Tribune*, April 29, 1928, section 7, p. 1.

35. *New Yorker* (April 21, 1928):3; and *New York Herald Tribune*, November 10, 1928, p. 28.

36. *New Republic* 55 (June 27, 1928):146.

37. Ibid., pp. 145, 146.

38. *New York Evening Post*, April 10, 1928, p. 18.

39. *New York Daily Mirror*, December 31, 1926, p. 3.

40. *Variety*, October 10, 1928, in *Diamond Lil* clipping file, Billy Rose Theatre Collection.

41. Clark, *The Painting of Modern Life*, pp. 109–110.

42. West, *Diamond Lil* (Shubert Archives script), Act 1, p. 15.

43. West, *Diamond Lil* (Library of Congress script), Act 1, pp. 28–29.

44. West, *Diamond Lil* (Shubert Archives script), Act 1, pp. 23–24.

45. *New York World*, February 6, 1930.

46. Advertisement for *Diamond Lil* at the Flatbush Theater, Brooklyn, September 1929, held in *Diamond Lil* clipping file, Billy Rose Theatre Collection.

47. Press release dated October 8, 1927, in Texas Guinan clipping file, Billy Rose Theatre Collection.

48. See, for example, Lewis Erenberg, *Steppin' Out: New York Nightlife and the Transformation of American Culture, 1890–1930* (Westport, Conn., 1981).

Chapter Six: "I'm the Queen of the Bitches"

1. *New York Herald Tribune*, October 2, 1928, p. 20.

2. *New York Evening Post*, October 2, 1928, in *Pleasure Man* clipping file, Billy Rose Theatre Collection of the Performing Arts Research Center, New York Public Library at Lincoln Center, New York City.

3. *New York World*, October 3, 1928, pp. 1, 4.

4. *Variety*, August 8, 1928, p. 1.

5. *Variety*, September 19, 1928, p. 47.

6. *New York Times*, October 2, 1928, pp. 1, 34.

7. Mae West quoted in the *New York World*, October 3, 1928, p. 4.

8. Esther Newton, *Mother Camp: Female Impersonators in America* (Chicago, 1972), pp. 6–7.

9. Robert C. Toll, *On With the Show* (New York, 1976), p. 256.

10. *Variety*, October 27, 1916, p. 3.

11. The following discussion of female impersonation in vaudeville owes much to the insightful analysis in Toll, *On With the Show*, pp. 239–263. On its origins in the minstrel show see also Robert C. Toll, *Blacking Up: The Minstrel Show in America* (New York, 1974).

12. Toll, *On With the Show*, p. 247.

13. Ibid., p. 239.

14. Ibid., p. 243.

15. Uncited, undated review of Eltinge's skit *The Fascinating Widow*, in Julian Eltinge clipping file, Billy Rose Theatre Collection.

16. Quoted in Toll, *On With the Show*, p. 253.

17. Quote taken from page 6 of the New York district attorney's memorandum on the *Pleasure Man* case (Case #174,820–1/2, *New York v. Mae West et al.*), held in the District Attorney Case Files, Municipal Archives, New York City.

18. Police officers' observations are taken from the *New York Sun*, March 26, 1930, p. 27, and from the district attorney's memorandum cited in the previous note.

19. Mae West, *Pleasure Man*, Act 2, p. 5, manuscript held in the Mae West Collection, Manuscript Division, Library of Congress, Washington, D.C.

20. Ibid., Act 1, p. 10.

21. Ibid., Act 2, p. 1.

22. *New York Daily News*, October 2, 1928, p. 1.

23. West, *Pleasure Man*, Act 3, pp. 5–6.

24. Quoted in George Chauncey, *Gay New York: Gender, Urban Culture, and the Making of the Gay Male World, 1890–1940* (New York, 1994), p. 55; on "inversion," see Chauncey, *Gay New York*, pp. 47–63, and "Christian Brotherhood or Sexual Perversion? Homosexual Identities and the Construction of Sexual Boundaries in the World War I Era," in Martin Duberman et al., *Hidden From History: Reclaiming the Gay and Lesbian Past* (New York, 1989), pp. 294–317.

25. *Billboard*, October 13, 1928, p. 42.

26. *American Mercury* 15 (December 1928):501.

27. Quote taken from pp. 4–5 of New York district attorney's memorandum, *New York v. Mae West et al.*

28. Jimmy Durante and Jack Kofoed, *Nightclubs* (New York, 1931), pp. 54–55.

29. Information on Savoy is scanty, but see the brief discussion in Anthony Slide, *The Vaudevillians* (Westport, Conn., 1981), pp. 134–135.

30. *Dial* (August 1923), quoted in Roger Baker, *Drag: A History of Female Impersonation on the Stage* (London, 1968), p. 214.

31. *New York Herald*, April 14, 1895, in Female Impersonators clipping file, Billy Rose Theatre Collection.

32. Uncited, undated article from Julian Eltinge clipping file, Billy Rose Theatre Collection.

33. George Chauncey, "From Sexual Inversion to Homosexuality: The Changing Medical Conceptualization of Female 'Deviance,' " in Kathy Peiss and Christina Simmons, eds., *Passion and Power: Sexuality in History* (Philadelphia, 1989), pp. 87–117; Jonathan Ned Katz, *Gay/Lesbian Almanac* (New York, 1983), pp. 145–147.

34. *New York World*, April 4, 1931, p. 1.

35. *New York Morning Telegraph*, March 21, 1930, p. 1.

36. *New York World*, April 2, 1930, p. 13.

37. Slide, *The Vaudevillians*, p. 51.

38. For an analysis of the antigay backlash of the 1930s see Chauncey, *Gay New York*, pp. 331–354.

39. *Variety*, April 7, 1937, in Female Impersonators clipping file, Billy Rose Theatre Collection.

40. *New York World*, October 3, 1928, p. 4.

41. *New York Evening Post*, March 25, 1933, reprinted in Montrose J. Moses and John Mason Brown, *The American Theatre As Seen by Its Critics* (New York, 1934), pp. 305–307.

42. Pamela Robertson, "'The Kinda Comedy That Imitates Me': Mae West's Identification With the Feminist Camp," *Cinema Journal* 32 (Winter 1993):61.

43. Newton, *Mother Camp*, pp. 107–109.

44. Ethan Mordden, *Movie Star: A Look at the Women Who Made Hollywood* (New York, 1983), p. 123.

45. Quoted in ibid.

46. Parker Tyler, *The Three Faces of Film* (New York, 1967), p. 11.

47. George Davis, "The Decline of the West," *Vanity Fair* (May 1934):46, 82.

Chapter Seven: The Honor of White Womanhood

1. *Publisher's Weekly* (October 18, 1930):1818.

2. Mae West, *Babe Gordon* (New York, 1930), p. 147.

3. Quoted in Jervis Anderson, *This Was Harlem: A Cultural Portrait, 1900–50* (New York, 1981), p. 60.

4. David Levering Lewis, *When Harlem Was in Vogue* (New York, 1982), p. 107.

5. *Literary Digest* 100 (March 16, 1929):21.

6. Advertisement held in *Harlem* clipping file, Billy Rose Theatre Collection of the Performing Arts Research Center, New York Public Library at Lincoln Center, New York City.

7. *Literary Digest* 100 (March 16, 1929):22.

8. Ibid.

9. Lothrop Stoddard, *The Rising Tide of Color* (New York, 1920), p. 301.

10. Ibid., p. 90.

11. Quoted in Herbert G. Gutman, *The Black Family in Slavery and Freedom, 1750–1975* (Oxford, 1976), p. 544.

12. Stoddard, *Rising Tide of Color*, p. 301.

13. West, *Babe Gordon*, p. 147.

14. Ibid., p. 156.

15. Ibid., p. 155.

16. Anonymous East Texas man quoted in John D'Emilio and Estelle Freedman, *Intimate Matters: A History of Sexuality in America* (New York, 1988), p. 217.

17. West, *Babe Gordon*, pp. 279–282.

18. Ibid., p. 236.

19. For more on this point—and for an argument relevant to this chapter in general—see bell hooks's discussion of Madonna in *Black Looks: Race and Representation* (New York, 1992).

20. Quoted in Investigator's Report, Barron's Exclusive Club, West 134th Street, May 1928, in Box 37, Committee of Fourteen Papers, Manuscript Division, New York Public Library, New York City.

21. Charles Keil, *Urban Blues* (Chicago, 1966), pp. 56–57.

22. Jimmy Durante and Jack Kofoed, *Nightclubs* (New York, 1931), p. 113.

23. *New York Review,* November 7, 1931, in *The Constant Sinner* clipping file, Billy Rose Theatre Collection.

24. West, *Babe Gordon,* p. 239.

25. The script used for the production of *The Constant Sinner* is held in the Shubert Archives, New York City.

26. George Eells and Stanley Musgrove, *Mae West: A Biography* (London, 1984), p. 99.

27. Ibid., p. 80.

28. *New York Times,* October 4, 1931, section 8, p. 4.

29. Adele Gilbert, letter to the author, December 18, 1986.

30. George Haddad-Garcia, "Mae West, Everybody's Friend," *Black Stars* (April 1981):62–64.

31. Eells and Musgrove, *Mae West,* p. 83.

32. *American Mercury* 15 (December 1928):501.

33. Zora Neale Hurston, "Characteristics of Negro Expression," in Nancy Cunard, ed., *Negro Anthology* (New York, 1934), pp. 45–46.

34. Sander Gilman, "Black Bodies, White Bodies: Toward an Iconography of Female Sexuality in Late Nineteenth Century Art, Medicine, and Literature" in Henry Louis Gates, Jr., ed., *"Race," Writing, and Difference* (Chicago, 1985), pp. 223–261.

35. Bruce Kellner, *"Keep A-Inchin' Along": Selected Writings of Carl Van Vechten About Black Arts and Letters* (Westport, Conn., 1979), pp. 162–163.

36. *New Yorker* (September 26, 1931):26.

37. *New York Evening Post,* September 15, 1931, in *The Constant Sinner* clipping file, Billy Rose Theatre Collection.

Chapter Eight: Mae West Mania

1. *She Done Him Wrong* file, Motion Picture Association of America (MPAA) Collection, Margaret Herrick Library, Academy of Motion Picture Arts and Sciences, Beverly Hills, Calif.

2. See letter from Will Hays to Adolph Zukor, October 18, 1932, MPAA *She Done Him Wrong* file, which discusses the Resolution of October 31, 1930, and some of its contents.

3. Richard Maltby, "The Production Code and the Hays Office," in Tino Balio, ed., *Grand Design: Hollywood As a Modern Business Enterprise* (New York, 1993), p. 45. For more on the response to the movies see Daniel Czitrom, *Media and the American Mind: From Morse to McLuhan* (Chapel

Hill, N.C., 1982); Lary May, *Screening Out the Past: The Birth of Mass Culture and the Motion Picture Industry* (New York, 1980); and Garth Jowett, *Film, the Democratic Art: A Social History of American Film* (Boston, 1976).

4. See Jowett, *Film, the Democratic Art*, pp. 113–119.

5. MPPDA Resolution of June 19, 1924, reprinted in Jowett, *Film, the Democratic Art*, p. 466.

6. George Eells and Stanley Musgrove, *Mae West: A Biography* (London, 1984), p. 104; Maurice Leonard, *Mae West: Empress of Sex* (London, 1991), p. 103.

7. Quoted in Eells and Musgrove, *Mae West*, pp. 104–105.

8. Adolph Zukor, *The Public Is Never Wrong* (New York, 1953), p. 267.

9. Martin Sommers, "Up in Mae West's Room," *New York Sunday News*, February 26, 1933, p. 24.

10. Eells and Musgrove, *Mae West*, p. 108.

11. Maltby, "The Production Code and the Hays Office"; Richard Maltby, "*Baby Face*, or How Joe Breen Made Barbara Stanwyck Atone for Causing the Wall Street Crash," *Screen* 27 (March–April 1986):22–45; and Lea Jacobs, *The Wages of Sin: Censorship and the Fallen Woman Film, 1928–42* (Madison, Wisc., 1991).

12. Maltby, "*Baby Face*," p. 30.

13. Quoted in Maltby, "*Baby Face*," p. 31.

14. Jason Joy to Carl Milliken, July 7, 1932, MPAA *Red-Headed Woman* file, cited in Maltby, "*Baby Face*," p. 31. For an extended study of sex films and their impact on the industry see Jacobs, *The Wages of Sin*.

15. Maltby, "The Production Code and the Hays Office," p. 24. *Virgins in Cellophane* is mentioned in the report from James Wingate to Will Hays, November 11, 1932, MPAA *She Done Him Wrong* file.

16. Will Hays to Adolph Zukor, November 23, 1932, MPAA *She Done Him Wrong* file.

17. Maurice McKenzie memo, November 29, 1932, MPAA *She Done Him Wrong* file. McKenzie worked in the MPPDA's New York office as an assistant to Will Hays.

18. Eells and Musgrove, *Mae West*, p. 110.

19. Quoted in John Kobal, *People Will Talk* (New York, 1985), p. 159.

20. *Variety*, February 14, 1933, pp. 12, 21.

21. Five successive drafts of the script can be found in the *She Done Him Wrong* file, Paramount Pictures Collection, Margaret Herrick Library, Academy of Motion Picture Arts and Sciences, Beverly Hills, Calif.

22. Jason Joy to James Wingate, February 5, 1931, MPAA *Little Caesar* file, quoted in Maltby, "The Production Code and the Hays Office," p. 40.

23. For an incisive analysis of these representational strategies see Jacobs, *The Wages of Sin*, pp. 27–105.

24. James Wingate to Will Hays, January 13, 1933, MPAA *She Done Him Wrong* file.

25. James Wingate to Harold Hurley, November 29, 1932; James Wingate

to Will Hays, December 2, 1932, both in MPAA *She Done Him Wrong* file.

26. James Wingate to Harold Hurley, November 29, 1932, MPAA *She Done Him Wrong* file.

27. For this draft, dated November 8, 1932, see Paramount Pictures *She Done Him Wrong* file.

28. Contrast, in particular, Bright's initial draft of November 8, 1932, with the release dialogue script, both in Paramount Pictures *She Done Him Wrong* file.

29. *New York Daily News*, February 11, 1933, p. 20.

30. James Wingate to Will Hays, January 13, 1933, MPAA *She Done Him Wrong* file.

31. *Variety*, February 14, 1933, pp. 12, 21.

32. *New York Daily News*, February 24, 1933, p. 18.

33. Ben Maddox, "Don't Call Her Lady!," unattributed 1933 movie magazine clipping in possession of the author.

34. *Variety*, February 28, 1933, p. 8, and October 17, 1933, p. 8.

35. *Nation* 136 (March 1, 1933):242; *New York Evening Journal*, February 10, 1933, p. 13; *New York Evening Post,* February 10, 1933, p. 12.

36. Undated letter from Sidney Kent to Will Hays, MPAA *She Done Him Wrong* file.

37. Maltby, "The Production Code and the Hays Office," pp. 29–30.

38. Telegram from Vincent Hart to James Wingate, February 3, 1933; Will Hays to James Wingate, February 27, 1933; James Wingate to Harry Cohn, March 2, 1933, all in MPAA *She Done Him Wrong* file.

39. The origins of *I'm No Angel* remain less than clear, like all West's films after *She Done Him Wrong*. Its basic premise—a circus dancer turned lion tamer who invades and conquers high society—developed out of a short story or treatment called "The Lady and the Lions" written by writer-publisher Lowell Brentano. From there the process of revision becomes more murky. My speculation that West contributed a skeletal plot is based on the fact that the film's narrative, particularly its early sequences, bears strong similarities to West's first play, *Sex.* In both West plays a notorious woman who is eager to escape her sleazy surroundings and who has a series of comic encounters—with her male protector (who accuses her of "getting high hat"), with an ingenue (whom she urges to find a rich lover), and with a suitor (who tries to embrace her and before whom she dances). In both she is implicated in a jewel theft and flees into a job as an entertainer, succeeding in enchanting a rich man until her past returns to haunt her.

40. Eells and Musgrove, *Mae West*, p. 121.

41. All quoted dialogue transcribed from *I'm No Angel* (MCA Universal Home Video).

42. *Variety*, October 3, 1933, p. 3.

43. "Making Love to Mae West," *Picturegoer* 3 (December 30, 1933):13.

44. "Why Mae West Went to Prison," *Picturegoer* 3 (December 23, 1933):13.

45. Ibid.

46. Vincent Hart memo, October 4, 1933, MPAA *I'm No Angel* file.

47. *New York Herald Tribune*, October 22, 1933, section 5, p. 3.

48. *New York Evening Journal*, October 14, 1933, p. 8.

49. Carol Ward, *Mae West: A Bio-Bibliography* (Westport, Conn., 1989), pp. 84–86.

50. Colette, *Colette at the Movies: Criticism and Screenplays* (New York, 1980), pp. 62–64.

51. George Jean Nathan, *Passing Judgements* (New York, 1935), pp. 266–268.

52. Gilbert Seldes, *Mainland* (New York, 1936), p. 119.

53. George Davis, "The Decline of the West," *Vanity Fair* (May 1934):46, 82; Parker Tyler, *The Hollywood Hallucination* (New York, 1944), pp. 95–99.

54. James Wingate to Vincent Hart, September 16, 1933, and James Wingate to Will Hays, September 20, 1933, MPAA *I'm No Angel* file.

55. Vincent Hart memo, October 4, 1933, MPAA *I'm No Angel* file.

56. *New York Sun*, October 14, 1933, p. 9; *New York Morning Telegraph*, October 14, 1933, p. 1.

57. *Variety*, October 31, 1933, pp. 8–10, 35; see also October 17, 1933, pp. 8–10, 36, and October 24, 1933, pp. 8–11, 62.

58. *New York Times Magazine*, April 2, 1933, p. 11, quoted in Hayden Herrera, *Frida: A Biography of Frida Kahlo* (New York, 1983), p. 175.

59. Quoted in Eells and Musgrove, *Mae West*, p. 147.

60. *Variety*, October 17, 1933, p. 19.

Chapter Nine: It Ain't No Sin

1. *Variety*, November 28, 1933, p. 2.

2. Paul Facey, *The Legion of Decency* (New York, 1974; originally published 1945).

3. Richard Maltby, *Harmless Entertainment: Hollywood and the Ideology of Consensus* (London, 1983), p. 101.

4. Sidney E. Goldstein, "The Motion Picture and Social Control," in William J. Perlman, ed., *The Movies on Trial* (New York, 1936), p. 218.

5. John Haynes Holmes, "The Movies and the Community," in Perlman, ed., *The Movies on Trial*, pp. 200–201.

6. Ibid., p. 205.

7. Francis G. Couvares and Kathy Peiss, "Sex, Censorship and the Movies: The National Board of Review, 1909–1922" (unpublished paper, n.d.), pp. 2–3. I am grateful to Kathy Peiss for supplying me with this paper.

8. "The Production Code of the Motion Picture Producers and Directors of America, Inc.—1930–1934" (Part 2, "Reasons Supporting Preamble of Code"), reprinted in Garth Jowett, *Film, the Democratic Art: A Social History of American Film* (Boston, 1976), pp. 468–472.

9. "Producers Cleansing Films, But Will Reform Last?" *Literary Digest* 118 (July 21, 1934):7.

10. Martin Quigley, *Decency in Motion Pictures* (New York, 1937), p. 6.

11. "Production Code of the Motion Picture Producers and Directors of America, Inc.," p. 472.

12. Ibid.

13. Ibid.

14. Ibid.

15. *New York Times*, November 16, 1926, p. 11.

16. Jowett, *Film, the Democratic Art*, pp. 220–231.

17. Henry James Forman, *Our Movie-Made Children* (New York, 1935), p. 147.

18. Ibid., pp. 222–223.

19. Ibid., p. 223.

20. *I'm No Angel* ad quoted in *Christian Century*, October 25, 1933, p. 1327.

21. James Wingate to William Botsford, September 18, 1933, *I'm No Angel* file, Motion Picture Association of America (MPAA) collection, Margaret Herrick Library, Academy of Motion Picture Arts and Sciences, Beverly Hills, Calif.

22. *Variety*, October 24, 1933, p. 23.

23. "Churches War Against Obscenity," *Literary Digest* 117 (March 3, 1934).

24. Lea Jacobs, *The Wages of Sin: Censorship and the Fallen Woman Film, 1928–42* (Madison, Wisc., 1991), pp. 16–17.

25. Quigley, *Decency in Motion Pictures*, pp. 35–36.

26. See, for example, Studs Terkel, *Hard Times: An Oral History of the Great Depression* (New York, 1970).

27. Quoted in Richard Maltby, "*Baby Face*, or How Joe Breen Made Barbara Stanwyck Atone for Causing the Wall Street Crash," *Screen* 27 (March–April 1986):44.

28. Nancy Woloch, *Women and the American Experience* (New York, 1984), p. 458.

29. Malcolm D. Phillips, "What Price Hollywood Now?" *Picturegoer* 3 (November 4, 1933):12–13.

30. Alice Ames Winter to Will Hays, November 21, 1933, Hays Collection, Indiana State Library, Indianapolis, Ind., quoted in Jacobs, *The Wages of Sin*, p. 108.

31. Jacobs, *Wages of Sin*, p. 109.

32. Maltby, *Harmless Entertainment*, pp. 97–99.

33. Ibid., pp. 106–116.

34. *Variety*, March 13, 1934, p. 5.

35. *It Ain't No Sin* (March 2, 1934, draft script), p. A–18, *Belle of the Nineties* file, Paramount Pictures Collection, Margaret Herrick Library, Academy of Motion Picture Arts and Sciences, Beverly Hills, Calif.

36. Ibid, p. B–11.

37. Ibid.; see also Joseph Breen's notes on the uncut film made from the script, MPAA *Belle of the Nineties* file.

38. John Mason Brown, review of *She Done Him Wrong*, *New York Evening Post*, March 25, 1933, reprinted in Montrose J. Moses and John Mason Brown, *The American Theatre As Seen by Its Critics* (New York, 1934), pp. 305–307.

39. Gerald Weales, *Canned Goods As Caviar: American Film Comedy in the 1930s* (Chicago, 1985), p. 39.

40. Joseph Breen memo, June 6, 1934, MPAA *Belle of the Nineties* file.

41. Joseph Breen's notes on *It Ain't No Sin*; Joseph Breen to John Hammell, June 2, 1934; and Joseph Breen's memo of June 6, 1934; all in MPAA *Belle of the Nineties* file.

42. My account of the scene, including the lines that follow, has been pieced together from several sources: the March 2, 1934, draft script of *It Ain't No Sin*, Paramount Pictures *Belle of the Nineties* file; and Joseph Breen's notes on the film, his letter to John Hammell of June 2, 1934, and his memo of June 6, 1934, all in MPAA *Bell of the Nineties* file.

43. *It Ain't No Sin* (March 2, 1934, draft script), p. A–13, Paramount Pictures *Belle of the Nineties* file.

44. Ibid., p. B–28.

45. Joseph Breen to William Botsford, March 7, 1934, MPAA *Belle of the Nineties* file.

46. Unattributed memo of March 7, 1934, MPAA *Belle of the Nineties* file.

47. Joseph Breen to Will Hays, March 7, 1934, MPAA *Belle of the Nineties* file.

48. Joseph Breen to John Hammell, June 2, 1934, MPAA *Belle of the Nineties* file.

49. Quigley, *Decency in Motion Pictures*, pp. 35–36.

50. Raymond Moley, *The Hays Office* (New York, 1945), p. 101.

51. *Variety*, March 13, 1934, p. 5.

52. Moley, *The Hays Office*, p. 146.

53. William Botsford to Joseph Breen, February 17, 1934, MPAA *Belle of the Nineties* file.

54. William Botsford to Joseph Breen, March 5, 1934, MPAA *Belle of the Nineties* file.

55. See Will Hays to Adolph Zukor, October 18, 1932, and November 16, 1932; Will Hays to James Wingate, November 22, 1932; Will Hays to Adolph Zukor, November 22, 1932, and November 23, 1932; all in MPAA *She Done Him Wrong* file.

56. Robert Stanley, *The Celluloid Empire: A History of the American Motion Picture Industry* (New York, 1978), pp. 86–87.

57. Joseph Breen to Will Hays, June 2, 1934, MPAA *Belle of the Nineties* file.

58. Ibid.

59. *Variety*, June 15, 1934, quoted in Maltby, *Harmless Entertainment*, p. 104.

60 Maltby, *Harmless Entertainment*, p. 104.

61. *Variety*, August 7, 1934, p. 1.

62. Maltby, *Harmless Entertainment*, pp. 101–102.

63. *Variety*, June 26, 1934, p. 5.

64. Will Hays memo, July 13, 1934, MPAA *Belle of the Nineties* file.

65. *New York Herald Tribune*, September 22, 1934, p. 10.

66. *Nation* 139 (October 10, 1934):420.

67. *New York Evening Post*, March 25, 1933, quoted in Moses and Brown, *The American Theatre as Seen by Its Critics*, p. 307.

68. *Nation* 139 (August 1, 1934):126.

69. *New York Herald Tribune*, October 14, 1933, p. 10.

70. *Variety*, September 25, 1934, pp. 8–11, 29.

Chapter Ten: Mae West in Exile

1. *Klondike Annie* file, Motion Picture Association of America (MPAA) collection, Margaret Herrick Library, Academy of Motion Picture Arts and Sciences, Beverly Hills, Calif.

2. John Hammell to Will Hays, June 29, 1935, MPAA *Klondike Annie* file.

3. Will Hays to John Hammell, July 2, 1935, MPAA *Klondike Annie* file.

4. John Hammell to Will Hays, June 29, 1935, MPAA *Klondike Annie* file.

5. Joseph Breen to John Hammell, October 22, 1935, MPAA *Klondike Annie* file.

6. Noted in Joseph Breen to John Hammell, September 4, 1935, MPAA *Klondike Annie* file.

7. Ibid.

8. Joseph Breen to John Hammell, September 5, 1935, MPAA *Klondike Annie* file.

9. Joseph Breen to Will Hays, December 31, 1935, MPAA *Klondike Annie* file.

10. Ibid.

11. The memo, unsigned and undated, was evidently leaked to Joseph Breen and can be found in the MPAA *Klondike Annie* file.

12. *Variety*, March 18, 1936, p. 1.

13. Uncited, undated review held in MPAA *Klondike Annie* file.

14. *Los Angeles Examiner*, February 28, 1936.

15. *Variety*, March 4, 1936, pp. 7–10, and March 18, 1936, p. 1.

16. *Variety*, March 4, 1936, p. 7.

17. Quoted in Ramona Curry, "Mae West As Censored Commodity: The Case of *Klondike Annie*," *Cinema Journal* 31 (Fall 1991):68.

18. *New York Times*, March 15, 1936, section 9, p. 3.

19. *Hollywood Reporter*, February 5, 1936, in MPAA *Klondike Annie* file.

20. *Pittsburgh Post-Gazette*, February 20, 1936, in MPAA *Klondike Annie* file.

21. Joseph Breen private memo, February 10, 1936, MPAA *Klondike Annie* file.

22. Joseph Breen private memo, February 10, 1936, MPAA *Klondike Annie* file.

23. George Eells and Stanley Musgrove, *Mae West: A Biography* (London, 1984), p. 130.

24. Quoted in Eells and Musgrove, *Mae West*, p. 135.

25. *New York Herald Tribune*, November 19, 1936, p. 19; *New York Times*, March 15, 1936, section IX, p. 3.

26. Joseph Breen to Emanuel Cohen, August 10, 1937, MPAA *Every Day's a Holiday* file.

27. Quoted in the *Hollywood Reporter*, February 16, 1938, in MPAA *Every Day's a Holiday* file.

28. Lea Jacobs, *The Wages of Sin: Censorship and the Fallen Woman Film, 1928–42* (Madison, Wisc., 1991), p. 153.

29. *New York Times*, January 27, 1938, p. 17.

30. Ibid.

31. *My Little Chickadee* file, Universal Pictures Collection, Doheny Library, University of Southern California, Los Angeles.

32. Eells and Musgrove, *Mae West*, pp. 192–198.

33. *New York Times*, March 16, 1940, p. 8.

34. *New York Times*, November 26, 1943, p. 29.

35. Mae West, *Goodness Had Nothing to Do With It* (Englewood Cliffs, N.J., 1959), pp. 220–221.

36. Mae West, *Mae West on Sex, Health, and ESP* (London, 1975), p. 112; see also West, *Goodness*, pp. 177–182.

37. West, *Mae West*, pp. 107–112.

38. West, *Goodness*, p. 166.

39. *New Yorker* 20 (August 12, 1944):38; *Nation* 159 (August 12, 1944):194.

40. Eells and Musgrove, *Mae West*, pp. 212–221.

41. Maurice Leonard, *Mae West: Empress of Sex* (London, 1991), p. 320.

42. John T. Alexander, *Catherine the Great: Life and Legend* (New York, 1989), p. 332.

43. Richard Meryman, "Mae West: A Cherished, Bemusing Masterpiece of Self-Preservation," *Life* 66 (April 18, 1969):62.

44. Maurice Zolotow, *Billy Wilder in Hollywood* (New York, 1977), pp. 156–158.

45. Wayne Koestenbaum, *The Queen's Throat: Opera, Homosexuality, and the Mystery of Desire* (New York, 1993).

46. Leonard, *Mae West: Empress of Sex*, pp. 268–269.

47. Grace Moore, *You're Only Human Once* (New York, 1946), p. 203.

48. Koestenbaum, *The Queen's Throat*, p. 133.

Chapter Eleven: The Queen of Camp

1. *Interview* 1, no. 1 (1969):2.

2. Robert Jennings, "Mae West: A Candid Interview With the Indestructible Queen of Vamp and Camp," *Playboy* (January 1971):78.

3. Andrew Ross, *No Respect: Intellectuals and Popular Culture* (New York, 1989), p. 137.

4. Susan Sontag, "Notes on Camp," *Against Interpretation* (New York, 1966), pp. 276, 287.

5. Thomas Meehan, "Not Good Taste, Not Bad Taste—It's 'Camp,'" *New York Times Magazine*, March 21, 1965, p. 30.

6. Ibid., pp. 30–31, 113–115.

7. Ross, *No Respect*, p. 139.

8. Sontag, "Notes on Camp," pp. 288–289.

9. Quoted in Steven V. Roberts, "Seventy-six—and Still Diamond Lil," *New York Times Magazine*, November 2, 1969, p. 72.

10. On the post–World War II domestic revival see Elaine Tyler May, *Homeward Bound: American Families in the Cold War Era* (New York, 1988).

11. George Eells and Stanley Musgrove, *Mae West: A Biography* (London, 1984), pp. 244–245.

12. Uncited, undated newspaper clipping in possession of the author.

13. Eells and Musgrove, *Mae West*, pp. 35–36.

14. Esther Newton, *Mother Camp: Female Impersonators in America* (Chicago, 1972).

15. Helen Lawrenson, "Mirror, Mirror, on the Wall," *Esquire* (July 1967):72–73.

16. George Melly, *Revolt Into Style: The Pop Arts in Britain* (London, 1970), p. 161.

17. For an illuminating analysis of the intellectual sources of 1960s sex radicalism see Richard Dyer, *Now You See It: Studies on Gay and Lesbian Film* (London, 1990), pp. 136–137.

18. For a good example of this attitude, see Richard Meryman's tongue-in-cheek account of West's 1960s revival in "Mae West: A Cherished, Bemusing Masterpiece of Self-Preservation," *Life* 66 (April 18, 1969):60+.

19. The term "pop-camp" is used by George Melly to denote the pop art appropriation of gay camp humor. See Melly, *Revolt Into Style*, pp. 132–133, 161.

20. Michael Bronski, "Judy Garland and Others: Notes on Idolization and Derision," in Karla Jay and Allen Young, eds., *Lavender Culture* (New York, 1978), p. 210.

21. Feminist Robin Morgan has been particularly vehement in making this argument, stating, "We know what's at work when whites wear blackface. The same thing is at work when men wear drag." Quoted in Michael Bronski, *Culture Clash: The Making of a Gay Sensibility* (Boston, 1984), p. 205.

22. Jan Dawson, "Once Is Not Enough," *Time Out* (September 29, 1978):17.

23. Wayne Koestenbaum, *The Queen's Throat: Opera, Homosexuality, and the Mystery of Desire* (New York, 1993), p. 133.

24. Ibid., p. 117.

25. *Big Reel* (August 1979):n.p.

26. Quoted in Eells and Musgrove, *Mae West*, p. 307.

27. Pamela Robertson, "'The Kinda Comedy That Imitates Me': Mae West's

Identification With the Feminist Camp," *Cinema Journal* 32 (Winter 1993):58.

28. Molly Haskell, "Mae West's Bawdy Spirit Spans the Gay Nineties," *New York Times*, August 15, 1993, p. 14.

29. Kevin Thomas, "Mae West: At One With Her Image," *Los Angeles Times Calendar*, November 30, 1980, p. 5.

30. Meryman, "Mae West: A Cherished, Bemusing Masterpiece," p. 62.

31. Jennings, "Mae West: A Candid Interview," p. 78.

32. Ibid.

33. Parker Tyler, *The Three Faces of Film* (New York, 1967), p. 11.

34. George Davis, "The Decline of the West," *Vanity Fair* (May 1934):46, 82.

35. Meryman, "Mae West: A Cherished, Bemusing Masterpiece," p. 62C.

36. *New York Times*, June 8, 1979, section 3, p. 10.

37. Eells and Musgrove, *Mae West*, p. 280.

38. Jennings, "Mae West: A Candid Interview," p. 78.

Epilogue

1. George Eells and Stanley Musgrove, *Mae West: A Biography* (London, 1984), p. 309.

2. Molly Haskell, "Mae West's Bawdy Spirit Spans the Gay Nineties," *New York Times*, August 15, 1993, pp. 11, 14.

3. Quoted in Ellis Nassour, "Mae West," *Club*, undated interview in Mae West clipping file, Billy Rose Theatre Collection of the Performing Arts Research Center, New York Public Library at Lincoln Center, New York City.

4. Mae West, "Sex in the Theatre," *Parade* (September 1929):12.

5. *Variety*, March 21, 1982, p. 2.

6. Maurice Leonard, *Mae West: Empress of Sex* (London, 1991), p. 352.

7. Eells and Musgrove, *Mae West*, p. 315.

8. Leonard, *Mae West: Empress of Sex*, pp. 341, 373.

9. John Kobal, *People Will Talk* (New York, 1985), p. 153.

Bibliography

ARCHIVAL SOURCES

Beverly Hills, Calif. Academy of Motion Picture Arts and Sciences. Margaret Herrick Library.

Motion Picture Association of America Collection
Belle of the Nineties
Every Day's a Holiday
Go West, Young Man
Goin' to Town
I'm No Angel
Klondike Annie
She Done Him Wrong

Paramount Pictures Collection
Belle of the Nineties
Every Day's a Holiday
Go West, Young Man
Goin' to Town
I'm No Angel
Klondike Annie
She Done Him Wrong

Brooklyn, New York. Brooklyn Public Library.
Brooklyn History Collection
Greenpoint Clipping File
Mae West Clipping File

Los Angeles. University of Southern California. Doheny Library.
Universal Pictures Collection.
My Little Chickadee

New York. New York Public Library. Manuscript Division.
Committee of Fourteen Papers

New York. New York Public Library at Lincoln Center. Billy Rose Theatre Collection of the Performing Arts Research Center.
The Constant Sinner Clipping File
Diamond Lil Clipping File
Female Impersonators Clipping File
Harlem Clipping File
Robinson Locke Collection of Dramatic Scrapbooks: #450, 1079, 2541
Pleasure Man Clipping File
Sex Clipping File
Julian Eltinge Clipping File
Texas Guinan Clipping File
Walter Johnson Burlesque Scrapbook

New York. Municipal Archives.
· District Attorney Case Files
Case #168495 (*The People of the State of New York vs. C. William Morganstern et al.*)
Case #174,820-1/2 (*The People vs. Mae West et al.*)

New York. Shubert Archives.
The Constant Sinner
Diamond Lil

Washington, D. C. Library of Congress. Manuscript Division.
Mae West Collection
Diamond Lil
The Drag
Pleasure Man
Sex
The Wicked Age

PERIODICALS

American Mercury. New York: 1926–28.
Billboard. 1928.
Interview. 1969.
Literary Digest. 1911, 1929, 1934.
Los Angeles Examiner. 1936.
Movie Mirror. New York: 1933.
Nation. New York: 1932, 1933, 1934, 1944.
New Republic. New York: 1926, 1928, 1933.
New York American. 1913, 1927.
New York Daily Mirror. 1926–27.
New York Daily News. 1928, 1933, 1980.
New York Evening Post. 1926–28, 1931, 1933.
New York Herald Tribune. 1926–28, 1931, 1933–36.
New York Morning Telegraph. 1927, 1930, 1933.
New York Sun. 1930, 1933.
New York Times. 1912, 1914, 1926–1944, 1979.
New York World. 1911, 1913, 1927–28, 1930–31.
New Yorker. New York: 1926, 1928, 1931, 1944.
Picturegoer. 1933.
Publishers Weekly. 1930.
Theatre Arts Monthly. New York: 1927–28, 1933.
Variety. New York: 1908, 1912–38, 1982.

BOOKS AND ARTICLES

Addams, Jane. *The Spirit of Youth and the City Streets*. New York, 1912.

Allen, Robert C. *Horrible Prettiness: Burlesque and American Culture*. Chapel Hill, N.C., 1991.

Ames, Winthrop. "Censorship of the Stage: A Counter-Proposal." *Review of Reviews* 75 (April 1927):399.

Anderson, Jervis. *This Was Harlem: A Cultural Portrait, 1900–50*. New York, 1981.

Armbruster, Eugene L. *Brooklyn's Eastern District*. Brooklyn, 1992; originally published 1928.

Asbury, Herbert. *The Gangs of New York: An Informal History of the Underworld*. New York, 1928.

Babuscio, Jack. "Camp and the Gay Sensibility." In *Gays and Film*, edited by Richard Dyer, pp. 40–57. New York, 1984.

Bailey, Peter. "Ally Sloper's Half-Holiday: Comic Art in the 1880s." *History Workshop* 16 (Autumn 1983):4–31.

Baker, Roger. *Drag: A History of Female Impersonation on the Stage*. London, 1968.

Bergman, Andrew. *We're in the Money: Depression America and Its Films.* New York, 1971.

Bernheim, Alfred A. *The Business of the Theatre.* New York, 1932.

Bessie, Simon Michael. *Jazz Journalism.* New York, 1938.

Bourdet, Edouard. *The Captive.* Translated by Arthur Hornblow, Jr. New York, 1926.

Bronski, Michael. *Culture Clash: The Making of a Gay Sensibility.* Boston, 1984.

———. "Judy Garland and Others: Notes on Idolization and Derision." In *Lavender Culture,* edited by Karla Jay and Allen Young, pp. 201–212. New York, 1978.

Caffin, Caroline. *Vaudeville.* New York, 1914.

Chauncey, George. "Christian Brotherhood or Sexual Perversion? Homosexual Identities and the Construction of Sexual Boundaries in the World War I Era." In *Hidden From History: Reclaiming the Gay and Lesbian Past,* edited by Martin Duberman et al., pp. 294–317. New York, 1989.

———. "From Sexual Inversion to Homosexuality: Medicine and the Changing Conceptualization of Female 'Deviance.'" In *Passion and Power: Sexuality in History,* edited by Kathy Peiss and Christina Simmons, pp. 87–117. Philadelphia, 1989.

———. *Gay New York: Gender, Urban Culture, and the Making of the Gay Male World, 1890–1940.* New York, 1994.

———. "The Way We Were: Gay Male Society in the Jazz Age." *Village Voice,* July 1, 1986, pp. 29–30, 34.

Cheney, Sheldon. *The Art Theatre.* New York, 1917.

Clark, T. J. *The Painting of Modern Life: Paris in the Art of Manet and His Followers.* New York, 1984.

Colette. *Colette at the Movies: Criticism and Screenplays.* New York, 1980.

Curry, Ramona. "Mae West as Censored Commodity: The Case of *Klondike Annie.*" *Cinema Journal* 31 (Fall 1991):57–84.

Curtain, Kaier. *"We Can Always Call Them Bulgarians": The Emergence of Lesbians and Gay Men on the American Stage.* Boston, 1987.

Czitrom, Daniel J. *Media and the American Mind: From Morse to McLuhan.* Chapel Hill, N.C., 1982.

Davis, George. "The Decline of the West." *Vanity Fair* (May 1934):46, 82.

Davis, Michael M. *The Exploitation of Pleasure: A Study of Commercialized Recreations in New York City.* New York, 1911.

Dawson, Jan. "Once Is Not Enough." *Time Out* (September 29, 1978):17.

D'Emilio, John. *Sexual Politics, Sexual Communities: The Making of a Homosexual Minority in the U.S., 1940–1970.* Chicago, 1983.

D'Emilio, John, and Freedman, Estelle. *Intimate Matters: A History of Sexuality in America.* New York, 1988.

Durante, Jimmy, and Kofoed, Jack. *Nightclubs.* New York, 1931.

Duryea, Brian. "Vaudeville: Where the Acts Come From." *The Green Book Magazine* (September 1915):545.

Dyer, Richard. *Now You See It: Studies on Gay and Lesbian Film*. London, 1990.

Eames, John Douglas. *The Paramount Story*. London, 1985.

Eaton, Walter Prichard. *At the New Theater and Others*. Boston, 1910.

Edwards, Richard Henry. *Popular Amusements*. New York, 1915.

Eells, George, and Musgrove, Stanley. *Mae West: A Biography*. London, 1984; originally published New York, 1982.

Erenberg, Lewis. *Steppin' Out: New York Nightlife and the Transformation of American Culture, 1890–1930*. Westport, Connecticut, 1981.

Facey, Paul. *The Legion of Decency*. New York, 1974; originally published 1945.

Felter, William L. *Historic Greenpoint*. Brooklyn, 1918.

Fleming, Karl, and Fleming, Anne Taylor. *The First Time*. New York, 1975.

Forman, Henry James. *Our Movie-Made Children*. New York, 1935.

Gilbert, Douglas. *American Vaudeville*. New York, 1963; originally published 1940.

Gilman, Sander. "Black Bodies, White Bodies: Toward an Iconography of Female Sexuality in Late Nineteenth Century Art, Medicine, and Literature." In *"Race," Writing, and Difference*, edited by Henry Louis Gates, Jr., pp. 223–261. Chicago, 1985.

Gomery, Douglas. *The Hollywood Studio System*. London, 1986.

Green, Abel, and Laurie, Joe Jr. *Show Biz: From Vaude to Video*. New York, 1951.

Haddad-Garcia, George. "Mae West, Everybody's Friend." *Black Stars* (April 1981):62–64.

Hamilton, Jack. "Raquel Welch, Mae West Talk About Men, Morals and *Myra Breckinridge*." *Look* 34 (March 24, 1970).

Harlow, Alvin. *Old Bowery Days: The Chronicles of a Famous Street*. New York, 1931.

Hartt, Rollin Lynde. *The People at Play*. Boston, 1909.

Haskell, Molly. "Mae West's Bawdy Spirit Spans the Gay Nineties." *New York Times*, August 15, 1993, p. 14.

Henderson, Mary C. *The City and the Theatre: New York Playhouses From Bowling Green to Times Square*. Clifton, N.J., 1973.

Hewitt, Barnard. *Theater USA: 1665–1957*. New York, 1959.

hooks, bell. *Black Looks: Race and Representation*. New York, 1992.

Hurston, Zora Neale. "Characteristics of Negro Expression." In *Negro Anthology*, edited by Nancy Cunard, pp. 39–46. New York, 1934.

Jacobs, Lea. *The Wages of Sin: Censorship and the Fallen Woman Film, 1928–42*. Madison, Wisc., 1991.

Jay, Ricky. *Learned Pigs and Fireproof Women*. New York, 1986.

Jennings, Robert. "Mae West: A Candid Interview With the Indestructible Queen of Vamp and Camp." *Playboy* (January 1971):78ff.

Jowett, Garth. *Film, the Democratic Art: A Social History of American Film*. Boston, 1976.

Kasson, John F. *Amusing the Million: Coney Island at the Turn of the Century.* New York, 1978.

Katz, Jonathan. *Gay American History: Lesbians and Gay Men in the USA.* New York, 1976.

———. *Gay/Lesbian Almanac.* New York, 1983.

Keil, Charles. *Urban Blues.* Chicago, 1966.

Kellner, Bruce. *"Keep A-Inchin' Along": Selected Writings of Carl Van Vechten About Black Arts and Letters.* Westport, Conn., 1979.

Kennedy, Hubert C. "The 'Third Sex' Theory of Karl Heinrich Ulrichs." In *Historical Perspectives on Homosexuality*, edited by Salvatore J. Licata and Robert P. Peterson, pp. 103–112. New York, 1981.

Klaprat, Cathy. "The Star as Market Strategy: Bette Davis in Another Light." In *The American Film Industry*, edited by Tino Balio, pp. 351–376. Madison, Wisc., 1976.

Knight, Howard R. *Play and Recreation in a Town of 6,000.* New York, 1915.

Kobal, John. *People Will Talk.* New York, 1985.

Koestenbaum, Wayne. *The Queen's Throat: Opera, Homosexuality, and the Mystery of Desire.* New York, 1993.

Lawrenson, Helen. "Mirror, Mirror, on the Wall." *Esquire* (July 1967):72–73.

Leonard, Maurice. *Mae West: Empress of Sex.* London, 1991.

Lewis, David Levering. *When Harlem Was in Vogue.* New York, 1982.

Lunbeck, Elizabeth. "'A New Generation of Women': Progressive Psychiatrists and the Hypersexual Female." *Feminist Studies* 13 (Fall 1987):513–543.

McCabe, James D., Jr. *Lights and Shadows of New York Life; or, The Sights and Sensations of a Great City.* Philadelphia, 1872.

MacGowan, Kenneth. "The Crisis on Broadway." *Harpers Magazine* 158 (December 1928):112–118.

McNamara, Brooks. "'A Congress of Wonders': The Rise and Fall of the Dime Museum." *Emerson Society Quarterly* 20 (3rd Quarter, 1974):216–232.

Maltby, Richard. "*Baby Face*, or How Joe Breen Made Barbara Stanwyck Atone for Causing the Wall Street Crash." *Screen* 27 (March–April 1986):22–45.

———. *Harmless Entertainment: Hollywood and the Ideology of Consensus.* London, 1983.

———. "The Political Economy of Hollywood: The Studio System." In *Cinema, Politics and Society in America*, edited by Philip Davies and Brian Neve, pp. 42–58. Manchester, England, 1981.

———. "The Production Code and the Hays Office." In *Grand Design: Hollywood as a Modern Business Enterprise*, edited by Tino Balio, pp. 37–72. New York, 1993.

Manning, Bishop William T. "Power of the Theater for Good." *Theater Magazine* 47 (March 1928):15.

May, Elaine Tyler. *Homeward Bound: American Families in the Cold War Era.* New York, 1988.

May, Lary. *Screening Out the Past: The Birth of Mass Culture and the Motion Picture Industry*. New York, 1980.

Meehan, Thomas. "Not Good Taste, Not Bad Taste—It's 'Camp.' " *New York Times Magazine*, March 21, 1965, pp. 30–31, 113–115.

Melly, George. *Revolt Into Style: The Pop Arts in Britain*. London, 1970.

Merritt, Russell. "Nickelodeon Theaters, 1905–1914: Building an Audience for the Movies." In *The American Film Industry*, edited by Tino Balio, pp. 83–102. Madison, Wisc., 1976.

Meryman, Richard. "Mae West: A Cherished, Bemusing Masterpiece of Self-Preservation." *Life* 66 (April 18, 1969):60ff.

Miller, Tice. "George Jean Nathan and the 'New Criticism.' " *Theatre History Studies* 3 (1983):99–107.

Moley, Raymond. *The Hays Office*. New York, 1945.

Mooney, Michael Macdonald. *Evelyn Nesbit and Stanford White: Love and Death in the Gilded Age*. New York, 1976.

Moore, Grace. *You're Only Human Once*. New York, 1946.

Mordden, Ethan. *Movie Star: A Look at the Women Who Made Hollywood*. New York, 1983.

Moses, Montrose J., and Brown, John Mason. *The American Theatre as Seen by Its Critics*. New York, 1934.

Nathan, George Jean. *Art of the Night*. Rutherford, N.J., 1972; originally published 1928.

———. *Passing Judgements*. New York, 1935.

Newton, Esther. *Mother Camp: Female Impersonators in America*. Chicago, 1972.

Peiss, Kathy. *Cheap Amusements: Working Women and Leisure in Turn-of-the-Century New York*. Philadelphia, 1986.

Perlman, William J. ed. *The Movies on Trial*. New York, 1936.

Quigley, Martin. *Decency in Motion Pictures*. New York, 1937.

Rahill, Frank. *The World of Melodrama*. University Park, Pa., 1960.

Roberts, Steven V. "Seventy-six—and Still Diamond Lil." *New York Times Magazine*, November 2, 1969, pp. 70ff.

Robertson, Pamela. "'The Kinda Comedy That Imitates Me': Mae West's Identification With the Feminist Camp." *Cinema Journal* 32 (Winter 1993):57–72.

Rosow, Eugene. *Born to Lose: The Gangster Film in America*. New York, 1978.

Ross, Andrew. *No Respect: Intellectuals and Popular Culture*. New York, 1989.

Russo, Vito. *The Celluloid Closet: Homosexuality in the Movies*. New York, 1981.

Seitz, Don. "Selling Sin." *The Outlook* (February 23, 1927):241.

Seldes, Gilbert. *Mainland*. New York, 1936.

Simmons, Christina. "Companionate Marriage and the Lesbian Threat." *Frontiers* 4 (Fall 1979):54–59.

Singal, Daniel Joseph. "Towards a Definition of American Modernism." *American Quarterly* 39 (Spring 1987):7–26.

Slide, Anthony. *The Vaudevillians*. Westport, Conn., 1981.

Snyder, Robert W. *The Voice of the City: Vaudeville and Popular Culture in New York*. New York, 1989.

Sobel, Bernard. *Burleyque: An Underground History of Burlesque Days*. New York, 1931.

Sontag, Susan. "Notes on Camp." In Sontag, *Against Interpretation*. New York, 1966.

———. *Styles of Radical Will*. New York, 1969.

Spitzer, Marion. *The Palace*. New York, 1950.

———. "Ten-Twenty-Thirty: The Passing of the Popular-Priced Circuit." *Saturday Evening Post* (August 22, 1925), pp. 40, 42, 48.

Stanley, Robert. *The Celluloid Empire: A History of the American Motion Picture Industry*. New York, 1978.

Stansell, Christine. *City of Women: Sex and Class in New York, 1789–1860*. New York, 1986.

Staples, Shirley. *Male-Female Comedy Teams in American Vaudeville, 1865–1932*. Ann Arbor, 1984.

Stein, Charles W. *American Vaudeville as Seen by Its Contemporaries*. New York, 1984.

Stevens, Ashton. *Actorviews*. Chicago, 1923.

Stoddard, Lothrop. *The Rising Tide of Color*. New York, 1920.

Street, Julian. "Oh, You Babylon!" *Everybody's Magazine* 27 (August 1912):177.

Sumner, John S. "Padlock Drama." *Theater Magazine* 47 (May 1928):11–12, 62.

Taylor, William. *In Pursuit of Gotham: Culture and Commerce in New York*. New York, 1992.

Terkel, Studs. *Hard Times: An Oral History of the Great Depression*. New York, 1970.

Thomas, Kevin. "Mae West: At One With Her Image." *Los Angeles Times Calendar*, November 30, 1980, p. 5.

Toll, Robert C. *Blacking Up: The Minstrel Show in America*. New York, 1974.

———. *On With the Show: The First Century of American Show Business*. New York, 1976.

Trimberger, Ellen Kay. "Feminism, Men and Modern Love: Greenwich Village, 1900–1925." In *Powers of Desire: The Politics of Sexuality*, edited by Ann Snitow, Christine Stansell, and Sharon Thompson, pp. 131–152. New York, 1983.

Tucker, Sophie. *Some of These Days*. Garden City, N.Y., 1945.

Tuska, Jon. *The Films of Mae West*. Secaucus, N.J., 1973.

Tyler, Parker. *The Hollywood Hallucination*. New York, 1944.

———. *The Three Faces of Film*. New York, 1967.

Walker, Stanley. *The Nightclub Era*. New York, 1938.

Ward, Carol. *Mae West: A Bio-Bibliography*. Westport, Conn., 1989.

Weales, Gerald. *Canned Goods as Caviar: American Film Comedy in the 1930s*. Chicago, 1985.

West, Mae. *Babe Gordon*. New York, 1930.

———. *Goodness Had Nothing to Do With It*. Englewood Cliffs, N.J., 1959.

———. *Mae West on Sex, Health, and ESP*. London, 1975.

———. *Pleasure Man* [novelization]. New York, 1975.

Wilson, Garff B. *Three Hundred Years of American Drama and Theater*. Englewood Cliffs, N.J., 1973.

Woloch, Nancy. *Women and the American Experience*. New York, 1984.

Zeidman, Irving. *The American Burlesque Show*. New York, 1967.

Zolotow, Maurice. *Billy Wilder in Hollywood*. New York, 1977.

Zukor, Adolph. *The Public Is Never Wrong*. New York, 1953.

UNPUBLISHED PAPERS AND THESES

Buckley, Peter G. "The Culture of Leg Work: The Transformation of Burlesque After The Civil War." Paper presented to the American Historical Association, December 1986.

Buckley, Peter G. "To the Opera House: New York Theatre and Culture, 1820–1860." Ph.D. thesis. State University of New York at Stony Brook, 1985.

Couvares, Francis G. and Peiss, Kathy. "Sex, Censorship and the Movies: The National Board of Review, 1909–1922." Unpublished paper, n.d.

Maltby, Richard. "From the Implausible to the Unspeakable: The Censorship of Sexuality From Mae West to Shirley Temple." Unpublished paper, n.d.

Index

Abdul Kadar (Adolph Schneider), 4
actors:
 black, 165–166, 171
 fascination with, 198
 gay, 60, 67–68, 138, 141–144, 152
Actors Equity, 75
Actor's Theater, 90
Addams, Jane, 10–13, 73–74
advertising:
 for *Babe Gordon,* 153, 159
 for *Diamond Lil,* 109, 133–134
 of *Harlem,* 163
 of Harlem nightclubs, 164
 of *Sex,* 50, 252
 see also publicity
African-Americans, *see* blacks
Albee, Edward, 32, 33, 36–37
alcohol, 66, 79
 Keith Circuit ban on, 34
 Prohibition and, 94, 156
 in Raines Law Hotels, 109
 at Victoria Theater, 29
All God's Chillun Got Wings (O'Neill),
  165–166
American Mercury, 84, 90, 97–98,
  143
Ames, Winthrop, 80, 92
Anderson, John, 84, 90
Andress, Ursula, 242
anti-Semitism, 196
Asbury, Herbert, 116
Astor family, 65
Astor Hotel, 65
Atkinson, Brooks, 84, 88–91
Atlas Corporation, 211
audience:
 for burlesque, 22, 23–24, 74
 for *Captive,* 91, 97–100
 censorship and, 72–75
 for cheap theater, 9–13
 for *Diamond Lil,* 107, 111, 117,
  124–125, 129, 132–133

"dirty-play" controversy and, 77–78,
  91–92, 101
division between entertainers and,
  23–24, 34, 42
for *Drag,* 96
fairy impersonators and, 145–146
for film, 174, 186, 192–193,
  197–201, 207, 209, 228
gay men as, 238–239, 240, 246–247
for Keith Circuit, 20, 27, 33–37
modernist view of, 91–92, 101
provincial, 21
for *Sex,* 69, 105–106
for Tanguay, 40–44
for variety theater, 23, 33–34
for vaudeville, 20, 21, 27, 30–37, 74,
  138–141
Victorian view of, 73
West's view of, 21, 27, 57, 66, 69,
  93, 96, 122, 135, 207, 245, 247,
  248
autographs, 254

Babe Gordon (West), 153–162
 original title of, 154
 rape in, 160–161
 title competition for, 154
 unpleasant taste left by, 162
Back Street (film), 178
Bank Holiday, 186
Barron's Exclusive Club, 163
Bartholomew, Robert, 11
Bayes, Nora, 47
Beatles, 236
"Beef Trust" ("elephantine") choruses,
  24
Belle of the Nineties (film), 213–217,
  219, 226
Benchley, Robert, 69, 170
Bergen, Edgar, 227
Bernhardt, Sandra, 254
Better Public Shows Movement, 75

Beyond the Horizon (O'Neill), 97
Big Tess, 65–66, 144
Billboard, 24, 47, 143
Biltmore Theater, 136, 137
birth control, 12
Birth of a Nation, The (film), 160, 186
bisexuality, 55–56
Black and White, see *Babe Gordon*
blackface, 165
blacks, 2, 154–172
    as actors, 165–166, 171
    in *Babe Gordon,* 154–155, 159–162
    in *Constant Sinner,* 163, 164–165, 171
    dancing of, 26, 163, 169
    men vs. women, 163–164
    middle class, 164
    sexuality of, 159, 161–162, 169
    West influenced by, 26, 168–169
    see also Harlem; interracial sex
Blair, Mary, 165
Blake, Peter, 236
blind selling, 203, 223
block booking, 203, 223
Blonde Venus (film), 178
blood-and-thunder melodrama, 9, 10
B'nai Brith, 194
body, attitudes toward, 11–14
    cheap theater and, 11–12
    female purity and, 12, 14
    social reform and, 11–12
    of tough girls, 13
body language and mannerisms, 2
    in *Diamond Lil,* 125–128, 133
    in *Sex,* 53, 54, 55
body type:
    in burlesque shows, 24, 55
    in 1890s, 118
    in 1920s, 118
    respectability and, 54, 55
    of Tanguay, 38
    of West, 192, 241–242
Bogart, Humphrey, 81
Bolitho, William, 133
Botsford, William, 210
Bourdet, Edouard, 57, 79–84, 88–93
    see also *Captive, The*
Bowery, 31, 66, 93, 106–117
    burlesque shows on, 22, 23, 28, 66
    in *Chatham Square,* 106
    in *Diamond Lil,* 106, 107, 109–117, 123–124, 127–128, 134
    Durante on, 65, 66

    in *Every Day's a Holiday,* 226
    folklore of, 110–116, 119, 124, 134
    history of notoriety of, 108
    melodramas about, 110–113, 115
    in *She Done Him Wrong,* 183–184
    Victoria's acts' debt to, 30
"Bowery, The" (song), 111–112, 114, 117
Bowery Boy, 112, 113
Bowery Gal, 112, 113, 115
boycotts:
    Broadway, 71, 79, 102
    film, 195, 222–223
Boys in the Band, The (Crowley), 248
Brackett, Charles, 125
Breen, Joseph, 202–203, 207–213
    Every Day's a Holiday and, 226
    Klondike Annie and, 220–222, 224–225
Bright, John, 180, 182, 184
British burlesque, 22
Broadway, 46–172
    corruption of, 84–85, 91
    female sexual expressiveness on, 54–55
    freedom of expression on, 48
    Hollywood compared with, 174, 187
    legitimate performance styles on, 49, 51, 69; see also "dirty-play" controversy
    as legitimate stage, see legitimate stage
    West boycott planned on, 71, 79, 102
    West's invasion of, 46–69
    women's responsibility for dissolution of, 78
    see also specific plays
Brodie, Steve, 112, 113, 115, 116
Bronx Opera House, 137
Brooklyn, N.Y., West's background in, 2, 6–9, 12
Brooklyn Elks Club, 7
Brooks, Alan, 148
Brooks, Louise, 253
Brown, John Mason, 125, 126, 216
"buffet flats," 156
Burkan, Nathan, 148
burlesque, 2, 9, 22–27
    audience for, 22, 23–24, 74
    comic "bits" in, 24
    cootch dancing in, 25
    Drag and, 62, 66, 67
    as European import, 22

fairy impersonator compared with, 145
Hammerstein and, 28, 29
prostitutes and, 24, 53, 67, 110, 145
Sex compared with, 52–53, 55, 67, 76
striptease in, 24, 52
Tanguay's ties to, 38, 39–40
West's work in, 45, 47–48, 126, 254

cabarets, 31, 94, 166
Caffin, Caroline, 29, 37
camp, 1, 151–152, 235–250
    acknowledged, 246–247
    cultural recycling and, 237–238, 240–242
    derision and, 241, 242
    in *Drag*, 68, 246
    gay men and, 151–152, 235–240, 242–243, 245–250
    Koestenbaum's view of, 243–244
    outrageousness and, 237
    in *Pleasure Man*, 151, 246
    Sontag's essay on, 236–237, 243
    use of term, 151, 236, 237, 246
Canby, Vincent, 248
Cantor, Eddie, 127
Capitol Palace, 164
Captive, The (*La Prisonniere*; Bourdet), 66, 79–84, 88–93
    audience for, 91, 97–100
    court ruling on, 100–101
    Drag compared with, 57, 80, 81, 84, 92–93
    modern theatrical aesthetic of, 84, 88–91, 97–99
    plot of, 80–81
    police raid against, 70, 84, 100
    reviews of, 57, 84, 91, 97–99
    success of, 57, 71
Carman, Florence, 4
Catherine Was Great (West), 231–233
Catholics, Catholic Church, 174
    Legion of Decency of, 194–197, 203, 207, 210, 212
censorship, 71–77
    of film, 71, 74–75, 102, 173–175, 177–189; *see also* Motion Picture Producers and Distributors of America; Production Code; Production Code Administration; Studio Relations Committee

Keith Circuit and, 34–37, 182
Smith's opposition to, 102
see also "dirty-play" controversy; *specific regulatory groups*
Century Club, 134–135
Charleston News and Courier, 158
Chatham Square (Linder), 106
Chauncey, George, 62–65, 143
cheap theaters, 9–13
    regulation of, 74, 79, 101
    see also burlesque; melodrama; vaudeville theater
Chekhov, Anton, 82
Cheney, Sheldon, 86, 91
Chicago, Ill., Elite Number One in, 26
Chicago Examiner, 42
Chicago World's Fair (1893), 25
Chinatown, 93
Circuit (Mutual Burlesque Wheel), 47, 52, 105
circus, 33
    in *I'm No Angel*, 188, 190
Citizens' Play Jury, 75–76, 77
Clansman, The (Dixon), 160
Clarendon, Hal, 9, 10
Clark, T. J., 129
class relations:
    in *Diamond Lil*, 121–124
    in *Sex*, 120–121
    see also middle class; middle-class women; working class; working-class women
Cline, Edward, 229
clothing:
    of black chorus girls, 163
    in burlesque shows, 24
    in *Diamond Lil*, 117–118, 128
    in *Drag*, 61, 62
    female sexuality and, 54
    in *Sex*, 128
    of Tanguay, 38, 39, 40
    of tough girls, 13
Club Pansy, 95
Cochran, Charles, 107, 110
Cohen, Emanuel, 178, 211–212, 225
Colette, 192
Columbia, 230
Columbus Journal, 44
combination houses, closing of, 74
comedy-dramas of life, of West, 67, 71; *see also Drag, The; Sex*
Committee of Fourteen, 52–53, 164

concert saloons, 22, 33–34, 35, 144
  in Coney Island, 65–66
Coney Island, 40, 65–66
Confidential, 168
Congress, U.S., 157, 203, 223
Connors, Chuck, 112–116
Conrad, Ethel, 5
Constant Sinner, The (West; novel), see
  Babe Gordon
Constant Sinner, The (West; play), 150,
    154, 162–172
  blackface in, 165
  critics' views on, 163, 171
  failure of, 171–172, 176
  film adaptation of, see *Belle of the*
    Nineties; It Ain't No Sin
  municipal unease as influence on,
    163–164
  obscenity charges against, 171
  tour of, 171–172
  West's curtain speech in, 166–167
  West's wariness and, 165–171
contraception, 12
Conway, Jack, 137
cootch dancing, 25–26, 28, 48, 190
Cosmopolitan Pictures, 222
Cotton Club, 94, 134, 164
courtesans, mythical, 129
Coward, Noël, 166
Coy, James, 148
crime, 68
  Bowery and, 108, 109, 114
  cheap theater and, 10
  in *Diamond Lil,* 107, 109
  in film, 177, 207–208, 214
  homosexuality as, 58–59
  Prohibition and, 94
  see also killers and near-killers
cross-dressing, see female imperson-
    ation, female impersonators
Crowley, Mart, 248
Curtain, Kaier, 56

Dainty Marie, 5
Dame aux Camélias, La (Dumas), 129
dance halls, 26
  in *Diamond Lil,* 106, 107, 116–117
  middle-class women in, 2, 15
  tough girls in, 13, 14
dancing:
  black influence on, 26, 163, 169
  in cheap theater, 9, 11
  cootch, 25–26, 28, 48, 190

Egyptian, 25
  muscle, 19, 26, 27, 62
  shimmy, 26–27, 48, 169, 190
  social reformers' criticism of, 11, 13,
    26
  spieling, 13, 14
  of tough girls, 13
  of Wallace, 15
  of West, 19, 25–27, 48, 169, 188,
    190
Darling, Candy, 237
Davies, Marion, 222
Davis, George, 152, 192
Davis, Hartley, 36
Davis, Michael, 72–73
Davis, Owen, 10
Decca Records, 236
decorum:
  Keith Circuit and, 35–37
  legitimate theater and, 50, 85
  minstrel shows and, 139
  Tanguay's assault on, 43
  of West, 170–171
De Leon, Millie, 25, 26
Democrats, Democratic party, 102
Depression, Great, 176, 201–202
Destry Rides Again (film), 229
Diamond Lil (West), 103–135, 163,
    246
  audience for, 107, 111, 117,
    124–125, 129, 132–133
  on banned list, 173–177
  Bowery in, 106, 107, 109–117,
    123–124, 127–128, 134
  costumes in, 117–118, 128
  critics' views on, 104, 105, 107,
    109–110, 116–119, 125–127,
    133, 150
  film version of, see *She Done Him*
    Wrong
  financing of, 94
  Linder's influence on, 106
  music in, 111–112, 117, 118, 120,
    170
  national renown of, 174
  1940s revivals of, 118, 238
  nostalgia in, 116–120, 124, 125
  original vs. opening night script of,
    120–123, 130–132
  plot of, 106–107, 109, 115, 116
  popular imagery recycled in, 116
  realism of, 109–111, 116, 127, 128,
    174

rehearsals of, 122–123
Sex compared with, 105, 107, 109, 110, 116, 120–121, 122, 126–130, 134
success of, 105, 107, 116–120, 125, 150, 171
Diamond Tony's, 65–66
Dietrich, Marlene, 229, 243, 252
dime museums, 9, 28, 29, 33
Dinah East (film), 235
"dirty-play" controversy, 70–103
  legislative response to, 101–102
  modernists and, 71, 80, 84, 86–93, 101–102, 103
  nightlifers and, 71, 78–79, 92–97, 102
  Padlock Law and, 101–102
  social reformers and, 71–79, 101, 102, 103
divorce, 17
Dixon, Thomas, 160
Doctorow, E. L., 6
Doelger, Matilda, *see* West, Matilda Doelger
Doll's House, A (Ibsen), 89
Drag, The (West), 46–47, 48, 55–69, 76, 79–81, 246
  as antigay propaganda, 56
  audience for, 96
  boycott of, 71, 79, 102
  Captive compared with, 57, 80, 81, 84, 92–93
  cast recruited for, 60
  criticism of, 72, 96, 134
  drag ball in, 61–62
  film version rejected for, 249
  as freak act, 67–68
  message of, 58–59, 60
  Pleasure Man as restaging of, 138, 142–143
  plot of, 57–58
  premieres of, 71, 96
  as product of cultural moment, 66
  realism of, 56, 67–68, 109, 110, 134
  rehearsals of, 60–61
  research for, 56, 59
  slumming and, 96–97
  social injustice combatted by, 57
drag shows and balls, 2, 31, 65–66, 242, 252
  in *Drag,* 61–62
  in *Pleasure Man,* 138, 142–143
drugs, 52, 66, 108, 182

in *Diamond Lil,* 106, 107, 109, 116
Dumas, Alexandre, 129
Durante, Jimmy, 65–66, 144, 145, 164

Eaton, Walter, 88
Edna May, 65–66, 144
education, 8–9
  sex, 59–60, 65
Education Department, New York, 74
Edwards, Richard Henry, 14
Eells, George, 18, 165
effeminacy, culture of, 64–65, 94–95, 141–144
Elite Number One, 26
Elks, 194
Ellis, Havelock, 63, 147
Elsner, Edward, 60, 61
Eltinge, Julian, 139, 140–141, 145, 146–147, 149
Emergency Council of Fraternal Organizations, 194
Empire Theater, 90
Every Day's a Holiday (film), 219, 225–228
expression, freedom of, 48

fairy impersonators, 144–146, 150, 151
family, instability of, 202
Farewell to Arms, A (Hemingway), 178
Farmer, Frances, 253
Fatima, Mademoiselle, 4
Faulkner, William, 178
Federal Council of Churches of Christ, 194
female impersonation, female impersonators, 137–152
  appeal of, 139–141
  banning of, 149
  fairy impersonators and, 144–146, 150, 151
  in *Pleasure Man,* 137–139, 141–144, 249
  "queerness" assumption about, 138–139
  respectability of, 139, 140
  West as, 1, 150–152, 235–236, 240, 244
  West imitated by, 243, 249–250
  West influenced by, 150–151
feminism, 242, 245
Fields, W. C., 229, 237, 241

film, film industry:
  audience for, 174, 186, 192–193,
    197–201, 207, 209, 228
  banned list in, 173–175
  boycotts of, 195, 222–223
  censorship of, 71, 74–75, 102,
    173–175, 177–189; *see also*
    Motion Picture Producers and
    Distributors of America; Produc-
    tion Code; Production Code
    Administration; Studio Relations
    Committee
  commercialization of, 196
  fear of, 174
  intimacy and, 198
  legitimate stage compared with,
    90–91
  as mass medium, 197
  sound in, 174
  theater compared with, 173–175,
    180, 187, 198
  vaudeville vs., 48
  West's comeback in, 232, 235–236,
    244–248
  West's decline in, 1, 225–230
  West's start in, 1, 173, 175–177
  see also Hollywood; *specific films*
Fitzgerald, F. Scott, 193
Follies, 55
Fonda, Jane, 242
Ford, Helen, 18
Forman, Henry James, 199–200
"Formula, the," 175
"Fougere, Mademoiselle," 39
"Frankie and Johnny" (song), 170, 239
freak acts, 32, 42
  Drag as, 67–68
  humbugs and sleazy curiosities in, 4,
    9, 28–29
  of publicity, 4–5, 9, 29–30
  West's development of, 6, 30
Freud, Sigmund, 56, 59, 60
"Funny Old Gal" (minstrel show stock
    character), 139
Furnas, Joseph, 190

gangs, 94
Gangs of New York, The (Asbury), 116
gangster films, 177
Garbo, Greta, 252
gay men, 31, 119
  artistic success of, 248–250
  in burlesque, 110

  camp and, 151–152, 235–240,
    242–243, 245–250
  culture of effeminacy and, 64–65,
    94–95, 141–144
  in *Dinah East,* 235
  as female impersonators, 137–139,
    141–147, 149, 150, 151
  flamboyance of, 2, 60
  in *Pleasure Man,* 137–138, 141–143,
    151, 166
  subculture of, 60, 62–66, 95, 143,
    147, 156
  as West audience, 238–239, 240,
    246–247
  West influenced by, 150–152,
    235–236, 240, 249
  West's contact with, 55–56
  as West's rivals, 248–250
  see also *Drag, The*
Gay Nineties, 1
  Diamond Lil nostalgia and,
    118–119, 125
  Diamond Lil revivals and, 118
gender boundaries:
  female impersonators and, 141
  nineteenth-century, 65
  sexual revolt and, 95, 238
gesture, Bowery, 113
Ghosts (Isben), 85–86
Gilbert, Adele, 167–168
Gilded Age, sexual indulgence of, 6
Gilman, Sander, 169
Givot, George, 165
glamour, sex films and, 178
Goin' to Town (film), 219, 226
Goldsmith, George, 76
Goldstein, Sidney, 195
Go West, Young Man (film), 219, 225
Graham, Lillian, 4–5
Grand Street Follies, 127
Grant, Cary, 152, 191
Grant, Madison, 157
Gray, Thomas, 20, 44
Great Depression, 176, 201–202
Greenpoint, West's childhood in, 7, 12
Greenwich Village:
  gay subculture in, 60, 62, 94–95
  modernist theater in, 87
Griffith, D. W., 160
Grizzly Bear, 26
guidebooks, New York City, 31, 93
Guinan, Texas, 134–135, 175
gun sales, 5

"Guy What Takes His Time, A" (or "Slow Motion Man") (song), 187
Gyp the Blood, Mrs., 32

"Half Woman, The," 28
Hamilton, Jack, 57
Hammell, John, 209, 219–220, 221
Hammerstein, Arthur, 28, 32
Hammerstein, Oscar, I, 27, 28, 32
Hammerstein, Oscar, II, 27
Hammerstein, Willie, 3–5, 27–33, 42
  death of, 32
  dime museum evoked by, 28, 29
Hammersteiners, 30–31
Hammond, Percy, 76, 104, 105, 125
Happy Rhone's, 164
Harlem, 52–53
  in *Babe Gordon*, 154–155, 159–162
  as commercial fantasy, 155, 156, 163
  in *Constant Sinner*, 163, 164
  gay subculture in, 62, 65, 156
  history of, 155–156
  peak of white fascination with, 154
  rent parties in, 156–157
  "slumming" craze in, 2, 31, 94, 95, 134, 163–164
Harlem (Thurman and Rapp), 156–157, 163
Harlow, Jean, 178
Hart, Vincent, 187, 189, 192
Hartig, Emma, 109
Haskell, Loney, 29
Haskell, Molly, 245, 252
Hays, Will, 173–175, 177–181, 185–188, 202
  Breen's correspondence with, 208, 209, 211–212
  government intervention feared by, 187
  Hammell's correspondence with, 219–220
Hays Office, *see* Motion Picture Producers and Distributors of America
Hearn, Edward, 152
Hearst, William Randolph, 68, 102, 222–223
Heat's On, The (film), 230, 236
Helburn, Theresa, 80
Hell's Kitchen, 62
Hemingway, Ernest, 178
Herbert, Hugh, 16

Hollywood, 172–231
  blacks and, 172
  Broadway compared with, 174, 187
  in 1960s, 241
  West's status in, 1, 225–228, 233–234
  see also film, film industry; *specific films*
Hollywood A Go Go (TV series), 237
"Hollywood Was Never a Honky Tonk Town" (song), 253
Holmes, John Haynes, 79, 195–196
homosexuality, 182
  ban on depiction of, 101, 143
  controversy over, 69, 71; *see also* *Captive, The;* "dirty-play" controversy; *Drag, The*
  as crime, 58–59
  medical views of, 56, 58, 59, 147
  see also *Captive, The; Drag, The;* gay men; lesbianism
honky-tonk, black, 2
Hornblow, Arthur, Jr., 90–91, 198
Houdini, Harry, 141
Hoyt, Charles M., 112, 114
Huber's dime museum, 28, 29
humor:
  in *Babe Gordon*, 161–162
  Bowery, 112, 113, 115
  in *Diamond Lil*, 130–132
  in *Drag*, 62, 67
  gay, 66, 151
  in *My Little Chickadee*, 229–230
  in *Red-Headed Woman*, 178, 183
  in *Sex*, 51–52, 53, 67
  in *She Done Him Wrong*, 183, 184
Hurley, Harold, 181
Hurst, Craig (Craig Russell), 242–243, 249–250
Hurston, Zora Neale, 168–169

Ibsen, Henrik, 85–86, 87, 89
identity, sex and, 95–96, 119, 144, 151
immigrants, 7, 9, 13, 108, 158
  film and, 174
I'm No Angel (film), 151, 187–193, 216–217
  audience for, 200–201
  Hays Office and, 188, 189, 202
  as hit, 192–193, 195
  publicity for, 188–189
  reviews of, 191–192, 201, 202, 209
  setting of, 188

I'm No Angel (film) (*cont.*)
  West's screenwriting credit in,
    187–188
interracial sex, 158–163, 165–168
  fear of, 158–160
  West's denial of, 166–168
  West's deriding of, 162
Interview, 235
irony, 150
  in *Babe Gordon,* 161
  in *Diamond Lil,* 130–132, 135, 170,
    191
  in *I'm No Angel,* 191, 192
It Ain't No Sin (film), 194, 203–213,
    217
  direct borrowings from play in,
    203–204
  plot of, 203–205
  revision of, see *Belle of the Nineties*
  She Done Him Wrong compared
    with, 204, 205

Jacobs, Lea, 227
Jews, 174, 194
Johnson, Jack, 29
Johnson-Reed Act (1924), 157
Jolo (Joshua Lowe), 6, 20
jooks (black bawdy houses), Hurston's
    views on, 168–169
journalism, 96
  Bowery and, 113–114
  Lexow and Mazet committees and,
    108
  sensationalism and, 5, 10, 32, 68
  see also specific newspapers
Joy, Jason, 177–178, 182

Kahlo, Frida, 193
Keith, B. F., 32, 33, 36–37
Keith Circuit, 20, 21, 27, 32–44
  censorship and, 34–37, 182
  female impersonators on, 138, 140
  Hammerstein granted monopoly by,
    28
  Palace Theater opened by, 32
  United Booking Office (UBO) of,
    35–36, 37
  vaudeville consolidated by, 33
  vaudeville style promoted by, 32–37,
    48
  West's work for, 20, 21
Kelly, Rev. Thomas J., 230–231
Kent, Sidney, 186–187

killers and near-killers:
  in *Babe Gordon,* 160–161
  female, 4–5
  male, 3, 29–30, 160–161
Klondike Annie (film), 218–225
  Hearst's criticism of, 222–223
Kneeland, George, 24
Knights of Columbus, 194
Kobal, John, 254
Koestenbaum, Wayne, 234, 243–244
Kofoed, Jack, 94, 95
Krafft-Ebing, Richard von, 56, 59, 147
Ku Klux Klan, 157–158

labor unions, 8–9
language:
  of Bowery, 113, 115
  of burlesque, 24
  censorship of, 34
  of *Drag,* 61, 62, 63
  in *Sex,* 52, 54
  of tough girls, 13
  see also slang
Las Vegas, Nev., West in, 239–240
La Tour, Babe, 22, 39
Laughlin, Harry, 19
Laurel and Hardy, 237
Le Baron, William, 175–176, 211
Lefty Louie, Mrs., 32
Legion of Decency, 194–197, 203, 207,
    210, 212
legitimate stage:
  artistic mission of, 80
  film compared with, 90–91
  middle class and, 50–51, 54, 78, 85,
    91–92
  regulation of, 71, 75–77, 79, 80, 92,
    101–102
  respectability of, 72
  sexual subject matter and, 50–51
  use of term, 48
Lehman Brothers, 211
Leon, Francis, 139, 140
lesbianism, 119
  fear of, 83–84
  see also *Captive, The*
Lexow committee, 108, 109, 110, 112,
    114
Library of Congress, Copyright Office
    of, 120
Life, 69, 233, 245
Linder, Mark, 106
Literary Digest, 197, 201

Little Coney Island, 28
Loew, Marcus, 20
Loew Circuit, 20–21, 44
London Observer, 227
Look, 57
Lord, Father Daniel, 195, 197, 198
Los Angeles Examiner, 222–223
Lowe, Joshua (Jolo), 6, 20
Lower East Side, 52–53, 62, 93
Lubitsch, Ernst, 224
Lulu Belle (play), 50, 51, 55, 66, 174

Macaulay's, 153–154
McCardell, Roy, 112
McGurk, John, 109
Madden, Owney, 94, 156, 175, 185
Madison Square Garden, 65
  Roof Garden Theater of, 3
Madonna, 254
Mahoney, Jeremiah, 100–101
Maltby, Richard, 174
Marbury, Elisabeth, 78
Marx Brothers, 237
Masons, 194
Max, Peter, 236
Mayer, Louis B., 211
Mazet committee, 108, 109, 114
medical profession, homosexuality and,
  56, 58, 59, 147
melodrama, 33
  blood-and-thunder, 9, 10
  Bowery in, 110–113, 115
  Diamond Lil as, 115
  Pleasure Man as, 138
Mencken, H. L., 97
Menken, Helen, 70, 81, 99
men-only entertainment, 22
  concert saloons as, 33–34
  dime museums and, 28
  see also burlesque
mental health, of tough girls, 14
Meryman, Richard, 233, 245
Metro-Goldwyn-Mayer (MGM), 178,
  211
middle class:
  black, 164
  Coney Island and, 40
  in *Diamond Lil,* 121–122
  disintegration of worldview of, 36,
    50–51, 77–79, 147
  female impersonation and, 138–141,
    146–147
  female purity and, 12, 14, 36

  inhibitions of, 124
  Keith Circuit and, 20, 33–36
  legitimate stage and, 50–51, 54, 78,
    85, 91–92
  modernist view of, 87
  Protestant, film feared by, 174
  Tanguay and, 40
  theater of, 9, 11, 20, 27, 30, 33–36,
    50–51, 69, 85, 86, 87, 91–92
  urban vice as fascination of, 31
  Victorian, 2
middle-class women:
  Broadway's dissolution and, 78
  clothing of, 2, 54
  legitimate stage and, 78, 85
  love and, 87
  minstrel shows and, 139
  modernist view of, 91–92
  rebellion of, 2
  at *Sex,* 69
  tough-girl style adopted by, 14–15
  at vaudeville theater, 30
Midler, Bette, 254
Midwest, West's touring in, 15–16
Milholland, Inez, 29
Miller, Gilbert, 88, 89
Milwaukee, Wisc., West in, 15–16
Milwaukee Works Progress Administration, 16
Minsky theater chain, 52
minstrel shows, 139
Miranda, Carmen, 242
miscegenation, *see* interracial sex
modernists, modernity:
  "dirty-play" controversy and, 71, 80,
    84, 86–93, 101–102, 103
  film as viewed by, 198
  in postwar years, 238
  psychology and, 77, 87–88
  sex and, 118–119, 159
Monroe, Marilyn, 253
Montez, Maria, 242
Montez, Mario, 237
Moore, Grace, 234
Morgan, J. P., 211
Morganstern, Clarence, 76
"Mother Superior," 68
Motion Picture Herald, 197, 223
Motion Picture Producers and Distributors of America (MPPDA; Hays
  Office), 173–175, 177–189
  board of directors of, 177, 179
  gangster films and, 177

Motion Picture Producers and Distributors of America (MPPDA;
Hays Office) (*cont.*)
I'm No Angel and, 188, 189, 202
It Ain't No Sin and, 205–213
Klondike Annie and, 219–225
My Little Chickadee and, 229
Paramount and, 178–180, 187–189,
202, 205–214, 219–228
sex films and, 178–189, 199, 202,
205–214
Studio Relations Committee of, 177,
179–184, 202–203, 213
Motion Picture Research Council
(MPRC), 199–200
muscle dance, 19, 26, 27, 62
musclemen, in West nightclub revival,
239–240
music, 193, 228, 236
black, 163–164, 170
Bowery in, 110–112, 114
in cheap theater, 10, 11
in *Diamond Lil,* 111–112, 117, 118,
120, 170
in *Drag,* 62
in *She Done Him Wrong,* 183, 187
of Tanguay, 39, 41, 43
Mutual Burlesque Wheel (or Circuit),
47, 52, 105
My Dress Hangs Here (Kahlo), 193
My Little Chickadee (film), 229–230,
241
Myra Breckinridge (film), 232,
235–236, 244, 247

Nathan, George Jean, 84, 89, 90,
97–99
on *I'm No Angel,* 192
on *Pleasure Man,* 143, 168
Nation, 216
national marketing of New York
drama, 85
NBC radio, West banned from,
227–228
Nesbit, Evelyn, 3–6, 10, 29–30
Newark Theater, 193
New Republic, 69, 116, 119–120,
125–126
Newton, Esther, 138
New York American, 68, 72, 102
New York City:
collapse of nightlife in, 176
end of class segregation in, 114

gay subculture in, 60, 62–66, 143,
147, 156
mainstream America vs., 174–175
opening of *I'm No Angel* in,
192–193
prostitutes in, 2, 66, 94, 108, 109,
156
public fascination with urban vice in,
27, 31
slumming craze in, 2, 31, 66, 93–95,
103, 163–164
vaudeville theater in, 2–6, 9, 27–45
see also specific neighborhoods
New York Daily Mirror, 49, 68, 96,
102
New York Daily News, 68, 102
New York Dramatic Mirror, 40
New Yorker, 49, 125, 164
New York Evening Graphic, 68, 102
New York Evening Post, 84, 90, 110,
127, 170
New York Herald Tribune, 49–50, 51,
76, 101, 104, 190, 215
New York Journal, 113–114
New York Society for the Suppression
of Vice, 77
New York State Assembly, 71
New York State Board of Motion Pic-
ture Censorship, 71, 74–75, 101,
102, 213–214
New York State Board of Theater Cen-
sorship, 72, 76, 79
New York State Legislature, 101
New York Times, 84, 88–89, 90,
99–100, 138
camp in, 237
West's curtain speech in, 166–167
on West's films, 228, 230, 248
New York Tribune, 85–86
New York World, 68, 113–114, 119,
148
nickelodeons, 9
Night After Night (film), 175–176
nightclubs, 31, 79, 94–95, 154,
166–167
in *Babe Gordon,* 159
Harlem, 94, 134, 159, 163, 164, 170
race mixing in, 164
West revival in, 239–240
nightlifers:
black sexuality and, 159, 161–162
"dirty-book" controversy and, 71,
78–79, 92–97, 102

Nordics (Northern Europeans), mongrelization fears of, 157–159
Norr, Ray, 202
nostalgia, in *Diamond Lil,* 116–120,
  124, 125
"Notes on Camp" (Sontag), 236–237
nudity, in burlesque, 24
Nugent, Frank S., 230

obscenity charges:
  against *Constant Sinner,* 171
  against *Pleasure Man,* 136–137, 144,
    148–149
  against *Sex,* 70; *see also* "dirty-play"
    controversy
Oddfellows, 194
O'Malley, Frank Ward, 112
O'Neill, Bobby, 19
O'Neill, Eugene, 77, 90, 97, 165–166
Oriental, 164
Our Movie-Made Children (Forman),
  199–200
Outlook, 77
Outrageous! (film), 249–250

Padlock Law (1927), 101–102
Page International, 235
Palace Theater, 47
  opening of, 32
Paramount, 174–193, 203–229
  financial problems of, 178, 211
  Hays Office and, 178–180, 187–189,
    202, 205–214, 219–228
  publicity department of, 185–186,
    188–189
  West's break with, 225–229
  West signed by, 173, 175
Paramount Theater, 193, 228
Parsons, Louella, 176
Partisan Review, 237
Passing of the Great Race, The (Grant),
  157
Patterson, Nan, 4
Peiss, Kathy, 113
penny dailies, 68
performance style, 1–2, 18–22
  body language and mannerisms in,
    see body language and manner-
    isms
  burlesque influence in, 22, 25–26,
    27, 126
  critical views on, 20, 22, 26, 27,
    44–45, 125–127

explicit sexuality in, 19–20, 21, 44
family background and, 6–7
in film, 176, 185, 187, 189–191,
  216, 217, 221, 224–225, 226
freak acts and, 6, 30
gay influence on, 150–152, 235–236,
  240, 249
Hurst's view of, 243
in *Sex,* 53, 54, 55, 126–127
Tanguay's influence on, 44
tough girl as influence on, 2, 6, 18
Philadelphia, Pa., vaudeville in, 19–20
Philadelphia North American, 25
Phillips, John, 253
Physique Pictorials, 240
Playboy, 246
Pleasure Man (West), 136–152
  camp in, 151, 246
  critics' views on, 136, 137–138, 143,
    150–151, 168
  female impersonation in, 137–139,
    141–144, 249
  novelized version of, 249
  obscenity charges against, 136–137,
    144, 148–149
  original titles of, 137
  police raid on, 136, 138, 141–142
  premiere of, 136
  preview performance of, 137
  rehearsals of, 137, 150
  as restaging of *Drag,* 138, 142–143
  West's defense of, 138
police force, Bowery and, 108
Police Gazette, 117, 118, 120
police raids:
  on Broadway, 70, 71, 84, 100, 102,
    136, 138, 141–142, 222
  on gay community, 147
  interracial casts and, 165, 166
pornography, 102, 195–196
  burlesque and, 23, 47
  West's plays and, 46
Porter, Cole, 193
Possessed (film), 178
power:
  commercial Harlem and, 163
  sexual, 14, 18
pregnancy, 12, 16
Prisonniere, La, see *Captive, The*
Production Code, 175, 177, 197, 203,
  208, 212–213
  drafting of, 195
  end of, 241

Production Code Administration
    (PCA), 213, 215, 217, 218, 221,
    227, 229
Prohibition, 157, 163, 172, 174, 175
    alcohol and, 94, 156
prostitutes:
    in *Babe Gordon*, 154
    burlesque and, 24, 53, 67, 110, 145
    in *Diamond Lil*, 107, 116, 121–122,
        128–129
    economics and, 53
    history of theatrical presentation of,
        129
    in *It Ain't No Sin*, 204
    in *Lulu Belle*, 50, 55, 66
    male, 66, 108, 109
    in New York City, 2, 66, 94, 108,
        109, 156
    Prohibition and, 94
    respectable women compared with,
        79, 118
    in *Sex*, 46, 49, 52–55, 67, 126–30
    in *Shanghai Gesture*, 50, 66
    in *She Done Him Wrong*, 1, 180,
        182, 184
    suicide of, 109
    tough girls compared with, 2, 13, 14
Protestants, 194
    film feared by, 174
Proust, Marcel, 192
Provincetown Players, 87, 165–166
psychics, 230–231
psychology:
    in *Captive*, 81–84
    in modernist theater, 77, 87–88
    of tough girls, 14
Public Enemy, The (film), 154
publicity:
    freak acts of, 4–5, 9, 29–30
    Paramount, 185–186, 188–189
Pulitzer, Joseph, 68, 113
purity, female, 12, 14, 36, 160

Queen's Throat, The (Koestenbaum),
    234
Quigley, Martin, 197, 201, 209

race mixing, in nightclubs, 164
racial fear, 157–167
racketeers, 94
Raft, George, 175
Ragtime (Doctorow), 6
Raines Law (1896), 109

Raines Law Hotels, 109
Rajah, Princess, 28
rape, 160–161
Rapp, William, 156–157, 163
realism:
    of *Diamond Lil*, 109–111, 116, 127,
        128, 174
    of *Drag*, 56, 67–68, 109, 110, 134
    of film, 183, 185–186, 197–198
    of *Sex*, 51, 53, 54, 55, 67, 109, 110,
        116, 127, 134
    social, 87
Red-Headed Woman (film), 178, 183,
        186
Reed, Rex, 245
religion:
    in *Diamond Lil*, 121–122, 123
    film and, 174, 194–197
    spiritualism and, 230–233
rent parties, 156–157
revival theaters, 236, 237
Reynolds, Burt, 251
Richman, Harry, 47
Rivera, Diego, 193
Robertson, Pamela, 150
Robeson, Paul, 165
Rockland Palace, 65
Roof Garden Theater, 3
Roosevelt, Franklin D., 186
Rorty, James, 216
Ross, Andrew, 237
Royale Theater, 136, 162
Rubaiyat, 94–95
Russell, Craig (Craig Hurst), 242–243,
        249–256

Sales, Soupy, 237
saloons, 13, 109
    concert, 22, 33–34, 35, 65–66, 144
    in *Diamond Lil*, 109, 116–117
Sanctuary (Faulkner), 178
Sands, Dorothy, 127
Sarne, Michael, 235
Savoy, Bert, 144, 145
Schenck, Joseph, 12
Schneider, Adolph (Abdul Kadar), 4
Schulberg, B. P., 177
Scott, Randolph, 152
scripts, parlor vs. whore, 76
Seitz, Don, 77
Seldes, Gilbert, 192
self-improvement:
    theater and, 11, 14, 73, 77, 86, 88

working-class, 8–9
sensationalism, 215–217
  Broadway commercialism and, 91
  cheap theater and, 10
  Hammerstein's taste for, 28, 32
  in *It Ain't No Sin*, 205, 207, 210
  in publicity for *She Done Him
      Wrong*, 186
  Sex and, 46
  urban, 6, 10, 27
  vaudeville and, 4–5, 9, 28–30
  West's love of, 12
"separate spheres" ideology, decline of,
      147
*Sergeant Pepper's Lonely Hearts Club
    Band* (album), 236
Sex (West), 46, 48–55, 66–70, 254
  advertising of, 50, 252
  burlesque compared with, 52–53, 55,
      67, 76
  Citizen's Play Jury ruling on, 75–76
  as cult hit, 69
  Diamond Lil compared with, 105,
      107, 109, 110, 116, 120–121,
      122, 126–130, 134
  humor of, 51–52, 53, 67
  Hurston's views on, 168–169
  jooks as influence on, 168–169
  police raid on, 70, 103, 322
  as product of cultural moment, 66
  profits of, 68
  realism of, 51, 53, 54, 55, 67, 109,
      110, 116, 127, 134
  reviews of, 46, 49–50, 51, 55, 103,
      127, 134
  success of, 46, 68–69, 105–106
sex, sexuality:
  in *Babe Gordon*, 159–162
  black vs. white, 159–163
  burlesque and, 23–25
  cheap theater and, 9–12
  in *Constant Sinner*, 163, 165
  in *Diamond Lil*, 128–132
  identity and, 95–96, 119, 144, 151
  interracial, *see* interracial sex
  in *It Ain't No Sin*, 205–207
  modernity and, 118–119, 159
  recreational, 95
  of Tanguay, 39–40
  of tough girls, 13, 14
  Victorian, 2
  West as adventurer and, 12, 15–18,
      225–226

  West's first experience and, 2, 12
  as West's weapon, 18
sex education, *Drag* as, 59–60, 65
sex films, 178–193
  ambiguity in, 182, 184, 191, 221
  Hays office and, 178–189, 202,
      205–214, 219–228
  in 1960s, 241–242
  reform movement and, 187,
      194–203, 212–217, 222–223
Sextette (film), 236, 247, 248, 250
  reviews of, 244, 245
  West's performing problems in, 251
sexual parody and self-mockery, 1, 2,
      54, 129–134, 150, 226, 229,
      239
sexual repression, 87, 159
sexual revolution, 241–242
sexual scandals, 3–5, 29, 68
Shakespeare, William, 224
Shanghai Gesture, The (play), 50, 51,
      66, 174
She Done Him Wrong (film), 1, 107,
      173–187, 193, 202
  black maid in, 184
  Brown's view of sexual style in, 216
  decoy material for, 180–181
  Hays Office and, 173, 178–187
  It Ain't No Sin compared with,
      204–205
  muffling of stage origins of, 180,
      184–185
  publicity for, 185–186
  sordid realism avoided in, 183
  success of, 186, 187, 189
Shekla, 4
She Wronged Him Right (cartoon),
      193
shimmy, 26–27, 48, 169, 190
Shooting Stars, (Those Two Girls), 5, 6,
      29, 32, 42
Short, Rev. W. H., 199
short stories, Bowery, 110–115
Shostac, Perry, 99
Shubert, J. J., 165
Shubert Organization, 85, 166, 171,
      176
Silverman, Sime, 20, 22, 30, 44–45
Simmons, Christina, 83–84
Singal, Daniel, 87
slang:
  gay, 61, 63, 65, 66, 142–143, 151
  stage, 30

slumming craze, 2, 31, 66, 93–97, 103,
    134–135, 163–164, 186
  in *Babe Gordon,* 159
  in *Diamond Lil,* 124
  in *Diamond Lil* advertisement,
    133–134
  Drag and, 96–97
Smart Set, 97
Smith, Al, 101, 102
Smith, Bessie, 170
Smith, Willie (The Lion), 156
Snyder, Ruth, 106
"socially prismatic" characters,
    114–115
social workers (social reform):
  burlesque as viewed by, 23–24
  cheap theater criticized by, 9–12,
    72–73
  Committee of Fourteen, 52–53, 164
  dancing criticized by, 11, 13, 26
  "dirty play" controversy and, 71–79,
    101, 102, 103
  film and, 187, 194–203, 212–217,
    222–223
  Lexow and Mazet committees and,
    108
  race mixing and, 164
  tough girls as viewed by, 13–14, 17
Sometime (musical), 18, 47, 48, 169
Sontag, Susan, 236–237, 243
speakeasies, 31, 79, 102
spieling, 13, 14
Spirit of Youth and the City Streets, The
    (Addams), 10
spiritualism, 230–233
Sporting Widow, The (playlet), 15
stage slang, 30
star system, 198
Stephens, Harmon, 201
Stevens, Ashton, 42
"stock burlesque" operators, 52–53
stock market crash (1929), 176
Stoddard, Lothrop, 157, 158–159, 169
striptease, 24, 52
Studio, 60
Studio Relations Committee (SRC) 177,
    179–184, 202–203, 213
Suicide Hall, 109, 116
Sullivan, Tim, 109
Sumner, John, 77
Sunset Boulevard (film), 233–234
syphilis, as drama theme, 85–86

Tanguay, Eva, 5, 38–44, 127
  critics of, 38–43
  lunacy of, 40–43
  salary of, 41, 42, 43
  West compared with, 42–44, 132
Taylor, William, 31, 114
Tenderloin, 62, 93, 155
"ten-twent'-thirt'" circuit, 10, 115
Thaw, Evelyn Nesbit, 3–6, 10, 29–30
Thaw, Harry, 3, 10, 29–30
theater:
  Broadway, *see* Broadway; legitimate
    stage; *specific plays*
  cheap, 9–13, 74, 79, 101; *see also*
    burlesque; melodrama;
    vaudeville theater
  commercialization of, 85, 91
  film compared with, 173–175, 180,
    187, 198
  of middle class, 9, 11, 20, 27, 30,
    33–36, 50–51, 69, 85, 86, 87,
    91–92
  modernist, 71, 77, 80, 84, 86–93,
    101–102, 103
  revival, 236, 237
  variety, 22–23, 33–34
  Victorian values and, 11, 73, 77, 86,
    87, 88
  West as actress in, 2, 18, 46, 48, 49,
    52–55, 104–105, 125–137,
    150–152, 166–167, 231–233;
    see also specific plays
  West as playwright for, 2, 46–49,
    104–149, 162–172; *see also spe-*
    cific plays
  see also specific theaters and plays
Theater Arts Monthly, 92, 125
theater community, "dirty-play" con-
    troversy and, 71, 79–93, 96–103
Theater Guild, 90
Theater Royale, 104
Theater Supervisory Board, 71, 79, 80,
    92, 102
Theater Syndicate, 85
Thomas, Kevin, 245
Thompson, Harlan, 188
Three Ambler Brothers, 5
Three Gertzes, 5
Thurman, Wallace, 156–157, 163
ticket prices:
  Broadway, 48, 50, 68
  of movies, 197
  at Victoria Theater, 30

Time, 237
Times Square, 79, 140, 176
  legitimate district of, 48
  Palace Theater in, 32, 47
  slumming in, 94, 95
  see also Victoria Theater
Timony, James, 60, 76, 103
tough girls, 13–15
  in burlesque shows, 24
  contempt for, 14, 17–18
  defined, 2
  as hypersexuals, 169
  mental health of, 14
  middle-class women influenced by,
    14–15
  prostitutes compared with, 2, 13,
    14
  social worker critique of, 13–14, 17
  as victims, 14
  West as, 2, 6, 13–15, 17–18, 25–26,
    27, 151, 169
touring companies, touring:
  conformity required by, 15, 17
  of West, 15–16, 17, 20–21, 169,
    171–172, 239
transvestism, 147
  see also female impersonation, female
    impersonators
Trip to Chinatown, A (Hoyt), 112
Troy, William, 215
Tucker, Sophie, 30
Turkey Trot, 26
Tuska, Jon, 47, 254
Tyler, Parker, 152, 192, 246

UCLA students, 241
Ulrich, Leonore, 55
Ulrichs, Karl, 56, 59
United Booking Office (UBO), 35–36,
  37
Universal Pictures, 173, 177, 229–230
urban sensationalism, 6, 10, 27

Vanderbilt family, 65
van Druten, John, 92
Vanity Fair, 90, 152
Van Vechten, Carl, 170
Variety:
  on Breen, 203
  burlesque reviewed in, 23
  as Diamond Lil, 116, 118, 119, 125,
    128
  on *Drag,* 60–61, 66, 96

  on female impersonators, 137–138,
    139, 141, 149
  on film clean-up campaign, 212, 213
  "Half Woman" criticized in, 28–29
  on Hammersteiners, 30
  Keith Circuit mission announced in,
    37
  on *Pleasure Man,* 137–138
  on *Sex,* 51, 68, 69, 76, 103
  on West's films, 181, 184–185, 188,
    193, 194, 210, 223
  on West's vaudeville performances, 6,
    20, 22, 44–45, 169
  on *Wicked Age,* 105
variety theater, 22–23
  in concert saloons, 33–34
vaudeville theater, 25–45
  audience for, 20, 21, 27, 30–37, 74,
    138–141
  consolidation of, 32–33
  female impersonators in, 138–149
  freak act in, 4–5, 6, 9, 28–30, 32, 42
  Keith Circuit in, *see* Keith Circuit
  Loew Circuit in, 20–21, 44
  movies vs., 48
  persona required by, 20
  in *Pleasure Man,* 137
  roots of, 33–34
  social reformers' view of, 72–73
  touch of class required in, 20, 21
  West's problems in, 20, 21, 42–45,
    48
  West's work in, 2, 5–6, 9, 18–22,
    25–32, 42–45, 47, 48, 126, 169
Victorian values:
  female cultural role and, 78
  female impersonators and, 140
  female purity and, 14, 160
  Legion of Decency campaign and,
    196
  modernist critique of, 86–87
  policing of cultural activity of poor
    and, 74–75
  racial fears and, 157–162
  revolt against, 2
  theater and, 11, 73, 77, 86, 87, 88
  tough girl and, 2
  West's shattering of, 252, 253
Victoria Theater, 3–6, 9, 27–33, 67
  audience for, 27, 30–31, 32
  collapse of, 32
  cost of, 30
  freak acts ended by, 32

Victoria Theater (*cont.*)
  monopoly of, 28
  Nesbit at, 3–6, 29–30
  origins of, 27–28
  Tanguay's connection to, 5, 38, 42
  West's performances at, 5–6, 9, 30,
    43–44
Vim, 240
violence:
  in *Babe Gordon,* 160–161
  in cheap theater, 10
  in *Diamond Lil,* 107
Virgins in Cellophane (film), 178
Volstead Act, 94

Wald, Lillian, 13
Waldorf, Wilella, 170–171
Walker, Jimmy, 102
Wallace, Frank (Frank Szatkus),
    15–18
  divorce of, 17
  silence maintained by, 16
  West sued by, 17
Wallace, James, 144
Warhol, Andy, 237
Warner, Harry, 173, 177
Warner Brothers, 173
Washington, D.C.:
  Constant Sinner in, 171
  I'm No Angel in, 193
Washington Square Players, 87, 90
Watts, Richard, 215, 216
Weales, Gerald, 205
Welch, Raquel, 242
West, Beverly (formerly Mildred;
    sister), 8
West, John Edwin (brother), 8
West, John Patrick (father), 6, 7–8, 16
West, Katie (sister), 8
West, Mae (Mary Jane West):
  aging of, 232–233, 240, 244–245
  ambition of, 8, 31–32, 45, 47, 48
  appearance of, 19, 125, 167, 176,
    192, 241–242, 252
  as apprentice to cheap theater, 9–12
  arrests of, 70, 102, 136–137
  autobiography of, 21, 47, 55–56,
    180, 230, 231, 232, 252
  A vs. B, 233, 245
  in burlesque, 45, 47–48, 126, 254
  camp and, 1, 151–152, 235–250
  child parts of, 9
  contraception used by, 12

dancing of, 19, 25–27, 48, 169, 188,
    190
death of, 251–252
debut of, 7, 9
defiant grandeur of, 231–234
earnings of, 16–17, 175, 229
education of, 9, 59
end of obscurity of, 46–47, 102–103
family background of, 2, 6–9, 169
as female impersonator, 1, 150–152,
    235–236, 240, 244
film career fall of, 1, 225–230
film career start of, 1, 173, 175–177
film clean—up campaign and,
    194–203, 212–217, 222–223
film comeback of, 232, 235–236,
    244, 248
film critics' views on, 176, 186,
    190–193, 209, 210, 216, 217,
    226–227, 229–230, 238, 244
film persona of, 190–191
first sexual experience of, 2, 12
flamboyance of, 48, 191, 229, 239,
    243, 247
frustration of, 248
funeral of, 245
health problems of, 251
imitations of, 127, 243, 249, 250
lawsuits of, 17, 168
mannerisms of, *see* body language
    and mannerisms
marriage of, *see* Wallace, Frank
moral influence of, 216
in *My Little Chickadee,* 229–230,
    241
in *Myra Breckinridge,* 232, 235–236,
    244, 247
nadir in career of, 45, 47
in *Night After Night,* 175–176
nightclub review of, 239–240
1960s revival of, 236–238, 240–244
as "Norma Desmond," 233–234
at Paramount, 175–193, 203–229;
    see also specific films
peak of popularity of, 192–194
performance style of, *see* perfor-
    mance style
as playwright, 2, 46–49, 104–149,
    162–172; *see also specific plays*
at *Pleasure Man* obscenity trial,
    148–149
as pop culture icon, 1, 2, 238,
    240–244, 252